LOVE OF THE WORLD

Love of the World
Essays

JOHN MCGAHERN

Edited by
STANLEY VAN DER ZIEL

Introduction by
DECLAN KIBERD

faber and faber

First published in 2009
by Faber and Faber Ltd
Bloomsbury House
74–77 Great Russell Street
London WC1B 3DA

Typeset in Minion by RefineCatch Limited, Bungay, Suffolk
Printed in England by CPI Mackays of Chatham

A CIP record for this book
is available from the British Library

ISBN 978–0–571–24511–6

2 4 6 8 10 9 7 5 3 1

Contents

V PREFACES AND INTRODUCTIONS

VI REVIEWS

CONTENTS

CONTENTS

Introduction

Declan Kiberd

Thoughts and ideas seldom outlast the period in which they are enunciated, but a lucid style may live forever. For John McGahern nothing was nobler than an accurate description of the world as it is. The Celtic nature poetry which he loved was almost completely devoid of ideas, arguments, judgements: lyricists simply gave the image which they received. McGahern, who valued a calm, orderly life, kept his main energies for writing and reading. His home in rural Leitrim was filled with classic books which he read and re-read: Homer, Flaubert, Tolstoy, Chekhov, Yeats and Proust.

Current literature he read with gentle curiosity. He was never a harsh but ever an exacting reader. Praises of the second-rate seemed to him like robberies of the truly deserving: and so he became a quiet but convincing advocate for past writers whose work had been neglected (such as John Williams) or for current authors (like Alistair MacLeod) whose subtle, elegiac modes seemed to be drowned out by noisier artists. He was hard to please, but utterly generous about those whose work he admired. Intent above all on creating his own fictional world, he did not set down his critical thoughts at any great length. He never felt the need to work the literary circuits of London or New York, so there is no archive of long, selfregarding essays taken from their major literary reviews. He was more likely to write a short piece on invitation from an editor whom he liked in the *Leitrim Guardian*, the *Irish Times* or Dublin's *Evening Herald*.

His essays are in consequence a gathering of fugitives – occasional pieces done at the mercy of time and chance. He hoarded his best energies for his stories and novels, and once his few hours of daily writing were done, preferred to walk the fields. He wrote some essays on travel whenever he found the destinations interesting; and if people whom he respected invited him to give a lecture or a talk, he would do so, once he felt assured that he had something to say. In his later years, and particularly after the success of his novel *Amongst Women*, he was often asked to write essays on such themes as social change, the rights of women, the role of the Catholic Church, or the decline of rural villages. Editors who knew of his literary preferences would ask him to write reviews concerning his favourite authors. What is so remarkable about these pieces is how little he offers in the way of opinion but how steadfastly he describes the experience of reading through the text in question. He held that it was the duty of a reviewer to report as exactly as possible the very process of moving from page to page through a narrative: how he felt, what thoughts occurred, the final feelings on closing the volume. Precisely because his reviews were occasional, there is an elegiac quality, a sense of sadness in shutting not just a book but a window on a world which may never be seen again.

That note sounded with amazing clarity in the stories of Alistair MacLeod. McGahern once gave a copy of MacLeod's stories as a gift to every member of a postgraduate class in University College Dublin, asking only that anyone who didn't enjoy the volume would return it to him, so that he might present it to somebody else. Not one of the twenty-four students felt the need to give back the copy. The long, lingering titles favoured by MacLeod – 'As Birds Bring Forth the Sun', 'The Closing Down of Summer' – seem to be echoed in that given by McGahern to his last work of pure fiction *That They May Face the Rising Sun*. It is based, like MacLeod's laments for the ebbing rituals of the Maritimes in Canada, on the notion that a tradition may live on in the very lament for its passing, and that the account of the dying of a code will invariably become the central narrative of the world which takes its place. The motif of the swan-song is present in so many of McGahern's writings – but also of time regained and life redeemed by the act of giving a shape to it. This second look at an experience can transform a person from one who is imprisoned by it to one who is set free to place it in a far wider pattern of human significance. What marks an artist off from a journalist is the fact that he is never at the mercy of the immediate moment, never one who suffers that provincialism of time and mind which leaves him a captive to merely personal concerns. So in more than one of his essays McGahern could see the moment of Irish 'freedom' in 1921, not as a qualified triumph of nationalism, but as a conjuncture when responsibility for management of the decline of rural Ireland was passed from one elite group to another.

In this longer view, more anthropological than political, nothing is ever completely lost, for change is so gradual and slow that people may console themselves with the sentiment that if things aren't getting greatly better, then at least they are not getting much worse. But some changes in individual lives are quite exhausting. McGahern noticed how the adjustment to life in the capital city of Dublin used up the intelligence and feeling of many bright scholarship boys and girls who had come into the civil service or teaching profession from a childhood passed on remote farms: and that it was often left to the next generation in such families to carry the inheritance of ideas and emotions onto a new plane. This may indeed be the best cultural explanation so far given for the emergence of that confident, even brash generation which helped to create the Celtic Tiger.

McGahern was pleased that people in the new Ireland had more money and more choices, but he feared a loss of the old courtesies in a world of push, rush and bustle. He knew that manners have a moral dimension, enabling people to relate more easily to one another in the very process of respecting privacies. Far from being an artificial impediment to relationship, good manners were what made candour, openness and kindness possible. The people of rural Leitrim still had beautiful, considerate manners ('no misters in this part of the world', says one of his characters, 'nothing but broken-down gentlemen'), traceable to the modes of a lost Gaelic aristocracy, which survived still in forms of address ('*a dhuine uasail*' meaning 'noble person'). McGahern's characters often bear themselves like ruined noblemen, for whom the exchange of money is a vulgar embarrassment and in whose eyes ancient custom is far more valuable than any modern law. Such a world is built on mutual trust. The old Gaelic notion of *comhar na gcomharsan* (by which neighbours exchanged days of work) would eventually be denounced by some sociologists as a form of licensed mutual terror, but it was also a case of rural *noblesse oblige*, rooted in the values espoused not only by a poet such as Dáibhí Ó Bruadair but also by a novelist such as Jane Austen. Like Austen, McGahern believed in neoclassical tact: the need for people to exercise self-restraint, even and especially when in the presence of disagreeable persons. Both sought to find a mode of existence for their critical attitudes within rather than beyond society.

This ideal of courtesy – a desire not to invade the space of other people – was what led McGahern to the declaration that an author can never know everything about a character, even a character of his own devising. His impatience with some writers was attributable to their assumption of omniscience, but he treated his characters with the sort of tact which they needed to show one another in order for the community to survive as such. Even if we can categorize acquaintances, those who are on terms of intimacy with us remain finally indecipherable. A person is in the end a mystery, each one protecting a locked room which nobody else should presume to enter without clear permission. And an artist is just like a complete person. Confronted with a good book, McGahern always knew when to draw back, when to be silent and display the energy of a powerful reticence.

That silence was not based on anything so vulgar as the idea of an art that eludes analysis. For McGahern it was the act of reading that was sometimes incommunicable. If happiness was something to be felt but never fully described as it was being experienced, the same was also true of reading. Its risky pleasures can be hinted at, anticipated or reconstructed as an experience, but never with the full cohesion of the elements that made those moments. It was in fact as difficult to offer a convincing account of a reading as it was to evoke the modes of personal fulfilment. All of life is a kind of erotics, based on the challenge of reading and misreading other persons and so in his introduction to John Williams's *Augustus* McGahern quotes from the work: 'erotic love is the most unselfish of all the virtues: it seeks to become one with another, and hence to escape the self'.

At the centre of McGahern's artistic practice is a prioritization of pleasure. The culture which produced him often qualified the noun 'pleasure' with the adjective 'guilty' and it was not alone in making that dismal equation. Even in the zones of the contemporary novel and its criticism, the pursuit of pleasure is a distinctly unfashionable, even unmentionable, thing. Many current novelists, though they proclaim anti-puritan ideas, are often 'hard work', suspicious of a pure delight in language such as may also be found in music. McGahern, despite having little or no ear for music, brought many of the feelings associated with its making and reception into literature. The Catholic Ireland of his youth offered little by way of aesthetic experience, except through the sights, sounds and smells of the Mass or Benediction, May altars or Easter rituals. At its most moving moments, that church offered an altar but no pulpit, a ceremonial of flowers, incense and song. The melancholy truth was, however, that these were but rare moments in a religious practice whose once-beautiful rituals were being replaced by merely ethical injunctions. Repeatedly in his essays, McGahern invoked the distinction made by E. R. Dodds in his book *The Greeks and the Irrational* between morality and religion: whereas the former sought only to regulate men's relations to one another, the latter concerned itself with nothing less majestic than man's relation to fate, the gods, destiny itself. The poet W. B. Yeats took a similar view, arguing that if a novelist like George Eliot had had more religion, she would have had fewer morals, for he held that the moral impulse and the religious destroyed one another in the end. The religious person is forever in a mode of celebration; the moralist too often is denying or banning something. Irish Catholicism had declined from its pre-Famine gaiety into a rule-bound set of practices, scruples and interdictions: and McGahern, whose early novel *The Dark* was banned by the government censorship board, apparently for depicting a scene of masturbation, knew the full wrath of such a raw, overweening authority.

His dismissal from his post as a primary teacher in 1965 was an outcome of this regulatory ethic, the direct consequence of an intervention by Archbishop John Charles McQuaid, whose subordinates argued that a man married in a registry office could not be a fit catechist of young boys. But that sacking was also based on a puritanical, middle-class propriety which had slowly but surely replaced the old, joyful world of wakes and pattern-days, festivals and carnivals. Some elements of that world lingered on even a century after the Famine in the Leitrim of

McGahern's childhood. He recalled affectionately the Hardyesque landscape in which no haystack was ever safe from the cavorting of couples after a July dance, 'and the whole parish filled with people going off like alarm-clocks'. In his eyes the new moralists of the socially relevant novel were in secret collusion with the Catholic rule-keepers who announced an end to dancing in private houses or to wakes in remote hillsides.

France attracted McGahern not just because it offered an instance of a peasant society undergoing secularization and modernization some decades before Ireland, but also because the French seemed able to hold on to their regional identities and accents, their style as a way of being in the world, their earthiness. For them the rules which terrified so many Irish people existed only to be broken. One reason for this stubborn resistance to central authority was an honest pride in local culture and this was something which McGahern noticed and praised for its persistence in the *remoter* parts of Ireland. If Charles de Gaulle could ask in despair how any leader could hope to unite a country with 365 varieties of cheese, McGahern liked to describe Ireland as an island composed of thirty-two separate self-governing republics called counties.

The Leitrim in which he grew up in the 1940s was truly remote. To cycle fifteen miles in any direction was to encounter the exotic Other. Neutral Ireland might have been a sheltered, inward-looking place, which liked to dismiss a world war as a mere 'emergency', but in many respects it was much less monocultural than it is now, when incomers and natives congregate in the same shopping malls, approve the same television programmes, and so on. In those years, to enter a new townland even slowly by bicycle was to invade an area of strangeness, which brought the traveller also into contact with the stranger within himself or herself. The people's way of talking, of moving their bodies as they walked, of planting flowers or vegetables, was radically different from all that the traveller knew – and their accents were exceedingly strong and difficult to follow, as difficult in all probability as the visitor's own.

The colour of locality informed every utterance in those days, as it does the dialogue (and often the narrative) of McGahern's own fiction. It was for these qualities that he loved Synge's Aran, Kavanagh's Monaghan, Yeats's Sligo, Joyce's Dublin. People in that order of things were so rooted to their own spot that they felt no need to lay claim to other ideas, other territories, other worlds, and least of all to emulate the distant fashions of London or New York. The nation and the national themselves appeared as rather distant, abstract entities, as remote to Leitrim as to Tomás Ó Criomhthain's Blasket islanders, whose Irish contained no word for 'republic' and who regarded state pensions as strangely modern perversions. Even the county loyalties, so fiercely whipped up every year by supporters of Gaelic football, had somewhat artificial roots in a British shire system, and must have seemed a little confusing to a child who crossed regularly by bicycle from Leitrim to Roscommon. The real unit of culture, as in France, was the parish, the local church spire being its epicentre and the sound of its bell marking out the limits of its intimate, familiar world.

This world appeared to be dissolving in the decades of McGahern's writing career, as the Irish embraced modernity with more and more people living in cities and towns. He and his wife Madeline bucked that trend, returning in the 1970s to live in a lakeshore farmhouse in Leitrim (then the least fashionable of Irish counties but now immortalized by his art). This act of withdrawal was a characteristic declaration of resistance to the siren-calls of the literary cliques. The Dublin pubs which he had known in the 1960s had been filled with writers, often embittered and spiteful because there was so little wealth to share: and McGahern, deeply unimpressed, chose to move away from the quarrels and alliances, even before the post-censorship culture of celebrity had taken hold.

Insofar as McGahern had a theme in his reading and criticism, it was his search for information about how traditions come to an end. He was convinced that whenever a world was about to disappear, a writer emerged to give utterance to it. If that world had been cut off by the facts of nature from a wider society, it achieved this complex articulation through its own resources, evoking that intense form of writing which is poetic, even if formally offered as prose. Ó Criomhthain's *An tOileánach* (*The Islandman*) was his model for such a work, but so also was Synge's treatment of Aran in his travel book, Yeats's ferocious keen for Anglo-Ireland in *Purgatory*, Kavanagh's angry lament for Monaghan in *The Great Hunger*, or Kate O'Brien's epitaph on the Victorian Catholic upper crust in *The Ante-Room*. The Blasket epic was paradigmatic in the stoicism of its author and in its Homeric–Joycean conviction that the day was the unit by which life might be seized and rendered. The islanders' motto when on a spree – '*níl ann ach lá dár saol*', 'it's just a day of our lives' – might also have been the epigraph to *Ulysses*. All of these texts, which McGahern admired, offered an archaeology of lost worlds.

So, whenever he presented a linked set of seminars, he chose these as central exhibits, which lived on by sheer grace of style. The search in *The Aran Islands* was the same as Synge had found in Pierre Lôti, 'for some sign of the persistence of the person'. Compared with the austere, pared-back language of the travelogue, the baroque language of *The Playboy of the Western World* was (in the words of one of McGahern's fictional characters) 'eejity stuff'. Yeats's *Purgatory* was a study of that phase in Anglo-Irish decline when all that was left to the members of that class was their style: McGahern's review of a book about the twilight of the ascendancy was tender and affectionate, but also astringent enough to quote Friedrich Engels on the awful expropriations behind such opulence and charm. Somerville and Ross's *The Silver Fox* was one of the half-forgotten books which he rescued by his attention to it, showing just how fully the Anglo-Irish began to understand Ireland at that very moment when they were losing possession of it – a moment to be repeated at the climax of *Amongst Women* when Moran only comes into imaginative understanding of the beauty of Great Meadow as he is about to lose it forever.

But the most astonishing choice in McGahern's series of seminars was kept for last: Primo Levi's account of existence in the concentration camp of Auschwitz, *If This Is a Man*. McGahern always said that some people are born to be writers and that others become writers through a traumatizing event which calls out for final narration – the killings of the War of Independence made Ernie O'Malley an artist and in some-what similar manner the horrors at Auschwitz impelled a chemist like Levi to produce his account of 'the end of days'. O'Malley's *On Another Man's Wound* chronicled the death of a revolution; *If This Is a Man* analysed not only the exhaustion of a people but of the very language which might describe their sorrow. For McGahern the most rending and mysterious statement was Levi's contention that if the suffering had gone on any longer, a wholly new language would have had to be invented to meet it. It may be added that McGahern's own fictions were probably not the work of a born writer but of one who had been made into an artist by the death of his mother when he, her eldest son, was only ten.

In the library of a local Protestant family, the Moroneys, he developed in the subsequent years a love of reading. The early experience of death was, he said much later, 'my first real experience of the world as a lost world and the actual daily world as not quite real'. In his eyes the world was always well lost for a day with a book. As a writer he was genuinely and pleasantly surprised every time one of his stories found a reader in a mysterious moment of coupling, seeming at once arbitrary and pre-destined. He enjoyed the rather random ways in which texts came to him, some knowingly placed by editors with a shrewd sense of his interests, others quite capriciously sent to the house in Foxfield.

Although he invariably stressed the pleasure which he took in a text, the works he loved most had little sense of self-gratification. Writers like Ó Criomhthain and Synge, Flaubert and Proust, were all humble in that they allowed their entire traditions to speak through them. They became original by going back to origins. Reading was indeed like sex: for the reader – much as the writer before him – seeks both to affirm the self and then to lose it in a moment of bliss. Such pleasure was quite unconnected with the late-twentieth-century equation of freedom with consumption McGahern was aware that the pleasure of self-gratification was now one of the major elements of modern culture, with the liberties once taken only by rare artists being casually treated as a common entitlement in matters of 'lifestyle'. Yet alongside this hedonism in the entertainment and consumer culture went a strange puritanism in the higher arts. In them almost any emotion – abasement, abjection, sexual frenzy, halluci-natory insight, the death-drive itself – was conceivable: any, that is, but the impulse to take pleasure in a tale well told.

McGahern's tactic was one of simple disobedience to the rule-keeper's mantra, which held that 'it's only a sin if you take pleasure in it'. The authorities might control the mating of couples and even the publica-tion of books, but they could not finally censor private acts of reading. The expressive pleasures of the plastic arts of painting and sculpture had proved beyond the purses of most Irish people, as unthinkable as the acquisition of a beautiful building: but a book could be read by almost anyone. The censorship accordingly focused not on the painting, sculpture or music favoured by the wealthy, but on those pleasures more bounteously available to the middle ranks and to the poor.

McGahern's style expressed, without strain or sweat, the calm, unhurried assurance of a craftsman, an ability to sink into the sought experience and to possess it utterly. His sentences are pared but splendid, honest yet patiently formed, and so quite at odds with the utilitarian mind that is devoted to efficiency, productivity, hurry. The sin of the utilitarian class, right across the world, was to have reduced a literature of daily vision to a series of pedagogical tests for the examination and recruitment of its own administrative elites. The Nigerian novelist Chinua Achebe once received a letter from a youth which said: '*Things Fall Apart* is a marvellous work but it has one flaw – you did not supply any sample questions at the end.' That dismal process could be reversed, nonetheless, as the narrator of *The Leavetaking* realizes when he leaves college: 'no longer the dull slog of exams but ways of seeing one's own world for the first time'.

Much contemporary writing is too obviously destined from the outset for the school syllabus and college seminar, with its panoply of mythic reference, learned citation and quotable lines, all designed to fill the student's notebook. Instead of urging people to raise themselves to the level of the classics, the dominant culture has generated writers who lower their thresholds to the level of their mechanistic, moralizing, harried readers. All this is supposed to be deeply democratic, an effect which allows the ordinary man or woman to read books that are 'difficult', 'searing', 'sensational'. McGahern was the truer democrat, however. He wished to slow down the speed of our reading, so that people might learn again how to identify and savour the everyday. The ordinary, as Joyce joked, was the proper domain of the artist: the extraordinary could safely be left to journalists. Intrepid, self-admiring intellectuals lusted after the exceptional, castigating the everyday as banal and routine: but McGahern rendered the dignity of ordinary people's lives.

One element of that dignity is openness to accident, to the random. A sense of the unexpected and of the capricious is central to McGahern's idea of pleasure, as something which may overtake us unexpectedly and for no obvious reason. Good works of art are beyond causal explanation, just mysteriously *there*, as arbitrary and secretive as great-creating nature itself. The distrust of pleasure in a risk-averse society is linked to a fear of the accidental. Criticism is often an attempt at repressive control of fictions which nonetheless insist on their freedom from anyone's over-riding intentions for them. The pleasure of any book comes in pulses, which are quite the opposite of mere sensation, for sensation is always sourced not in the usual but the exceptional, not in the slow assimilation of felt experience but in a surge of an emotional overload. Whereas pleasure offers one of the highest experiences of life – life when it is wholly itself – sensation is now sought most desperately by those who fear that they may not be living at all. They wish to be shocked rather than pleasured, in order to convince themselves that they still have the capacity to feel.

If McGahern's tastes were fastidious, his instincts were democratic, but rooted in the conviction that there is something inherently beautiful about a silent experience of pure imagination. Like writing, reading presupposes a marked degree of silence in a culture. *That They May Face the Rising Sun* emphasizes the successful collaboration of two men over many years based on shared silences. One of the men, the Shah, has the natural courtesy and lovely manners of an aristocrat, although he can neither read nor write:

Often he sat in silence. His silences were never oppressive and he never spoke unless to respond to something that had been said or to say something that he wanted to say. Throughout, he was intensely aware of every other presence, exercising his imagination on their behalf as well as on his own, seeing himself as he might be seen and as he saw others.

McGahern knew how to immerse himself in the exacting silence of a reading: for him a bore was someone who took away your solitude but offered nothing in its place. The quietness of the world before the advent of transistor radios, television and motor cars was a thing to be envied and, as far as possible, repossessed: but the problem was that the search for pleasure once conducted in art was now carried on in the noisy electronic media. All of these pleasures were programmatic, measurable, lacking in surprise and designed for consumption by passive receivers, unlike the active reading of books by self-reliant citizens.

What for him were the sources of readerly pleasure? Although the satisfactions of work or play are usually communal, the intense delight of the reader is solitary. T. S. Eliot once said that we isolate a thing in order to enjoy it. That sounds predatory but isn't so, since it simply indicates the need to surround an admired object with a space sufficient for contemplation. McGahern was a slow, ardent reader and his relaxed but vigilant attention was a kind of prayer. A friend who called once upon him found an anthology of poetry open at Matthew Arnold's 'Dover Beach'. Months later, that friend returned, only to find the volume open at the same page. 'I'm still looking at it,' McGahern laughed, 'except that now it has started to look back at me.' If paintings need space in which to be truly engaged, so also do poems and books.

The requirement of academic courses that students read many classic texts in fairly rapid succession sometimes dismayed him. 'How can they have enough time to read them?' he would ask in sadness. Hence he curtailed his time in universities (even though he loved talking to the young) and he rejected some potentially lucrative offers. In the classroom his method was not dialogic. He would blurt out stunningly original comments with a take-it-or-leave-it insouciance, curious as to the response of those whose opinions differed, but offering none of the mediation ('on the one hand, on the other hand . . .') of the more usual type of seminar leader. He had a rural Irish respect for anything well made (quite different from the do-it-yourself constructions of a mass culture).

The distrust of pleasure among so many intellectuals today arises from a misconception that the deeper realities of life are encountered in pain, adversity and suffering. This view has, however, a scandalously ancient lineage, from the tip of pagan stoicism, through Christian ideas of self-denial, down to our own revolutionary asceticism. But what if it isn't true? What if it is the capacity for playful pleasure which makes us human and distinguishes us from all other animals? McGahern was something of a stoic, who knew when to accept the inevitability of pain, but who could also find in it a call back to the potential fullness of another kind of life.

Reading was not an interpretation but an experience in itself. The joy of reading was a sharing in the creative power of the writer. The texts which he encountered most intensively have been changed and enriched by his re-readings of them: and his own creative writing is an intrinsic part of that re-reading. Whether by Ó Criomhthain, Yeats or Synge, O'Malley, Levi or MacLeod, each of these texts records a deep sense of loss, but in every case the satisfaction of an accurate narration affords a new kind of expressive dignity.

Editor's Preface

John McGahern had been a voracious reader ever since he first befriended the neighbours whose house contained a nineteenth-century library from which the future novelist would take away a number of volumes each week in an old oilcloth shopping bag. In later years he would remember his first encounters with books about the Rocky Mountains and novels by Dickens and Zane Grey. In those days, as he recalls in a marvellous and much reprinted essay, 'The Solitary Reader', he read indiscriminately, for nothing but pleasure. He never relinquished that guiding principle for the rest of his life (and it is invoked in a number of the essays collected in this volume), even after he discovered new authors and different ways of reading and thinking about books in his early maturity in the Dublin of the 1950s, where he read Proust and Tolstoy in his bedsit on the Howth Road between visits to city-centre dancehalls. As Mrs Waldron in McGahern's late story 'Creatures of the Earth' also considers, such favourite books can come to act as Proustian images that 'lightened and deepened life, gave recognition and pleasure.'[1] It seems only appropriate, then, that McGahern's recollection of the timeless pleasure of reading should silently borrow its opening sentence from Proust's essay *On Reading*: 'There are no days more full in childhood than those days that were not lived at all, the days lost in a favourite book.'[2]

Among his favourite books McGahern included not only the great novels of Austen, George Eliot and Beckett, stories by Tolstoy and Alistair MacLeod, the poems of Auden, Larkin, Kavanagh and Yeats, and plays by Chekhov and Shakespeare, but also classic works of criticism, like Proust's *Contre Sainte-Beuve*, Auden's *The Dyer's Hand*, Bergson's *Laughter*, E. R. Dodds's *The Greeks and the Irrational* and Paolo Vivante's *The Homeric Imagination*, and their presence can be felt throughout his own occasional prose. He was also a keen reader of the letters and journals of certain writers whose style he admired, such as Chateaubriand, Stendhal, Flaubert and John Butler Yeats. He had an instinctive dislike of the rigid, artificial distinctions drawn by academics and the book trade between various genres. As he explained in an interview,

> . . . there is no difference between those books. You wouldn't say a bad book of Irish poems is inferior to . . . [*rethinks sentence*] – that *The Homeric Imagination* is inferior to a bad novel or a bad book; that's nonsense . . . I think there is just writing, that a lot of those categories are just snobbery. There used to be a theory that verse was superior to prose, and that both of them were superior to drama and movies. But a good movie certainly could be better than a sonnet or a novel or anything.[3]

McGahern's own forays into criticism and non-fiction were sporadic, but they usually offered some tantalizing insights into the author's preoccupations, the scope of his reading and thinking or the circumstances of his past. Throughout the essays gathered in this collection, the style and voice are recognizably that of the author of the great novels and stories (because style springs from personality, no matter what the subject or genre, as McGahern himself suggests in his essay on *An tOileánach*), even when the subject matter sometimes appears very far removed from the familiar territory of his fiction – as for example in the account of a trip to Morocco or the review of a novel by Georges Simenon.

This volume also reveals a side of McGahern that is likely to be unfamiliar to readers not previously acquainted with McGahern as essayist, reviewer or public speaker. The extent of McGahern's wide reading in the literature of Europe was everywhere present but rarely visible in his fiction, mainly because he took great care not to turn fiction into a self-conscious exercise in namedropping, choosing instead, as Ovid counselled, to use art to conceal art. Only in the fiction of the 1970s are other authors sometimes named outside the context of a schoolboy's compulsory reading list, and even then only very occasionally: Proust,

Freud and Matthew Arnold in *The Leavetaking*, Chekhov in *Getting Through*, Merriman and Pirandello in *The Pornographer*. Yet the influence of these authors and others pervades all of the fiction, from *The Barracks* to *That They May Face the Rising Sun*, as well as his *Memoir*. In the occasional prose – in travelogue, autobiographical sketch and literary criticism alike – many of the same authors are never far away. Sometimes they are explicitly cited, but the prose also harbours many echoes of such great predecessors as Beckett and Yeats, Auden and Flaubert. Their presence pervades McGahern's language like the ghost of Plato who materializes as a corrective teller of truths out of one of Yeats's late poems into the conclusion of McGahern's last essay, 'God and Me': 'Still sings the ghost, "What then?"' [4]

The pieces collected here were written over the course of almost four decades: from McGahern's first published essay, the 'Prologue to a Reading' given at a university in the United States in 1966 (shortly after the publication of the US edition of *The Dark*), which appeared in the Northern literary magazine *The Honest Ulsterman* two years later, to an essay on the role of religion in twentieth-century Ireland (a theme to which many of the pieces collected in this book return again and again) published only a matter of weeks before his death in *Granta*, edited by Ian Jack, with whom he had established an amicable professional rapport during the final years of his life.

Between these bookends McGahern published a surprising number of book reviews and essays on a variety of topics, from the literary to the social and historical, from the analytical to the deeply personal, in a wide range of publications on both sides of the Atlantic. Often these publications were one-offs: like his essay on the forgotten Belfast novelist Forrest Reid in another Northern journal, *Threshold* ('*Brian Westby*'), or his foreword (printed here as 'Mr Joyce and Mr Yeats') to an exhibition catalogue of rare first editions of James Joyce's books at Colgate University in upstate New York, an institution with which McGahern had had a long association ever since he first went there in 1969 as a visiting professor, a position to which he would return regularly over the course of the next three decades. The *Exhibition Catalogue* (which appeared as an issue of the journal of the Colgate University Library) was edited by his friend

Neill Joy, who taught alongside McGahern at the English Department at Colgate. Sometimes, also, McGahern engaged in relatively long-standing connections with certain newspapers, as when he contributed a series of short reviews to the Dublin *Evening Herald* in 1986–7, when the books pages of that paper were edited by Ferdia MacAnna, to whom he was well-disposed. This was an extraordinary flurry of reviewing for a man who generally published so sparingly – yet even those reviews of the most superficial interest usually contain at least one thought or sentence that is startling for its truth or beauty, or the clarity of its expression. A more drawn-out association with the books pages of the *Irish Times* began in 1989, first under the literary editorship of the novelist John Banville and later that of Caroline Walsh. He also wrote occasionally for the *Irish Independent*, the *Listener*, the *Times Literary Supplement*, the *Leitrim Guardian* and the *New York Times*, as well as contributing to books and, sporadically, to academic journals.

Many of the occasional pieces came out of friendships with individual editors, or the love of certain classic authors like Joyce, John Butler Yeats, Forrest Reid or the American novelist John Williams – sometimes, also, he promoted living writers who he thought had not been enough noticed, like the Canadian short-story writer Alistair MacLeod or the local histories of his cousin Liam Kelly. Essays were sent to people he had met and liked for inclusion in books and magazines: Mary Massoud in Cairo, Ian Jack in London, Denis Sampson in Montreal, Derek Mahon in Dublin. Such contributions would be either original works or existing essays he wanted to reprint, always in a slightly reworked version, for McGahern rewrote these incidental pieces just as he rewrote, on those rare occasions when the opportunity arose, the fiction which was always of more consummate interest.[5]

For this collection, McGahern's essays have been divided into six sections. Any such division will always be somewhat arbitrary, and the different sections are not nearly as autonomous as the subheadings might suggest. Often autobiography and travelogue will turn into literary criticism, if only sometimes for a sentence or two. But the opposite is also true. Essays about other writers will often start from recollections of defining moments in his own past, like his memory of attending

Ernie O'Malley's State funeral in 1957 or of finding O'Malley's literary notebooks by accident at around the same time. The brilliant essay on Tomás Ó Criomhthain's *An tOileánach* (which has become something of a minor classic in its own right) circles back in the final paragraphs to McGahern's memory of his own mother: the essay that begins by asking 'What is my language?' ends by analysing that of the beloved who is also the true subject of McGahern's story of his own life in *Memoir*. Autobiography and the examination of social or historical issues are even more inextricably linked, and are therefore placed together in the same section – the most purely autobiographical pieces at the beginning of that section, followed by those essays that draw on autobiography in the pursuit of writing a historical account. If all good history is local history, a conviction that is repeated in many of these essays, then for McGahern the perception of a historical era is also inextricably bound up with the story of *personal* development and growth.

I WRITING AND THE WORLD

A small number of abstract utterances about the nature of art and writing and the artist's place in the world form the opening section of the book. McGahern habitually refused to discuss the process of artistic creation. He was not an author who enjoyed discussing his own work, much less sermonizing on how to write or giving lectures on technique. Those who asked him about the significance of particular elements in his novels or stories would invariably be told that 'it's not for me to say'[6] – a refrain that reverberates through many of the interviews he gave throughout the latter half of his career like Bartleby's well-mannered 'I would prefer not to.'[7] As a result all the pieces collected in this first section are short, and only three of them were published during McGahern's lifetime (and that modest count includes *two* versions of 'The Image'). They are all concerned with aspects of the creative process that are central to McGahern's aesthetic – and in that they are unusual within the McGahern corpus since, like those of many other practising writers, McGahern's moments of artistic self-revelation are usually thinly veiled as comments on the work of other writers (McGahern himself remarked that Beckett's early book on *Proust* 'tells more about Beckett than it tells about Proust'[8]). It is no accident, then, that so many critics have found a description of the timeless and placeless art of *Amongst Women* in McGahern's comments on the epic world of *An tOileánach*.[9]

The opening section contains two versions of 'The Image', McGahern's first published piece of non-fiction. Originally conceived as a 'Prologue to a Reading' during the first decade of his career as a novelist, the aesthetic principles delineated in 'The Image' can be seen at work in all of McGahern's fiction. It describes the task of the artist as a constant struggle 'to pull the image that moves us out of the darkness'[10] (a quality which McGahern also ascribed to Patrick Kavanagh in his review of a book about that poet). This is in itself a distinctly Proustian undertaking,[11] although it becomes clear from a humorous anecdote about an early reading of 'The Image' at an American college, which appears elsewhere in this collection, that its original inception may owe as much to a sentence from Thomas Aquinas: 'The image is a principle of our knowledge. It is that from which our intellectual activity begins, not as a passing stimulus, but as an enduring foundation',[12] a statement which McGahern also recalls being quoted by Patrick Swift during the summer of 1960. The subtitle of the original 1968 version of the essay, 'Prologue to a Reading', moreover, probably deliberately recalls Proust's 'Prologue' to *Contre Sainte-Beuve*, which describes the same process whereby

. . . as soon as each hour of one's life has died, it embodies itself in some material object, as do the souls of the dead in certain folk-stories, and hides there. There it remains captive, captive forever, unless we should happen on the object, recognise what lies within, call it by its name, and so set it free. Very likely we may never happen on the object (or the sensation, since we apprehend every object as sensation) that it hides in; and thus there are hours of our life that will never be resuscitated: for this object is so tiny, so lost in the world, and there is so little likelihood that we shall come across it.[13]

The ideas expressed in 'The Image' also appear to closely resemble those of McGahern's lecture on Herman Melville's 'Bartleby, the Scrivener', delivered to a packed audience at the Belfast Arts Festival on 24 November 1967. Some of that lecture was recalled years later by the poet Richard Murphy, who was close to McGahern in the 1960s:

If style is creative memory, as he suggested, may I be forgiven for remembering creatively that John said, 'Art is as mortal as life, whether it lasts one year or a million years, like us it must die. It's a game, the most interesting game there is. It's not religion, but false religion: the writer sets up as God, king and counsellor . . .'[14]

Regrettably, the lecture itself has not been preserved – nor have those on other favourites like Primo Levi's *If This Is a Man* or Yeats's *Purgatory*, both given as part of a series on Modern Writing when McGahern was writer in residence at NUI Galway and University College Dublin during the 1990s.

A revised text of 'The Image' is included alongside rather than instead of the original essay, as it shows an interesting shift in emphasis. In either version, 'The Image' is probably the single most important articulation of McGahern's artistic aims.

'The Image' is as much a prose poem as a manifesto, and many of its phrases and references are probably deliberately elusive and obscure. The same can be said of the piece that opens the collection, the elliptical 'Five Drafts', whose peculiar structure recalls Beckett's late prose master-piece *Worstward Ho*, in which each paragraph revises the imperfect utterance of the one that preceded it – a process that creates its own refrains. 'Five Drafts' could only have been written by a man with a deep love of the world in an effort to understand it. That desired understanding is of the nature of love, particularly of physical or erotic love[15] – which is the deepest kind of love, as McGahern argues in his essay on John Williams's *Augustus*, as it forms a gateway to the 'other' who would otherwise remain completely separate from the self, a theme which is also dealt with in the preface to the second edition of *The Leavetaking*. (Those two pieces should ideally be read side by side as expressions of the same fundamental belief about the troubled relationship between the self and the 'other' or the 'beloved'.) Because all life is mortal, and all love potentially threatened or temporary, the love of another as well as that of the world 'carries within it the seeds of calamity as well as the promise of total happiness'. That final line of 'Five Drafts' recalls the narrator's observation in *That They May Face the Rising Sun* that Bill Evans leaves himself open to disappointment by hoping, dreaming and looking forward to a weekly outing: 'He was no longer living from moment to moment, from blow to blow, pleasure to pleasure, refusing to look forward or back: he was now living these bus rides on Thursday in the mind as well. The seeds of calamity were sown.'[16] Real happiness, perhaps, is only possible when we know that the cause for that happiness can be snatched away at any moment and cannot be taken for granted. 'Five Drafts' is a celebration of the temporal world and of human love.

The other pieces collected in the first section are more straightforward and do not need as much commentary. I have included a brief reflection on the physical nature of words ('Playing with Words'), as well as an extract on the subjective nature of all written history, a theme that is central to much of McGahern's fiction (particularly to *The Leavetaking*) – as it is to that of Claude Simon, a writer whom he much admired but who is mentioned only once in these essays. 'The Local and the Universal' expresses McGahern's thoughts on the relationship between those two seeming opposites. The distinctive central phrase of that essay, 'The universal is the local, but with the walls taken away', was borrowed from the Portuguese writer Miguel Torga[17] – but it also recalls a comment James Joyce had made about his native city: 'I always write about Dublin, because if I can get to the heart of Dublin I can get to the heart of all the cities of the world. In the particular is contained the universal.'[18] All good writing, McGahern believed, is 'local' in the best sense of the word, because 'Everything interesting begins with one person, in one place.'[19] Sometimes novels can become political or philosophical tracts that lose sight of the particular sights and sounds of the world in their pursuit of 'the great questions which, for all that, adjust themselves very well without his aid', as Joyce wrote in a letter which McGahern quotes with approval. McGahern's own fiction worked in the opposite direction from such books: from the specific could be gleaned the universal – 'representations of particular lives' become representations of 'all of life', as he writes about Joyce's *Dubliners*.

'Madness/Creativity', finally, argues against the ever-fashionable cult of insanity as a source of great Art. Those writers who foster a deranged persona, McGahern argues, are often either dilettantes or shrewd practitioners who use madness as a theme. In a longer typescript draft of the essay, McGahern quotes Philip Larkin's essay on Sylvia Plath to support that argument. Her poems, Larkin suggests, seem to enter neurosis, or insanity, and exist there in a prolonged high-pitched ecstasy like nothing else in literature . . . [Madness] was her subject; together they played an increasingly reckless game of tag. Mad poets do not write about madness: they write about religion, sofas, the French Revolution, nature, their cat Jeoffry.[20]

Such a demand for the artist to maintain at all times an intelligent and fully conscious critical distance from experience is not far removed from Wordsworth's famous imperative for 'emotion recollected in tranquillity'. Raw emotions, like mental breakdown, may be the subject of poetry, but they should always be reworked in the cold light of day by a disciplined author fully in control of his creative powers: art should always be 'the calm that is an ordered passion' (a phrase which McGahern borrowed from W. B. Yeats), not 'a general flailing about'. The dismissal of self-expression as the opposite of art recurs, perhaps unfairly, in the course of McGahern's assessment of George Moore (whose novels *A Drama in Muslin* and *The Lake* were among his favourites) at the beginning of his essay on *Dubliners*.

II PLACES AND PEOPLE

The second section begins with a short essay about a collection of photographs of County Leitrim taken by Leland Duncan in the 1890s, which were discovered by McGahern's cousin Liam Kelly. The essay was first published as a foreword to Kelly's collection of those photographs, and it probably says as much about the art of photography, or by extension the art of fiction, or poetry, or any art, as it does about Leitrim, or about those particular photographs. McGahern's conclusion that in such early photographs of subjects still largely unaware of the process of photography 'Time has become reflection' is very close to another phrase that runs as a leitmotif through some of these essays: that borrowed by McGahern from Donald Gordon's description of Yeats's poetry as an art that 'abolishes time and establishes memory'.[21] Much of McGahern's thinking on Yeats was influenced by Professor Gordon, whose memory is invoked briefly but affectionately in a note at the conclusion of McGahern's essay on the poet's father, John Butler Yeats.

McGahern's fiction was always rooted in specific places. Like the rural migrants to Dublin who appear in many of his short stories and in the novels of the 1970s, *The Leavetaking* and *The Pornographer*, imaginatively McGahern hardly ever left his native Leitrim and Roscommon even when he was teaching in Newcastle, Reading or upstate New York, or travelling to Cairo or Tokyo in the later years of his life. He shared this imaginative rootedness with great predecessors like Joyce and Beckett, who had both written about Dublin and the Wicklow hills from their homes in Trieste, Zurich and Paris; or Yeats, who, while living in London and Dublin for most of his life, made the Sligo of his childhood the well-head of his 'permanent or impermanent images'. (McGahern liked that same rootedness in other writers, too. And he not only found it in authors like the Orkney poets George Mackay Brown and Edwin Muir or the Dubliner Kevin Lehane (who published under the pseudonym Tom Corkery), but also, perhaps more unexpectedly, in Albert Camus, who is celebrated here as a recorder of familiar native places rather than in his more usual guise as one of the great innovators of twentieth-century thought.)

It seems appropriate, then, that the section on places and people should begin in the familiar confines of County Leitrim, which is recalled here in loving and sometimes humorous detail, occasionally repeating images that have also found their way into the fiction. After such local beginnings, the essays in this second section move gradually into the wider world: first to Galway and its hinterland (where the McGaherns had briefly lived, in Cleggan, when they first returned to live in Ireland in 1970, before making their permanent home on Laura Lake in County Leitrim) and Trinity College Dublin, where McGahern spent a year as writer in residence in the early 1990s; before finally, after a stop at Blake's pub in Enniskillen, venturing beyond Ireland to Newcastle, Paris and Morocco. McGahern made even the medinas and the harsh mountain landscape of North Africa his own, savouring the smallest telling detail, as when he observes how 'outside Marrakesh, the land grew flat and stony. I thought it beautiful.' The phrase is typical of the observer who had also noticed the stunted trees on the coast road near Cleggan: 'There are also small trees that I find very moving, sometimes standing alone, other times in weak rows. Their shapes show that all the time they lean away from their scourge, the ocean. The salt and wind strip the outer branches of bark. Even in the full leaf of summer these trees appear to wear a crown of bones' in the essay on Galway; or who had written of the Shah's transformative gaze of the stunted birch trees of Gloria Bog in *That They May Face the Rising Sun*.[22]

There are many vivid moments in these essays when McGahern's eye is drawn to the simplicity or even poverty of certain sights: in Leitrim, Galway and North Africa, as well as in that of the houses of Mennonite settlers in rural Indiana which he thought 'beautiful in their plainness' ('In the Beginning Was the Word'). His imagination is often drawn to such humble, unpretentious images – more the eye of a 'dirty low-down Low Church Protestant'[23] like Samuel Beckett than that of the boy who had marvelled at the baroque beauty of the ceremonies of the Catholic Mass. McGahern's instinctive love of such plainness (not surprising for someone who had grown up in a region which, apart from the occasional splendours of the Catholic Church, was so poor that the passing crow was said to bring a packed lunch) is also manifested in his bare, restrained prose style, closer to that of frugal masters like Beckett, Ó Criomhthain and the Joyce of *Dubliners* than to the exuberant excess of Flann O'Brien or the later Joyce of *Finnegans Wake*.

The remainder of this section is made up of recollections of friends. The tribute to Michael McLaverty, published in the *Sunday Independent* soon after the older novelist's death, is particularly moving. The evocative portrait of the painter Patrick Swift, written from memory many years after the events it describes, is noteworthy since besides honouring the memory of a dead friend it also gives a vivid impression of a period in McGahern's own life which his *Memoir* had all but ignored. *Memoir* was designed to give the impression that the author's formative years had ended after his childhood and youth,[24] but 'The Bird Swift' deepens our sense of McGahern's intellectual formation with its recollection of discussing books (Ellmann's *Joyce* and Painter's and Maurois's lives of Proust) and of looking at paintings with Swift during the summer of 1960. It is fascinating to learn that McGahern preferred a little Constable to the whole of the Picasso retrospective that he went to see with Swift at the Tate Gallery. On another occasion, McGahern also expressed his admiration for other restrained depictions of ordinary life: the 'little Velasquez' of *An Old Woman Frying Eggs* and the work of Vermeer ('that catching of a mysterious moment which is full of ordinariness. There is no grand subject but somehow, in the way it's done, it is surrounded by mystery and grandeur . . .'), as well as Giotto's *Flight into Egypt*,[25] a reproduction of which appears on the postcard sent by Jim and his family to Jamesie and Mary from an Italian holiday in *That They May Face the Rising Sun*.[26]

An affectionate portrait of the journalist Dick Walsh completes this section. The two men had first met in Dublin in the late 1950s, and Walsh had defended McGahern when *The Dark* was seized by customs and banned in Ireland in 1965. Not long before his death in 2003 he was to recall about the furore that surrounded the publication of that novel how 'Later [McGahern] was a source of great admiration for the rest of us. He had looked Irish life in the face in a way it didn't like being looked at.'[27] Walsh's rigorous and erudite journalism is also remembered in another essay later in the collection.

III AUTOBIOGRAPHY, SOCIETY, HISTORY

These essays all to some degree combine elements of personal recollection or memoir with reflections on Irish institutions and attitudes in the second half of the twentieth century. They illustrate how local or personal histories are often far more evocative than accounts of the great affairs of state. The first seven essays are all concerned with McGahern's intellectual formation. They discuss his discovery of books and the pleasures of reading in that nineteenth-century library in a Protestant big house near his home, his education at the Presentation Brothers' new school in Carrick-on-Shannon and St Patrick's College Drumcondra, where he trained to be a teacher between 1953 and 1955, and his early days as a writer. It also includes his reaction, recalled from the steady ground of later maturity, to the banning of *The Dark* in 1965 (which also led to his dismissal from his teaching post in a Church-run National School system), as well as a humorous anecdote about the unnerving experience of giving an impromptu lecture at an American college not many years after, when he was still a young novelist. A witty piece on the processes of literary prizegiving is also included in this section.

The remainder of the third section comprises occasional essays about Irish social and cultural history, mostly dealing with the 1950s. Many of these essays were commissioned by the *Irish Independent* and the *Irish Times* on occasions such as the 1989 and 1992 General Elections (the essay on the latter campaign also comments in no uncertain terms on the Abortion referendum of the same year), a backward glance at the 1950s at the turn of the new millennium, the seventy-fifth anniversary of the Easter Rising in 1991, or simply the festival of Christmas. The immediacy of the occasion of the two election pieces has resulted in what are probably the least restrained utterances in the present collection, whose tone contrasts noticeably even with the essays that immediately succeed them, those on the Ireland of McGahern's youth and early maturity. These valedictory essays are concerned with the repressive moral and intellectual climate of mid-century Ireland. But McGahern's vision ultimately transcends the general darkness of those decades as he allows his gaze to be lifted by the image of the spires of Illiers which Proust had described in a letter, in order to restore to an institution that had been so much criticized some of the dignity and the credit McGahern believed it deserved, if only because the Church had first taught him about grace and beauty and ceremony.

The last three essays in this section are concerned with the death of the rural world and the imminent disappearance of the Irish countryside as McGahern had known it in his childhood and for most of his mature life. One essay returns to the Protestant class to which McGahern owed the experience of his first library, and describes not only the fate of dwindling Southern Protestant communities but also (by reflection) the Northern Troubles. In his reflections on the decline of the Irish rural landscape, socio-historical reflections again give way to a celebration of the written word as the great Nova Scotian storyteller Alistair MacLeod gets the final say about the demise of rural Ireland when the awareness of the dwindling stature of the Mohill cattle mart reminds him of the stories in *The Lost Salt Gift of Blood*. In MacLeod's account of a world 'poised on the edge of eclipse or change' in a country across the Atlantic, McGahern found expressed, with elegance and precision and without sentiment, a version of what he saw happening around him in rural Leitrim and Roscommon. And his description (in the longer essay on the same author) of MacLeod's miners and fishermen who 'take joy from that very oblivion of which they so movingly sing' probably deliberately recalls W. B. Yeats's concept of 'tragic joy': when the tragic hero experiences a 'sudden enlargement of their vision, their ecstasy at the approach of death . . . Tragedy must be a joy to the man who dies.'[28] The humble world of MacLeod's Cape Breton is ennobled by this 'tragic joy', and McGahern's own celebration of the last moments of a world changing rapidly beyond all recognition may be read in that same mode of perfect joyous utterance in the moment of a culture's final passing.

IV AND VI LITERATURE AND REVIEWS

Since McGahern primarily saw himself as a writer who just happened to live on a farm, just as he had once been a writer who happened to be a teacher,[29] it is hardly surprising that well over half of this collection is made up of writing about literature: of book reviews and extended essays about certain books and authors, as well as rare explicit utterances about the process of artistic creation.

The first two essays in the section on literature are both concerned with the relationship between the writer and his public or the writer and his critics. In the first, McGahern warns the writer against pandering to the tastes of prescriptive critics in a bid to sell more books or to be included in university syllabi; in the other, he offers a sympathetic engagement with the burden placed on certain writers by their critics. The provocative 'A Literature without Qualities', unpublished during McGahern's lifetime, argues against the commodification of literature and the tyranny of prescriptive 'aesthetic labels'. The shape of McGahern's recurring preoccupation with 'the poor gaudy beads of local colour' (as he refers to them in a review of a collection of stories by George Mackay Brown) came largely out of his reading of Borges, and may be read alongside that writer's classic essay on 'The Argentine Writer and Tradition'.[30] Its proximity to Borges's essay may also account for its tone and style, which are unlike that of any of the other pieces in the collection.

McGahern's attitude towards critics and criticism was often ambivalent at best. In an unpublished lecture given in Sligo he remarked about a brand of literary tourism that:

. . . in an age which has so many loud diversions away from the original printed word, may I say that the great heart of Yeats, the magical words, will not be found in these diversions or even in Dromahair or Drumcliffe Churchyard, but in *The Collected Poems* and *The Collected Plays* which stand on our shelves – or in Mr Keohane's bookshop – and do not even ask to be opened.[31]

McGahern's distrust of an academic publishing machine that threatened to overshadow those individual voices it ostensibly sought to promote is sharpest in his reviews of two posthumously published books by F. Scott Fitzgerald; but it is imagined most poetically – and most poignantly – in a striking image in the essay printed here as 'Mr Joyce and Mr Yeats' which ironically recalls Austin Clarke's famous image of Yeats as a mighty oak tree casting his formidable shadow over the Irish imaginative landscape: 'Yeats was rather like an enormous oak-tree . . . which, of course, kept us in the shade and of course we always hoped that in the end we would reach the sun, but the shadow of that great oak-tree is still there.'[32] In McGahern's knowing reworking of Clarke, Yeats is no longer an intimidating presence but a cautionary example of a writer under threat from critics who demand too much from 'the poor written word'.

Notwithstanding his sceptical attitude to critics, McGahern's own literary criticism, when it came, was always insightful and sprang from a genuine love of certain works. Sometimes these were works which he thought had been unfairly forgotten, like the novels of John Williams, the letters of John Butler Yeats or Forrest Reid's novel *Brian Westby*. As he explained in an interview,

I've never really written fiction unless I wanted to, out of the need. I've done very little criticism; and the reason I've done it is sometimes for money, and also to draw attention to books that I liked that didn't get attention. For instance I wrote the introductions to *Stoner* and *Augustus* by John Williams, simply because I thought he was a wonderful writer and he had gone completely out of recognition, and now actually he is being reprinted in America because of this . . . His writing is so good that I couldn't understand why it had . . . [*pauses*] you know. I think we all become extinct eventually but there was no reason why this man should become extinct so quickly.[33]

McGahern's essays on J.B.Y.'s letters and *Brian Westby* should both be read as part of a sustained effort to get those works back into print (he succeeded in this with Yeats; Reid's book remains out of print to this day). The J.B.Y. letters had been part of his imaginative landscape ever since he first read them in the 1950s, and references to and echoes of them appear in many of the essays collected here. McGahern sought for opportunities to have them reprinted throughout the 1970s and 1980s: he was at one point going to include them in a projected *Faber Book of Irish Prose*, to be edited by him, in the early 1980s,[34] but it was eventually through an offer from a French publisher that they were reissued, with McGahern's own introduction, in 1999. His advocacy of *Brian Westby* was equally intense. In 1966, McGahern wrote to Michael McLaverty (who shared his admiration of Forrest Reid's style) to ask him for a copy of *Brian Westby*. He tried unsuccessfully to persuade Charles Monteith, his editor at Faber and Faber, to reprint the novel, before sending the copy borrowed from McLaverty for consideration to Knopf in New York, who had just published McGahern's own novel, *The Dark*.[35] Over the course of the next decade he conceived a number of other schemes to have the novel republished, all to no avail.

McGahern's idealized Solitary Reader is a close relative of Virginia Woolf's Common Reader, who 'differs from the critic and the scholar . . . He reads for his own pleasure rather than to impart knowledge or correct the opinions of others.'[36] Those same qualities are recognizable in McGahern's criticism and reviews. He was always a sympathetic and undogmatic critic who believed that 'the best criticism surely grows out of love', and that 'All that survives does so by acquiring lovers.' Books one does not like, he repeatedly counselled in the good manners of the mind, should be put aside with regret rather than venom. His ideal literary critic or reviewer, unprescriptive and motivated by nothing more or less than a love of the subject, is embodied perfectly by two of the lecturers described in one of the final chapters of *The Dark*:

. . . there were one or two who simply spoke about their subject with love, and their quiet excitement was able to come through, one frail grey-haired woman in a botany class, a younger man at mathematics who continually brushed imaginary chalk specks from his gown as he spoke and you came away wanting to learn and share, both were beautiful and young in some way.[37]

McGahern's attitude towards the proper relationship between literature and criticism was made abundantly clear when, speaking at an
academic conference, he concluded one version of the anecdote about a
public appearance at a Mennonite college which forbade readings of
original works but tolerated criticism (an anecdote which was recycled
for use on various occasions) with a sly criticism of his own: 'I tell this
by way of apology for a reading as I know that there are some Joyceans
who while not as strict as the Mennonites prefer commentaries to any
readings on an occasion such as this.'[38] His own criticism often showed
the opposite tendency. As a critic, he preferred to let work speak for itself
in the hope that genuinely good writing might attract some new lovers,
and what is striking about many of his essays on favourite authors
(particularly those on Forrest Reid and Alistair MacLeod) is how exten-
sively McGahern quotes from the work. A just cause needs no advocate.
McGahern believed passionately that a writer's only responsibility is to
the language: to 'get the words right'.[39] And so to say simply that he or
she wrote well was the highest form of praise that could be afforded to
any writer, in whichever genre they happened to work – and that conclusion summed up the achievements of authors as various as Chekhov and
Alice Munro, Lawrence and J. R. Ackerley.

V PREFACES AND INTRODUCTIONS

The remainder of the book is made up of McGahern's introductory notes
to some of his own works. The prefaces to *The Leavetaking* and *Creatures
of the Earth* may be read alongside the elliptical pieces in the first section
of this volume, as they give a further insight into some of McGahern's
ideas about the nature of fiction. The two introductions to *The Power of
Darkness* – that to the 1991 stage version and that to a revised text for
radio, recorded in 2005 – comment on the nature of revision and adaptation, his affinity with Tolstoy, and the serious repercussions of the
repressive nature of the mid-twentieth-century moral climate in Ireland.

It is clear from everything he wrote that John McGahern had a deep 'love
of the world', a phrase borrowed from Hannah Arendt[40] which he also
used as the title of one of his last short stories. Through seeing and

reading and writing ('the pleasures of the mind'), this love of all that surrounds life was allowed to develop in the constant wonder that any of it existed at all – not least of all the self, since the chances of any individual having been born at all were remote and dependent largely on accident, as the narrator of *The Leavetaking* also considers.[41] The finite, transitory nature of existence was not in the end something that should be regretted or feared, as the constant sense of an ending lent an added vividness to every moment, giving a sense of wonder to the most ordinary of sights. As he writes in *Memoir*:

We grow into an understanding of the world gradually. Much of what we come to know is far from comforting, that each day brings us closer to the inevitable hour when all will be darkness again, but even that knowledge is power and all understanding is joy, even in the face of dread, and cannot be taken from us until everything is. We grow into a love of the world, a love that is all the more precious and poignant because the great glory of which we are but a particle is lost almost as soon as it is gathered.[42]

With its constant savouring of every meticulously observed detail, McGahern's writing, like the ideal act of literary criticism he envisaged, is always an act of love; and his style, like the loving perspective on her own familiar reality that is suddenly identified by Mrs Waldron in 'Creatures of the Earth', is 'ever watchful and lively and at ease.'[43]

Stanley van der Ziel
April 2009

NOTES

1 John McGahern, *Creatures of the Earth: New and Selected Stories* (London: Faber and Faber, 2006), p. 323.
2 Cf. Marcel Proust, *On Reading* [1905], translated and edited by Jean Autret and William Burford (London: Souvenir Press, 1972), p. 3.
3 Stanley van der Ziel, 'An Interview with John McGahern' [October 2004], Appendix II in *Medusa's Mirror: Art, Style, Vision & Tradition in the Fiction of John McGahern* (PhD dissertation, University College Dublin, 2008), p. 364.
4 Cf. W. B. Yeats, 'What Then?', *The Poems*, edited by Richard J. Finneran, revised edition (London: Macmillan, 1991), p. 302.

5 Some of McGahern's short stories were revised – sometimes drastically – between publications, and so were the second part of *The Leavetaking* (for the revised 1984 edition) and the play *The Power of Darkness*. The latter was produced in three substantially different versions in just over three decades: for BBC Radio in 1972, at the Abbey Theatre in 1991 and for RTÉ Radio in 2006. McGahern accepted the fact that a novelist – unlike poets, short-story writers or playwrights – is not usually afforded the opportunity for revision once the work is published, but he was grateful for opportunities when he *could return to a work*. The prefaces and introductions in section V all dwell on the urge for revision and on the various circumstances under which it had been possible.

6 Van der Ziel, 'An Interview with John McGahern', p. 366.

7 Herman Melville, 'Bartleby, the Scrivener: A Story of Wall-Street' [1853], *The Norton Anthology of American Literature*, Sixth edition (5 Vols), general editor Nina Baym (New York and London: Norton, 2003), Vol. B: 2,330–55, *passim*.

8 Denis Sampson, 'A Conversation with John McGahern', *Canadian Journal of Irish Studies* 17.1 (July 1991): 13–18, p. 17.

9 See for example John Cronin, 'Retrenchment and Renewal: John McGahern's *Amongst Women*', *Irish University Review* 22.1 (Spring/Summer 1992): 168–76, pp. 170–1, 176; Denis Sampson, *Outstaring Nature's Eye: The Fiction of John McGahern* (Washington, D.C.: The Catholic University of America Press, 1993), pp. 221, 239, 248–9; and Declan Kiberd, 'John McGahern's *Amongst Women*', *Language and Tradition in Ireland: Continuities and Displacements*, edited by Maria Tymoczko and Colin Ireland (Amherst and Boston: University of Massachusetts Press, 2003): 195–213, pp. 198–200, 203, 209.

10 Arminta Wallace, 'Out of the Dark' (interview with McGahern), *Irish Times* 28 April 1990: Weekend 5.

11 The phrase from the Wallace interview is itself an unmistakable echo of Proust's *A la recherche du temps perdu*: 'The only things that come from ourselves are those we draw out of the obscurity within us, which can never be known by other people.' Marcel Proust, *In Search of Lost Time*, general editor Christopher Prendergast (London: Allen Lane, 2003), Vol. 6: *Finding Time Again*, translated by Ian Patterson, p. 188.

12 Cf. St Thomas Aquinas, *Philosophical Texts*, selected and translated by Thomas Gilby (London: Oxford University Press, 1951), p. 234.

13 Marcel Proust, *By Way of Sainte-Beuve*, translated by Sylvia Townsend Warner (London: Chatto & Windus, 1958), p. 17.

14 Richard Murphy, *The Kick: A Memoir* (London and New York: Granta, 2002), p. 262. See also two other eye-witness accounts: Ray Rosenfield, 'John McGahern Gives Insight on Melville', *Irish Times* 25 November 1967: 10; and Seamus Heaney, 'Shedding the Skin of Youth' (review of *The Leavetaking*), *Sunday Independent* 26 January 1975: 9.

15 A number of the recurring thoughts and phrases in 'Five Drafts' clearly echo John Williams's descriptions of the protagonist's renewed understanding of the nature of love in *Stoner*: 'In his forty-third year William Stoner learned what others, much younger, had learned before him: that the person one loves at first is not the person one loves at last, and that love is not an end but a process through which one person attempts to know another . . . [H]e began to know that [love] was neither a state of grace nor an illusion; he saw it as a human act of becoming, a condition that was invented and modified moment by moment and day by day, by the will and the intelligence and the heart.' John Williams, *Stoner* [1965] (London: Vintage Classics, 2003), pp. 194–5.

16 John McGahern, *That They May Face the Rising Sun* (London: Faber and Faber, 2002), p. 212.

17 Miguel Torga, *The Creation of the World* [1937–81], translated by Ivana Rangel-Carlsen and Patricia Odber de Baubeta (Manchester: Carcanet, 2000), quoted on the back cover. McGahern began to use that aphorism in many of his public appearances from about 2000 or 2001, concurrent with the publication in English of the complete edition of *The Creation of the World*. He told Eamon Maher that this was the origin of the phrase. See Maher, 'Catholicism and National Identity in the Works of John McGahern: Interview', *Studies: An Irish Quarterly Review* 90.357 (Spring 2001): 70–83, p. 81.

18 Quoted in Richard Ellmann, *James Joyce* [1959], revised edition, with corrections (Oxford, New York, Toronto and Melbourne: Oxford University Press, 1983), p. 505.

19 Clíodhna Ní Anluain (ed.), *Reading the Future: Irish Writers in Conversation with Mike Murphy* (Dublin: Lilliput, 2000): 137–55, p. 150.

20 Quoted by McGahern in an untitled typescript. NUIG P71/1069. Cf. Philip Larkin, *Required Writing: Miscellaneous Pieces 1955–1982* (London: Faber and Faber, 1983), p. 281. McGahern changed the order of the sentences from Larkin's original.

21 D. J. Gordon, *W. B. Yeats: Images of a Poet: My Permanent or Impermanent Images*, with contributions by Ian Fletcher, Frank Kermode and Robin Skelton (Manchester: Manchester University Press, 1961), p. 43.

22 See McGahern, *That They May Face the Rising Sun*, pp. 35–6.

23 Samuel Beckett, *More Pricks than Kicks* [1934] (London: Calder, 1993), p. 184.

24 See Stanley van der Ziel, Review of *Memoir*, *Irish University Review* 35.2 (Autumn/Winter 2005): 463–9.

25 See Nicholas Wroe, 'Ireland's Rural Elegist' (profile of McGahern), *Guardian* 5 January 2002: Saturday Review 6–7, p. 7. The quotation is from Colm Tóibín.

26 McGahern, *That They May Face the Rising Sun*, p. 108.

27 Quoted in Wroe, 'Ireland's Rural Elegist', p. 6.

28 W. B. Yeats, *Essays and Introductions* (London: Macmillan, 1961), pp. 522–3. Elsewhere, Yeats had also written about 'that despair which is a form of joy' which is a central feature of 'poetical tragedy' as he saw it. W. B. Yeats, *Explorations* (London: Macmillan, 1962), p. 296. The phrase 'tragic joy' itself appears in the poem 'The Gyres', *The Poems*, p. 293.

29 *John McGahern: A Private World*, directed by Pat Collins. RTÉ 1 Television, 11 January 2005.

30 See Jorge Luis Borges, *Labyrinths: Selected Stories and Other Writings* [1964] (London: Penguin, 2000), pp. 211–20.

31 Untitled typescript. NUIG P71/uncatalogued.

32 Quoted in *Reviews and Essays of Austin Clarke*, edited by Gregory Schirmer (Gerrards Cross: Colin Smythe, 1995), p. xi.

33 Van der Ziel, 'An Interview with John McGahern', p. 365.

34 I am indebted for this information to Denis Sampson.

35 See three letters to Michael McLaverty from the second half of 1966, in *Dear Mr McLaverty: The Literary Correspondence of John McGahern and Michael McLaverty 1959–1980*, edited by John Killen (Belfast: Linen Hall Library, 2006), pp. 45–6.

36 Virginia Woolf, *The Common Reader*, new edition (London: Hogarth Press, 1929), p. 11.

37 John McGahern, *The Dark* (London: Faber and Faber, 1965), p. 174.

38 Untitled manuscript. Private Collection.

39 Wallace, 'Out of the Dark', p. 5.

40 I am indebted to Madeline McGahern for remembering the origin of the phrase. See also Elisabeth Young-Bruehl, *Hannah Arendt: For Love of the World* [1983], revised edition (New Haven and London: Yale University Press, 2004).

41 See John McGahern, *The Leavetaking* (London: Faber and Faber, 1974), p. 35.

42 John McGahern, *Memoir* (London: Faber and Faber, 2005), p. 36.

43 McGahern, *Creatures of the Earth*, p. 326. That phrase itself echoes a sentence from Jane Austen's *Emma* (Harmondsworth: Penguin, 1985), p. 241.

Editor's Note and Acknowledgements

Many of these essays appeared previously in various books and magazines. For inclusion in this volume, spelling and punctuation have been regularized throughout. Quotations from other texts have been checked where possible and silently corrected where necessary. The aim of the current text is above all to be readable; and so scholarly interjections have been kept to a minimum. Footnotes are mine. Occasional omissions, usually of substantial repetitions of material between essays, are indicated by ellipses in square brackets: [. . .].

As he points out in one of the essays collected here, John McGahern's Irish was far from fluent, and I am indebted to Declan Kiberd for correcting McGahern's usage of occasional Irish words and phrases; my debt to Professor Kiberd also extends to his invaluable advice on other elements of the editorial work and the preface. Particular gratitude is owed to Fergus Fahey, the keeper of the John McGahern Collection at the James Hardiman Library, NUI Galway, who kindly provided me with copies of some of the relevant archival material; and to Neil Belton and Kate Murray-Browne at Faber and Faber for expert guidance. I also wish to thank the staff of the libraries of University College Dublin, Trinity College Dublin and the National Library of Ireland, as well as Irene Stevenson at the *Irish Times* and Frank Coughlan at the *Irish Independent*. Denis Sampson, Neill Joy and Patrick Lonergan have all sent me hard-to-get pieces or suggested useful leads in my hunt for McGahern's published non-fiction. I owe a special debt of gratitude to Jana Fischerova and Graham Price for invaluable suggestions and advice.
  SvdZ

I

WRITING AND THE WORLD

Five Drafts

We are sexual from the moment we are born until we die, and love is the human act of becoming, modified moment by moment, making all that is dear to us more precious still as it passes, until it becomes the rich gift of the life and self, taken and given to us for a time from the black jewel case.

We are sexual from the moment we are born until we die. In the beginning we could not come into any wholeness of being without the other, the beloved. That love eventually suffuses everything around the beloved and goes out to all of life we feel precious. In the mind alone this must grow old or fail, unless the mind before the body goes.

We are sexual from the moment we are born until we die. The church I was brought up in turned this powerful and abiding instinct that suffuses everything we feel as precious or hold dear into the functional act of human reproduction, surrounding it with shame and sin, as it sought to turn the human act of becoming, which is modified moment by moment and day by day, away from the love of what is merely human into the love of God.

We are sexual from the moment we are born, it grows as the body grows and fails with the body until we die: by then it has become part of the mind, the will and the intelligence and heart, which grows in the human act of becoming as the body fails, and suffuses everything we hold precious or dear. The church I was brought up in sought to turn this powerful and abiding instinct into the functional act of procreation, surrounding it with shame and sin, as it directed this human act of becoming modified moment by moment, day by day, year by year.

We are sexual from the moment we are born until we die, it grows as the body grows and fails with that body, but by then it has become part of the mind as well, the will and the intelligence and heart, which continues to grow even as the body fails and suffuses everything we hold precious or dear. The church I was brought up in sought to limit this powerful and abiding instinct to the functional act of procreation, surrounding it with shame and sin, as it directed this human act of becoming away from the passing world in which it is set to God and Eternity. What we love first is never what we love last, but without that first love we would never have been made whole or allowed into the world of love, and that entrance has to be through another person. When that passion is concentrated on another person, first or last, it carries within it the seeds of calamity as well as the promise of total happiness.

The Image: Prologue to a Reading at the Rockefeller University [1968]

When I reflect on the image two things from which it cannot be separated come: the rhythm and the vision. The vision, that still and private universe which each of us possess but which others cannot see, is brought to life in rhythm, and by rhythm I think of the dynamic quality of the vision, its instinctive, its individual movements; and this struggles towards the single image, the image on which our whole life took its most complete expression once, in a kind of grave, grave of the images of dead passions and their days.

For art is, out of the failure of love, an attempt to create a world in which we can live: if not for long or forever, it is still a world of the imagination over which we can reign, and to reign is to purely reflect on our situation through this created world of ours, this Medusa's mirror, which allows us to celebrate even the totally intolerable. And we absurdly reign over this imaginary world in the illusory permanence of false gods, and it may be this need of permanence that creates in its turn the need for shape or form.

So we cannot live, we can only absurdly reign, and we have no reason or right to reign, but it is not possible to live when confronted with the immovable solidity of the world, so we transform it into another way because of nothing more than our instinctive need. And as we reign alone there on our cuckoo throne the subjects we summon up are images.

Image after image flows involuntarily now, and still we are not at peace, rejecting, altering, shaping, straining towards the one image that will never come, the lost image that gave our lives expression, the image that would completely express it again in this bewilderment between our beginning and end, and then the whole mortal game of king would be over, and all games. It is here, in this search for the single image, that the long and complicated journey of art betrays the simple religious nature of its activity: and here, as well, it most sharply separates itself from formal religion.

Religion, in return for the imitation of the formal pattern, promises us the eternal Kingdom. The Muse, under whose whim we reign, in return for a lifetime of availability, may grant us the absurd crown of style, the 'revelation' in language of this private and unique world each of us possess, as we struggle for what may be no more than a yard of lead piping we saw in terror once.

The Image [1991]

When I reflect on the image, two things from which it cannot be separated come: the rhythm and the vision. The vision, that still and private world which each of us possesses and which others cannot see, is brought to life in rhythm – rhythm being little more than the instinctive movements of the vision as it comes to life and begins its search for the image in a kind of grave, grave of the images of dead passions and their days.

Art is an attempt to create a world in which we can live: if not for long or forever, still a world of the imagination over which we can reign, and by reign I mean to reflect purely on our situation through this created world of ours, this Medusa's mirror, allowing us to see and to celebrate even the totally intolerable.

We cannot live, we can only reign, and we have no reason or right to reign, nothing more than our instinctive need; so we reign in the illusory permanence of false gods; and it may be this need of the illusion of permanence that creates in its turn the need for shape or form. As we reign on our cuckoo thrones the subjects we summon up are images.

Image after image flows involuntarily now, yet we are not at peace – rejecting, altering, shaping, straining towards the one image that will never come, the image on which our whole life took its most complete expression once, that would completely express it again in this bewilderment between our beginning and our end; and then the whole mortal game of King would be over, and all games.

It is here, in this search for the one image, that the long and complicated journey of art betrays the simple religious nature of its activity: and here, as well, it most sharply separates itself from formal religion.

Religion, in return for the imitation of its formal pattern, promises us the Eternal Kingdom. The Muse, under whose whim we reign in return for a lifetime of availability, may grant us the absurd crown of Style, the revelation in language of the unique world we possess as we struggle for what may be no more than a yard of lead piping we saw in terror or in laughter once.

Playing with Words

I write because I need to write. I write to see. Through words I see.

As with most serious things, it began in play, playing with the sounds of words, their shape, their weight, their colour, their broken syllables; the fascination that the smallest change in any sentence altered all the words around it, and that they too had to be changed in turn. As in reading, when we become conscious that we are no longer reading romances or fables or adventure but versions of our own life, so it suddenly came to me that while I seemed to be playing with words in reality I was playing with my own life. And words, for me, have always been presences as well as meanings. Through words I could experience my own life with more reality than ordinary living.

Work often begins with an image or a rhythm or a line of dialogue that stays in the mind and will not go away until it is written down. Often, after it is written down, it goes away, it is nothing; sometimes it results in work that lasts for months or years. I write to see into what world those phrases and images that will not go away will lead me, to give that world being and shape.

Almost twenty years ago I printed 'The Image', which described all that I felt about writing. It is true for me now as then.

If I have any quarrel today with 'The Image', it is that it is perhaps too serious. I remember David Hume's stricture on the uselessness of arguing about religion because its base is faith not reason. The same is true of art. Most good writing, and all great writing, has a spiritual quality that we can recognize but never quite define. In his wonderful little piece on Chateaubriand, Proust recognized this quality both by its presence – the blue flower on the earth – and its absence from the more worldly glittering prose of diplomat and traveller. Call it moral fragrance or style or that older, healing word – magic.

The Local and the Universal

Everything interesting begins with one person in one place, though the places can become many, and many persons in the form of influences will have gone into the making of that single woman or man. No one comes out of nowhere; one room or town or locality can be made into an everywhere. The universal is the local, but with the walls taken away. Out of the particular we come on what is general, which is our great comfort, since we call it truth, and that truth has to be continually renewed. What is general and true has to be found again. If we resort to what is already general in this quest, all we are likely to find is the stale air of the imitative.

Listowel seems to have been more fortunate than most places, in that a number of extraordinarily talented people have gone into the creation of this week. The law of singularity seems to have prevailed here as well since the dear late John B. Keane told us that when he and the other distinguished presences took their walks in the attractive town square here in Listowel, they often moved in different circles.

History (On meeting J. C. Beckett)

I admired the histories of the late Professor J. C. Beckett, especially the clarity of his writing, and when we met and I told him so, he was glad. As he thanked me, he remarked, 'Of course, they're prejudiced,' with a very sly twinkle. What this has always seemed to me to imply is that there is no such thing as a 'true' history. Each is a version of what has taken place, and everybody who writes is coming from somewhere.

   [. . .]

Madness/Creativity

I have to say at once that I feel nothing but unease when confronted with such a theme.

Madness, like banality and boredom and murder, can be written about; but when they are, the writing itself can never afford to be any of these things. For instance, prose has never to be more alert to every shade of nuance than when writing about boredom, which is the opposite to the state it is attempting to reflect and bring to life.

There are great works that approach the themes of madness or break-down. I think of Melville's 'Bartleby, the Scrivener', Gogol's 'Diary of a Madman', Pirandello's 'The Rivers of Lapland'. Ultimately, these works are chilling in their sanity, and they use madness as a method to show what we call reality or the human condition in uncompromising light. Chekhov, a practising doctor, avoided all such methods when he came to write 'Ward 6'.

The history of art is littered with movements that link creativity to madness and systematic derangement of the senses, with drugs or other violences. They have come about through fashion or boredom with the mainstream, or, more seriously, they have been attempts to enter deeper into the very subconscious that lies like laughter at the dark heart of life. It seems to me that the results that have come back to us, whether from Dada or the Beats, remain uncertain. Often among the shrewder practitioners can be found a critical intelligence masquerading as creative. Could the fur-lined cup have passed for wit if the common glaze did not have such a long and useful and unexamined life?

When I was young there was a slogan linked to a fashionable

psychoanalytical movement: Break down to break through. It posited madness as the norm and exalted self-expression. I have always felt that self-expression is the opposite of creativity – the clear mirror, the reflection of personality that we call style, everything removed from it that is not itself. Self-expression becomes like the crowded beaches Montale referred to in his diary-essay 'Flaubert's House': Ascona and Capri, 'rendez-vous of Nordic nudists and misunderstood geniuses'.

In work, there comes a time when we have to abandon the purely rational and trust to instinct and strong feeling and imagination, but it cannot be forgotten that the very abandonment is sanctioned by an intelligence aware of its own rational limit. What results is always tested by the same intelligence which decides finally between truth or sense or dross.

In Irish the most moving phrase for a mad person is one who belongs to God, *duine le Dia*, placing that person outside human jurisdiction. Confronted with such a phenomenon we can only turn away in pity and terror, knowing that even the greatest works of art belong to the luxury trades.

II

PLACES AND PEOPLE

Time Regained:
Photographs of County Leitrim

Foreword to *The Face of Time: Leland Lewis Duncan 1862–1923:
Photographs of County Leitrim*, edited by Liam Kelly

I enjoyed Liam Kelly's history of his own parish of Kiltubrid when it was published – I find these local histories often far more moving than accounts of the great affairs of state – and I did not know then that he had come on this remarkable collection of photographs by Leland Duncan in the course of his research.

They have the fascination of nearly all old photographs. Time that is still our element has already washed over these lives, and they seem to look at us out of a depth of time or waters in fashions that have ceased. What an added pleasure it is to see how unselfconscious these people are. They could not imagine how they would look in a photograph. Their mute presences are more eloquent than an idea of self. This is further reinforced by the relatively rudimentary techniques of the period Duncan was working in. He had to be able to see the picture in his mind's eye beforehand; he could not add or subtract anything later in the darkroom, so that whatever he saw in his viewfinder before the shutter clicked was the finished picture.

At first glance, the photographs seem to be the work of an extremely gifted amateur, but a more careful look points to their being something more. They document a society in a time and place, and all the images are picked with care. That he chose to focus on a poor cottage, a bare-footed woman in a doorway, two servant girls in their Sunday finery, is significant; but more telling of the eye which he brought to his craft is the angle of the house, the broom next to the doorway, the placing of the birdcage and wheel. I believe he had a sure grasp of the limitations of photography, its built-in objectivity, and that he was able to use it to express his patent sympathy with the people he was photographing. How, otherwise, could these pictures speak to us so movingly across all the years?

The best pictures are full of what I can only describe as a delightful tact (and what, after all, is true tact but a kind of mind-reading?). They speak to us out of a world that has disappeared; but such is the magic and mystery of art that they do so with a richness and depth that life rarely gives. Time has become reflection.

County Leitrim: The Sky above Us

We live in the poor heart of the island of Ireland. The large centres of population are almost all the same distance from where we live: Dublin is a hundred miles away; Belfast is a hundred and twenty; Galway is ninety. In the richer parts they claim that when the crow flies over Leitrim he takes his lunch along. It does not help to know that in Madrid and Barcelona they say that when the eagle flies across the proud province of Granada he takes bread and cheese and a half bottle of wine, because, compared to the poor crow, the eagle with his bottle of wine resembles a royal procession.

Not many people live in Leitrim, not many live in any of the western border counties. The towns are small, the county's principal town is Carrick-on-Shannon, which is smaller than the lesser towns of most other counties. Small here is mostly plain. A few have individual charm, but many are made up of one wide street, the houses in such tired argument with one another that they take on a drab sameness; and they are particularly weary in rain.

Yet the people scattered so sparsely around the countryside love these towns, and that changes them on certain days and hours – on market days, or some feasts of the saints, especially when feast and market coincide, and always in the excited crowded bustle of late-night Saturday shopping.

There is nothing dramatic about the landscape, but it is never dull. On the low drumlins around the countless lakes the soil is hardly an inch deep. Beneath it is either channel-compacted gravel or daub (a sticky blue clay), and neither can soak up the heavy rainfall. Irregular hedgerows of whitethorn, ash, green oak, holly, wild cherry, sloe and sycamore divide the drumlins into rushy fields. The hedges are the glory of these small fields, especially in late May and early June when the whitethorn foams out into streams of pink and white blossom. The soil's very poorness is what saved these hedges from the bulldozer, when great trees and old shrubs were being levelled and 'rationalized' for machinery through Europe in the 1960s and 1970s.

The sally is the first tree to green and the first to wither; the rowan berries are an incredible orange in the light from the lakes each September. The hedges are full of mice and insects and small birds, and sparrow hawks can be seen hunting all through the day. The snipe and the otter, the pheasant and the grey-suited heron, the fox and the hare are common. Along the lake edges and river banks there are private lawns speckled with fish bones and blue crayfish shells, where the otter feeds and trains her young. The foxglove is here and the orchid, with thousands of other wildflowers. Yet everywhere the ruined cottages in their small shelter of trees remind me of what the goat said to the farmer when he insisted the animal climb on to the roof to graze: 'The view up here is great, but there's nothing to eat, and even I am in danger of sliding off.'

One such small ruin stands on the shore of Laura Lake. The two thick, round piers, common to this area and on which the gates were hung, are no more than ten paces from the water, obscured by fuchsia bushes. The gates are gone, as are the roofs of the buildings within, but the stone walls are intact. Although a sturdy sycamore has taken root in the main living room, it is easy to see from the shapes that remain how delightful it must have been when it was a working farm.

A Mr Gallagher lived here with his family. All the accounts speak of an easy-going, charming, handsome man. The fragments of beautiful blue platters that can still be found in the shallows of the lake in front of the house also tell of relative prosperity. They had a pony and trap. Every Thursday Mr Gallagher drove into town in the trap, and when he had his business done went to Hoey's Hotel, owned by his cousins, where he drank the best whiskey the house possessed, and then the pony took him home. All his children were tall and handsome. The last of his sons held a big auction in 1953. He wanted to follow his girl to New York, where he married her and joined the fire department. The auction is still remembered; an enormous crowd gathered by the lake's edge, and the cattle, the farm machinery, the tools, the household utensils, the pony trap, were all sold.

County Leitrim has no coastline, other than an absurd couple of miles that squeeze out to the Atlantic between Donegal and Sligo. From there Leitrim wanders shapelessly south and east to where the Shannon leaves the county at Roosky. The long sheet of water called Lough Allen splits Leitrim in two. The upper Shannon flows out of Lough Allen past the tiny village that gives the county its name, passing through Carrick, Jamestown, Drumsna to Roosky. The Iron Mountains run for miles through the county and cross the border into Northern Ireland at Swanlinbar. Both the Irish customs post and the British Army checkpoint lie in the shadow of these low mountains. Generally, the Irish will glance out of the window and wave each car through, especially if it is raining.

At the British Army checkpoint it is very different. People have been killed here. There are ramps and screens and barriers and a tall camouflaged lookout tower. A line of cars waits behind a red light. A quick change to green signals each single car forward. In the middle of this maze armed soldiers call out the motor vehicle number and driver's identification to a hidden computer. Only when they are cleared will the cars be waved through. Suspect vehicles are searched. The soldiers are young and courteous and look very professional.

Sometimes they remark on my wife's New York driving licence and enquire about Kojak and Manhattan. Their look seems also to ask what on earth is she doing in this godforsaken place beneath the mountains, but they are too polite to put it into words. Only once were the assembly-line formalities broken. As the soldiers were checking our identification, an officer appeared and asked if we were going to Enniskillen. His upper-class English accent defined his rank; an Irish officer would have had much the same accent as his men. When we told him that we were on our way to Enniskillen and would be returning within a few hours, he asked us if we would bring him two loaves of wholewheat bread. On our return, as we proffered the brown parcel, the soldiers were edgy, their machine guns at the ready. 'Just a few loaves of wholewheat bread,' we said in as conciliatory a tone as possible. 'Your officer asked us to bring them.'

'Oh, that nutcase,' a soldier said, just as the officer himself appeared, pulling money from inside his combat jacket. 'Thank you very much indeed. We were completely out of wholewheat bread.' When the money was refused – 'with the compliments of the country' – he looked at a loss for a moment, before coming to attention and honouring us with one of the sharpest salutes I have ever seen, out there beneath the mountains, in the middle of the wilderness. I wish the whole commerce of Northern Ireland could be as simple as that human request.

The town of Enniskillen is on an island, on a lazy sweep of the River Erne. We began to travel regularly across the border to Enniskillen many years ago, during the long postal strike in the South, to post and collect our mail. We grew fond of the town and its people and continued going there to shop after the strike had ended. The whole feel of the place is refreshingly of another country. The town is large and prosperous, neater and better kept than most Southern towns, and on a true summer's day the many-islanded Erne can seem to sparkle like no other river. English newspapers are on sale, the churches are numerous and diverse. There are monuments and war memorials, and the neat dress of the people is noticeable, their humour dry and sarcastic. The shop assistants are more helpful and polite than those in the South.

The Protestant work ethic is pervasive. If there are tensions dividing the inhabitants, they are hidden carefully in the interests of business. And when, in 1987, a bomb concealed by the IRA in an empty building near the War Memorial exploded and killed eleven bystanders, the town united in mourning.

The Portora Royal School is here mostly for the sons of upper-middle-class Protestants. Wilde and Beckett were among its pupils. And in the Hollow, down from the Catholic cathedral, is one of the most beautiful bars in Ireland: Blake's of the Hollow. The counter is of white marble, and there are great varnished barrels on the shelves and chromed brass lamps and an intricate tongue-and-grooved ceiling. Up the stairs are alcoves like compartments in a railway carriage. In one of them, for years, a man sat every Thursday morning drinking a bottle of champagne while perusing the *Financial Times*.

I like Enniskillen best during the Thursday market, a throng of people moving between stalls, haggling over chains and tractor parts outside the cattle market or just standing and chatting pleasantly away to one another, while across the road, outside the Railway Hotel, a Nonconformist sect thumps out 'The End Is Nigh'.

The whole region is dominated by water. As the Erne is in the North, the Shannon is the great river of the South, and it rises in the low chain of mountains that crosses the border. In the nineteenth century the two rivers were joined by a network of canals through the many lakes. The venture turned out to be a financial disaster but, as I write, the canal is being made navigable again. By the time the river reaches Carrick-on-Shannon, it is deep and sluggish. Houseboats are for hire. Some of them sleep as many as eight people. The most interesting journey is up the river, through wide Drumharlow Lake and into the narrow gentle tributary, the river Boyle, passing through Oakport Lake and the lock gates into Lough Key, anchoring at villages along the way.

The river banks are beautiful, and parts of them are wooded. In the 1919 War of Independence, and in the Civil War that followed, there were men who fought the boredom and humiliation of jails by walking together in their imagination up one bank of the Shannon in the morning, returning down the opposite bank in the evening, each man picking out what others had missed on the way. They knew the river stretches like their own lives.

Once a boat passes Knockvicar Bridge, in County Roscommon, the whole feel of the Shannon becomes English, with its walks and woods and lock gates and the water sliding evenly over the weir. It could have been painted by Constable. For generations this area, containing some of the richest limestone in Ireland, was owned by the Stafford King-Harmans. In the nineteenth century the family was so wealthy that they were able to bring John Nash from London to redesign their white house above Lough Key, in which, it was said, there was one window for every day of the year. What looks like the ruin of a medieval castle stands on an island in the lake, but it is, in fact, a nineteenth-century folly. Rockingham House burned down in 1957, but the Gothic gardens and harbour, the great beech walk, the racehorse stables, the gatehouses and the roofless chapel of ease are well kept.

A hideous concrete lookout tower has been added, that manages to look cold and grey even in the sun. The last baronet, Sir Cecil Stafford King-Harman, was buried in 1987 within the family's chained plot in Ardcarne churchyard; on the headstone the index finger of a partly closed fist points toward heaven, above the inscription 'Spes Tuttissima Coelis' (Our most certain hope of Heaven). The King-Harmans also owned the town of Boyle, where their town house, later a British military barracks, is now being restored.

Nearby, along the river Boyle, there is a well-preserved twelfth-century Cistercian abbey, one of the finest in the country. The monks drew on the same landed wealth as the King-Harmans. Some miles south, in the pleasant town of Strokestown, is Strokestown Park House, open to the public. It was the home of the Pakenham Mahons, related through marriage to the King-Harmans, and has been successfully restored. As if to correct any rush toward Anglo-Irish sentiment, the young and able curator, Luke Dodd, is setting up a Famine museum side by side with that symbol of a life of privilege and gentility.

Though I have written only about a small area, less than thirty miles, it would nevertheless be considered enormous by the local people. Except for football and politics, the county divisions mean little to them. For those who live around Mohill, Rockingham, eighteen miles away, might as well be Syracuse (New York or Sicily). It is each single, enclosed locality that matters, and everything that happens within it is of passionate interest to those who live there. 'Do you have any news, any news?' But once the news crosses a certain boundary, eyes that a moment before were wild with curiosity will suddenly glaze: news no longer local is of no interest.

The dramas can be as funny or mundane or heartbreaking as the point of view. A man visits the Garda station, complaining about the trespassing cattle of a close neighbour.

'The law wouldn't want to get involved. Why don't you have a word with him yourself? The two of you together could come to some agreement,' the Donegal guard advises reasonably.

'We're not speaking.'

'Why aren't you speaking?'

'We haven't spoken to one another in years.'

'What is the cause?'

'To tell you the truth I forget. It happened such a long time ago that I can no longer remember.' The situation is not dissimilar to what is taking place on a larger scale in Northern Ireland.

Their neighbours would not have forgotten. They know everything about one another. Each scrap of news is added gleefully to an enormous store. In these towns both the individual and the family are held in high regard. Everyone attends the same church, shops in the same shops, drinks in the same bars: 'You go where your comrades go.' There is no getting away from the Drumshambo wind.

A boy from Fenagh who had newly arrived in New York City went looking for a cousin who had joined the police force. He found him on duty near the East River. A piercing January gale blew off the water. As soon as they had shaken hands, the boy turned his back to the river, saying, 'Michael, there's no escaping the wind from Drumshambo.'

Our village is Fenagh, in south Leitrim. Two bars watch one another across a road: one Fianna Fáil, the other Fine Gael. The site of the one public telephone was a major focus. For some years now it stands outside the Fianna Fáil bar, but once it used to move with every change of government, all of thirty yards to the other side of the road. The public telephone is no longer the potent symbol of power it once was, and governments now change too often.

Overlooking the bars are two roofless fifteenth-century churches, all that remains of a once-great monastery founded by St Colmcille, which was famous as a divinity school under St Killian, leaving us the 'Book of Fenagh'. In the fields surrounding the monastery, paths between the rows of the monks' cells can still be traced in the short, rich grass. A purpose-built National School disfigures the ancient site.

A mile further on toward Mohill is the eyesore of a ruined ballroom that throbbed to the big bands of the 1950s. 'There wasn't a haycock safe for a mile around in the month of July.' All the money the ballroom made was lost on two other ventures – a motorcycle Wall of Death and an unheated swimming pool dug by hundreds of workers despite all the lakes around. On maps and signposts, the lake below our house is called Lough Rowan, but no one knows it other than as Laura Lake, 'the middle lake' in Irish, which is exactly what it is, a lake between two lakes.

Mohill is our town. In its plain way I think it beautiful. There is no desolate big street. The simple streets link perfectly into one another. A stark Catholic church on the hill dominates the town, the little Protestant church is hidden away in its graveyard garden at the bottom. Mohill is about as far south as the Ulster Plantation reached, and here Protestants can be found making a living on smallholdings as poor as those belonging to their Catholic neighbours.

I like the town best in winter, the outskirts glistening with frost, the excitement on the faces of people in from the countryside for the late Saturday-night shopping, children and parcels being dragged about under the street-lamps. When the shopping is done, they go to the bars to meet the people they know and to discover the news, each locality to its own bar. In early March, on a Thursday market day, once I see the bags of seed potatoes and bundles of cabbage plants – Early York and Flat Dutch, Greyhound and Curly – on the corner outside Luke Early's bar, each bundle tied with baler twine of all colours, I know the winter is almost over. I think of Mohill as one of the happiest towns in the world.

In Enniskillen, a few years ago, I heard a barman ask an elderly man with a thick Leitrim accent, 'I suppose you'd be from Leitrim?' The barman was young and cocky.

'Yes. Near enough,' the man said slowly.

'I suppose, now, there wouldn't be too much happening down in Leitrim?' the barman laughed.

'It's peaceable,' the man seemed to agree, 'but not too peaceable. Middlin' peaceable. What you want, like where we're from, across the river. Belçoo. Yes. Middlin' peaceable. What you want. The sky above us.'

In a not dissimilar situation, I like to remember and imagine John Walter Cross (whose first cousin, Leland Duncan, took remarkable photographs of Leitrim in the late 1880s and 1890s), sitting in an Oxford tea-room soon after George Eliot's death and overhearing a group of students mocking her seriousness. In their ignorance they might as well have been talking about Belcoo or Leitrim. As he left the tea-room, Cross approached their table. 'Excuse me for intruding, but she wasn't like that at all. She was serious but she was also great fun. I was married to her.'

Galway, Western Ireland's Lilting Heart

Galway is one of the liveliest and most attractive towns in the whole of Ireland. It is the undisputed capital of Connaught, the western province that contains Counties Galway, Leitrim, Mayo, Roscommon and Sligo. Built at the shallow, turbulent mouth of the river Corrib, protected from the Atlantic by a wide, deep bay, it falls somewhere between a large town and a city, with many of the advantages of both but without their attendant ills. It is the only university town the region boasts, and is a centre for medicine, fishing, light industry and tourism, with easy access to a richly varied hinterland.

The core of Galway first appears in 1124, when a castle was built at the mouth of the easily forded Corrib for Turlough O'Connor, King of Connaught. But, unlike most rivers on which medieval cities grew, the Corrib does not give access to fertile valleys or plains; the lands to the north through which it flows are wild and picturesque but mostly barren. Galway had to turn to the ocean and trade if it was to prosper, and Galway merchant princes developed links with Italy, Spain, Dublin, London and, in particular, the French ports. Trading houses were established in Nantes, La Rochelle, Bordeaux and Cádiz. Eventually, younger sons of the merchants were placed in the foreign countries, and trade extended even to the West Indies.

The handsome stone buildings we see in Galway today date mostly from the nineteenth century, when the medieval city walls were demolished and built upon. The railway link with Dublin, completed in 1851, opened up the town to tourism. This was certainly helped by the splendid Great Southern Hotel, built at the terminus, which dominates Eyre

Square today. From its rooms, in great comfort, you can either watch the trains move slowly into the small station or turn to the breathtaking views of the Atlantic. The railway was opened as the Great Famine (1845–9) was ending, and this human traffic was not one-way traffic only: while the porters were carrying the tourists' bags the short distance to the new hotel, hundreds were waiting with their third-class tickets to board the trains out of Galway in the hope of escaping poverty and starvation.

University College Galway was completed in 1849. The original architecture in the Gothic style is pleasing, even beautiful, when the Virginia creeper turns red on the stone. The university nearly closed a number of times because of the Roman Catholic hierarchy's opposition to non-denominational education. Not until well into this century did it start to prosper and grow. Now it is one of the most pleasant places to study in Ireland, attracting students from all over the world.

Because Galway is such an old city and has been attracting visitors for so long, many descriptions of it survive. In 1934, Virginia Woolf wrote to Katherine Arnold-Forster about the countryside close to Galway: 'It is a lovely country, but very melancholy, except that the people never stop talking.' A melancholic man who often passed through Galway on his way to or from the Aran Islands, about which he wrote so well, was John Millington Synge. A man who once carried Synge's bag from the docks to the station thought that because of its weight the bag must contain gold. On being informed that only books were in it, he was greatly disappointed: 'if it was gold was in it it's the thundering spree we'd have together this night in Galway.'

James Joyce's wife, Nora Barnacle, came from Galway. Joyce first visited the city with their son, Giorgio, in 1909 to meet Nora's mother. He again was there with Nora and their two children in 1912, when he wrote to his brother Stanislaus from the family house at 4 Bowling Green: 'Nora's uncle feeds us in great style and I row and cycle and drive a good deal.' Michael Healy, Nora's uncle, a Galway port official, gave the couple much help throughout their life, and when Joyce came to offer a copy of his *Pomes Penyeach* to University College Galway, he wrote the librarian in 1935 that it was in part 'a small acknowledgment of a great debt of gratitude to Mr Healy himself'.

Today No. 4 Bowling Green, now No. 8 Bowling Green, is the Nora Barnacle House, restored and furnished with great taste by Sheila Gallagher, who runs the tiny museum. The house consists of just two rooms. From the street, one enters directly into the small kitchen-living room and a narrow stair leads to the bedroom on the second floor. Around the house and on the walls are photos and mementos of the Joyces' life. The atmosphere is humbling in its smallness and total lack of any pretension.

At the top of Bowling Green is the Church of St Nicholas, which dates back to 1320 and is one of the largest medieval churches in Ireland. Although it was mutilated by Cromwell's soldiers, many interesting things survive. Floor memorials display symbols depicting the crafts of those who are buried there (a hammer with a crown for a goldsmith), and the wealth of the merchants is recorded in various guises.

On Market Street, beside St Nicholas's Church, there is a charming Saturday-morning market. People come in from the countryside to sell honey, jams, preserves, homemade cheese and butter, all kinds of fresh vegetables and flowers. The stalls vary. Sometimes lace and silver and small antiques can be found.

Why is Galway today so appealing? Not, I think, for any single reason. Not even for the summer horse races, when the rich and famous helicopter in and the rest pour in by bus, train or car – any old way they can – and the town doesn't seem to sleep for a good week. Not for the Cuirt Poetry Festival, which attracts an international gathering of writers and readers and the small halls are full of people attending to the spoken word. Nor, either, for the September oyster festivals, when the delicious Galway Bay oysters are washed down with gallons of stout and jokes and stories.

I like Galway in all these festivals and weathers, but what I like best is the variety that this small city affords – the islands, weirs, harbour, the ocean, the university, canals, the once salmon-rich Corrib, the bridges from where the small trout can be seen swaying or still in the tidal pools out from the arches, the ungainly carnival of swans huddled by the river's mouth or sailing proudly on the rising tide. There's no more pleasant place to watch the sight of swans and wheeling gulls and boats (and capsizing canoeists) than from a table in Nimmo's Restaurant by the Spanish Arch, an extension of the medieval walls in the place where Spanish ships once were moored. They serve excellent seafood, good inexpensive wine, and the service is refreshingly quiet, and the room is beautiful.

For as long as I remember it, the centre of Galway has been a vibrant, bustling place, but in recent years it has benefited much from a government policy that gives grants and tax concessions toward the renewal of inner towns and cities. Old mills and warehouses and courtyards have been restored as restaurants, shops, galleries and apartments. There's a Gaelic theatre, Taibhdhearc na Gaillimhe, where the plays and shows are all in Irish, and the Druid Theatre Company, founded not so many years ago by a talented group of former university students. There are many restaurants and hotels, from Nimmo's near the pier to the Great Southern on Eyre Square, to the more modest Atlanta in Dominick Street, where actors from the Druid often gather with theatre and literary people for a late-night drink. On the same handsome street is O'Maille's Drapery Store, full of the finest Irish linen, tweeds and beautifully styled knitwear.

Everything is near, which makes Galway a perfect town for walking in or strolling about. Especially enjoyable is joining the slow human flow through the narrow streets on a late evening in summer, all languages floating about in the warm air – French, Italian, Irish, Spanish, German, the English of the different nations and accents from every corner of Ireland. The doors of all the bars are open, people carry the drinks outside to stand talking in groups on the pavements or sit on windowsills. From within the bars the sound of a tin whistle is joined by an accordion and a lively fiddle. Close to the harbour, hurrying groups of young people and heavy rhythmic vibrations tell of a rock band in session.

The roads that lead out of Galway give access to as much, or even more, variety than the city. To the south is Clare and the Burren, a limestone wilderness; and, where the shale and limestone meet, whole streams disappear underground for miles, and in rich fissures between the rocks grow gentian, cranesbill, rich saxifrages. A few miles to the west is the Gaeltacht, where Irish is spoken. Ferries or small planes go each day to the Aran Islands, except in the worst weathers.

Between Galway and Clifden, to the west, is the pleasant town of Oughterard, on the shores of Lough Corrib. Lough Corrib and Lough Mask form a long corridor of water, dotted with many islands, that is broken into two lakes by a ridge of land between the towns of Clonbur and Cong. The lakes are long famous for their trout and can be dangerous in rough weather. Beyond Oughterard are the wild mountains, a wilderness of bog and heather, the odd lake, many sheep and the multicoloured plastic bags used for gathering turf or peat, the occasional house and shop and white cottage. The small black-and-white sheepdogs can be seen on foot with their masters or riding past on tractors.

Clifden must be one of the most attractive market towns in Ireland, at the head of the north arm of Clifden Bay, under the Twelve Bens, mountains wonderful for walking and climbing. Like Galway, Clifden is a centre, giving access to spectacular views of ocean and mountain and bog, lakes and rivers, quiet inlets and harbours. Guest houses and hotels abound, some of them famous, as do bars and restaurants. From Clifden, I'd take the direct road to the little fishing village of Cleggan, some ten miles to the north. For miles the road runs through unfenced moorland and bog, and then without warning, in one heart-stopping moment, sky and ocean seem to merge into one another and run all the way out above Cleggan Head to the islands.

From Cleggan north to Achill Island is little more than sixty miles, but it is a long drive. I'd want to drive slowly, and with bog holes on either side of the narrow road, hairpin bends and resting sheep, it is dangerous as well as wasteful of all there is to see to drive fast. Along the way is Kylemore Abbey, across the serene expanse of Pollacappul Lough, sheltered by a thick growth of rhododendrons and exotic shrubs and trees. A mountain rises sheer behind the abbey and looks across the quiet lake into farther mountains. Ahead the road curves around one side of the long narrow inlet of the ocean that is Killary Harbour, and then winds dramatically beneath the mountains. Often the sides of the road are bare of anything but gorse and heather; then in valleys or around cottages are sudden patches of fuchsia, the red bells vivid here by the sea, and shiny cotoneaster. There are also small trees that I find very moving, sometimes standing alone, other times in weak rows. Their shapes show that all the time they lean away from their scourge, the ocean. The salt and wind strip the outer branches of bark. Even in the full leaf of summer these trees appear to wear a crown of bones.

Westport is a big town that I could happily spend days in, but I'd want to reach Achill by night. On the road from Newport there are beautiful long strands below Mulrany, before the bridge across the narrow sound onto Achill Island, the largest island in Ireland. After the town of Achill Sound, with its shops and hotels, the road passes between high walls of rhododendrons before entering the open island of moorland and mountain, white strands, sheer cliffs and hillsides, small fields in the sheltered valleys along the coast, scattered white cottages. There are three main villages – Keel, Dooagh and Dugort, the last a nineteenth-century Protestant missionary settlement; and two high mountains, Slievemore, from which the whole island can be viewed, and the slightly smaller but much more dramatic and dangerous Croaghaun. At the foot of Croaghaun is Keem Bay, where the rhythmic falling of the waves on the white sand has a magical sound under the high dark cliffs. Close to Keem is Corrymore House, once inhabited by Captain Charles Boycott, before his troubles with the County Mayo peasantry caused his name to enter the English language, and later by the extraordinary Major Freyer, who ran it as a hotel. The Freyer story is well remembered on Achill even today, and is worth lingering over.

The Major's father, Sir Peter Freyer, was one of the most brilliant medical students ever to graduate from University College Galway, gaining first place in every subject in each of his college years and first place in the entrance examination for the Indian Medical Service in 1875. In India he quickly gained a brilliant reputation as a surgeon. One of his patients was the Nawab of Rampur's brother, whose ambition was to become Nawab himself. Freyer performed on him a serious operation, and the patient eventually succeeded his brother. At his first durbar, or court, he made a public presentation of one hundred thousand rupees to Peter Freyer. The Indian Medical Service was outraged by the gift of such an enormous sum to one of its servants and demanded the money, with the later option of granting Freyer release from the service. Freyer refused to give up the money on the grounds that he had well earned it. Soon afterwards he was offered a consultancy in London and went on to become one of the most famous surgeons in England, with a practice in

Harley Street. He died in 1921 and is buried in Clifden, near where he grew up; each year a lecture in his name is given at University College Galway by a distinguished surgeon.

One of Sir Peter's dearest wishes was for his son to follow him into the medical profession, and with this in view he sent him to Oxford. His son Dermot, the future Major, had no intention of granting this wish. He served with the British Army in World War I, and then, soon after his father's death, moved to Achill. There, with a large library and a Gaudier-Brzeska sculpture of the philosopher's stone, he started the Corrymore House Hotel. One of the hotel's more eccentric features was that the guests were charged according to the Major's estimation of their entertainment value. If guests were boring or demanding, they were presented with a very stiff bill at the end of their stay. Guests who were entertaining or good company were charged only nominal sums, if anything at all. Very favoured guests were invited into the library for conversation and given the philosopher's stone to hold. All through the day the Major drank cold, strong black tea, and even on Achill he retained a passion for English country dancing. Every Sunday afternoon, the big dining room was cleared and all the English people living on Achill who still remembered their country dances were invited in to dance with the Major. These dances were sometimes interspersed with sword dances, in which long wooden laths were used.

Not having been on Achill for many years, I drove there a few weeks ago. Little had changed. The prosperity of Galway and Clifden seemed hardly to have touched Achill. I wondered if this could have anything to do with the character of the people. Perhaps they were too gentle, not aggressive enough in pursuit of the new wealth. In my experience, the Achill people have been the gentlest, the friendliest, the most mannerly and hospitable people to strangers in the whole of Ireland. The Achill land is poor. For generations they've had to emigrate, often as migrant workers, most commonly in groups, taking their island with them, and it is as if their own experience of exile had given them an imaginative sympathy with strangers.

The island was as beautiful as ever: the amazing Achill blues and purples were everywhere; the manners as gentle as before, and as slyly humorous. The spirit of the place was still primarily one of solitude.

Before I left, I climbed to Corrymore House. They last told me in Dooagh that it hadn't opened as a hotel for more than fifteen years. A small dog looked out at me from one of the ground-floor windows. Below lay the white cottages of Dooagh, the dark headlands, miles of ocean, a richness of views, but I found myself thinking of those English people arriving years before from all over the island in their Sunday finery for an afternoon of tea and English country dancing until I half expected the Major to come out of the house to see if there was any sign of his early guests.

'What Are You, Sir?' Trinity College Dublin

When I was young in this small country, Trinity College was so far removed from our lives and expectations that it seemed a complete elsewhere. We had read in the textbooks that Wolfe Tone had studied there, and Burke too, and Grattan and Goldsmith: but it was information we memorized and it never took on any life other than its textbook one. Maynooth was real because the priest went there, as were the colleges of the National University that gave us doctors, solicitors, vets, and the occasional semi-learned rake. Then, when it seemed that I too could attend university, I became aware that Trinity was an actual, living university like the others, that the scholarship was as valid at Trinity as in any of the other places but as a Catholic I could never study there: not only was it a mortal sin to attend but a Reserved sin to boot.

When I came to live in Dublin in the 1950s Trinity was a prominent part of the landscape of what was then a fairly intimate city: the front statues, the railings, the blue clock, the playing fields within the walls, the thin, human stream passing in and out of the front gate, the accents mostly the accent of command. I knew nobody who worked or studied there. I suppose the Reserved sin still hovered over the place, but by the time I rid my own mind of that childish darkness it was a place I had no connection with. Looking back, I think the Trinity of that time lived very much within its own pale within the city, and this had its origins, like the Reserved sin, in history, in caste and class.

At that same time, in an amusing way, I came on the fact that Trinity had a status more often associated with garrisons than universities. I was sharing digs with some barmen in the city. They were all from the

country, easy-going, fond of hurling and bike racing. One day I saw two
of them sporting Trinity scarves. I was surprised to learn that they had
bought the scarves, supposing that they had been left behind in one of
the bars by roistering students. They told me that because of the irregular hours they worked they had had difficulty picking up girls until they
discovered that if they hung about the front gate of Trinity on their day
off wearing the scarves they could pick up working-class Dublin girls
more easily than hunting through the city as plain barmen.

If someone had suggested then that thirty years later I would come to
live for six months in Trinity as the Writer Fellow, I would have laughed.
At that time, thirty years ahead appeared so far away that it was as incon-
ceivable as it was undesirable ever to reach, and coming to Trinity would
have only compounded the disbelief; but since those years this country
has changed more than during the entire previous century: the Reserved
sin has gone, the two traditions now work and study in the college.

I came to take up residency one wet, mild January evening. I was given
keys and shown to the house where I would be living, number 25 Rubrics.
XXV was cut on the stone lintel above the doorway. Wide, freshly
scrubbed stairs led to my room on the first floor. The dark brown door
was solid and heavy. The room was enormous. To the left of the door three
tall windows looked out on to the Front Square. I could see all the way
across the cobbled square to the archway at the front gate, a long sweeping view at that time of evening, with the rain falling beneath the lamps.
One side of the windows the branches of the huge Oregon maple reached
darkly up above the lawn. Each window had its own white wooden shutters, the wood warped with age. The long heavy brown curtains closed
easily. Across the room three similar windows looked out on New Square.
There was a writing desk, a single bed in a corner, a wardrobe, a brown
sofa, two brown armchairs, a plain table and a few chairs. The whole sense
of space was beautiful. A gas fire stood in the original fireplace, but the
white mantel and the surrounds hadn't been changed. A gaitered clergyman could be imagined easily in this room, a servant putting coal on the
fire, a horse tethered to the railing below. And it was freezing cold. Inside
the room it was colder than it was outside on the cobbles, and it took the
small gas fire more than a day to warm it. Behind a white door in
the corner I discovered the smallest kitchen I had ever seen.

That evening I managed to lock myself out, leaving the keys within the room. Shamefacedly, I set out for the porter's lodge. It must have been at the time the shifts change, for the lodge was full of porters. I had no ID card, nothing that could connect me with the college.

'What are you, sir?'

'A Visiting Fellow.'

'What kind of Fellow?'

'The Writer Fellow.' Even to my own ears it sounded unconvincing.

'You're a writer, then. What do you write?'

'Books.'

'Do you write anything decent?'

'No.'

At this point a porter took keys from the wall. We walked across the square to the Rubrics.

After he'd let me in and I'd recovered my keys and thanked him, I asked the whereabouts of the bathroom. It was outside, a few yards from the entrance to the house. A green door with ventilation slats screened a locked door that one of my keys opened. 'My solution to the problem is to keep a large, flowery teapot in my room,' a neighbouring Fellow explained to me a few days later, with comical precision. 'It looks very well – people often admire it – but I never use it for making tea.'

I grew to love that room, all the more watchfully since I knew I'd have to leave it in June. I could look on the square all day from one of those high windows: the students hurrying in all weathers between classes, sometimes eagerly, more often anxiously, greeting or meeting, avoiding each other, flirting, impressing, courting. A professor goes by in emphatic conversation with a favourite student, the student frozen into an attitude of listening as they walk. A group of academics slowly cross towards the Senior Common Room, their relative importance measured by the quantity of attention each receives. A white-hatted cook runs between buildings. The porters move from car to car, examining parking discs. A young faculty wife drives up and takes a baby in a basket from the back seat of her car. Always there was something of interest happening. For this reason the window at which I wrote and read was kept permanently shuttered, the heavy brown curtain drawn throughout the day.

One presence that was never shut out was the sound of bells, the great clamour of the bell at ten in the morning and the bell for Commons at 6.15, figures wearing or carrying gowns hurrying towards the Dining Hall from all quarters, and the bells striking the hours and half-hours all through the day and night, most movingly in the silence of early morning, the so-called hopeful hours, when each single strike seems to count against us.

To come down from the windows to the square itself is to lose at once the sense of its human traffic, the ebb and flow of the life of the college, and to feel instead the presence of the buildings that enclose the square. I love that space. The Front Square has a sense of gesture, and pride, and yet it has its own calm, and the scale of it remains completely human. To go left is to come face to face with the brute concrete of the Arts Block, which should not fit in but somehow does. A Calder stabile, badly in need of new paint, graces the lawn. Beyond are the library and playing fields and the Nassau Street railings.

I tried to keep my great room orderly, but in spite of my efforts it soon took on the untidiness of scattered books and papers, chairs and tables moved here and there. A woman came one day every week to clean the room. In less than an hour she'd have everything shining in its own place. She was a charming woman and often we talked as she cleaned. She told me how she waited each morning for the private bus at six o'clock that took the cleaners into Trinity, and that she was able to be home in time to cook the family dinner. She had the eye of a good novelist for the characters who lived in the rooms she cleaned. She described an attitude that I thought had long since ceased, concluding with: 'I've been cleaning his room for fourteen years. He's never once spoken to me. The woman before me cleaned his room for twenty-eight years. She told me he never once spoke to *her*. I used to say "Good morning" at first, but now I don't say anything, haven't for years. They say he's one of the cleverest men in the whole university, but I say he has the manners of a bowsie.'

To live in Trinity is to live in quiet in the very heart of Dublin. Everywhere I'd want to go in the city was but a few minutes' walk away. A favourite walk was to leave the room in Rubrics around ten at night, out by the front gate, up Suffolk Street, turning towards Exchequer Street, lingering at some of the menus outside the many restaurants,

combing back through the little streets off Grafton Street, perhaps dropping into a bar on the way back before returning to Trinity before the
front door closed at midnight.

To live in Trinity is to live in close awareness of the great dead who
worked and studied there. The person I found myself turning to most
often when I was there was John Butler Yeats. To live with his letters is to
live with some of the best company in the world, irascible, charming,
pigheaded, extraordinarily intelligent, always passionate:

I never joined that [Historical] Society though I often thought about it, and I
remember perfectly how now and again its debates used to have a real importance in College. Lecky of course was a constant speaker there. I kept to the
undergraduate Philosophical from some impression that the hard-headed
Philistine abounded too much in the historical . . .

In a way he continued being a student of genius throughout the whole
length of his long life:

My dear Willie – I am afraid you must sometimes think me very conceited – the
fact is not only am I an old man in a hurry, but all my life I have fancied myself
just on the verge of discovering the primum mobile . . .
My complaint is that all literature has gone over to the side of the schoolmaster and that it used to be carried on by the boys themselves.

I like to imagine him reading John Stuart Mill, 'that man who wore no
peacock's feathers', in his final year, when he won a university prize in
political economy; and whenever I look at Front Square I cannot but
think of his beautiful letter on dreaming, in which the spirit of Berkeley
surely breathes:

My theory is that we are always dreaming – chairs, tables, women and children,
our wives and sweethearts, the people in the streets, all in various ways and with
various powers are the starting points of dreams . . . Sleep is dreaming away
from the facts and wakefulness is dreaming in close contact with the facts, and
since facts excite our dreams and feed them we get as close as possible to the facts if
we have the cunning and the genius of poignant feeling . . .

Scattered everywhere throughout his letters are jewels that are often
echoed in his son's best lines:

Now a most powerful and complex part of the personality is affection and affection springs straight out of the memory. For that reason what is new whether in the world of ideas or of fact cannot be subject for poetry, tho' you can be as rhetorical about it as you please – rhetoric expresses other peoples [sic] feelings, poetry one's own.

And:

I have no belief in what is called a personal God, but I do believe in a shaping providence – and that this providence is what may be called goodness or love, and that death is only a change in a world where change is a law of existence . . .

Reading John Butler Yeats's letters, in that same place where the old man in a hurry walked and studied when young deepened the sense of the actual day of the college even more than the bells that rang out our hours. I was very happy living in Trinity, but happiness is its own completion and cannot be described.

Blake's of the Hollow

I have been going to Blake's of the Hollow for close to twenty years and think of it as one of the happiest and most beautiful bars in the whole of Ireland.

We live less than an hour's drive away from Enniskillen. I have always liked the town, and we'd often go there on market day. I was first drawn to Blake's by the handsome front, its paintwork an unusual fireman's red: that front alone cost Richard Herbert £400 after he bought the premises and had the whole bar remodelled in 1887. Mr Herbert must have been a wise as well as a wealthy man: the six months it took to complete the work he spent in Arizona.

Within the swing doors the bar is in perfect agreement with the front. Behind a counter of white marble, four huge sherry casks stand. Two of the casks remained in use until the 1920s, when whiskey was horse-drawn from the bonded warehouse in Market Street and hand-pumped into one of the first two casks on alternate deliveries.

The lamps along the bar are beautiful. They were once gas lamps, now converted to electricity, and the original brass is chromed. The ceiling and panelling are of pitched pinewood. At the end of the bar is a small room with a fireplace. High in the corner is a television set. Above this room is the office. Overlooking the whole bar, with its ornate lamps and glass, it could belong in a theatre or ship. Behind the office is a row of snugs along a wide landing. They remind me of first-class compartments in very old railway carriages or cabins aboard a ship. A short wide stairs leads to the landing. There are small tables by the snugs along the landing at which you can sit and watch the bar below. The patterned tilework of the floor is identical with that in the Catholic church a hundred yards or so above the Hollow which was built a decade or so before the bar was remodelled, but the tiles in Blake's are much more cracked and worn than the church tiles.

William Blake (1901–1981) bought this public house from the personal representatives of the then late Richard Herbert in 1929, and thereafter lived above the premises. He had retired by the time I started going to Blake's and his son Donal ran the bar, as he still does today. Mr Blake, or Boss as he was affectionately known, was an impressive figure in the bar, dressed in a loose woollen sweater, always wearing a tie, with his fine head and snow-white hair. When he smoked his pipe he could be the captain on the bridge of his ship looking out on a vessel-free horizon. Without any obvious word or gesture he could convey his displeasure of any small negligence instantly to the barmen. There were a few customers he talked to. They seemed to be more like old friends than customers – they were certainly both – but even with them he retained his impressive stillness. Mostly he listened, the listening interspersed with sharp inaudible questions or what looked like sly pointed comment. After some of these exchanges sometimes he smiled and when he did so his face was wonderful to see.

Johnny was the head barman then, Michael his very young assistant. Johnny was one of the best barmen I have seen or known. He was small, with neat black hair, his face creased with laughing and goodnature. If anxiety, other than to please, had made any contribution to the lines he never allowed it to show, and he was as friendly and outgoing as the Boss was reserved and silent. They were an extraordinary pair together. Johnny made all his customers feel special, knew them all by name and much of their histories, would greet someone who hadn't been in the bar for months as if he'd missed them and was just waiting for them to come in that very minute. He was kind, but could be sharp. He disapproved of one customer who liked to move from group to group in Blake's, 'The only man I know that can go on a pub crawl without ever leaving the bar he started out in.' He was quick and nimble on his feet and always cycled to and from Blake's. Each day at lunchtime he'd put on his bicycle clips, check the cardboard box on the counter where the pool coupons were kept, take his bicycle from the hallway, his voice muted in case he'd be delayed as he wheeled it past the customers and out the door.

He told me that for years on the Sunday of the Ulster Final he used to cycle from Enniskillen to Clones, to work all that day of huge crowds in a bar, help wash up at the end of the day, and cycle home to Enniskillen. He'd never seen an Ulster Final but heard so much about them that it killed any desire he might have had to go to see one for himself.

In early December each year he'd take several large sheets of paper and rule them into small numbered squares before pinning them on the panelling across from the bar for the Christmas Draw. Each customer wrote their own name or the names of friends in the squares and paid. There were at least twenty prizes, sometimes even more, from the Christmas hampers to the single bottle of wine or carton of cigarettes. On Christmas Eve all the sheets had to be cut up into the individual squares. The whole process must have been extremely time-consuming and laborious, and it was no wonder it was discontinued after Johnny's retirement; but it was enormous fun. Over the years nearly everybody won something there were so many prizes. I remember well my wife's pleasure the Christmas she won a bottle of port, the first time she'd won anything in a raffle. Straw was an affectionate nickname for Johnny and the raffle became known as Straw's Draw. Each Christmas I think we all felt we were Lloyd's Names, and it turned out that we were far less at risk in Straw's Draw than in the famous London company.

In the 1970s there was a long postal strike in the South and Donal Blake kindly allowed me to use 6 Church Street, Enniskillen as an address. Twice a week for months we'd go to Enniskillen to post letters and collect our mail in Blake's. I became a regular among regulars.

There was another 'regular' who appeared every Thursday for years in Blake's. He dressed in tweed suits with a flowing bow tie, and he always entered carrying a copy of the *Financial Times*. A young man chauffeured him to the bar around noon every Thursday and returned to collect him in the middle of the afternoon. He sat alone in one of the upstairs booths studying the pink pages of the *Financial Times* while drinking a bottle of champagne.

Blake's was selling 'White Powers' then, a whiskey they bottled themselves, and it came from the time William Blake bottled beer and stout and spirits for the retail trade. It must have been fifteen or twenty years in the casks before it was bottled and it was the most delicious whiskey I ever tasted. Eventually, they only sold it to regular customers. I used to buy 'White Powers' to give as presents. Now I wish I had kept some of those bottles for future occasions.

The pint of Guinness you get in Blake's is as good as you can get anywhere. Michael draws a perfect shamrock in the cream of the stout with a flourish so neat and quick it cannot be followed. They have delicious sandwiches neatly cut into squares with generous measures of tea in the old aluminium teapots. In cold weather the hot whiskies with cloves and lemon are delicious. They have excellent wines, and our Thursday man can surely vouch for the excellence of the champagne he drank so studiously for years. An honoured customer is Mrs Rankin of Florencecourt whose favourite drink – De Kuyper's gin – [has] embossed on the lovely old green bottle 'who De Kuyper nightly takes soundly sleeps and fit awakes.' When she celebrated her hundred-and-eighth birthday in Blake's recently she surprised everybody; she had the delicious hot rum with soup and sandwiches instead of her favourite glass of Hollands.

I was sorry when the postal strike ended. It was the most pleasant way ever of dealing with mail, but still, years later, the week is not complete without a visit to Blake's, even if it is only to drink warming tea from an aluminium teapot.

Johnny has retired but comes in from time to time. Michael has taken Johnny's place and the excellent home-made soup Michael makes each day has been added to the fare. Donal Blake still runs the bar, and is often there. Sometimes their children – on holidays from university or between jobs – serve behind the counter. The whole bar is as happy and as beautiful as when I was first drawn to it by the handsome front almost twenty years ago. I hope it continues forever.

Dreaming at Julien's

In the spring I got a call to ask if I'd travel to Morocco and write about that country. I had never been to any part of Africa and knew nothing about Morocco. 'We guessed that. It's one of the reasons we want to send you.'

Could I have time to think about the offer?

I trawled around to see if I could find even tenuous links with Morocco. I had seen the Warner movie *Casablanca*, which hadn't even been made in Morocco. I had read about Fez and Marrakesh and the High Atlas Mountains, but that wasn't knowledge. I recalled vivid evocations of Algiers and Oran in the essays of Camus, cities that share the same Mediterranean coastline, and picked up *Exile and the Kingdom*. The evocations of the places where Camus's life began were as fresh and compelling as when I first read them:

That silence is not always of the same quality, depending on whether it springs from the shade or the sunlight. There is the silence of noon on the Place du Gouvernement. In the shade of the trees surrounding it Arabs sell for five sous glasses of iced lemonade flavoured with orange-flowers. Their cry 'Cool, cool', can be heard across the empty square. After their cry silence again falls under the burning sun: in the vendor's jug the ice moves and I can hear it tinkle.

Algeria, with Tunisia and Morocco, are the countries of North Africa most closely linked to France, and I found that the little acquaintance I had with anything Moroccan derived from the early 1970s when my wife and I lived briefly in Paris: the richly coloured rugs and coverlets in galleries and shop windows, the fine Moroccan binding on rare books, the beautiful geometric designs on plates and bowls and pitchers.

One such blue and white plate with intricate geometric designs hangs on a wall in the house. The plate was given to us by a young Englishman we knew in Paris. He had spent a year teaching English to the King of Morocco. While he spoke eloquently of the cities and the people, the mosques and markets and the Moroccan countryside, never once did he mention the King or the royal family, though he had lived with them for a year in several of their palaces. I still remember his understated manners and the tact with which he'd change the conversation if our questions were too pointed. When he was leaving Paris he gave us the blue and white plate which he had been given as a member of the royal party on a visit to Fez.

At that time, we used to frequent a restaurant called Julien near the Arc in Strasbourg Saint-Denis. The long rectangular room was an art nouveau palace fallen on hard times, and it was the cheapest and most colourful place to eat in the whole of Paris. All the waiters were Moroccan, and a Moroccan red wine, Amarante, was served, not as rough as the *vin ordinaire* and a favourite with the regulars.

Into the once plush wall seating and on bentwood chairs hundreds were crammed each evening; porters from the shops and markets, all kinds of workers, often in the distinctive blue of their work clothes, students, tourists, the many prostitutes who worked the streets and small hotels around Saint-Denis, and people like ourselves astray in Paris with plenty of life and little money. Clouds of cigarette smoke would drift across the designs of the ornamental glass roof while the pre-Raphaelite ladies on the tiled walls, in their innocent pastoral poses, stood far above the rushing waiters, the harassed shouts and the noise. The huge wall mirrors deepened and enlarged the room, holding the crammed diners side by side with the flared peacocks on the opposite wall in their depths. In the middle of the heat and noise the small black-ened fans circled helplessly overhead.

At Julien's we had to be careful in our choice of dishes. Tomato salad was safe and delicious. The bread was always good. Steak and chips were popular and reliable. A green salad was risky; it could come with snails. Once I ordered a fish and received two; the second fish was a small fish the larger fish on the plate had swallowed.

Because of the way people were crowded together it was easy to fall into conversation with people studying in Paris, with workers or tourists. I remember all the people were extremely polite. Often we found ourselves at a table of prostitutes. With their thick makeup and wigs and bright clothes, they looked like birds of paradise. As the Amarante was liberally poured, sometimes they'd discuss their clients in tones of ribald mockery. Once I heard an unacceptable low offer being discussed. 'I told him,' she said amidst laughter, 'that for such a price I wouldn't let him use my pot' (*J'lui ai dit, a ce prix-la, faut pas t'gener, pourquoi qu't'emportes pas les rideaux?!*). More often they discussed their children or their grandchildren, the price of food and clothes, where they bought bread and fish and vegetables and meat.

The tables were covered with rough white paper. At the end of the meal the waiter would tot up what was owed on a corner of the table between the breadcrumbs and wine stains. The waiters were courteous and appreciative of even small tips. On the way out we'd pass long queues waiting for tables beside the ornate mahogany bar.

Yet, we were never hurried or rushed; we could linger as long as we wished over our glasses of Amarante.

We always walked to Julien's, crossing the Pont Neuf to the Quai de la Mégisserie, passing the pet and garden shops that stayed open late along the quay and the many cafés around the Châtelet before reaching the Rue Saint-Denis. At the time, the markets of Les Halles were still in Paris. The Rue Saint-Denis ran alongside the markets and was always crowded. There were many small hotels. In the hallways of these hotels, behind the glass doors, stood the ladies of the night and beckoned. They were lit like a display of flowers. They were all attractive, and some looked beautiful. I suspect these hallways were cunningly lighted.

These flowers looked very different from the ladies we had dined with at Julien's. After the Rue des Pêcheurs there were fewer hotels and the ladies plied their trade in doorways and at street corners. From Julien's we often came through the markets and would see the long-distance lorries from all parts of France being unloaded in a white, blinding electric light: cauliflowers, bags of onions, fruit, carcasses of beef and lamb.

In the days that followed the telephone call there was much rain in Ireland, not beating rain but rain dripping down every day from low skies, and the sun of Morocco gradually started to take on a powerful allure. When I was called back I said I'd be glad to go to Morocco if I could travel by way of Paris. I explained about the inexpensive restaurant with the Moroccan waiters and the red Amarante. I'd have a known place to start from; otherwise, I'd be travelling blind.

'That restaurant must be Julien's,' the woman said, to my amazement, on the phone. 'I ate there a few times. You could eat for next to nothing.' She didn't recall it as being particularly beautiful; it was the birds of paradise and the cheapness she remembered.

I had been back to Paris many times since I lived there, but it was always on business. Often I'd go thinking I'd have time to see the city I knew, but, except for a few snatched hours here and there, it never happened. It is the most beautiful city I know. Increasingly, like most cities, it is harder to see because of the traffic. Some months ago I and many others were caught for several hours in a Paris television studio during a technicians' strike. At the last possible minute the dispute was settled, the show recorded, and we got out of the lighted concrete cavern off the Champs-Elysées after midnight and had dinner in a late-night brasserie. At two o'clock the night was cold but clear and I decided to walk across the city to my hotel in Montparnasse.

I crossed the river at the Pont des Invalides. There was hardly any traffic, the city was almost silent. I could hear the hours and the half-hours being struck. I have never seen anything as beautiful as this silent, naked city. The walk took over two hours and I wished it had been longer.

This time I had nothing to do in Paris but return to where we once lived and walk from there to Julien's. The quarter has become fashionable and expensive. The narrow streets close to the river between the Place Saint-Michel and the Rue Dauphine were built at the beginning of the seventeenth century. Inside the heavy red gate of the old hotel is a cobbled courtyard. On one side is a successful two-star restaurant that has been there for many years. While we lived there I saw a number of restaurants start up in the same place and fail. It must be one of the most dispiriting sights in the world. It is like watching a dream fail in public. The shape is nearly always the same. There is an enormous sense of excitement before it opens; the kitchens are being prepared, the decor chosen, the cooks and waiters hired, and hundreds of other things. A gala opening with celebrities and politicians takes place. We saw the mayor of Paris at one such opening. As we crossed the courtyard with all the doors thrown up, the congratulations and the laughter and champagne, it was as if all we had to do was to reach out and we'd touch the dream. Then, passing in and out through the courtyard over the months that followed we'd see it fail – waiters standing in the doorway, the tables behind them empty, quarrelling voices of recrimination. Then, one day, the glass that displayed the menu would be empty, the doors closed. Eventually, one restaurant opened, in much the same way as all the others, and succeeded, almost without our noticing. Happiness is its own completion.

Today, across the courtyard is a second new restaurant, but when we first lived there it was the workshop of a family of locksmiths, with two craftsmen and three or four apprentices. They wore leather aprons over the traditional blue work clothes. As well as locks and keys they made shutters and grating. There was much busy shouting and hammering and showers of sparks.

The apprentices travelled about to sites on mopeds with hanging satchels. They had a van for transporting the shutters and gratings. They always greeted us with a great cheerful shout that still retained a strict formality as we passed in and out. They were replaced by an art gallery, now the restaurant. On the corner, where a Breton couple used to have a small supermarket, is a glittering shop that sells expensive teas and chocolates.

The evening we arrived in Paris was warm. The trees were almost in full leaf. The tables outside the cafés we passed were crowded. At one such table I noticed a single daffodil set in a wine glass. There were lovers in the stone alcoves of the Pont Neuf, but their courting seemed to take the form of photographing one another rather than embracing. There were more pet shops than I remembered along the quay. The small hotels with the glass doors on the Rue Saint-Denis have disappeared. Near the Rue des Pêcheurs there were many sex shops: 'Pomme d'Or', 'Paris Sexy', 'Libraire Erotique'. A crowd had gathered round a coloured boy who was dealing out three cards on an upturned cardboard box. I was beginning to think the ladies of the night had disappeared with the small hotels until I reached the Rue des Cygnes. In the alleys and the doorways they were as plentiful as ever. The only change I noticed was that most of them were now coloured and all the pretty ones were black.

I think my heart paused when I saw that Julien was still there. A uniformed doorman stood outside. Inside, it was far more beautiful than I remembered, an art nouveau palace, lit like a jewel. The pre-Raphaelite ladies could be observed clearly. The spacious mirrors still held the flared peacocks in their depths; their designs and the rich colours of the glass roof were spectacular. As it was early, we were shown to a good table. The wall seating had been upholstered in plush burgundy. There was a tablecloth of immaculate linen and generous spacing between the tables. At the next table an elegant French woman was dining alone and reading what looked like a company report between courses. All the waiters were French, discreet and helpful. The oysters we had were fresh, the sole a little dry, but the medallions of monkfish with wood mushrooms in a cream sauce were perfection. There was no Amarante on the wine list, but the house Sancerre was delicious. The fare was incomparably better than in the old Julien and incomparably more expensive, but not as expensive as a similar restaurant in Dublin.

As we ate I noticed that the blackened fans that used to turn above the heat and noise were now painted an attractive yellow – and were still. The bentwood racks where our coats used to hang in heaps above the tables were now decorated with hats and bonnets in fashions that had long ceased.

As we left, a busload of German tourists were being shown to their tables. For all its brightness and beauty, it had more the feel of a museum than the poor vibrant living eating palace it once was. At the door are brochures with the information that Julien is now a listed historical building, one of the finest examples of art nouveau, created for the 1889 Universal Exhibition by Trézel. When I used to eat there I knew nothing other than that it was beautiful, cheap and great fun.

On the plane to Rabat, a young American was in the window seat. On his shirt he wore the name of a computer firm he worked for in Salt Lake City.

'This is great. You guys speak English,' he greeted. 'I've been here ten hours and haven't met anybody who spoke English.'

'You can hardly be too surprised to hear only French spoken in France?' I suggested as gently as possible.

'I don't buy any place where they don't speak English.'

'It's a very definite view,' I said.

'That's where I'm coming from anyhow,' he said. 'I have a bad feeling about this trip. I nearly turned back on the way to the airport yesterday.'

'It's too late now,' I said. 'We are in the air!'

Morocco, the Bitter and the Sweet

In Rabat there was dust on the tarmac, dust on the leaves, dust on the burned grass, but the dry heat was pleasurable. The sky was overcast. There was to be rain later in the evening. As soon as the luggage came off the plane it was surrounded by poor, hungry-looking porters. When I went to pick up my bags, an old, gaunt porter protested. I showed him that I hadn't as yet acquired any Moroccan money. He responded with a gesture more eloquent than words. Thin, delicate fingers plucked an offering to his mouth. He needed to eat.

At the Rabat Hilton, porters in traditional white uniforms – white shoes, long white stockings, white pantaloons and the red fez – took our luggage. The hotel gardens were well kept. Bitter orange trees and colourful flowers and plants flourished within borders of rosemary and bay. Two men in long white robes and white headdress walked up and down the paths in the gardens at dusk.

In the morning, Madeline and I drove past the miles of pink palace walls until we saw signs for La Plage. A rutted track ended at a bare, concrete café beside the beach. The beach was crowded, and all kinds of ball games were being played. Above it, close to the city walls stood an enormous graveyard. All the headstones were uniform, their backs to the sea, the plain Arabic inscriptions facing the city walls, so that they seemed to march in rows toward Mecca. Covering all the graves was the same crawling plant of tiny shiny leaves, bees moving between the small red and yellow flowers. In the middle of the cemetery an entire family was gathered beneath a large black umbrella. Outside the shade of the umbrella, a few old men shielded their heads from the merciless sun with newspapers.

The road out of Rabat ran for miles through woods. '*La Forêt est la Source de la Vie*,' a sign proclaimed. The forest gave way to vineyards, olive groves, orchards, sloping fields of grain only a few inches tall and whole fields of deep blue and bright yellow wildflowers. Nobody knew their names. Along the margins of the road all kinds of goods were for sale: potatoes displayed in pyramids on raised mounds of earth, little string bags of nuts and snails, trays of olives and lemons, heaps of oranges, fowl and black turkeys. What was common to this road and all the other roads we travelled was the sight of shepherds guarding their flocks of goats and sheep grazing the margins of the orchards and vineyards and fields of grain.

On the outskirts of Fez we acquired two youths on motorcycles, calling the names of different hotels at each traffic light. They seemed to be glued to the sides of the car. At the Palais Jamai Hotel, an official guide approached us as the hotel porters took the luggage. He wanted to know if we had been much set upon on our way into the city: 'You were wise to ignore these boys. Sometimes they lead cars into the back streets of the medina where they are robbed.'

That evening thunder and lightning crisscrossed the medina, and the mountains seemed to draw closer. In the middle of the storm the last of the five prayers of the day sounded from the main mosque, loud, formal, passionate, imploring. As soon as there was a pause, it was filled by prayer from the smaller mosques, until it seemed that voice was answering voice across the city and the mountains with the same dark, echoing entreaty. Then, as suddenly as the prayer began, it stopped. Throughout Morocco these prayers were to be heard all through the day, but nowhere were they as impressive or as moving as in Fez.

Early the next morning, we met our official guide to the medina, a Berber from the north. Though young, he had already many of the utterances and mannerisms of a patriarch. Here and elsewhere, nobody approached us while we were accompanied by an official guide. He led us quickly to the extraordinary Qarawiyin Mosque. Founded in the ninth century, it still has its original minaret, the oldest in Morocco, built in 956. The mosque has fourteen gates, 275 pillars, three fountains, can hold twenty thousand worshipers, and for a time was the most famous university in the Arab world, drawing such scholars as Avicenna and

Averroes within its walls. Since it is barred to non-Muslims, we could only glimpse its shape and magnificence through the graceful arches.

But for all the strange beauty of the mosque, it was the medina itself that was the most compelling. Sixty thousand people live and work within the medina. Each street by law must have a bakery, a fountain and a bathhouse. Under its straw covering, the Attarine souk displayed heaps of red and yellow spices. We came into streets of metal workers, brass workers in the 'Street of Yellow', streets where wedding clothes were made, where olives, butter, jam and honey were sold. We passed a master tailor sewing an elaborate gown on a raised platform while overseeing four apprentices at lesser tasks below, a shoemaker on a raised platform finishing the uppers of a shoe. At the fountain three girls drank from a communal cup.

As we approached the tanneries, there was the distinct smell of animal entrails. A narrow, winding stair led to flat roofs. Below us, in concrete pools or pits of dye, boys and young men were soaking the skins. There must have been a hundred workers in or around the different pits of dye in shades of red, white, brown, yellow and blue. In workshops above the pits, craftsmen were working the skins.

We crossed the river of Fez by a narrow bridge that divides the city in two. The shallow, fast-flowing river was a ripe yellow. On the way through, the streets cry 'Balak!' and hug the walls to allow the laden mules and donkeys to pass. Most of the donkeys wore nosebags to prevent them from plucking greens from other baskets.

On the way to look at carpets, we turned into an alley that opened into the sudden magnificence of a restored palace. Four floors ascended to a domed glass roof. On one floor five girls worked antique looms. Downstairs, we were shown to luxurious sofas. Mint tea was brought. The salesman poured tea above a low table. He had a well-honed pitch in French and English. 'There is no obligation. We can sit and enjoy the tea. Mint tea is an aphrodisiac.'

Six men spread out the carpets on the tiled floor. Two small rugs were chosen. A kind of frenzy now entered the dealing. They would take a credit card, but they needed a deposit of foreign money as well. For what? 'As a deposit, foreign money as deposit.' It did not occur to me until afterward that the cash must have been the salesman's commission.

The previous night we had eaten in the Moroccan restaurant of the Palais Jamai. The food was delicious. There was music and a belly dancer. I asked the guide if one could find a restaurant without music and dancers. He said that in a Moroccan restaurant it was necessary to have the 'spectacle' and recommended the restaurant Al-Firdaous.

The restaurant was another restored palace, empty when we arrived. It had magnificent tall pillars and alcoves and draperies. We sat in the vast emptiness for a while before deciding to take a table. An hour later there were still no other customers. Three musicians entered and began to play. There was one waiter. The first course, an assortment of salads, was pleasant, but the succeeding courses were barely edible. We sat there like the king and queen of emptiness, when suddenly the music quickened and a veiled woman entered and began to dance. Toward the end, she drew money from beneath her brassiere and shook it as she danced. We paid her and she left. With relief we thought that was the 'spectacle'. We were wrong. A colourful troupe entered in a representation of a country wedding. We hadn't sufficient cash to pay such a company and were trying to get the bill and leave when the music struck up more loudly and an even larger group gathered round the table. Their aggression was unmistakable. There was no choice but to outface them, and finally they left. The musicians departed sadly. There was no sound but the rain dripping from the roof outside in the vast and sumptuous emptiness.

The next morning, we drove with our guide out toward the mountains, from which there were striking views of the city. We parked at the mellah, where the Jews of Fez were moved in 1438. We walked in the Jewish cemetery, which has been restored, orange and olive trees planted. The streets of this quarter were far wider and many of the houses had balconies of wood and wrought iron decorated with plants and flowers. On the way back, the guide asked if we'd visited the restaurant the night before. I had a feeling that he already knew all that had taken place.

'Was it good?'

'Not very. We were the only people there.'

'Usually it is full,' he said firmly.

During our time together, our guide expressed himself on many subjects: Shakespeare, women, Fez, his desire to see other countries. Some of his views were naive but none were unintelligent. I felt we had been lucky, but I knew nothing about him.

The midday heat in the medina was intense. A row of donkeys tied to a wall were suffering. A single donkey had rolled over on the ground with its pack and was breathing heavily. Farther on, a mule lay dead in the middle of the street. It had been stripped of whatever it had been carrying, except for a poor piece of cloth worn beneath the saddlebags.

Later that evening, I tried to go for a walk on my own. Not more than a few hundred yards from the hotel, a boy attached himself to my side like a voluble shadow, offering even not to speak at all once we were within the medina, and would not leave me until I turned back to the hotel.

Even though there was little traffic, it was difficult enough to find our way out of Fez the next day, but within a mile of the city we were passing carts laden with white flowers, girls in coloured dresses driving flocks of sheep, mules drawing water tanks.

We were in the foothills of the mountains. Higher in the mountains we came on women washing wool at the side of a stream, while above them a man was ploughing a small clearing between the rocks with a mule and a wooden plough. There was little traffic. The roads were good. There were times in the wide expanse of earth and sky when the sensation was more like flying. We broke the journey at a small modern hotel in the middle of the wilderness, near Khenifra. In the foyer, a photograph of a monkey in a little-boy suit holding a bunch of bananas was hung beside a studio portrait of Charlie Chaplin.

The landscape was often reminiscent of some of the tilework in the mosques in that it was always the same and yet infinitely various. On the outskirts of Marrakesh a young women in a blue dress was carrying sacks of grain on her head through a cornfield. Even though it was rush hour in Marrakesh, we acquired two boys on motorbikes immediately, and, as soon as they lost heart outside the closed windows, they were replaced within a hundred yards by yet two more.

The next morning at our hotel, the Tichka Salam, we met our guide, who was small, humorous and extrovert. He spoke in a rapid staccato out of the corner of his mouth. Several times he yawned on the way into the city. He was a Berber from the south.

As we drove through avenues lined with rows of small orange trees, he said, 'They are very bitter. The religious refugees brought them from Seville.'

We walked in the great Jemaa el Fna, the square where crowds used to assemble for the beheading of criminals. It was now filled with monkeys on leads, snake charmers, fortune-tellers, storytellers from the Sahara. To catch any eye for even a moment was to be drawn into one kind of commerce or another. One look and the snake charmers started to play. The medina was more colourful than Fez, more extrovert, more prosperous and more touristy.

We were becoming an increasing disappointment to our guide. He took us to pottery shops, rug shops, a shop that sold spices. 'A big welcome,' they would all say. 'Even though you buy nothing, we are still smiling.' Sometimes they ran after us, offering goods at a quarter of the price they had been asking in the shop. After a number of times the guide saw my inquiring look. 'They like to bargain. They'd like to sell cheap because tomorrow they are closed.'

The Islamic Sabbath fell the next day. In Marrakesh it was hot and dusty. Essaouira, by the sea, was only two hours away. Once we left the olive groves and orchards outside Marrakesh, the land grew flat and stony. I thought it beautiful. Mounds of rock were gathered here and there in the fields to clear a space for grass or cultivation. Nobody was working in the fields. There was no traffic. When we slowed, approaching goats and sheep by the roadside, the shepherds often raised their hands in acknowledgement. Close to Essaouira there was a herd of beautiful black goats standing on their hind legs like dogs, their front feet planted on the branches of olive trees while they plucked at the leaves.

At first the town looked dull and dusty, the flat-roofed white houses unprepossessing. We turned down several roads that looked as if they would lead to the ocean, but they went nowhere. Then a stream of people appeared. We followed them, found a crowded street and parked. A huge market on waste ground that sold everything from bicycle wheels to oranges and artichokes stood outside a big stone archway. Going down a narrow street from the market to the sea, we came on a charming eighteenth-century hotel, the Hotel Riad al Medina. In the tiled courtyard, two fountains were surrounded by potted plants and flowers, and rose petals floated in the water. We had a mint tea in the courtyard. The bedrooms that we looked at were cool and comfortable.

Not far from the hotel, stone steps led to a lookout post guarded by antique cannon. Away to the right were sand dunes, below us the harbour and the ocean, and beyond a crowded beach. Reluctantly, we turned back through the narrow streets, where a woman was selling a tray of sea urchins.

From Marrakesh we crossed the Atlas Mountains to Taroudant. At times we were only a few hundred feet below the snowline. My abiding sense was of a tiny car clinging like an insect to the side of the mountain, a sheer drop of thousands of feet into ravines below.

Even in this mountainous wilderness there was much life: terraces of small fruit trees in white blossom, women washing clothes at the edge of a rushing river, bright rugs spread out on rocks, red houses carved into the mountainside. In a sleepy village, the windshields of the trucks were covered with brown paper bags against the fierce sun. We passed many flocks of small mountain goats. Very high up, a white tent was perched on the edge of a ravine, and in front of the closed tent eighty-four flat beehives were arranged in rows. There were times when we thought that we would never get to the other side of the mountain, and it was with a certain disbelief that we found ourselves driving into Taroudant.

While the Palais Jamai in Fez was the most deserving of its five stars, the hotel with the happiest atmosphere was the Palais Salam in Taroudant. The atmosphere of the city was also relaxed, and we were able to walk without interference. We arrived for the big open market, sheep and goats and fowl sold at one end, a flea market at the other. In between, mounds of fruit and vegetables were spread out on the ground.

All that I saw during the days in Morocco has retained an extraordinary vividness, perhaps because of its very strangeness and rich colours. When I think of the many people working in the fields, the teeming markets, the mosques, there is a single image that keeps returning and will not go away. At the very top of the medina in Fez, as it is closing down in the midday heat, a boy sits astride a tall mule. Both the boy and the mule are splattered with dried blobs of mortar. They must have been carrying cement and sand to some building site within the medina and taking rubble away. The boy isn't more than fifteen, and is counting silver coins in his hand. So absorbed is he that he seems to be unaware of the minor obstruction he is causing. Nobody yells for him to move or get out of the way. They look up impassively at what he is doing before edging politely and silently past the mule, which is standing like a stone amid the flies and dust. The boy doesn't pay me or anybody else any attention. He is still counting and recounting the coins in his hand as I move away.

An Irishman in Newcastle

'Hallo, kidders! How's yor luck,' Jimmy Learmouth used to open at the Newcastle Hippodrome.

The pale blue half-circle of the Tyne Bridge meets you coming into Newcastle. The blue stars of the Scottish and Newcastle breweries shine above the bars in the evenings. The same half-circles of riveted blue steel and glass roof the great covered market, where deer and hare, with their heads in little plastic caps, hang beside cheap tennis rackets. There is the red and gold of the first Marks and Spencers bazaar among hundreds of stalls and the blue Weigh House, where once I saw an enormous woman with a hat have herself weighed for two pence on one scale while a porter weighed a tray of hearts for one pence at the next.

By way of Nun Street you enter the Cloth Market, fruit and vegetable stalls pitched on the cobbles, Indians selling coloured bales, a china stall that sells factory seconds cheaply, some little flaw in the glaze or print; and at the very bottom you come to the last music hall in England – Balmbras.

Here, Keith Wilson, the host of Balmbras, will welcome you. 'You never know, do you! I started out as a *chef de cuisine*, and here I wind up running Balmbras,' he laughs with characteristic straightforwardness and charm.

Balmbras began in 1862. 'I took the bus frae Balmbras and she was heavy laden,' is a line from 'The Blaydon Races'. As a music hall it suffered from the wheel of fashion, was for long a billiard hall, but the decor was never pillaged, and when it opened again as a music hall in 1962 it was almost as if it was a hundred years before.

It must be one of the loveliest rooms in Newcastle. It is like the inside of an enormous gilded barrel, the same half-circle of the bridges and market, ironware of oriental design in shapes of six by four breaking the regular curve of the ceiling into arches. The empty spaces in the ironwork glow a velvet blue above the lamps. The stage is framed in the same half-circle, and the heavy circular tables claw the floor. Woodcuts of Newcastle folk heroes, like Coffee Johnny, act out their lives along the walls.

It is, perhaps, the most unlikely place to find an Irishman, except that there seems to be always an Irishman, as if God appointed one to all the most unlikely places; and as the plush red curtain parts to show an old Newcastle street scene, and as the organ fades, the name PAT HEALEY shows up on a red card, and an Irish voice says 'Welcome to Balmbras Music Hall': Pat Healey steps up to the brass rail and starts to act and sing.

Pat Healey and Edna Selkirk and Les Carmichael, the percussionist, are the stars of the show. When Edna comes on, in long black skirt and a blouse of red silk, the ostrich feather sweeping back from the red roses in the hat, Les comes charmingly to life on the drums. He seems as much on the stage as Edna, playing backward and forward to [ ] as Pat Healey bows off. They do everything with such ease of timing that they make the others look clumsier than they probably are. Carmichael's face becomes a Chinese study again after Edna goes, and he stomps out the obligatory rhythm to the contortions of the drag artist. All three are old troopers. Only when she comes among the tables and you see the frail hands under the nylon can you begin to believe Edna is seventy. Lizardlike, Carmichael is ageless above the drums. Even in daylight Healey hardly looks his sixty years.

'I was born in Monastereven, in Drogheda Row. There were fourteen of us, and I was called Bonna. The old boy in the pub used to keep his cattle in Bonnaderragh, and we used to go for the cattle for him, but I could never get my tongue round Bonnaderragh, and so they called me Bonna. When I went back there a few years ago, I got a terrible shock: it was only a little way off, and I thought it was miles. My father used to cut and sell firewood for a living. When I got a job one summer in John McCormack's stables, I thought that the biscuits for the racehorses were for eating.

'Then we went to Mallow. I was always a bit of an athlete. In 1934 I hurled for the Mallow Minor Team that won the County Championship. We beat St Finnbar's in the Final, and Jack Lynch was hurling for them that day.

'My brother had gone to Galway to be a hairdresser, and I followed him. He stayed there all his life. He owned Caesar's Salons. It was there I started to play for Corinthians, and I came to London to see the England v Ireland match. The ticket was twenty-eight bob. I met a fellow that was homesick, and sold the return half for fourteen.

'I got my first break in the Pride of Erin Dancehall in Tottenham Court Road. The Caseys ran it then. I used to sing "Pennies From Heaven". Someone from the E. G. Heng Agency heard me and signed me on. It was how I began.

'I must have played in every music hall in Britain, in the second-class theatres as well as in the first. If you wanted to work the fifty-two weeks of the year, you had to play the second as well as the first.

'Collins Theatre in Islington, I played the Empire in Woolwich. City Variety in Leeds. I was "Boots" Healey there, Canada's Singing Cowboy. There was this old horse we had that we used to have to walk around the streets before we went on, but once didn't he open up on stage.

'Queens in Dundee
Hippodrome in Aberdeen
Shakespeare in Liverpool
Empire in Newcastle

They're just some. I could fill a page. They're all gone now. I was "on the green" in those days. And isn't it strange I find it hard to remember some of the great theatres in which I made my living, while I remember every one of the names of the people I went to school with.

'We were bombed out too. We'd just finished the show in Grinsay when it was hit. All the sea lions were killed. Lucky enough, we were booked down the road in Scunthorpe. Then we went to the Hippo- drome in Hamilton and we were burned out of there the first Saturday night. That's the worst of the stage – no show, no pay.

'Once we played in Lyme Regis, and hardly anybody showed up. "What's the matter?" the manager asked. "Didn't the bills go up?" "O they don't read bills round here." "What do you do?" "You get the town crier." So we got the town crier and he charged us a half a crown. And the next day myself and the manager were playing billiards when we heard the bell going, and we stopped and looked out the window. There was the town crier, with the top hat and the bell, shouting, "Hear ye! Hear ye! Hear ye!" announcing the show, and there wasn't a sinner about. "O my God," the manager said. "That's another bloody half-crown down the drain," and we went back to playing billiards.

'I was understudy for Josef Locke, which meant I was juvenile lead. You sang a bit, fed the comics, danced with the girls, and then, if Locke went sick or temperamental, you got your chance. I got mine at Doncaster, and I filled the house two weeks running, and the same at Newcastle. I was billed as England's greatest tenor, but then this looked like becoming too much of a good thing [ ] come back. Patrick O'Hagan was my understudy for a while. Someone showed me an interview with O'Hagan in some circus magazine a while back, and he asked, "Whatever happened to Pat Healey?" Each man in his time plays many parts.

'Afterwards, when my voice started to go, I was glad of my years as juvenile lead. I wasn't dependent on my voice. I could hold an audience for a whole night.

'Once you have an audience you can never let them go. If you do it's impossible to get them back. All you can say afterwards is tonight I have died a little; tomorrow I'll live again.'

I notice lines of Shakespeare running through his own speech and bring it to his attention.

'Shakespeare is soaked into the old greasepaint. I was sick a while back, and there was nothing to read in the house but a Collected Shakespeare. I didn't finish much of it, but there was hardly a page that there wasn't some line I already knew. That's what I miss most about the road. We went from one town to another all over England, but always to the same digs. We were all together, like in one family, without having to bother about the family. I played for two weeks at Aberdeen once and it was only years after that I realized I was at the bloody sea all that time. Since you always went back to the same digs, going to a new town was like going home, without having to put up with home.

'I played in the Olympia in Dublin too, with Alpedosta and his accordion band. Cecil Sheridan was on the bill. It was the only place I ever nearly got beaten up. There was a big fellow up in the gods who kept shouting that I wasn't Irish, and I said to him, "Come back stage after the show," and he bloody well did.

'In 1952 I got ill. It was touch-and-go. The road days were over. I thought I might as well throw in the towel, and I got a job selling TVs; but I couldn't stay away. It's something in the blood. I started to play the local pubs, and when Balmbras started I went there.'

Another night at Balmbras is almost ended. The bar has stopped serving, the girls are tiredly washing glasses. The audience is singing, an inscrutable smile on Les Carmichael's face as he taps out the rhythm with ironical little flickers. The artists have joined hands, to sing and dance out the chorus. Edna is in tails now with a top hat and riding crop. They have all taken their bows except Pat Healey, and Edna says, '. . . And the biggest hand of all for Pat Healey, the man who strings the show together.'

The silence is all the more silence because it is so sudden once the hall is empty. Keith Wilson is counting the takings. The girls are clearing the tables. Les Carmichael is putting away his instruments.

George Knowles, the baritone, has his cap and coat on, so has Vic the organist, the [ ] girls, Cynthia and Cathy, the drag artist from North Shields, Edna and Pat Healey. They are having a last drink in the alcove beside the bar.

'You were great tonight, Edna,' Pat Healey says, as he sips his pint of ale. 'You had them eating out of your hand.'

'They were a very nice audience,' she says quietly and just turns her whiskey and soda round in her glass. Les Carmichael is dressed for the night now too. He pauses at the alcove, as if considering how a few good drum taps might improve the whole s[ ], and then nods curtly, and goes out.

'Les is something out of the ordinary.'

'Wasn't he the resident drummer in the Grand – was it in Byker? – for thirty years?'

'And I'm waiting for my chauffeur,' Pat Healey breaks into elfin laughter. 'And if anybody ever asked you, tell them that the Irish did a lot of architectural work round Newcastle.'

The Bird Swift

I had heard of the 'Bird Swift' in the bars around Grafton Street when I was young, and the pun 'Fried Bacon' they had coined to describe his work. 'He could charm fivers out of patrons' pockets like the birds out of the bushes,' was said to me in a gloomy mixture of envy and admiration of his social expertise. Though he had long left Dublin, he still possessed a fame of a sort in the bars.

Through the youngest of the Swifts, Tony, I had come to know most of his family. In the small house in Carrick Terrace, which was stuffed with the mother's extraordinary energy and charm, I saw his drawings and paintings for the first time – I remember with particular vividness a small watercolour of a Rialto sweetshop – and it was there I was given *Come Dance with Kitty Stobling* to read in a typescript Jimmy Swift had made for Kavanagh at that time.

I met Patrick Swift in London in 1960, and saw him over a few weeks of that hot summer. He was living with Oonagh and their daughters Katty and Julie in a basement flat in Westbourne Terrace. As well as painting and drawing, he was editing the magazine *X* with David Wright, and they had accepted the first piece of prose I published. Sometimes I stayed with him over night and we spent whole days together. The flat had a charming front room with books and paintings, a bedroom and a kitchen at the back. A long, narrow hallway ran the length of the flat, with the bathroom at its end, and the spare bed was in an alcove in the hallway. The flat had very little light. I think he worked in borrowed studios and was looking for a permanent studio. I remember going with him to look at rooms for rent, but they were all either too expensive or depressing.

On one of those searches, we met a painter Paddy knew who had a studio in the particular house and who specialized in car crashes, working from photographs. Paddy examined the paintings courteously, asking questions about this angle or that, but as we walked away from the house he said, 'God, it's sad. The poor fellow hasn't a bull's clue. He was probably the star of some art school and now he thinks he's an artist, when he could have been happy as a plumber or carpenter or mechanic.'

We often walked across Kensington Gardens to the Victoria and Albert, where I remember him enquiring about obtaining a ticket to the Reading Room with a view to working there on some essays he was planning to write for *X*. We always looked at the Constables. It was he who first told me how well Constable wrote in his letters about trees and clouds and light and water. Walking back across the gardens, we enjoyed the great trees, especially the plane trees, with their peeled strips of bark – 'They soak up the polluted air' – and he quoted a favourite line, 'Bring in the particular trees / That caught you in their mysteries', mentioning that he preferred trees to flowers. I remember him pausing at the Peter Pan statue beside the ornamental ponds and fountains at Lancaster Gate and that he admired especially the small rodents at its base.

He was tall, with thick black hair that sometimes fell across his face as he argued, and he had inherited his mother's bird-like features. He wore casual, inexpensive clothes, black or blue shirts, and he was one of those people who always look elegant no matter what they wear. He moved at ease among all kinds of people. Only once did I ever see him socially flustered or angry. He liked to argue and was in the middle of an argument one evening in the French pub when a man who had known him at Synge Street entered. He was dressed like an engineer or accountant and very drunk. Paddy didn't notice at first and the man stood quietly at the counter listening while he waited for his drink. As soon as he had it in his hand he bellowed, 'The star of Synge Street Debating Society is still at it.' Paddy's detachment was so complete that it was unusual for anything to provoke more than irony or amusement, but some days later I heard him make scathing remarks about middle-class drunks loosed from their cages.

Most of our evenings ended in Soho. They would start quietly enough near Lancaster Gate in a genteel bar with deep carpets, polished brass rails, bowls of flowers. Because of the hot weather, all doors to bars seem to have been eternally open on to the street all through that summer. Sometimes there would be an argument between Paddy and David Wright as to whether to travel into Soho by the underground or by taxi. Paddy usually won. He loved travelling by taxi. We would go to the Swiss pub and then to the French. He seemed more to dance into bars than to move to counter or corner. He knew many people and his charm around them was also a kind of dance. Later we would climb the narrow stairs to Muriel's, then end the evening dancing into the hopeful hours at the Mandrake. 'All Men Are False Said My Mother' was a hit that year. Elizabeth Smart played it over and over on the jukebox. After such a night Paddy would be up at seven the next morning, bathe Katty and Julie, bring Oonagh tea or coffee in bed, toss the girls high into the air, playing and laughing with them as he dressed them and gave them breakfast. Then he would go to whatever borrowed studio he had.

Sometimes he would need to go into town to buy paints or canvas or on business connected with *X*, to see printers or to look for advertising, and I would go with him. I think he enjoyed this. Crafts and trades fascinated him. Once we watched a long line of trainee nurses from Paddington Hospital, in their blue and red capes. 'Look how attractive every one of those girls are in their uniforms,' he said. 'Allow them self-expression, to pick the clothes they like and tart themselves up according to the fashions, and I bet there's hardly one you'd look at twice.' We always walked. We enjoyed walking, always looking around, talking about what we saw or something he was reminded of. None of this was in the least bit self-conscious but part of a vital energy, and he was as good a listener as talker. He had a list of set questions too that were uncomfortably like an examination text. 'What does a young man do in Dublin?' 'What does a young man do for artistic company in Dublin? For intellectual company?' 'How does a young man pick up girls in Dublin?' 'Who are the main reviewers in the newspapers now?' 'Where would you go to the cinema or theatre in Dublin?' I could answer readily enough that to go into McDaid's or any of the bars around Grafton Street on any Saturday night was enough to cure me of desire for artistic company for at least a month.

'Well, Kavanagh is at least a man of some genius. Why don't you try to see more of him?'

I told him that I had no inclination to go through the barrage of insult and abuse that seemed the necessary initiation to the doubtful joy of Kavanagh's company and that I preferred to read the work. I suggested that it might have been easier for him because he was from the city and a painter.

'Not at all,' he laughed. 'The first time we met I was told that I was nothing but a gurrier and a fucking intellectual fraud.'

'What happened then?'

'Naturally after that I ignored him. Then one day Patrick McDonough took me to lunch – he was a Guinness rep, as well as a good minor poet and a charming man. After lunch we went into a bar and had a brandy at the counter. Kavanagh was at the back of the bar, with newspapers, probably the racing pages, and he was coughing and muttering and shifting around all the time we were there. McDonough had a business appointment and couldn't stay. As soon as he left, Kavanagh came up to the counter and demanded, "What are you doing with that fraud McDonough?" As soon as I explained, he said, "You shouldn't be wastin' your time with fucking phoneys like that. I've been thinking about you and I think you may well be the real thing!"'

To my surprise, he hadn't told the story to Jimmy Swift, and when I told it to Jimmy, who knew Kavanagh, he went into hoots of laughter: 'I think we can safely say that it was no sudden critical insight that led to that conversation.'

I asked Paddy once how he rhymed Kavanagh's often boorish self with the sensitive and delicate verses. 'My dear boy, separation of Art and Life,' he laughed outright. 'All those delicate love poems are addressed to himself, even if it is sometimes by way of God. Such sensitivity would be wasted on a mere Other. He once told me that he often used to dip into American poetry anthologies to put him into an inspirational mood in the mornings, but nowadays I think the very thought of his own importance is sufficient to get him into orbit.'

I think he understood perfectly the mixture of child and monster, fool and knave that went into the wayward intelligence of Kavanagh's genius. Out of the understanding had grown a deep, comic sympathy. 'Once, when we were staying at John Farrelly's, he pointed out a particular grass. "I love that grass. I've known it since I was a child. I've often wondered if I'd be different if I had been brought up to love better things." He could be a dreadful coward as well as a bully. Once I got a frantic phonecall and found him sulking in Pembroke Road. There was a bunch of Americans at O'Faolain's who wanted to meet him. He wouldn't go unless I came with him: "We will be moving into enemy territory." We went out to O'Faolain's and he was like a mouse all evening. Of course there were roars afterwards; yet he can be funny and marvellous sometimes . . .'

He loved David Wright and David Gascoyne. He admired George Barker in much the same way as he admired Kavanagh, and Barker's life provided him with almost as much comic detail as Kavanagh's did. He had irrational hatreds; for instance, all clergymen, and the tone in which he referred to their collars was always violent, striking in his case since his usual tone was amused, detached, ironic even in heated arguments. Writers he didn't approve of received the same treatment as clergymen, and some of them were true writers – Chekhov was one, definitely a clergyman, Henry James another – and since poor artists of all kinds outnumber the good – many times over – this floating violence had the appearance and weight of authority. He appeared to be much more at ease talking about writing than painting, but I believe this was only superficially true. Reading through his articles I think it can be seen that he hadn't a natural feeling for language. What interested him was ideas and the conflict of ideas and their power when seen through the fascination of a powerful personality. That drunken arrow all the way from Synge Street may have gone deeper than had been intended.

Often, as we walked between meetings or had lunch in a bar, a couple of half-pints of bitter and pork pies with mustard, we talked of his family. As with painting, he hardly ever spoke of his mother, probably because she was too close. When I visited Carrick Terrace, his father liked to talk to me about the country. At the time, he had casual work with the Racing Board, and went as a steward to race meetings all over the country. He was also a keen fisherman. Paddy had vivid, painful memories of being taken on fishing trips as a boy. 'It was crucifying. Out in some field along the Liffey, trying to kill time for a whole day, grasping at butterflies that wavered about along the river bank, not able to shout or laugh or sing, afraid of your life to make any noise in case it would disturb the bloody trout.'

Of all his family, he spoke most of his older brother Jimmy; of the books Jimmy had encouraged him to read, of the extraordinary evenness of his behaviour at all times. 'I was always getting into some stupid row or other in the house, attacking someone, shouting, just being a terrible nuisance, until Jimmy would have to take charge and physically throw me out into the street. An hour or so later I'd feel miserable, ashamed of my life to meet Jimmy, feeling horrible. He'd just smile as if nothing at all had taken place and ask if I'd be interested in wandering down to McCauley's for a drink.'

'Why doesn't Tony exhibit?' he asked another time. 'He has a drawing talent.'

'He doesn't seem to want to.'

'He has far more talent than most of the people having shows in Dublin. I know he was well thought of at the College.'

'He says he's not prepared to make that commitment. He'll paint or draw when he feels like it and he wants to leave it at that. Aren't there far too many books and shows as it is?'

'Wouldn't it stir up a bit of life? Girls and money would be around. With his good looks he could have a ball, while as things stand he might just as well be scratching himself.'

I remember letting it rest, though I thought the line of argument exceedingly strange in his case. He had had one exhibition, which was notable for the acclaim it received, and never exhibited again. I felt like asking him why he was urging Tony to exhibit while patently unwilling to exhibit himself, but I knew instinctively that the questions would not be welcomed.

He was having his portrait painted by Tim Behrens, and some mornings Katty and I went with him. He complained that he disliked sitting for his portrait, and I asked the obvious, 'Well, why do you do it?'

'I suppose if you have to ask other people to sit for you, from time to time you have to do the same yourself.'

Behrens's studio was in one of those great London squares built around private gardens enclosed by high railings. Either the gates were open or, more likely, Paddy had got the key from Behrens, and Katty and I waited in the gardens. Katty must have been about three at the time. She was a grave, charming child, who plainly adored her father, and it was pleasant sitting or playing with her in the empty gardens surrounded by the trees and tall cream-coloured houses in the endless good weather. The last morning we were there Tim Behrens joined us with Paddy at the end of the sitting and we went to a nearby pub for a drink. Behrens was serious and soft-spoken, with understated good manners, and after twenty minutes or so he left us, saying that he had to get back to work. 'What's his work like?' I asked. 'It's good. In fact, he may well be the best of the younger people around, but what gets me about all these young people is that they are so damned serious. Work is important but it's not the be-all or end-all of everything, but if you listened long enough to these people you'd begin to believe there was nothing else in life.' He then told me that Behrens's understated manner had been nurtured by an enormous fortune. Paddy had met his father, Lord Behrens, and seemed to have detailed knowledge not only of the extent of the family wealth but also of its sources. I think Paddy was fascinated by wealth and power, and suffered more than most people the constraints of his relative poverty while living in a great city like London. He told me that Stevie Smith was the best company of all the people he had met in London. She had come to their house for dinner once and the reason they didn't continue to see her was they were too poor. 'She prefers to have drinks in the Savoy and dine out with rich people, and who can blame her.'

Often Paddy and I went to galleries together, and I think they were the best times. His usual argumentative self disappeared and was replaced by something close to diffidence. 'You can't write about painting,' he asserted. 'The whole thing is tactile. The canvas is either alive or it isn't. You can only look.' I mentioned Proust on Chardin and Vermeer, Rilke's monograph on Rodin. 'I don't mind that sort of writing but it doesn't really say anything about the painting. They use the paintings as starting points for themselves. Anyhow, everything Rilke writes about becomes pure Rilke, but it is far better than the usual judgemental guff.'

He preferred Maurois's hero-worshipping biography of Proust to Painter's, which he thought essentially bogus, pretending to an exactitude that wasn't ever possible about one's own life, never mind the life of another, and was, anyhow, irrelevant, never more so than when applied to a man of genius, where the abiding life is always in the private world of the spirit. In this regard, he felt even more strongly about Ellmann's life of Joyce. He felt a truer picture was always more likely to emerge through the lens of antipathy or admiration than the falsely scientific, which was no more than a modern, tarted-up version of the old academy. Sometimes we would wander through the commercial galleries around Bond Street. He was particularly excited by a small show of Giacometti's sculptures, and he admired L. S. Lowry. He said then that anybody with enough money to buy a Lowry would make a fortune. It was always a pleasure to look at paintings with him, but I knew that I could never be more than a very lame follower. We talked about this: that I hadn't the vocabulary, how what I liked or disliked was completely haphazard, that I could never feel or see through paint the way I could with words. He argued that it was better to approach painting or sculpture with clear unprejudiced eyes rather than with a mass of opinions or preconceptions. That might have been true if I had possessed a strong natural visual talent as he did, but it did not apply in my case. I have often reflected with amusement that his words could be applied more truly to the opinions he brought to writing than the lack of them in my weak visual sense. That weakness was depressingly present when we went together to the Picasso retrospective at the Tate Gallery. I remember it vividly – the hot afternoon, the torpor along the river, the scanty dresses, the faint breeze and the hot stone. There was a le Brocquy prominently displayed above the entrance as we bought our tickets. He looked at the painting in mock seriousness and asked in a matching tone, 'How many dinner parties would you estimate it took to get that put up there?'

Picasso meant nothing to me. I found the variety of styles and colours dispiriting. I said I'd bow out and was happy to sit and watch the human show. He was wonderfully easy in such situations and went about his own enjoyment. I remember saying to him as he rejoined me and we were leaving the gallery, 'I'm afraid I'd give the whole show for one small Juan Gris.' Paddy countered, 'I think it's true that no single painting works by itself in the exhibition, but when you see them all together it's breathtaking; it's the variety, the colour, the vitality, the sheer exuberance. There's a certain type of good painter who disappears or is diminished in a big show, and there are others – none more than Picasso – who need a big show to bring the work to life.'

We crossed London on the top of a bus to Aldgate. Whatever was showing in the Whitechapel Gallery didn't interest either of us for long. We walked the streets, the lane of Jewish silversmiths, the lane where poultry were plucked, the men sitting in open boxes amid the stench of blood and feathers, Brick Lane, the Whitechapel Road with its open market, Lemon Street. I knew the area well. I had lived there. As we walked towards London Bridge and lunch, we came on a small bomb site, part of a still lived-in terrace, that had turned into a sort of wild garden, dominated by an elder tree. Both of us loved the small Constable that used to hang in the Municipal Gallery, of an elder tree in blossom beside a wheelbarrow under a grey orchard wall. I remember particularly that it delighted Paddy how the wilderness had taken over the blasted concrete. 'If I had four or five acres in the country I'd let the whole thing go wild. Wouldn't it be much more interesting to watch it growing rather than have one of those big bloody formal gardens?'

Often we went to the National Gallery. Usually we split up. I was always sure to find him in the Rembrandt Room. A couple of times when he was pressed for time we went there directly. 'It's all so simple, such magic, so much life and death in one canvas,' he said once. When I look at some of the portraits of his mother I am reminded of the portrait of Maria Trapp which he so much admired.

Paddy wanted to make a drawing of me to send back as a present to his mother, and started it after lunch the day before I was to return to Dublin. He was having difficulty, and after several starts abandoned it, and we went to see a Disney film which was showing in the Paddington Cinema around the corner. He delighted in the pictures of the deer crossing the Arctic wastes along with the train of predators. The next morning he finished the drawing. I packed it with my bags, and we had the whole of the idle day together until the 8.40 left Euston.

We walked across Kensington Gardens to the Victoria and Albert and strolled back between the great plane trees. We sat for a while by the fountain before crossing to a bar on the Bayswater Road that had outside tables. We sat at one of the tables and started drinking gin. The roar of traffic amid the petrol fumes on the Bayswater Road was so constant that it was like silence. Paddy had no money but I had more than enough. He was worried about this until I showed him what I had and assured him that there would be a teacher's paycheck waiting for me in Dublin when I got back there in the morning. I had always found him proud and correct about money, in spite of his reputation in Dublin bars for charming fivers out of pockets, and this was especially true with people with as little money as he at the time. This correctness at that time was not usual in my experience of the bohemian circles. He rang Oonagh from within the bar to see if she could join us with Katty and Julie. As we sat in the heat and noise and drank gin, the talk turned to Stendhal – *Naples and Florence*, *Memoirs of an Egotist*, the Journals. 'It would be obscene to be anything but a romantic in this conformist age,' Paddy asserted, and I disagreed, thinking it was more a matter of temperament and background.

By way of the many beautiful girls that passed along Bayswater Road, the talk turned to Balbec and the sea, to the great passage on memory in St Augustine's *Confessions*, and finally to the Image, how all artistic activity centres on bringing the clean image that moves us out into the light. On that we could agree. We could even order a large gin on the strength of it. Paddy quoted Aquinas: 'The image is a principle of our knowledge. It is that from which our intellectual activity begins, not as a passing stimulus, but as an enduring foundation.' And the 8.40 out of Euston was still hours away.

A Poet Who Worked in Prose:
Memories of Michael McLaverty

Years ago when I was an evening student at UCD – one of those National Teachers Flann O'Brien observed as they came into Earlsfort Terrace after work on their bicycles – I saw that Michael McLaverty was to speak to the L&H. I'd read and enjoyed all his books, and went to hear him.

He was a short but robust looking man, his hair combed flatly across his receding forehead, and he spoke confidently and forcefully, with dry humour, patent sincerity and, above all, kindliness.

Towards the end of the discussion, which I seem to remember revolving round O'Connor and O'Faolain and the Russians, he complained about the neglect of Daniel Corkery, especially the stories, and appealed directly to the student audience to read certain stories – one was 'A Vision' – and invited us to write to him if we found them true or enjoyable. I had liked *The Threshold of Quiet*, but had been put off by the nationalistic essays, which at that time were more in vogue than his fiction. Because of McLaverty, I went and read Corkery's stories, and I wrote to him telling as well of the pleasure his own books had given me.

He replied warmly, which led to a correspondence of sorts, all about books or writing. On his next visit to Dublin he invited me to meet him in the little hotel he was staying in at the bottom of Harcourt Street, and we had tea together. I grew very fond of him. Behind a bluff headmasterly manner that had been acquired – at some cost I suspect – he was a shy, sensitive, obstinate and, I think, a very lonely man. In conversation he could be amazingly open, even dangerously unguarded.

Apart from his talent and intelligence, I believe that he was perfectly in tune with the simplicities of the Catholicism and green Nationalism he had grown up in, and these beliefs he adhered to piously throughout his long life. As well as being a source of strength, they may have taken some toll. In the novels in particular, there is sometimes a sense of a turning away from any disturbing grain in the material into the safe/unsafe paths of convention. I think this is true of his most interesting novel, *The Three Brothers*; but there are at least two paths in every wood, and if he had taken any other he would not have recorded his society as he did.

Tolstoy he loved – 'The Death of Ivan Ilych', 'The Kreutzer Sonata', 'Family Happiness' perhaps more than the great novels; all of Chekhov, including the letters; Gerard Manley Hopkins, Joyce, Katherine Mansfield, Edwin Muir and Corkery are the names I remember.

Some of the writers I was taken with at the time he could not abide. Flannery O'Connor was one exception. The originality of Kavanagh's talent he noticed from the beginning, but felt that after *The Great Hunger* and *A Soul for Sale* Kavanagh had gone wrong in Dublin. 'Poor Kavanagh,' he would murmur. He had a certain Northerner's view of Dublin as an envious, idle, incestuous, destructive place, and approved of Cyril Connolly's description: 'A warm pool full of smiling crocodiles.' He loved Thomas Kinsella's first book *Another September*, and was fond of quoting 'My love has sweets and grapes to eat / The air is like a laundered sheet.'

Though I was less than half his age, there was never a trace of condescension in his manner. Writing was too serious and spiritual for him ever to behave as a literary gent or successful author (which belong in an imaginary bestiary anyway), and he was as far from Bohemia as he was from the salon.

I remember talking with him once about the unsuitability of Life for work, how it always has to be re-imagined, rearranged or reinvented in order to be believable. I gave an example of a teacher I knew. He never had missed a day in school in thirty-eight years. His mother had died that August, and his daughter let slip that Daddy's prayers had all been answered. Every night, for years, the family had said a Hail Mary asking God that whenever He decided to take the grandparents to Himself, He would do so during the school holidays. To my surprise, he not only found the story believable, but was so delighted by it that he worked it into the fabric of his last novel.

I visited him twice in Belfast and had the pleasure of meeting his wife and daughter in their spacious, comfortable house in Derramore Drive. The first time he met me at Victoria Station, and as we left I noticed several porters waving or saluting. 'You seem to have a wide circle of acquaintances, Michael,' I said mischievously, since I knew it was unlikely to be true. 'We have very good parents at St Thomas's,' he responded stiffly.

Another time, on an excursion my own school made to Belfast, I was able to leave the school party and take a bus out to St Thomas's. He showed me round his school with pride, and before I left he said, 'There's a young fellow just out of Queen's in here that I want you to meet. He's going to go far. He has them all wild about poetry,' and he introduced me to the young Seamus Heaney. Heaney's work and success were a great source of pride and joy to him over the years after he stopped writing.

He was open and fair about *The Dark*, fair about what he liked and what he found unacceptable. The whole foolish scandal that surrounded the publication would have been anathema to him, and it did not help a tenuous relationship that I had been disappointed by his last novel. Also, there were hints in his letters that he was no longer well.

I did not hear from him again for several years. Then, out of the blue, he wrote to me in the late 1970s about a story of mine he had read in a magazine. He didn't say whether he liked it or not – he probably didn't – but, typically, said it was a story a young writer could learn a lot from. (If we had discussed it we would have disagreed, since I believe writing cannot be taught and that the only way a writer can learn from another is through osmosis.)

Again, we corresponded briefly. It turned out that he was making fairly extensive motoring trips around Ireland. He had even visited Boyle, Cootehall and the Forest Park. With some of his old vigour, he told me he'd been making enquiries about the McGaherns, and informed me gleefully that they were considered to be a highly respectable family. The implication was plain: I had not added much to that desirable state; and I remembered that, in spite or because of his

nationalism, he was fond of signing backsliding teachers into the attendance book in green ink whenever they were late. I invited him to call if
he ever motored into Leitrim, but he never did. I have never thought
about him with anything but affection and respect since we first met.

In 1989 I had the privilege of speaking at a birthday celebration in his
honour at The Arts Club in Belfast, but because of his illness and
absence there was a sense of valediction about the evening. Now only the
work remains.

I feel certain that his best work will endure. The charming 'The Poteen
Maker' is known far and wide, but there are many greater stories: 'The
White Mare', 'Uprooted', 'The Road to the Shore', 'The Game Cock', 'The
Schooner' are a few, and there are more.

Scattered throughout all the books are moments of vividness, of
beauty and truth. His work has 'a moral fragrance', to use the phrase of
fellow Ulsterman Forrest Reid, whose prose he admired. I see Michael
McLaverty essentially as a poet who worked in prose and honoured that
medium. I can think of many beautiful examples of his work, but none
more fitting than the following passage from 'The White Mare':

He might be in time; they'd hardly have her in the boat yet . . .

He thought of his beast, the poor beast that hated noise and fuss, standing
nervous on the pier with a rope tied round her four legs. Gradually the rope
would tighten, and she would topple with a thud on the uneven stones while the
boys around would cheer . . .

Nearer it came, gathering speed. A large wave tilted the boat and he saw the
white side of his mare, lying motionless between the beams. They were opposite him now, a hundred yards from him. He raised his stick and called, but he
seemed to have lost his voice. He waved and called again, his voice sounding
strange and weak. The man in the stern waved back as he would to a child. The
boat passed the rock, leaving a wedge of calm water in her wake. The noise of
the oars stopped and the sail filled in the breeze. For a long time he looked at
the receding boat, his spirit draining from him. A wave washed up the rock,
frothing at his feet, and he turned wearily away, going slowly back the road that
led home.

Dick Walsh Remembered

Foreword to *Dick Walsh Remembered:*
Selected Columns from the Irish Times *1990–2002*

Dick Walsh wrote uncommonly well: he had intelligence and feeling, wit and humour, a gritty, fearless integrity.

Most political columns disappear with the events that brought them into being, yet many of the pieces collected here remain as fresh as on the day they first appeared. This is largely due to the quality of the writing, but a number of other things play a part. In the time that they cover, rapid change was being forced on the institutions that had governed and shaped our lives. Habits of thought, unexamined for so long that they had acquired tacit legitimacy, came under open scrutiny. The simple certainties began to look simple but no longer certain. North and South were unable to ignore either one another or the wider world in which they were set; undreamed-of wealth came suddenly to a country long accustomed to poverty and the poor mouth; our first woman president was elected. Reluctantly, it seemed, we were realizing that the country was ours at last, while forces honed at home and elsewhere were poised to take it off our hands. All this was observed through the eyes of a fascinating political intelligence that believed passionately in freedom and democracy, its institutions and safeguards. That he also had a social agenda of his own, a vision of what constituted a just society, gave an edge to everything he wrote:

We need more scepticism (not more cynicism); we need class politics (not a retreat from it); and we need a vigorous opposition that ensures exposure is followed by action.

This is not to propose the left's return to the bad old days of half-baked jargon masquerading as Marxism but to suggest a cool, clear look at the way things are in the country.

In any civilized society, he believed, there should be state protection for the weak and disadvantaged, a level below which it was unacceptable to allow people to fall. There should also be curbs on the rich and powerful to prevent them from devouring everything around them; he did not see enterprise and fairness as incompatibles:

There is a suggestion that not only are equity and efficiency mutually exclusive, the efficient by the very nature of their enterprise are special cases – are entitled to cut corners.

But cutting corners, as we've seen, leads to some riding roughshod over the planning laws, company laws, financial regulations and other controls designed to ensure that in this Republic every citizen is bound by the same code.

The style he forged is highly individual. Mixing the language of the street and field and public house with clear English, it is immediately engaging. The nonchalance is illusory, masking a deadly seriousness. Not surprisingly, from time to time he engaged directly with political language: 'If thought corrupts language, then language can also corrupt.' He saw Orwell's reference to the effect of Stalinism on western thinking as equally applicable to the 1990s, and he detailed how 'the slovenliness of language makes it easier for us to have foolish thoughts':

Jargon and cliché combine to cover real meanings and so avoid upsetting us by bringing us face to face with reality. The expression used by some American services – 'terminate with extreme prejudice' – was obviously chosen to make killing more acceptable to the squeamish. Every force engaged in killing has its own deadly lingo: the Provisional IRA talks about legitimate targets.

Fellow journalists who worked alongside him, covering elections and conventions or state visits outside the country, speak of the intimidating rigour and pace at which he worked. No report or speech or manifesto went unread, no fact unchecked, every reference was hunted down. His ease when he came to write was based on mastery:

Paddy Smith of RTÉ announced lately that ostrich farming had begun in

England; and he wondered if it might take on here. I was surprised he hadn't noticed: we've been growing our own for years.

Not, I may add, without success. A foreign correspondent who was here for the general election asked why it was that candidates in Ireland invariably *stood* for office while in the United States and Britain they *ran* for it. The answer of course is that you can't run for anything with your head in the sand; and some of our home-grown ostriches have made it to the top while maintaining this well-known national position.

There are people, especially in Fianna Fáil, who accuse him of bias and animosity towards that party. Walsh himself came from an old Fianna Fáil family in the Clare heartland. As our biggest political party, its grassroots in every corner of the land and with one of the longest records of government in parliamentary democracy, he saw Fianna Fáil, together with the Catholic Church, as the organization that had the most profound influence on all our lives. In his moving tribute to Jack Lynch, he describes the nature of the party that Lynch joined. In this early innocence, Walsh reads the seeds of its later vices. That party, seeing the nation and itself as one, had hardly any need of programmes and rules. Broad national aims were sufficient. Pragmatism was elevated to the point of principle, and policy was whatever the leader said it was, but that was when the leader lived within his means, and words such as patriotism and honour and honesty had meaning. This grew to become a demand that the leader and the party should be unquestioned, he wrote in 1990, 'like an overbearing heavyweight in late-night company who cannot see how anyone can take a different view and, in certain circumstances, why anyone should be allowed to do so'. The great power and influence Fianna Fáil wielded was the very reason it should be scrutinized, Walsh believed, and this he did with a clinical savagery, though, at the same time, he was willing to praise individual members and contributions, such as Bertie Ahern's imaginative and courageous response to Northern Ireland.

The mindset was what he hated, its willingness to speak to different audiences in different voices in order to hang on to power at any cost. That the party hadn't the courage to legislate for change was to lead into the sorry moral mazes around contraception, family planning, divorce and abortion – he does not exempt the other parties from this cowardice, but they hadn't anything like the same power – and this moral ambiguity was to surface in other forms in the various tribunals. Dick Walsh takes us through those mazes with a formidable lucidity. During the divorce referendum, when there was much scaremongering that the institution of marriage would collapse if the right to divorce was granted, he argued that the logic of this is 'like saying that the existence of coronary units encourages heart attacks'. On abortion he writes:

The number of women going to Britain for abortions stands at more than 4,000 a year. Since the State refuses to allow clinics here – which would be the most sensible and least hypocritical thing to do – the traffic is bound to continue . . . When we discuss abortion and related issues, we stand at a crossroads where politics, religion, medicine and law intersect and the woman, who is faced with choice, is in danger of being left alone while gatherings of men, often middle-aged or elderly, some bound by celibacy, argue the toss.

On the North, he saw little to choose between Republican and Unionist dogmatism. 'On either side, whether fired by the Covenant or the Proclamation, only one feeling was stronger than suspicion and fear. It was the unshakeable sense of being right.' When he went to work in the North, he was nettled to discover that his own stereotypical view of the place was matched by a similarly clichéd view of the South as a corrupt, priest-ridden place. Where he saw hope was not in those walled simplicities but in some 'who've carried the heaviest workloads – tireless, patient people like Seamus Mallon, Reg Empey, Seamus Close, Monica McWilliams and David Ervine'.

In Dick Walsh's company, there was a sense that he spoke out of an accumulated wealth of local knowledge from many parts of the country, the terrain, the people, mentalities, their varied histories and stories and strategies – a present-day that was informed by a long past. I believe it is this quality that gives his columns depth beyond the events of the day, that gave them their first relevance. This quality is present everywhere, and is probably most visible in the piece he wrote on the Famine.

He recalled a simple myth we all grew up with – of grain being exported to pay the rack-rents while the people starved – another vague episode in the terrible history of Irish nationalism and race suffering. Many times in the course of the columns, he turns back to Clare and his influential father, the National School teacher. He tells of accompanying him fifty years ago when, after school, he visited old people collecting the folklore of East Clare. They often visited two brothers, Con and Solomon O'Neill, who were in their eighties and nineties. The brothers were most forthcoming about holy wells and pattern days and the various activities of the Clare fairies but, when asked about the Famine, they would say only that their family had nothing to do with it. This echoes a larger silence. He recalled, then, his excitement when the various works of scholarship, particularly those of Cormac Ó Gráda, came out, enabling him to see the past not only in its suffering but also in its complexity. Visiting his aunt with this knowledge years later, he enquired about the brothers' reticence. 'She pointed to a field by a stream we knew as the Sandy River and said people went there to eat the clover and a type of sorrel which grew between the woods and the Shannon. When I asked who they were she said: "Mountainy people. Poor auld *spailpíns*. They used to find them dead in the ditches."'

The *spailpíns* were the poorest of the poor, landless labourers: it was the class system that decided who survived, and even prospered, and who died. The enemy was not just the absentee landlords or English landlords, but landlords of *whatever* nationality or religion who used the system for exploitation.

Dick Walsh began his career on the desk of the *Clare Champion* and, in the best sense of the word, remained a local reporter all his life. The local, when the walls are taken away, becomes the universal. He spent his career removing such walls – walls of lies and violence, prejudice and certainty, privilege and deprivation, silence and bullying. The list is endless.

I had the pleasure of his friendship for many years. This is irrelevant here other than to say that the man and his writing were of one piece. He spoke always in his own voice, even to strangers. His later years were afflicted with illness and disability, which he carried with such extraordinary lightness that he gave heart to others. With a smile he would tell how as he waited for his taxi on D'Olier Street, bent over because of his illness, a woman would stop to help him search for coins or whatever he was missing on the pavement.

He was wonderful company and great fun, and he loved to talk. He spoke almost as well as he wrote, with a beautiful rhythmic phrasing. Unlike many who love to talk, he listened intently, and he had the habit of repose. Out of that repose or silence he would sometimes chant mischievously, 'Love-ly peop-le . . . Plen-ty of mon-ey . . . *No* man-ners.'

III
AUTOBIOGRAPHY, SOCIETY, HISTORY

The Solitary Reader

I came to write through reading. It is such an obvious path that I hesitate to state it, but so much confusion now surrounds the artistic act that the simple and the obvious may be in need of statement. I think reading and writing are as close as they are separate. In my case, I came to read through pure luck. I had great good fortune when I was ten or eleven. I was given the run of a library. I believe it changed my life and without it I would never have become a writer.

There were few books in our house, and reading for pleasure was not approved of. It was thought to be dangerous, like pure laughter. In the emerging class in the Ireland of the 1940s, when an insecure sectarian state was being guided by a philistine Church, the stolidity of a long empty grave face was thought to be the height of decorum and profundity. 'The devil always finds work for idle hands' was one of the warning catchphrases.

Time was filled by necessary work, always exaggerated: sleep, Gaelic football, prayer, gossip, religious observance, the giving of advice – ponderously delivered, and received in stupor – Civil War politics and the eternal business that Proust describes as 'Moral Idleness'. This was confined mostly to the new emerging classes – civil servants, policemen, doctors, teachers, tillage inspectors. The ordinary farming people went about their sensible pagan lives as they had done for centuries, seeing all this as one of the many veneers they had to pretend to wear, like all the others they had worn since the time of the Druids.

During this time I was given the free run of the Moroneys' library. They were Protestants. Old Willie Moroney lived with his son, Andy, in their two-storeyed stone house, which was surrounded by a huge orchard and handsome stone outhouses. Willie must have been well into his eighties then, and Andy was about forty. Their natures were so stress-free that it is no wonder they were both to live into their nineties. Old Willie, the beekeeper, with his great beard and fondness for St Ambrose and Plato, 'the Athenian bee, the good and the wise . . . because his words glowed with the sweetness of honey', is wonderfully brought to life in David Thomson's *Woodbrook*.

Willie had not gone upstairs since his wife's death, nor had he washed, and he lived in royal untidiness in what had once been the dining room, directly across the stone hallway from the library, that dear hallway with its barometer and antlered coat rack, and the huge silent clock. The front door, with its small brass plate shaped into the stone for the doorbell, was never opened. All access to the house was by the back door, up steps from the farmyard, and through the littered kitchen to the hallway and stairs and front rooms.

David Thomson describes the Moroneys as landless, which is untrue, for they owned 170 acres of the sweetest land on the lower plains of Boyle, itself some of the best limestone land in all of Ireland. The farm was beautifully enclosed by roads which ran from the high demesne wall of Rockingham to the broken walls of Oakport. The Moroneys should have been wealthy. They had to have money to build that stone house in the first place, to build and slate the stone houses that enclosed the farm-yard, to acquire the hundreds of books that lined the walls of the library: David Thomson, though, is right in spirit, for Willie and Andy had all the appearance of being landless.

Most of Andy's time was taken up with the study of astronomy. Willie lived for his bees. He kept hives at the foot of the great orchard. They both gathered apples, stored them on wooden shelves in the first of the stone houses of the farmyard, and they sold them by the bucketful, and seemed glad enough of the half-crowns they received. As a boy, I was sent to buy apples, somehow fell into conversation with Willie about books, and was given the run of the library. There was Scott, Dickens, Meredith and Shakespeare, books by Zane Grey and Jeffery Farnol, and many, many books about the Rocky Mountains. Some person in that nineteenth-century house must have been fascinated by the Rocky

Mountains. I didn't differentiate, I read for nothing but pleasure, the way a boy nowadays might watch endless television dramas.

Every week or fortnight, for years, I'd return with five or six books in my oilcloth shopping bag and take five or six away. Nobody gave me direction or advice. There was a tall slender ladder for getting books on the high shelves. Often, in the incredibly cluttered kitchen, old Willie would ask me about the books over tea and bread. I think it was more out of the need for company than any real curiosity.

I remember one such morning vividly. We were discussing a book I had returned and drinking tea with bread and jam. All I remember about that particular book was that it was large and flat and contained coloured illustrations, of plants and flowers probably, and these would have interested Willie because of the bees. The morning was one of those still true mornings in summer before the heat comes, the door open on the yard. Earlier that morning he must have gone through his hives – the long grey beard was stained with food and drink and covered his shirt front – and while he was talking some jam fell into the beard and set off an immediate buzzing. Without interrupting the flow of his talk, he shambled to the door, extracted the two or three errant bees caught in the beard, and flung them into the air of the yard.

I continued coming to the house for books after the old beekeeper's death, but there was no longer any talk of books. Andy developed an interest in the land, but, I fear, it was as impractical as astronomy. Because of my constant presence about the house, I was drawn into some of those ventures, but their telling has no place here.

I have often wondered why no curb was put on my reading at home. I can only put it down to a prejudice in favour of the gentle, eccentric Moroneys, and Protestants in general. At the time, Protestants were pitied because they were bound for hell in the next world, and they were considered to be abstemious, honest, and morally more correct than the general run of our fellow Catholics. The prejudice may well have extended to their library. The books may have been thought to be as harmless as their gentle owners. For whatever reason, the books were rarely questioned, and as long as they didn't take from work or prayer I was allowed to read without hindrance.

There are no days more full in childhood than those days that were not lived at all, the days lost in a favourite book. I remember waking out of one such book in the middle of the large living room in the barracks to find myself surrounded. My sisters had unlaced and removed one of my shoes and placed a straw hat on my head. Only when they began to move the wooden chair on which I sat away from the window did I wake out of the book – to their great merriment.

Nowadays, only when I am writing am I able to find again that complete absorption when all sense of time is lost, maybe once in a year or two. It is a strange and complete kind of happiness, of looking up from the pages, thinking it is still nine or ten in the morning, to discover that it is past lunchtime; and there is no longer anyone who will test the quality of the absence by unlacing and removing a shoe.

Sometimes I have wondered if it would have made any difference if my reading had been guided or structured, but there is no telling such things in an only life. Pleasure is by no means an infallible critical guide, W. H. Auden wrote, but it is the least fallible. That library and those two gentle men were, to me, a pure blessing.

A time comes when the way we read has to change drastically or stop, though it may well continue as an indolence or pastime or drug. This change is linked with our growing consciousness, consciousness that we will not live forever and that all human life is essentially in the same fix. We have to discard all the tenets that we have been told until we have succeeded in thinking them out for ourselves. We find that we are no longer reading books for the story and that all stories are more or less the same story; and we begin to come on certain books that act like mirrors. What they reflect is something dangerously close to our own life and the society in which we live.

A new, painful excitement enters the way we read. We search out these books, and these books only, the books that act as mirrors. The quality of the writing becomes more important than the quality of the material out of which the pattern or story is shaped. We find that we can no longer read certain books that once we could not put down; other books that previously were tedious take on a completely new excitement and meaning: even the Rocky Mountains have to become an everywhere, like Mansfield Park, if they are to retain our old affection.

That change happened to me in the Dublin of the 1950s. Again, I think

I was lucky. There were many good secondhand bookshops in which one could root about for hours. One book barrow in particular, on a corner of Henry Street, was amazing. Most of the books found there then would now be described as modern classics. How the extraordinary Mr Kelly acquired them we never asked. Those were times when books were discussed in dance halls as well as in bars. It was easy then to get a desk in the National Library. The staff were kind and even would bring rare books on request. There were inexpensive seats at the back of the Gate Theatre, and there were many pocket theatres, often in Georgian basements. Out in Dun Laoghaire there was the Gas Company Theatre where we had to walk through the silent showroom of gas cookers to get to see Pirandello or Chekhov or Lorca or Tennessee Williams.

The city was full of cinemas. I remember seeing *Julius Caesar* with Gielgud and Brando playing to full houses in the Metropole. At weekends, cinema tickets were sold on the black market. One such black-marketeer, a pretty girl I knew, showed me a fistful of unsold tickets one wet Sunday night shortly before eight o'clock and said, 'If I don't get rid of some of these soon – and at bloody cost at that – I'll have to let down me drawers before the night is out.' And there was the tiny Astor on the quays where I first saw *Casque d'Or, Rules of the Game* and *Children of Paradise.*

Much has been written about the collusion of Church and State to bring about an Irish society that was insular, repressive and sectarian. This is partly true, but because of the long emphasis on the local and the individual in a society that never found any true cohesion, it was only superficially successful.

I think that women fared worst of all within this paternalistic mishmash, but to men with intellectual interests it had at the time, I believe, some advantage. Granted, we were young and had very little to lose, but the system was so blatantly foolish in so many of its manifestations that it could only provoke the defence of laughter, though never, then, in public. What developed was a Freemasonry of the intellect with a vigorous underground life of its own that paid scant regard to Church or State. Even an obscene book, we would argue, could not be immoral if it was truly written. Most of the books that were banned, like most books published, were not worth reading, and those that were worth reading could be easily found and quickly passed around. There is no taste so sharp as that of forbidden fruit.

This climate also served to cut out a lot of the pious humbug that often afflicts the arts. Literature was not considered 'good'. There was no easy profit. People who need to read, who need to think and see, will always find a way around a foolish system, and difficulty will only make that instinct stronger, as it serves in another sphere to increase desire. In no way can this clownish system be recommended wholeheartedly, but it was the way it was and we were young and socially unambitious and we managed.

The more we read of other literatures, and the more they were discussed, the more clearly it emerged that not only was Yeats a very great poet but that almost singlehandedly he had, amazingly, laid down a whole framework in which an indigenous literature could establish traditions and grow. His proud words, 'The knowledge of reality is a secret knowledge; it is a kind of death', were for us, socially as well as metaphorically, true.

The two living writers who meant most to us were Samuel Beckett and Patrick Kavanagh. They belonged to no establishment, and some of their best work was appearing in the little magazines that could be found at the Eblana Bookshop on Grafton Street. Beckett was in Paris. The large, hatted figure of Kavanagh was an inescapable sight around Grafton Street, his hands often clasped behind his back, muttering hoarsely to himself as he passed. Both, through their work, were living, exciting presences in the city. I wish I could open a magazine now with the same excitement with which I once opened *Nimbus*:

> Ignore Power's schismatic sect,
> Lovers alone lovers protect.

(The same poet could also rhyme *catharsis* with *arses*, but even his wild swing was like no other.)

When I began to write, and it was in those Dublin years, it was without any thought of publication. In many ways, it was an extension of reading as well as a kind of play. Words had been physical presences for me for a long time before, each word with its own weight, colour, shape, relationship, extending out into a world without end. Change any word in a single sentence and immediately all the other words demand to be rearranged. By writing and rewriting sentences, by moving their words endlessly around, I found that scenes or pictures and echoes and shapes began to emerge that reflected obscurely a world that had found its first expression and recognition through reading. I don't know how long that first excitement lasted – for a few years, I think – before it changed to work, though that first sense of play never quite goes away and in all the most important ways a writer remains a beginner throughout his working life. Now I find I will resort to almost any subterfuge to escape the blank page, but there seems to be always some scene or rhythm that lodges in the mind and will not go away until it is written down. Often when it is written it turns out that there was never anything real behind the rhythm or scene, and it disappears in the writing; other times those scenes or rhythms start to grow, and you find yourself once again working every day, sometimes over a period of several years, to discover and bring to life a world through words as if it were the first and (this is ever a devout prayer) last time. It is true that there can be times of intense happiness throughout the work, when all the words seem, magically, to find their true place, and several hours turn into a single moment; but these occurrences are so rare that they are, I suspect, like mirages in desert fables to encourage and torment the half-deluded traveller.

Like gold in the ground – or the alchemist's mind – it is probably wise not to speak about the pursuit at all. Technique can certainly be learned, and only a fool would try to do without it, but technique for its own sake grows heartless. Unless technique can take us to that clear mirror that is called style, the reflection of personality in language, everything having been removed from it that is not itself, then the most perfect technique is as worthless as mere egotism. Once work reaches that clearness the writer's task is ended. His or her words will not live again until and unless they find their true reader.

I think every writer imagines he writes in complete freedom, within the limitations of language and talent; and the people I knew in the Dublin of the time acted as if they had complete freedom to read and think whatever they wanted. So it was a sharp shock when my own novel, *The Dark*, ran foul of our authorities. For me it brought in something unpleasant, something alien, for all that ever mattered to us was whether the work was any good or not; but if I hadn't considered our institutions to be serious up till then, there was no reason to begin to think otherwise because I was now in the public domain. People in Paris wanted to draw up a protest petition. Beckett agreed to sign it, among others; but he was the only one who insisted that I must be asked first if I wanted a protest. I was grateful to everyone, but I wanted no protest. Years later when *The Dark* was unbanned and Carmen Callil sent me a telegram from Panther books – THE DARK UNBANNED STOP PRESS TV RADIO WANT YOU STOP – I remained where I was. To have anything to do with the unbanning, for the sake of a few sales, would have been even worse than protesting about the banning in the first place: 'The minute the writer takes up a pen he accuses himself of unanswerable egotism and all he can do with any decency after that is to bow.' Chekhov's words were one of our early texts in the 'good manners' of the mind.

Coming from such a background, I was well aware of the incongruity of my situation as I sat in a dress suit in the big car as it swept silently through St James's Park around Trafalgar Square and down Fleet Street and past St Paul's to the Guildhall, where the Booker Prize ceremonies were to take place. My novel *Amongst Women* had been named a finalist and the winner was about to be announced. I know that no matter how society attempts to legislate for literature, with its prizes, its honours, its book clubs, university courses or censorship boards, it all finally comes to that essential and potentially subversive figure alone with a book. Without him or her the word is spiritually dead.

The Guildhall itself was lovely to look at and, as well as the tension, there was plenty of fun and laughter, and only one unpleasantness in the whole long Booker evening. Soon after the result was announced, Kenneth Baker, the Chairman of the Conservative Party, came over to our table and said how much he and his wife enjoyed *Amongst Women*. I saw it as a courtesy and kindness. The English critic A. N. Wilson, who was at the next table, got up at once and said, 'Do you realize, Mr Baker, that the novel glorifies the IRA?' W. H. Auden wrote: 'Very few of us can truthfully boast that we have never condemned a book or even an author on hearsay, but quite a lot of us that we have never praised one we had not read'; and it is probably best to leave it at that.

Amongst Women glorifies nothing but life itself, and fairly humble life.

All its violence is internalized within a family, is not public or political; but is not, therefore, a lesser evil. If the novel suggests anything, it is how difficult it is for people, especially women who until very recently had no real power at all in our society, to try to create space to live and love in the shadow of violence. How they manage to do that in the novel becomes their uncertain triumph.

In that light, Mr Wilson's statement, to put it mildly, sounded bizarre in the Guildhall's splendour; but I like to think that my training in all those secret Dublin years was not lost. I thanked Mr Baker for his courtesy. I bowed to A. N. Wilson.

Censorship

I have never spoken on censorship before other than to answer questions about my own case in various interviews, and I refused to take part in the public controversy that followed the banning of *The Dark* and my subsequent dismissal as a National Teacher.*

This I refused for a number of reasons, some of them simple enough.

I did not believe my case was very important or that the Irish Censorship Board – or even the Archbishop – were all that important either. On a relative scale, consider a great writer like Isaac Babel who was forced into silence for years, then put in a concentration camp, where he was shot or died of typhus, in spite of having praised Stalin's prose style in public. To take away a life must always be the ultimate unpardonable act of censorship.

---

* In June 1965, McGahern's second novel, *The Dark*, was banned in Ireland under the Censorship of Publications Act, and in October of that year McGahern was dismissed from his job as a primary teacher at St John the Baptist's National School in Clontarf, Dublin. The reason for the sacking consisted of a combination of the offence given to official clerical sensibilities by the 'dirty book' and McGahern's marriage to a Finnish divorcée in a foreign registry office during his leave of absence from the school. The teachers' union INTO (Irish National Teachers' Organization), of which McGahern was a member, refused to come to his defence. When the scandal over the banning of *The Dark* and the sacking became public knowledge in February 1966, Owen Sheehy Skeffington argued the 'McGahern Affair', as the sorry confluence of events became known, before the Irish Senate. He also published a thoughtful essay on the case. See Sheehy Skeffington, 'McGahern Affair', *Censorship: A Quarterly Report on Censorship of Ideas and the Arts* 2.2 (Spring 1966): 27–30.

I have always looked on art as a luxury, a great luxury, yes, but a luxury. While it may be an important part of my life, it can never be confused with essentials such as food or shelter, education or medicine. 'I work in the luxury trade,' was Flaubert's phrase. When I was interviewed by the General Council of the INTO around the time of the sacking, the then secretary, Mr Kelleher, said: 'If it was just the auld book, maybe we might have been able to do something for you, but by going and marrying this foreign woman in a registry office you have turned yourself into an impossible case entirely.' The style is far from Flaubert's but the similarity of emphasis is unmistakable.

I came to whatever intellectual age I am in the Dublin of the late 1950s and early 1960s. There is not the time to dwell on it here, but I believe it's not too crude to say that Church and State had colluded to bring about a climate that was insular, repressive, sectarian. Anybody with eyes or ears could see that the whole spirit of the 1916 Proclamation had been grossly subverted. If literature was mentioned at all it was primarily in a Catholic context, often defining itself by what it was against rather than supporting anything. A childishness in religion and politics and art was encouraged to last a whole life long. It is only fair to say that most people were untouched by all this and went about their sensible pagan lives as they had done for centuries, seeing it as one of the many veneers they had to pretend to wear like all the others worn since the time of the Druids. I think it is no simplification to state either that the country was being run almost exclusively for a small Catholic middle class and its church.

I belonged to the first generation to be born into this Free State, and it grew clear before long that the whole holy situation I had grown up in was of our own making. Britain could no longer be blamed. In fact, certain British institutions, like Penguin Books, the BBC, the *Observer*, the *Sunday Times*, the *Listener*, became our windows on the world, and without them this place would have been far darker than it was.

For me and the few friends I had in the Dublin of the time there was no such thing as a Catholic literature – or even Irish literature. In fact, we were inclined to avoid the word 'literature' like the plague. There were just books that were well written, that cast light and gave pleasure or solace. Even in literary circles of the time, there was a kind of didactic judgemental violence that I link with a censorship mentality. Surely the good manners of the mind require us to put aside a book we do not like with regret, not with venom. We could appreciate Kavanagh's

> Posterity has no use
> For anything but the soul,
> The lines that speak the passionate heart,
> The spirit that lives alone

all the more because we knew Céline's powerful and equally true refutation: 'Invoking Posterity is like making speeches to worms.' Truth came in versions and was seldom simple and never simple-minded. Tempting as it is to dress up the presence of a censor possessed of impeccable taste, we discovered that most of the books being banned were, like most books published, not worth reading, and those that were could easily be found and quickly passed around. My belief is that literary censorship is nearly always foolish, since, invariably, it succeeds in attracting attention to what it seeks to suppress. There is no taste so tantalizing as that of forbidden fruit.

My own reaction to the banning was mostly one of dismay. The experience was not unlike listening to a bad joke that one had learned to dismiss, and then discovering that one had become part of the joke oneself. There was also the deep distaste of seeing a prurience become part of what was an aesthetic matter.

Finally, while I owe a silent debt of gratitude to many, I would like to recall two people, both now dead, Owen Sheehy Skeffington of Trinity College who made the case his own with intelligence, dignity and a passionate sense of fairness, and, as a lawyer might put it, was in receipt of much abuse for his trouble. People in Paris wanted to make a protest, and while collecting signatures approached Beckett. He said he'd have to read the book first, and after he'd read it said he'd be glad to sign, but demanded that first they ask McGahern if he wanted a protest. Because of Mr Beckett's thoughtfulness and courtesy no such protest was made.

Why the Booker Is Such a Hard Bet

As publishers and booksellers look to the weeks that run to Christmas, the season of literary prizes has come again.

As a writer, I have been lucky enough to have been honoured by prizes and, as well as being judged, I have belonged to a committee of judges and know to some extent what it is like to have to pick one book out of many. Faced with a selection of books, all of them chosen above other competing books, it appears at first sight to be an almost impossible task for one of them to reach a shortlist of four or six, never mind to win. Every serious reader has at least one book they resisted fiercely at first, a resistance that may have lasted for years to a work that was to become an important part of their life. A decision has to be made on all these books over a few, brief moments.

When I began to write there were few prizes and little hype. To try to write well had to be its own reward, and beyond that expectations were low. To be published at all was miraculous, and the activity then was as likely to bring trouble as honour or money.

Charles Monteith, my editor at Faber, encouraged me to enter for the first award, the AE Memorial, an award of £100, given every five years to an Irish writer under thirty-five. I was then completing *The Barracks*, and Charles wanted me to enter the finished sections of the novel. I was reluctant to enter, principally because I felt there wasn't a remote chance of winning. I wrote him my objections: I hadn't any reputation, not even a book published; the award had never been given previously to fiction; I would have the trouble and expense of organizing and submitting five copies of the unfinished novel. In the days before photocopying, that was a considerable expense.

He replied that he still wanted me to enter and Faber would pay the typing costs. I'd have to pay if I won. I entered and won and the cost of the five copies consumed most of the award. It just about allowed Mr Lightfoot, my dear old landlord, and myself, after having a perilous jig together at the foot of the stairs where the letter landed on the lino, to head in the direction of Harry Byrne's public house on the Howth Road. Later awards were never to be so exciting or sweet.

When the telephone call came to say that *Amongst Women* had been shortlisted for the Booker almost a quarter of a century later, it was a different world: for three weeks the telephone never stopped ringing with requests for interviews, signings, launchings; to give one's Booker-bound opinion of this thing and that. All of it was interesting, some of it pleasurable, but, overall, it was far from enjoyable. It was as if one's life was in abeyance as the days ground down to the Booker night.

While filming an interview on the roof of the Faber building in Queen Square I understood that the whole event had as much to do with television as with books. Much to my surprise, I learned that the entire Channel 4 crew were readers. They were knowledgeable and genuinely interested in books and they told me that this annual occasion was the only book programme they got to make during the year. If it wasn't for the Booker they wouldn't get to make any. As they wished me good luck they told me that they'd see me at the entrance of the Guildhall; they'd know then whether I'd lost or won, but they'd be sworn to secrecy.

We met at the entrance to the Guildhall. We shook hands and smiled. We all knew it was too late for luck. The rest is a blur, like the flashlights of the photographers as they demanded poses alone or with the other candidates. The Guildhall looked like an enormous lighted cathedral, full of famous faces, none of whom appeared to be having a particularly good time.

A dour Scottish gentleman upbraided me at the bar, 'What are you doing here?'

'I'm the Faber horse. What are you up to?' Without answering, he stalked away. He was not having a good time.

At eight o'clock the lights in the enormous hall changed. The battery of television monitors at the other end of the room showed that the broadcast was live. As we talked at the table and pushed the inedible food about on the plates and tried to partake as sparingly as possible of the excellent wine, a young man in a tuxedo lay beside us on the floor, his camera trained on my face, presumably to pick up whatever reaction showed when the result was called.

Yet, looking back, I am glad to have been through it all. I learned that it has nothing to do with writing or reading or reflection: everything about it has to do with publishing. The publishers had believed in the book from the beginning, had worked well and hard to get it noticed and now it was getting widespread attention and would get even more if it had won. It was their night, and I was glad enough to play my part.

When I was a judge myself, the first feeling was of dismay – so many books – and inadequacy. After all the books were read, there were some that demanded to be looked at again. There were five judges. Reputation counted for little. What was under scrutiny was the book itself, without reference to anything that had gone before.

The first stage of the committee process was the easiest. Books without any support were eliminated, while those with the support of even one judge were retained. From here on in the real difficulty began. No two judges had the same taste and at this stage all the rejected books had been admired and liked by someone. I, for instance, would have preferred a number of those books to the eventual winner. That novel barely limped into the shortlist, but it won. It hadn't acquired the passionate support that some of the others had, but neither had it fierce opposition.

When all was said and done, it finally got the most votes. One of the books that received no support went on to win that year's Booker Prize. Change a committee and you'll change most of the books on the short-list and, almost certainly, the eventual winner. While it is a crude process, probably it is also a fair enough reflection of what is on show. Two of the greatest works of our century did win the Goncourt in their year, one of the volumes of Proust's *Remembrance of Things Past* and Céline's *Journey to the End of the Night*.

The publishing business is by its nature a public activity. Reading and writing are essentially solitary. They impinge on one another – booksellers and publishers are often readers – and when the reader recommends a book he or she has enjoyed to someone else, the act is the most powerful single factor in the book business: the word-of-mouth.

Without the book business it would be difficult or impossible for true books to find their true readers and without that solitary (and potentially subversive) figure alone with a book the whole razzmatazz of prizes, banquets, television spectaculars, bestseller lists, even literature courses, editors and authors, are all worthless. Unless a book finds lovers among those solitary readers, it will not live . . . or live for long.

Schooldays: A Time of Grace

A secondary school was opened by the Brothers in the town. The word *Salamanca*, having endured for most of a century as a mighty ball booted on the wind out of defence in Charlie's field, grew oails again on an open oea, bocamo distant spires within a walled city in the sun. Race memories of hedge schools and the poor scholar were stirred, as boys, like uncertain flocks of birds on bicycles, came long distances from the villages and outlying farms to grapple with calculus and George Gordon and the delta of the River Plate.

This description of the Presentation Brothers opening a secondary school in Carrick-on-Shannon in 1947 from the story 'Oldfashioned' is slanted into a fictional narrative that is rooted in fact. Our football field belonged to Charlie Reegan; it was directly behind his bar/grocery in the village, close to the banks of the Boyle river. The visiting teams changed in the bar. The local team, St Michael's, always changed in Charlie's empty or half-empty hayshed, draping their Sunday suits over the tedders or mowing machines or carts. I don't think we ever had a winning team. Most of our football was played out of defence. Whenever an enormous relieving clearance was booted down the field on the wind, a hopeful shout of *Salamanca!* would scatter from the sidelines.

Much later I learned that during the Penal Laws the boys who had vocations from our part of the country travelled to Spain by foot and horseback and fishing-boat to study for the priesthood in Salamanca. Words, like people, sometimes have to travel about in disguise and double for something other than what they are, and for a long time Salamanca has stood for me as a symbol of the outer limits of the North Roscommon imagination, which is no mean leap.

At that time people lived very much within the walls of their own small, local worlds. We knew very little about the big towns or what went on there. Boyle and Carrick were our towns, both of them six or seven miles away. I did not know the Brothers had started a secondary school a year before until one day, around Easter, Brother Damien came on his bicycle. I was planting potatoes with my father on Cox's Hill. I can still see Brother Damien lean his bicycle against the stone wall and come towards us across the field. He was dark and could have passed for a Spaniard, and later, when I was attending his school, he gained a certain reputation for reading an Italian newspaper each week. Reputations of all kinds fastened easily to people in those days. He told us that he was a Presentation Brother, that they had opened a secondary school for boys in Carrick-on-Shannon and that they were looking for pupils. They were offering six scholarships at their entrance exams in June. I sat the exam that year and won a half scholarship: it was worth £4 a year for five years. I attended Presentation College, Carrick-on-Shannon from 1948 to 1953.

At that time secondary schooling was available only to the well-off and a few specially coached, academically bright students. The well-off and the lucky few attended Summerhill College or the Ursuline Convent in Sligo, thirty miles away, but the county town of Carrick had two secondary schools for boys as well as the Marist Convent for girls. I believe this to be entirely due to a Mrs Lynch, who must have been a remarkable woman for her time. A few years before she had started the Rosary High School, which offered commercial secretarial training to girls as well as secondary schooling to boys. A married woman in charge of a school of adolescent boys and girls must have set off all kinds of ecclesiastical alarms. I believe the Brothers were brought in to close her down. They didn't succeed. In fact, both schools got on well together. The result was that the poor hinterland of Carrick had one of the most open and competitive secondary-school systems at a time when such schooling was kept strictly within the domain of the privileged.

The College was in a wing of the monastery. It had once been a military barracks. The community of Brothers lived in the other wing. They never numbered more than six or seven, and were made up of Brothers who taught at the long-established National School on the hill as well as those from the College. The closest Presentation community was forty miles away in Enniskillen. I suspect the little community in Carrick had a great deal of freedom for that time.

Like all other boys from the country and outlying towns and villages, I cycled to school. The bicycles were stacked in the large downstairs room. The roads were poor. Most lunchtimes some boys could be seen with bicycles upside down in the big room, mending punctures. This room was between the sanded yard where we played soccer with a tennis ball and the handball alley at the back. Buckled wheels or broken chains had to be taken to Gill's Bicycle Shop across the road. At lunchtime there was always a race downstairs from classes to claim places in the alley. Often on dry evenings we'd stay behind after school to play handball before heading on our bicycles into the country and towards our main meal of the day.

The rough cement floor of the alley was ruinous on boots and shoes. Usually we played with the little 'Elephant' ball, but sometimes sponge and tennis balls had to serve instead. The 'Elephants' were expensive. Wild strokes would send them straying off the netting into the scrapyard of Gill's Garage. There, Aggie Gill was our scourge as she chased or tried to apprehend us while we searched among the scrapped cars and lorries and engine blocks and radiators for the precious little brown 'Elephant'.

Our lunches were carried with our bag of books, strapped or tied on the bicycle carriers: a bottle of milk with a few sandwiches, butter and jam or Galtee cheese between slices of plain loaf or soda bread; tomatoes and ham were luxuries. We ate these sandwiches around the alley on good days, watchful as hawks in case our places in the queue for games would be taken. On wet days we ate bread and drank milk between the rows of bicycles. The milk was often brought in old medicine bottles corked with rolled newspaper.

Our lunch hours were never supervised. The Brothers had lunch in the big dining room within the monastery, and afterwards, if the day was dry, they walked up and down the concrete path that ran from the monastery door to the front gate, separated by a lawn and some tall evergreens and one lilac tree from the sanded yard where soccer was played.

For a time, Mr Mannion was the only lay teacher. He taught English, loaned me Dickens from his own library, and was popular both with the

Brothers and the boys. He was tall and sandy-haired, came from Galway, had been an army officer, played golf with a half-swing, and drank. On certain days he would return excited from his lunch in town. Then his teaching could be erratic, and was often broken by attempts to kick more heat from the pot-bellied stove in the corner. He wore thick, sponge-soled shoes, and these efforts usually ended with a hurt foot or the smell of burning rubber.

Was the atmosphere of the school religious? Looking back, I do not think it was, certainly not oppressively so. Generally, it was a narrow, restrictive, inward-looking time, dominated by a dark Church that emphasized sin, guilt, death and damnation.

This atmosphere was all about us, like the damp and the wet weather. My feeling is that the wise Brothers thought this sufficient. They did not feel that they had to haul any more low-grade coal from Arigna to the eternal fire. The atmosphere of the school was casual, hard-working, cheerful, even worldly in so far as our low horizons could be said to be of the world. I liked Latin and grew fond of Horace, and when I attempted to smuggle some of his thought into my Irish essay, *Tuairim Phagánta** was written boldly in the margin in red ink, but more in a spirit of mockery or humour than correction. What was marked ruthlessly were grammatical and spelling errors.

Their attitude to what happened outside the classroom was similarly broad-minded and practical. I remember being badly beaten in a fight. Brother Placid would not hear of right or wrong, cause or effect. He ordered my opponent to take me to the hospital to have the wound stitched. As we trudged up the street to the hospital we began to feel like a married couple having to face out to Sunday Mass after a Saturday night shindig, our stupidity growing more painful than any wound with every knowing smile we had to pass.

Brother Damien was very keen that we – or anybody else – should never confuse the Presentation with the Christian Brothers. 'My dear boys,' he used to tell us as we prepared to scatter for the summer holidays, 'you will meet people who will assume, once they hear you are attending the Brothers, that *we* are the Christian Brothers. Now,

---

* A pagan opinion (Irish).

enlighten these people on my behalf that you are *not* attending the Christian Brothers, and that you may be Christian in the sense that you are not pagan, but in no other sense.'

Gradually, the school began to take scholarships and prized examination places away from the diocesan colleges. In my fourth year a second visit from the Brothers found my father and myself again in the potato field. This time it was October and we were digging and pitting the potatoes, and the visitor was Brother Placid, who had replaced Brother Damien as school principal. I had done well that summer in the Intermediate. Brother Placid had been checking the attendances and found that my record in the three years up to the Intermediate was poor. Most of the absences were at regular intervals: a few weeks for potato picking, a week or two around planting time, another two weeks in late April for the turfcutting. Brother Placid took my father to one side, but not out of hearing. He said I was one of his best students and could go far, but not if I was kept from school for several weeks on the way into the Leaving. They walked away together to where Brother Placid had left his bicycle out on the road and stood talking there for some time. My father was silent when he returned to the row of ridges. We worked on until the light began to fail.

As we were covering the new part of the pit with rushes, my father spoke as if he had given lengthy consideration to what he had to say. 'It seems the Brothers think they may be able to make something out of you if you're prepared to work. You better get yourself ready this evening to go to school tomorrow.' When I appeared in school the next morning, Brother Placid just grinned behind the spectacles he was so fond of removing to polish with a white handkerchief. He too was silent.

At a time when corporal punishment was widespread in the home and school, there was little in Carrick-on-Shannon. The personalities of Brothers Placid and Damien contributed to this lack, as well as the fact that there was little need. Almost everybody in the school realized that they were privileged to be getting a secondary education and were anxious to make all the use of it they could. We knew the trains were full of people heading for the night boat and building sites in Britain.

I look back on those five years as the beginning of an adventure that has not stopped. Each day I cycled towards Carrick was an anticipation of delights. The fear and drudgery of school disappeared: without realizing it, through the pleasures of the mind, I was beginning to know and to love the world. The Brothers took me in, set me down and gave me tools. I look back on my time there with nothing but gratitude, as years of luck and privilege, and, above all, of grace, actual grace.

My Education

I remember very vividly a certain day in school when letters on the page that until then had been a mystery – just signs – suddenly started forming into words and making sense. I experienced a feeling of triumph, or the coming into knowledge. I suppose I was four or five at the time.

My mother was a teacher and I went to school wherever she taught, which was a lot of schools. She had a permanent job, but it was in a small school and the numbers fell. She always had to go to where there was a vacancy at the time, because of a thing called the Panel.

In one school, I remember there was a very wicked teacher called Mrs McCann and I thought I'd pacify her, maybe, because my own mother was a teacher. I decided to bring her flowers, but the only flowers that were growing around our house were thistles. I thought these purple flowers were quite beautiful and I brought her a big armful. She took it as an incredible insult and I got an extra biffing for that!

I think that nearly all the children of that generation went to school in fear. The war was going on in England and there was always the hope that one of the bombs would be dropped on our school.

My mother was a very gentle sort of person. She came from a very clever family, but they were poor and they came from the mountains. She was the first person from that mountain ever to take up the King's Scholarship, but I think that it was a hard thing for her, in that she was uprooted from her own class and sent to boarding school in Carrick-on-Shannon. She had seven children in nine years, and then she died. We had a farm as well, because in those days it was easier to buy a farm in the countryside than it was to buy a house – you had to buy the land with the house – so she had a very busy life.

My father was a Garda sergeant and again it was a very strange house in the sense that we used to go to the barracks in the school holidays and he would come to the farm on his days off. He was stationed about twenty-two miles from home and of course there were no cars then. He often used to come on wet nights and I remember still the blue glow of the carbide lamp on his bicycle and its strange hissing noise.

I had a distant relationship with my father. He was an only child himself and didn't relate very easily with people. To a certain extent I suppose he was, with the great influence of the Church at the time, very much a kind of symbol of God the Father. My father was very conventional in the sense that he would do whatever would be approved of. He was exercising the law and he was going to see that he set an example, first and foremost.

There was a lot of superstitious talk then. For instance, we were told that the sun danced in the heavens for the joy of the Resurrection at Easter. I was always getting up early to see if the sun actually danced. I heard so much about heaven that I went in search of it. We had an old rushy hill at the back of the house and I remember climbing it and being terribly tired and thinking I would never get to the top. Eventually I reached the top and there was a valley and an enormous disappointment to find another hill at the end of the valley. I remember falling asleep and alarming everybody because they couldn't find me.

My mother died when I was ten. When news of her death came, I was shattered. Our farm was sold and we went to live with my father in the barracks. There was a succession of maids, as they were called then, or servant girls that looked after us.

The barracks was a very interesting place. We lived in the living quarters and all the activities of the police station actually happened in the house. It became part of our domestic lives. We would see the few prisoners that were there and we would witness the routine of the barracks. Nobody had anything much to do. They used to cycle around the roads and they used to write reports, which I think were one of my first glimpses of fiction. They used to call them the patrols of the imagination. On wet days they would hole up in some house, but then they would have to pretend that they had cycled and had to dream up what they had seen along the way. These reports were quite long, often a page and a half of the foolscap ledger. Often in the evenings the policemen would be bored, because one of them always had to be in the barracks. They would come up to play cards in the living room. We would hear them thumping up the stairs with their bed in the morning and taking it down again at night, where they slept beside a phone that never rang.

There would be enormous excitement on a court day, when they would all be polishing themselves up. They had to go into town to the court and they would put a few bets on the horses. There would also be great excitement when the superintendent came on inspection. He used to line them up and comment on their dress and that sort of thing.

They also had to measure the rainfall. There was a copper rain gauge out among the cabbages in the garden and that was one of the daily rituals. There were a whole lot of pointless ceremonies. They had to put out the thistle, ragwort and dock posters and notices about dog licences too.

I got a scholarship to go to secondary school in Carrick-on-Shannon. It was a very good school and the Presentation Brothers were marvellous people. I taught for the Christian Brothers myself afterwards, in Drogheda, and there was certainly a difference between the Presentation Brothers and the Christian Brothers. The Presentation Brothers were much more liberal and they encouraged reading. A lot of people got scholarships to university, from what was a very poor part of the country. Brother Damien was quite snobbish and he used to say that the people of this country are remarkably ignorant. 'If you tell them that you're going to the Brothers, they'll immediately assume that you are referring to the Christian Brothers. Add to their little knowledge by informing them that you are Christian in the sense that you are not pagan, but that you are not Christian in any other sense!'

[...]*

At the end of secondary school, a lot depended on how well one did at the exams. If you did well, you had choices. If you didn't do well, you

---

* The description of the Moroneys and their nineteenth-century library which appeared at this place in the original essay is also rehearsed at length in 'The Solitary Reader', as well as in McGahern's *Memoir*.

didn't have choices and you went to England. I got a number of scholarships, including the ESB and the civil service, but I went to the training college and trained as a teacher.

It was quite a shock going from Carrick-on-Shannon to the training college, because the Presentation Brothers were much more civilized than the people that ran the training college. We were not trusted. I don't think they seriously wanted to educate us. In fact you could get into trouble for reading books in the study hall. It is amazing to think that we were going out to parishes as teachers, but we were only allowed out from two to six on a Wednesday and I think from two to seven on a Saturday. You had to be in for all meals on a Sunday and you had to be in by ten o'clock at night. If you broke any of these rules, or if you didn't go to daily Mass, you'd find yourself expelled.

I received most of my education from the other students and by going to the Gate Theatre. There was a marvellous boy who was in the same class as me called Éanna Ó hEithir. He was a nephew of Liam O'Flaherty and a brother of Breandán. He was envied because he had the use of O'Flaherty's flat in Paris. He knew a lot about books and he would lend them to anybody interested in reading them or talking about them. But the whole atmosphere at the college was anti-intellectual. There was a small group of boys that came from some of the better colleges like Rockwell or Blackrock and they formed a debating society. They were nicknamed *Oideachas Éireann** and were hounded mercilessly. You would think debating would be a normal activity for any third-level college. Also, if you didn't unlearn your table manners, you would absolutely starve there! There was a crowd from Donegal I remember that used to work in tunnels in Glasgow during the summer holidays, big fellows, O'Donnells and Gallaghers, and they were quite formidable at the table.

You had to be academically bright to get into college. You had to get eighty or eighty-five per cent to get in, but you only needed forty per cent to get out, so there was really no examination pressure. One had leisure and one learned how to obey the rules – and use them for one's own purposes.

* Irish Education (Irish).

In 1955, I came out of Drumcondra and I started teaching the same year. I went to the Christian Brothers in Drogheda and I spent a year teaching there. I then started to go to university at night and got a teaching post at a school in Clontarf and of course that was a great help to one's income – I think we were paid £6 a week then.

I didn't enjoy teaching. I'm very suspicious of people who say they do. I think that if you do anything well, or even if you try to do anything well, it's hard work and it's painful. It means taking attention from yourself and giving it to the children, in the same sense that writing is simply giving it to the words; there is a certain discipline that is pleasurable, but I wouldn't call that enjoyable. I think that teaching is very honourable work, but it is also very hard work, and I don't think it is appreciated as much as it should be in society. They say about writing that, if the writer has a great time writing, the reader has a bad time reading. I think that, while people that enjoy teaching might be having a ball, the children may not be learning much. The real work is quite a hard struggle and out of the struggle you get moments of satisfaction, but you're really just working in order to put something across for the children to learn.

My teaching career in this country came to an abrupt end when my book *The Dark* was banned. There was an enormous pressure on me to be the decent fellow and resign. I was determined that I wasn't going to do that and I turned up at school even though I wasn't allowed into the classroom. I had taught with all the teachers for seven or eight years and we were a very good school. We had got the 'Carlisle and Blake' award the year before, which meant that every teacher had to be highly efficient. They were friends and colleagues and I am still very close to one of them.

When I turned up at the school, everyone was in a worse state than I was and we must have made endless cups of tea that morning. The headmaster was in an awful state. He had informed me that I wasn't allowed into the classroom. The parish priest couldn't face it – he had gone on his holidays and could only see me when he came back. I think he was hoping that he wouldn't have to see me at all. I met him when he came back off his holidays and he told me that he was very happy with me and why did I have to go and write that book and bring all this trouble down on him. He told me that he had nothing against me but that the

Archbishop, John Charles McQuaid, had told him to fire me. Everyone was strangely pleasant about the dismissal. It seemed as if nobody else wanted it and he was more or less saying that it wasn't his fault, that he was well disposed towards me.

It was unpleasant, but I suppose I was lucky in that I had been writing and had had two books published already. I certainly was interested in writing as much as in teaching, but I couldn't afford to live off my books. So I went and taught in London.

That was a very different experience to teaching in Clontarf. Where you have the father and mother interested in education, as most people in Clontarf were, it makes teaching much easier, but in the East End of London they couldn't care less. I remember teaching a class that couldn't read, but the beginning of teaching was to get them to believe in their lives. You didn't teach them formal English, you got the *Evening Standard* and taught them about football. I had about fourteen kids in that class and I think I taught about twelve of them to read. I remember getting a marvellous sentence from one of the kids: 'My granddad used to roll barrels at Whitbread's Brewery at London Bridge, but now he's puffed when he comes up the hill after his dinner from the betting shop.' I thought 'puffed' was a marvellous word.

Eventually, Professor Gordon at Reading liked my work and gave me a research assistantship at the University of Reading, so I left teaching in London. I had been four years teaching in London after the Dublin débâcle. I have taught at university level since but never again at primary level.

I am back in the rushy hills now, back in my own place. Life is the same everywhere. I think that the quality of feeling that's brought to the landscape is actually much more important than the landscape itself. It is the light or passion or love, if you like, in which the landscape is witnessed that is more important than whether it contains rushes or lemon trees. A writer knows that he is only as good as the next day's page. In that sense I think of a writer as being always a beginner, and the day you cease learning is the day that you're finished.

Ní bheidh sibh ar ais:
St Patrick's College Drumcondra

'*Ní bheidh sibh ar ais*,' the Dean of Students, Father Johnston, who was better known as the Bat, used to warn us regularly in our first year. *Ní bheidh sibh ar ais* meant that we would not be invited back for a second year and wouldn't therefore qualify as National Teachers. For most of us in the 1950s, that meant the night boat for England.

What concerned the Bat was our conduct and behaviour. He had no interest in our studies other than that they should lead us towards conformity. Some of the best young minds in the country were here. It took eighty per cent or more to get into St Patrick's and forty per cent to get out, and you were neither more nor less a National Teacher whether you sailed out or staggered out. The real pitfalls were expulsion for conduct unbecoming, or not being invited *ar ais*.

They gave us hardly any education, which considering what was on offer at the time was probably no bad thing. What education I picked up when I was there was from fellow students. A brilliant classmate, the late Éanna Ó hEithir, first put Joyce and Eliot in my hands. Attendance at daily Mass and evening Devotions was compulsory; and, extraordinary in a third-level institution, there wasn't a literary, historical, philo-sophical or – more surprisingly – even a Gaelic Society: but there were religious societies. We were being groomed as non-commissioned officers to the priests in the running of the different parishes through-out the country, cogs in an organizational wheel, secondary to the priest in all things, including education. Teaching was often described then as the second priesthood, and it was dangerous not to belong to one of the religious societies.

I have always liked the American writer Ambrose Bierce's definition of a coward as one who in an emergency thinks with his heels, and I joined the Society of St Vincent de Paul. I will not burden you with my adventures as a lay brother – the very contemplation of the idea is enough – but the cowardly ploy worked: I was invited *ar ais*. Never, though, could I have imagined that I would be *ar ais* in the honoured way I am today.

Often we have to lose what we possess in order to know that possession. When I had to leave this country, I taught for a number of years at primary level in London. The teachers I worked with there were often good, pleasant people, but they were not of the same calibre as the people I was trained with or had worked with in our own schools. They were even more poorly paid than teachers here, at a time when Britain was by far the wealthier country. This showed in the quality of the people the profession attracted. Neither were they held in anything like the same regard in their own society. When so much is being said against the Church, I believe it was the Church that was mainly responsible for the high esteem given to teaching and learning here, an old respect for the schools. Those non-commissioned officers who were scattered out from St Patrick's to the parishes of Ireland were, for the most part, exceptional people. They laid the foundation of an educational system without which much of what is good in our society would not have been able to grow, including, let it be said, the fabled and now ailing Celtic Tiger – and this was done often in the face of obtuse ideological direction from their masters. When I was teaching in Clontarf, I once did a quick tot and discovered that slightly more of the timetable for that particular day was given over to religious instruction and the teaching of Irish than to all the other subjects combined.

Any nation or society which does not place education in the very forefront of its values will soon have no sense of itself, apart from what Freud calls 'narcissistic illusion'. Without knowledge we can have no sense of tradition, which must be continually renewed; and tradition is civilization.

I would like to think that all the dedicated people who were sent out from St Patrick's and the other training colleges to the parishes all over Ireland are being honoured with me here, and that today we are all *ar ais*.

In the Beginning Was the Word

Many years ago when I was teaching at Colgate University I was invited to give a reading at a conference on Irish literature at the University of Notre Dame in Indiana. I flew into South Bend in the early evening and was met by a professor of English. He told me he wasn't from Notre Dame, but from a Mennonite school, Goshen College. Notre Dame had made some of the speakers available to smaller colleges in the area; they were delighted to see my name on the list, and the whole of Goshen College were looking forward to hearing me at eight o'clock that evening. This happy change hadn't been communicated to me. I hadn't expected to be speaking at all that evening, but wasn't alarmed.

We had a pleasant dinner. The professor was an energetic, serious man. He was steeped in Yeats's plays, fascinated by the religious symbolism, and to my surprise spoke fluently about my own work. I was beginning to feel quite happy about the unusual turn of events as we drove towards Goshen.

We began to pass plain houses standing back from the road, the windows bare, the spotless glass shining in the late evening. The houses were beautiful in their plainness. The professor told me they belonged to Mennonites, and spoke of the origins of the sect, their beliefs, their customs, their religious practices. Time passed agreeably. As we came into the town, the hands of a large public clock stood in the square at ten minutes to eight. I casually asked the professor if there was anything in particular he would like me to read. He showed immediate alarm. There were many things he would like to hear, he assured me, but I was not giving a reading; I was to deliver a lecture. The Mennonites didn't allow readings, since they believed that there was only one true Book. Lectures were permitted, since they were seen as commentaries on that one Book, while readings were viewed as rivals or counterfeit usurpers. I felt I was in the middle of one of those dreams that occur to people who have been through competitive educational systems: an important exam has to be faced in the morning and throughout the year no lectures have been attended, no text studied, and in terror we awake to the huge relief that we had been dreaming: but this was no dream. I had either to refuse flatly there and then to enter the College or attempt to improvise a lecture. At the time, I had given a few public lectures. I made quick notes of the main points of all of them.

The auditorium was full. The entire student body and faculty were present, not less than eight hundred people. There was a large electric clock at the back. The long minute hand jerked as it moved. The introduction was all too brief. At three minutes past eight o'clock I was on my feet. I began with my notes from a lecture on the Image: 'The Image is a principle of our knowledge. It is that from which our intellectual activity begins, not as a passing stimulus, but as an enduring foundation.' I remembered the quotation in full from Thomas Aquinas, but then found myself racing through every other word I was able to recall. When I got to the end, I looked at the clock. The big hand had only reached ten: the whole of the fifty-minute lecture had been exhausted in less than seven minutes. I turned to my notes on 'Herman Melville and an Idea of Transcendence'. Dear Bartleby the scrivener came to my aid with his eternal and mannerly 'I'd prefer not to.' I was halfway through the Melville lecture when I dared to look at the clock again. The hand jerked suddenly from twenty to twenty-one minutes past the hour as I looked. I was safe. Towards the end I was even able to circle back to 'The Image', like a fighter plane putting out decoy material in order to divert incoming fire.

The President of the College rose to say that it was one of the most profound lectures he had ever attended, a truly religious experience. There were parts of it he had difficulty in following, but he looked forward to rectifying that lack on one quiet evening with the text. Courteously he enquired if it had already been placed and the name of the journal in which it might appear. I replied that it still needed revision, but I would send him a copy as soon as it appeared.

The story is only to some extent an aside, and I tell it because I had no difficulty with the Mennonite attitude. It was the attitude I had grown up with. In the same way, I have no difficulty with Auden's castigation of people who read the Bible for its prose. Auden speaks with the certainty of a believer, but if we are unbelievers what can we read the Bible for but its story and its prose, the extraordinary fiction or myth that has pervaded our language, our thought, our art, and on which much of our very civilization has been built.

It's a Long Way from Mohill to Here . . .

The church was full for evening Mass in Mohill last Saturday. Outside, one of the political parties was setting out their stall, a few faithful gathered around the party van and loudspeaker. They began their election address as soon as the Mass ended, but people hardly looked in their direction as they drifted to their cars or made their way into town.

A few who looked made half embarrassed, half apologetic shrugs but they still continued on their way. Conspiratorial smiles and glances were exchanged here and there. 'It is all a racket and we are not taken in any more,' the smiles appeared to say.

Of course, the election is now fought elsewhere, on TV and radio and through the staged photocalls. I suspect they speak after Mass only out of old pieties, and I expect that to die away soon. It is the same when the canvassers call to the door. They are self-effacing and polite and sometimes even apologetic. There are no vigorous doorstep arguments as there used to be. They hand you the party leaflet. They say, 'You'll not forget us on the day' or 'You'll do the best you can for us', and more daringly, 'You'll give us the big one, the number one on the day.'

Once the whole congregation would have assembled round that van. There would be bands and flags, cheers and heckling. Insults would be traded with gusto, followed by cheers and counter insults, and people would have left in a high state of excitement, often arguing all the way home until they had to part at the separate lanes to the houses. Often there were plays within plays in this child's world.

One of the candidates for the Dáil when I was a boy was known to be illiterate but his wife was a schoolmistress. Before each election, she'd write him an elaborate speech and he'd learn it by heart like a schoolboy. The crowd at the chapel gates knew this and set out to harry him. Once seriously interrupted, he could never find his way back into his speech at the point where he'd left off. 'You've already told us that hours ago,' would be shouted as soon as he resumed. Eventually he'd become properly enraged, throw his wife's speech to the wind and lay into his hecklers and political opponents in a broad dialect, which was fluent and colourful, but not in any of the schoolbooks.

That age of politics now seems even more than a world away. Now politics like everything else is a business, but in Ireland it is hardly run like a successful business and it seems to be run more for the politicians than the people.

I have never seen so much apathy as in this election. There is a dangerous sense of helplessness. 'No matter who gets in or out, it will still leave you and me the same,' I was told, and it could be Lear speaking from his prison cell without the poetry and without the ecstasy. There seems to be a general incomprehension as to why the election was called and a slow anger: 'They did as good as they ever did over the past two years, all of them having to pull together for once, and the others were able to keep a watch on the crowd in charge.'

The people were prepared to accept the cutbacks, as they seemed to be necessary, and they were anxious that they be carried out evenly and fairly, and there seemed worse ways of doing this than by all-party agreement. Now there is a dark fear that even worse times are on their way and that a large majority is being sought in order to enforce them without check. The people are tired of the politics of opportunism. They know that the country has lived and is living beyond its means. The younger generation do not want favours. They want rights. If they do not get them, they will go elsewhere.

Part of the problem is that we are a poor and small state and yet we have the pretensions and paraphernalia of a great nation. An interesting agenda for the new Government might be to look for cuts at the top. Abolish the office of the President, and do the same with the Senate. Halve the number of seats in the Dáil. We do not need so many deputies to run such a small country.

Then, as they say, we might start to motor.

Shame in a Polling Booth

I have never seen such apathy and muted anger throughout the whole election campaign or so much general agreement among commentators. In particular, that the election was unnecessary and wanted by nobody. It was not that it was thought we had such a great Government but that it was as good as any other we were likely to get.

Fianna Fáil were no longer trusted with absolute power and the PDs were seen as efficient watchdogs. When I asked people what they thought they would answer with a shrug of intolerant amusement, 'The whole rag bag of them would sicken you. Don't you know by now that the whole thing is just an old performance?' Even the old factional voices seemed to have gone. 'We'll get you, we'll sort you out when we get in', and equally unpleasant, 'We'll look after you. We always look after our own', appeared to have disappeared into general apathy.* As each slow

* McGahern humorously described another version of such a politics without substance in an unpublished essay: 'Unlike God, Who could only be approached through prayer, the politician not only could be visited – they held clinics for that purpose – but could be voted out of office. A corrupt two-way traffic ensued, which at its pinnacle is now the subject of expensive but necessary tribunals. This also had its comic moments. "He didn't flash enough," I heard once given as the reason a politician failed to be re-elected. My amazement must have shown that indecent exposure was being added to the demands on our politicians, because it was quickly explained that the ex-TD was so insensitive to the presence of his constituents that he failed to flash his car lights when he passed them on the road. This clientelism did not displace political thought because it had never been instituted.' (Untitled typescript, written after the publication of *That They May Face the Rising Sun*. NUIG P71/1328).

minute of the TV debate between Reynolds and Bruton dragged towards its predictable inconclusiveness, the absence of Dick and Dessie began to tick in their favour, louder than a taxi meter in a rush-hour traffic jam.

No matter what the outcome of the election is, I believe that Mr Reynolds had very bad luck in his nine months as Taoiseach, even though much of it was of his own making. Among the recent cries of 'come back, Charlie, all is forgiven,' I think it is forgotten how widely welcomed throughout the country was Albert Reynolds's appointment as Taoiseach. This was strengthened by his promise to bring fairness and openness to Government and by some of his new Ministerial appointments.

What was being welcomed was change, the same need for change that swept Mrs Robinson against all the odds to the Presidency. In that, too, he was unlucky. Mrs Robinson has brought amazing life to what, previously, was a largely moribund office. Comparisons were inevitable, and will remain so, with the new Taoiseach whether it be Mr Reynolds or another.

Much has been made of the 'crap, crap, crap' response. The 'not for sale' on Articles 2 and 3, the 'de-humanization' of the Health Service. Anybody under pressure can make this blunder. If they had been infelicities or verbal blunders only, they would not have mattered an expletive. Why they became important is that they were seen as symptoms of something more permanent and they began far back with the claim that the moral high ground could no longer belong to the PDs.

Now, morality can be taken away from somebody, or even borrowed. The only way it can be claimed is by practice, never by assumption. Eddying out from that claim with every succeeding move, gradually it grew clearer that nothing at all had changed. The Beef Tribunal dramatized the fact that the promise of fairness and openness had been just another catch phrase. Self-justification coupled with denigration were as firmly in place as ever. Change was demanded, and when no change seemed to be forthcoming, disappointment and reaction were all the sharper.

Confronted with the three referendum papers in the voting booth, I felt nothing but shame. Here was I, an adult male, in a democratic country, which is a member of the European Community of nations, being asked to give or withhold the right of a woman to travel or obtain information. Why not vote that women should be confined to the same street or townland they were born into or forbid them access to science or mathematics?

The supply of negative capability in this country seems to be endless.

When I was young, one of the reasons for learning Irish that used to be advanced was that when it replaced English all foreign corrupting influences would be excluded. Now we find ourselves having to give back the right to travel and obtain information to women and it has all been brought about by politicians who were too cowardly and opportunistic to legislate on these matters when they had the chance. It is all the more galling since, in practice, it can apply only to the poor and ignorant. Anybody with a bank balance and telephone and a little knowledge of the world can get as much travelling and information as they want within a few minutes and do so with or without benefit of law.

It is said that when a language dies it becomes infested with grammaria. Instead of being used to express thoughts and feelings and common sense, it becomes merely a vehicle for parsing, and only the parser would come up with a phrase like the 'substantive issue'. Surely, when a woman becomes pregnant it is a matter between her and her family, if she has one, and her doctor and is nobody else's business. Neither lawyer, priest or politicians like moral ground that is elsewhere.

After having to listen for weeks to the Ministerial sincerity of Mr Flynn as he advanced his reasoning on the referenda and the substantive issue, it was revelatory to see a photograph of him during a campaign, high up on a cutaway bog among windmills. He would make a fine and stubborn Don Quixote. There would be no dearth of Sancho Panzas; finding a Rosinante, though, may be more difficult. Poor old Caitlin may no longer be willing to plod along as the blinkered beast of burden.

From a Glorious Dream to Wink and Nod

I think that the 1916 Rising was not considered to be of any great importance in the country I grew up in. In fact, it was felt secretly to have been a mistake. 'What was it all for?' was a puzzlement as widespread as the Rosary.*

Certainly, it meant little to the people in the crowded boat trains, the men who worked on the roads or had a few acres and followed de Valera's dream, to the men and women who waited till they were too old to marry. As well, there was a deep, hidden ambivalence to the whole arrangement that called itself a country.

I heard one side of the ambivalence expressed by a young and spirited Clare labourer on a London building site in response to a fellow labourer reading out the news from his local newspaper that there was another disastrous wet summer in Ireland and prayers were being offered in all the churches for the rains to cease. The Gaelic gift for invective flowed well and true in the foreign tongue: 'May it never stop. May it rise higher than it did for fukken Noah. May they all have to climb trees'; and he did not laugh or even smile as he lifted his barrow full of concrete.

By this time, there was a new class closely allied to the Church and State which led these prayers and were loudest in the responses; but they were the chosen few, and their bounty, more often than not, was

* This essay was written as a reaction to the commemoration of the seventy-fifth anniversary of the 1916 Easter Rising and the Proclamation of the Irish Republic, and to examine the fate of its legacy.

enclosed in individual families. They grew rich in sanctimoniousness as well as in power and money. They were the new horsemen.

What *was* historically important, then? The Land War, I think. The wounds of famine and eviction had not healed. People had noticed that the strong farmer did not starve. The lesson had been too well learned. The strangely pedantic phrase 'famine mentality' was part of the vernacular – *caint na ndaoine*, as it was termed* – and used to explain anti-social, even irrational acts of greed or miserliness, which were but symptoms of deep unhappiness and insecurity. Had the war been truly won and by whom was never questioned. Feelings ran too deep for questioning. Catholic Emancipation was important as well. The Church saw to that. The Civil War meant more than the War of Independence; it defined the political system, such as it was, and, for the most part, is.

Nineteen-sixteen wasn't far away, then. It probably was too close in time for the comfort of mythmaking. A local man, Paddy Moran, worked a machine-gun from the roof of the GPO. He was arrested during the aftermath of Bloody Sunday and hanged in Kilmainham. There is a wonderful, affectionate portrait of him in Ernie O'Malley's classic account of those times, *On Another Man's Wound.* [...]† In National School I was in the same class as his nephew and niece, and I do not think he was greatly honoured.

In direct contrast, de Valera was publicly revered as having fought in Boland's Mills and for being a signatory of the Proclamation, though privately his name was always slightly tainted by the fact that he alone, of all the signatories, had escaped execution. By then, he looked more like a lay cardinal than a revolutionary, and the Free State had become, in effect, a theocracy, in direct opposition to the spirit and words of the

* 'The speech of the people' (Irish). The phrase was coined by Fr Peadar
Ó Laoghaire, who led a movement to infuse writing in Irish with the language
of everyday speech. He wrote about the cultural effects of the Famine
in *Mo Scéal Féin* (My Own Story). His basic argument was that the pre-Famine
Irish were 'bold without being bad-mannered', while the people after the
Famine were 'bad-mannered without being bold' – an argument that would
have appealed to McGahern.
† McGahern's full account of Paddy Moran's role in O'Malley's memoirs is
printed in the essay on Ernie O'Malley.

1916 Proclamation. De Valera's famous phrase, "The people have no right to be wrong", can still be heard alive and well today in more plausible forms from the mouths of the Reverend Denis Faul and others in the present desert-storm that surrounds the humble condom.

In addition to the openness of the Proclamation to all the people of Ireland, I think that it was unlucky for the Rising that it took place around Easter. This placed it in direct competition with the Church's greatest festival. In the country I grew up in the doctrines and truths of the Church were realities besides which all worldly things were shadows, though the Church politic was increasingly intent on controlling and ordering the same shadow, to its own detriment and to that of the State; but things had to be kept in proportion: the risen people were nothing before the risen Christ. We were urged to get up at daybreak to observe the sun dance in the heavens in its joy at the Resurrection. At night there was another type of dancing, the dancing of flesh and blood that had to be chastened and severely disciplined, unlike the Irish reel or jig danced in daylight at the crossroads.

Many of the signatories of the Proclamation were poor writers and intellectuals. A more unlikely crowd to spark a nation to freedom would be hard to imagine; that the serious revolution was brought about mostly by British bungling does not lessen their place. What would have happened if they had waited, if that freedom would have come about anyhow without violence – and partition avoided – cannot be answered with any certainty. And it does not matter now. They did not wait. My feeling is that North and South would have separated anyhow in their need to out-bigot one another. What is certain is that the spirit of the Proclamation was subverted in the Free State that grew out of that original act of self-assertion in the General Post Office.

In the increasingly diverse and fragmented Ireland we live in – healthily fragmented, for the most part, in my view – I think that we can best honour 1916 by restoring those rights and freedoms that were whittled away from the nation as a whole in favour of the dominant religion. We should put the spirit of the Proclamation into our laws. What we are likely to get, though, are more of the outward shows – maybe even a grant or two – while Wink goes out in search of Nod.

Whatever You Say, Say Nothing

There were two sectarian states in place in the 1950s, North and South, inward-looking and ostensibly secure, secretly content with one another despite public claims and utterances. Each could point the other out in self-justification. They demanded that they be unquestioned and un-examined, and the demand was given widespread, mute acceptance. In the South individual speech and thought were equally discouraged. The moral climate can be glimpsed in the warning catchphrases: 'A shut mouth catches no flies'; 'Whatever you say, say nothing'; 'Think what you say but don't say what you think'; 'The less you say, the more you'll hear'; 'Mind you, I have said nothing.'

The demand for this subservience was driven most powerfully in the Republic by the Catholic Church. Against the whole spirit of the 1916 Proclamation, by 1950 the State had become a theocracy in all but name. The Catholic Church controlled nearly all of education, the hospitals, the orphanages, the juvenile prison system, the parish halls. It is difficult to think of an area of life that its power and influence did not enter, unless it was among writers and intellectuals, and they did not count.

Church and State worked hand in hand. Women and single men were in a lower scale in the public services, a higher scale was in place for married men. Retirement on marriage was compulsory for women. The breaking of pelvic bones took place during difficult births in hospitals because it was thought to be more in conformity with Catholic theology than Caesarean section, presumably because it was considered more natural. Minorities had already been deprived of the right to divorce.

Compulsory Irish was advocated as a means of keeping foreign corrupting influences out, but the Catechism was taught in English.

The huge waves of organized devotion that marked the Marian Year of 1954 were thought to be a greater triumph of Irish Catholic and national solidarity than the Eucharistic Congress of 1932. Many of the new housing estates built at the time in the major towns and cities had a shrine or Marian grotto at their centre, or at the gable end of streets. The Mother and Child Scheme is so well known as to need no telling. There were individual politicians, such as Jack McQuillan and Noël Browne, who tried to fight this tide, but they were easily sidelined or driven out. Seán Lemass had already started to work for change from within the system, but the results had no immediate effect and would not be felt until long afterwards.

With Catholic Ireland triumphant and unchallenged at home, the image that went round the world was Ronnie Delaney falling on his knees at the end of the race after winning the gold medal at the Melbourne Olympics in 1956, blessing himself and raising his gaunt face to heaven in a prayer of thanksgiving.

In his brilliant and provocative history, *Ireland 1912–1985*, Joe Lee writes: 'Few people anywhere have been so prepared to scatter their children round the world in order to preserve their own living standards.' Between 1951 and 1961 well over four hundred thousand people emigrated, far more than in any other decade in the entire century, nearly all of them to Britain. They were young, poorly educated for the most part, ill prepared. Names like Holyhead, Chester, Crewe were burned into the national consciousness; but this was a silent generation, and it disappeared in silence. The men sold their physical strength, the women their willingness to work long hours. They came home in summer, especially the women, bringing their children, and sometimes their English husbands.

'Cheers, Pa!' the English son-in-law said manfully when his wife's father took him to the pub and bought him a pint. 'Lord, son, don't cheer in here or we'll get put out,' ran the joke of the time.

The boats were hardly better than cattle boats, and the boat to Liverpool did carry cattle in its hold. The trains were no better. Strangely, these emigrants were looked down on by the new elite that had done well out of Independence: it was somehow all their own sin and fault that they had to go into unholy Britain to look for work.

People did not live in Ireland then. They lived in small, intense communities, and the communities could vary greatly in spirit and character, even over a distance of a few miles; and I believe the real pain or emptiness for many exiles was that the places they had left were far more real to them than where their lives were taking place and where their children were growing up with alien accents. There was a hidden bitterness, but sometimes it was not so hidden.

I heard it expressed clearly on a London building site in 1954. Many of the men were sent their *Roscommon Herald*s or *Western People*s from home every week. They read them greedily and often exchanged them at work. During a break from work a man was reading aloud from one of these newspapers. Another wet summer in Ireland was turning into a disaster and prayers were being offered in all the churches for the rains to cease. A young Clare man was in our gang. 'May it never stop,' he said without a trace of humour when the reading finished. 'May they have to climb trees. May it rise higher than it did for fukken Noah.'

People do not live in decades or histories. They live in moments, hours, days, and it is easy to fall into the trap of looking back in judgement in the light of our own day rather than the more difficult realization of the natural process of living, which was the same then as it is now.

That the climate was insular, repressive and sectarian is hardly in doubt, but there is also little doubt that many drew solace from its authoritarian certainties. And, in a society where the local and individual were more powerful than any national identity, much of what went on was given no more than routine lip service. The people it affected most were the new emerging classes closely linked to Church and State – civil servants, teachers, doctors, nurses, policemen, tillage inspectors.

Most ordinary people went about their sensible pagan lives as they had done for centuries, seeing all this as just another veneer they had to pretend to wear like all the others they had worn since the time of the Druids.

A ruined ballroom near where I live stands as a monument, its curved iron roof rusted, its walls unpainted. A local man, Patsy Conboy, built it with money he made in the US, and he hired famous dance bands all through the 1950s. It was the forerunner of the Cloudlands and the Roselands and all the other lands, and he called it Fenaghville. In spite of being denounced from several pulpits, Fenaghville prospered and Patsy Conboy became a local hero. People came by bus, by lorry, hackney car, horse trap, on bicycle and on foot to dance the night away. Couples met amid the spangled lights on the dusty dance floor and invited one another out to view the moon and take the beneficial air. 'There wasn't a haycock safe for a mile around in the month of July.' All the money Patsy Conboy made on the dancehall was lost in two less rooted ventures, a motorcycle Wall of Death and an outdoor, unheated swimming pool. It might have helped if they had been denounced.

Today the climate has swung to an opposite extreme in that everything religious is now held in deep suspicion. A new injustice may be replacing the old. It should be remembered that many who entered the Church at the time were victims themselves. Brothers were recruited then at a very young age, generally from poorer families glad to give over their upbringing into the respectability of the cloth. Many young men and women entered the convents and the priesthood for high and idealistic reasons, but with the stigma of leaving then so strong, what chance had they in an ancient, ruthless, autocratic organization? 'An only life can take so long to climb / Clear of its wrong beginnings, and may never', Philip Larkin wrote in 'Aubade' – if indeed those beginnings were ever wrong.

Dublin was more a provincial capital than a city then, much smaller, friendlier. It was easy to fall into conversation with people; sometimes it was harder not to. We walked everywhere, cycled, hopped on buses. An old comedian of a conductor would wallop the bell and shout out 'Lodger's Rest!' as the 54A approached Lawrence Road with its evening load of civil servants. It was an exciting place to be young and have intellectual interests.

[...]*

We paid little heed to the pieties of Church and State. The Censorship

---

* The paragraphs describing the excitement of the Dublin cultural scene in the 1950s which appeared at this point in the original essay are identical to those in 'The Solitary Reader'.

Board was thought to be a joke. [. . .] Hatred of Britain, like Civil War politics, appeared to be part of an old foolishness. British institutions, like Penguin Books and the *Listener*, were windows among other windows on the world.

I think of the decade beginning with the lighting of the paraffin lamps as darkness came on, the polishing of the globe, the trimming of the wicks, the adjustment of the flame, as it had been done for generations. By the end of the decade every house had electricity. Most people had radios, very soon they would all have television. The world that had stayed closed and certain for so long would soon see nothing but change.

The Church and Its Spire

I was born into Catholicism as I might have been born into Buddhism or Protestantism or any of the other isms or sects, and brought up as a Roman Catholic in the infancy of this small state when the Church had almost total power: it was the dominating force in my whole upbringing, education and early working life.

I have nothing but gratitude for the spiritual remnants of that upbringing, the sense of our origins beyond the bounds of sense, an awareness of mystery and wonderment, grace and sacrament, and the absolute equality of all women and men underneath the sun of heaven. That is all that now remains. Belief as such has long gone.

Over many years I keep returning to a letter Marcel Proust wrote to Georges de Lauris in 1903 at the height of the anticlerical wave that swept through France:

I can tell you at Illiers, the small community where two days ago my father presided at the awarding of the school prizes, the *curé* is no longer invited to the distribution of the prizes since the passage of the Ferry laws. The pupils are trained to consider the people who associate with him as socially undesirable, and, in their way, quite as much as the other, they are working to split France in two. And when I remember this little village so subject to the miserly earth, itself the foster-mother of miserliness; when I remember the *curé* who taught me Latin and the names of the flowers in his garden; when, above all, I know the mentality of my father's brother-in-law – town magistrate down there and anticlerical; when I think of all this, it doesn't seem to me right that the old *curé* should no longer be invited to the distribution of the prizes, as representative of something in the village more difficult to define than the social function symbolized by the pharmacist, the retired tobacco-inspector, and the optician, but something which is, nevertheless, not unworthy of respect, were it only for the perception of the meaning of the spiritualized beauty of the church spire – pointing upward into the sunset where it loses itself so lovingly in the rose-coloured clouds; and which, all the same, at first sight, to a stranger alighting in the village, looks somehow better, nobler, more dignified, with more meaning behind it, and with, what we all need, more love than the other buildings, however sanctioned they may be under the latest laws.

Proust's plea is for tolerance and understanding that come from a deep love, a love that is vigorous and watchful:

. . . let the anticlericals at least draw a few more distinctions and at least visit the great social structures they want to demolish before they wield the axe. I don't like the Jesuit mind, but there is, nevertheless, a Jesuit philosophy, a Jesuit art, a Jesuit pedagogy. Will there be an anticlerical art? All this is much less simple than it appears.

The Church grows in the very process of change, Proust asserts, and he argues that it had assumed an influence even over those who were supposed to deny and combat it, which could not have been foreseen in the previous century, a century during which the Catholic Church was 'the refuge of ignoramuses'. He names a number of great writers of the time to show that the nineteenth century was not an anti-religious century. Even Baudelaire was in touch with the Church, Proust argues, if only through Sacrilege.

There is no danger, even today, of the parish priest being excluded from a school ceremony in Ireland. In any of the small towns it would be as much as a person's social life was worth to try to keep him away, which does not make Proust's truth less applicable. If the eighteenth-century church in France was 'the refuge of ignoramuses', my fear is that the Church in twentieth-century Ireland will come, in time, to be seen similarly, and my involvement was when it was at the height of its power.

My early grammar was made up of images. The first image was the sky; in that, at least, it is in harmony with the spire of Illiers. Heaven was in the sky, and beyond its mansions was the Garden of Paradise. House of Gold, Ark of the Covenant, Gate of Heaven, Morning Star were prayed to each night. One of my earliest memories is of looking up at the steep, poor rushy hill that rose behind our house and thinking that if I could climb the hill I would be able to step into the middle of the sky and walk all the way to the stars and to the very gate of heaven. I could not have understood then that it was necessary to pass through death to reach that gate.

If heaven was in the sky, hell was in the bowels of the earth, but not our earth, an earth that was elsewhere. A great dark river overhung with swirling mists flowed past an entrance screened by mountains and great boulders. Across a wide desolate plain came the souls of the damned from the seat of judgement, naked and weeping, bearing only a single coin to give to the boatman to take them across the river and into eternal fire.

Between this hell and heaven purgatory was placed. It had no entrance and descriptions of it were vague, probably because everybody expected to spend some time there before gaining heaven, as the saints alone went straight to God. The physical heat of the flames was as great as in hell but the suffering was leavened by the expectation of the eternal happiness to come, the sight of the face of God in heaven.

Another part of purification was to relive transgressions committed in life in order to undo them. Yeats's play *Purgatory* revolves around this idea:

> she must live
> Through everything in exact detail,
> Driven to it by remorse, and yet
> Can she renew the sexual act
> And find no pleasure in it, and if not,
> If pleasure and remorse must both be there,
> Which is the greater?

More prosaically, I heard an old guard, who had been a shoemaker before joining the police, complain good-naturedly as he stitched a football one Sunday (there was only one football in the village: it had burst before an important match, and all manual work was forbidden on Sundays) that we were asking a great deal of him because he'd have to undo each hempen stitch with his nose in purgatory.

Situated between earth and purgatory was limbo. Grave-faced children or infants with no stain but original sin had to wait there through all eternity, but without pain. Once we learned that limbo was no longer open to us after baptism and that we were faced with the likelihood of hell or, at best, certain purgatory, limbo appeared to be not such a bad place at all.

All this was learned in the home, through answers to ceaseless questioning, later through the catechism learned by rote in school, reinforced by constant images and daily rituals: the Pope's hand raised in blessing, the lamp that burned all day and night before the Sacred Heart on the high mantelpiece, the silence that fell when the Angelus rang, the Rosary each night, the Grace before and after meals. We followed the life of Christ as a story that gave meaning to our lives through the great feasts of Christmas and Easter and Whitsun when it was dangerous to go out on water. There were even signs and manifestations. A boy in school was a seventh son, in a line unbroken by girls, who had the power of healing; and we were told that the sun danced for joy in the heavens on Easter Sunday morning in remembrance of the Resurrection. When the sun did not appear on certain Easter Sunday mornings, hidden in the rainy skies of spring, we were told that it was dancing more carefree than ever behind the clouds. The contradiction inherent in the universe having a memory did not strike us then, even as we memorized that all that was past or present or to be was but an instant in the mind of God.

The time came when the religious centre moved from the home and school to the church. This was a natural, unconscious movement, and almost certainly began with the reception of the sacraments. All the doctrinal and ritual preparations for First Confession and First Communion took place in the school. The preparation for Confirmation was more elaborate because we were going to be examined by the Bishop. This took up much schooltime, but part of our instruction was given in the church by the old parish priest, Canon Glynn. On good evenings Canon Glynn would walk up and down the avenue of limes that ran between the presbytery and church reading his breviary while we played among the evergreens and headstones in the churchyard. At the time, people kept guinea fowl, and there was a boy in our class who had learned to imitate their call. So perfect was his imitation that when he climbed high up in the cypress by the gate he was answered by the fowl in the farmyards around. It was a terrible shriek. Mikey Flanagan was his name but all his life long he was never known as anything but Guinea Flanagan. I remember little of Canon Glynn's instruction, other than the smallness of the class and overcoated priest in the empty vastness of the church, but I remember Guinea's call from high in the cypress branches with piercing clarity. The Bishop came that Easter. With his crozier and rich colours and tall hat he was the image of God the Father. At the altar rail he struck us lightly on the cheek. We were now soldiers of Christ. I became an altar boy, in scarlet and white, and began to take a more direct part in the ceremonies.

Before the printed word, churches were described as the Bibles of the poor, and they were my only Bible. I never found the church ceremonies tedious. They always gave me pleasure, and I miss them still. The movement of focus from the home and school to the church brought with it a certain lightness, a lifting of oppression, a going outwards, even a joy, that is caught in the very opening movement of the ordinary of the Mass:

> *Introibo ad altare Dei*
> *Ad Deum qui laetificat juventutem meum*
> (I will go unto the altar of God
> To the God who giveth joy to my youth.)

There were the great ceremonies of Christmas and Easter, but the ceremonies I remember best are the Stations of the Cross in Lent and the Corpus Christi processions. There were never more than a handful of people present at these Lenten Stations gathered beneath the organ loft. In the dimly lit church, rain and wind often beating at the windows, the church smelling of damp, the surpliced priest, three altar boys in scarlet and white, one with a cross in front, two bearing lighted candles, moved from Station to Station, the name of each echoing in the nearly empty church, 'Veronica Wipes the Face of Jesus', and the prayer,

> O Jesus who for love of me didst bear Thy cross
> To Calvary in Thy sweet mercy grant to me to suffer
> And to die with Thee

chanted at each Station.

Corpus Christi was summer. Rhododendron and lilac branches were taken by cart and small tractors from the Oakport Woods and used to decorate the grass margins of the triangular field around the village. Coloured streamers and banners were strung across the road from poles. Altars with flowers and a cross on white linen were erected at Gilligan's, the post office and at Mrs Mullaney's. The Host was taken from the tabernacle and carried by the priests beneath a gold canopy all the way round the village, pausing for ceremonies at each wayside altar. Benediction was always at the post office. The congregation followed behind, some bearing the banners of their sodalities, and girls in white veils and dresses scattered rose petals from white boxes on the path before the Host. Jung remarks in his letters that the Gospels in themselves are such crude and naive documents that the myth of Jesus could not have taken root and expanded over centuries throughout the world if it didn't echo both current and older myths of a divine messenger taking on human form. Surely the simple Corpus Christi procession was a symbol of the divine leaving the tabernacle and visiting the ordinary human village for one mortal-immortal hour beneath the sky.

In contrast, there was the Mission. Every few years Redemptorists came to the village like a band of strolling players and thundered hell and damnation from the pulpits for a whole week. Stalls selling rosaries and medals and scapulars, prayerbooks and Stations were set up along the church wall for the macabre carnival. There was a blessing of holy objects on the closing night. The distinguished poet and translator, the late Eoghan Ó Tuairisc, told me that on one such occasion an uncle of his, a keen fisherman, could find nothing but a wagtail in his pockets for the blessing and held it up with the scapulars and rosaries. That wagtail went on to catch more pike in the years that followed than any other bait that ever trawled the Suck.

These Redemptorists were brought in to purify through terror, but in my experience they were never taken seriously, though who can vouch for the effect they might have had on the sensitive or disturbed. They were evaluated as performers and appreciated like horror novels. 'He'd raise the hair on your head,' I heard often remarked with deep satisfaction. Poorer performances were described as 'watery'.

Some of the local priests were a match for these roaring boys, and while they were feared and accepted I don't think they were liked by the people, though they'd have a small court of pious flunkies. They were often big, powerfully built men. In those days it took considerable wealth to put a boy through Maynooth, and they looked and acted as if they came from a line of swaggering, confident men who dominated field and market and whose only culture was cunning, money and brute force. Though they could be violently generous and sentimental at times, in their hearts they despised their own people.

I remember a Canon Reilly well. He was so strong that he had once been able to lift railway gates off their hinges. The Canon was on his way to a sick call when halted by the closed gates. The railwayman had refused to open the gates because of the oncoming train. The Canon then lifted both gates from their hinges and drove across the railway track in front of the slow, puffing train. He ran little risk of collision. The narrow-gauged train had so little power that on the steep slopes the second-class passengers sometimes had to get out and walk. Canon Reilly was also famous for the burnt-out clutches in his cars. He had never learned how to change gears, and when he met someone he wanted to talk to he would just put his foot on the clutch. It was known to be a delicate balancing act for his interlocutors to catch his words above the engine while staying clear of the car in case the clutch was forgotten in the heat of conversation. Also, the Canon carried a length of electric flex in a small suitcase round to the schools with which he chastised various delinquents, and every Sunday after second Mass he stood by the church gate ready to pounce on any boy attempting to escape Master Gannon's catechism class, which took place in a corner of the church at the end of Mass. Generally, the boys were hauled back into church by the ear.

The Canon also involved himself in an outing my father made each year to the Ulster Final in Clones. When one particular year he decided to take me with him to hear second Mass in Ballinamore before setting out, I warned him that I did not think it a good idea because of the Canon and that it'd be safer to attend Mass in some town closer to Clones. He laughed at my opposition and it seemed to make him even more determined to go to Ballinamore. I kept as close as I could to my father as we left the church, but I hadn't much hope once I saw the Canon's huge bulk at the gate. I was seized by the ear.

'He's with me,' my father said.

'I don't care who he's with. Like every other boy he's going to attend catechism class after Mass.'

'We are on our way to the Ulster Final and it is already late.'

'I don't care if you're on your way to Timbuctoo.'

'I ask you to let go of his ear.'

'He's going back into his class like every other boy.'

'If you refuse to release his ear, I'm taking hold of your ear.' My father, in plain clothes for the football match, was the sergeant in charge of a small barracks, but it was twenty miles away, and well outside the Canon's jurisdiction.

Even looking back on it across the years from a totally changed society it was an extraordinary act. The catechism declared it a sacrilege to touch or defile a holy person, place or thing. Some young priests played football and I had heard serious debates as to whether it was permissible or not to shoulder-charge an anointed priest within the rules of the game.

In this manner, under the sanctuary lamp before the high altar, my father, the Canon and I stood, and after some verbal wrangling it was agreed that if I was allowed to join Master Gannon's class in the side chapel I would be asked one question, and if I answered it we could leave straight away for Clones. Ears were then released.

'Ask this fellow one question and if he answers it he can leave,' the Canon said to Master Gannon.

There was a twinkle of amusement in the teacher's eyes that did not reassure me till he asked, 'Who made the world?'

'God made the world.' I hadn't expected such an easy question. I stood in terror in case the question was difficult and I failed and was detained.

'Go. Both of yous go before I lose control of myself,' the Canon roared.

Another kind of priest was a Dr McLaughlin, who was thought to be a brilliant man, mostly, I suspect, because of his doctorate. He was, plainly, disturbed and remained a curate all his life. 'Great minds are close to madness,' was widely quoted. He was often seen driving around with his ancient mother, but on Sundays he would shout dire warnings against all feminine allurements. 'You may consider them visions of paradise when they are painted and powdered and dressed to kill on a Saturday night, but see them on Monday mornings when the powder and paint is taken off!' More strangely, he used to fulminate against those who had recourse to the Last Sacrament too frequently: 'There are some individuals in this parish who have enough oil on them to float a battleship!' On the eve of great feasts, when there were long queues outside all the other confession boxes, the queue outside his was either nonexistent or noticeably short. There was always the possibility of an eruption from within the darkness of his box: 'How dare you come in to me with a soul like this!' and all eyes would fasten on the penitent's curtain to wait for the emergence of the disgraced sinner.

In contrast was a young and intelligent priest who took over for a few months when the Canon had to go into hospital. His sermons were short and simple and delivered quietly. They related Christianity to the lives of people and stated that quiet reflection on the mystery of life was in itself a form of prayer; and they dealt with character assassination, vindictiveness, marital violence, child beating, dishonesty, and the primary place of love and charity of mind. Prominent people were furious, and some of the worthies in the front seats lifted up the heavy kneelers and let them down with a bang while he spoke to show their disapproval. They rejoiced when he left. Their satisfaction took the form of a deep and troubled censoriousness. What they really wanted was hell and damnation, which they could apply, like death, to other people: it is no accident that funerals remain our most frequent and important carnivals. Religion, like art and politics, can only safely reflect what is on the ground.

Church and school and state worked hand in hand. Years later when I was a National Teacher I totted up the teaching hours and discovered that slightly more than half the *clar* of that particular day had gone on religious instruction and the teaching of Irish. How the children received a rudimentary education is difficult to imagine, and probably the truth is that many of those less fortunate in the kind of homes they came from did not.

I left National School to go to the Presentation College in Carrick-on-Shannon. A few years earlier a Mrs Lynch opened the Rosary High School in the town, which provided secretarial training as well as secondary schooling. The Marist Convent for girls had been long established. A woman in charge of a school of adolescent boys and girls must have set off all kinds of ecclesiastical alarms, and the Presentation Brothers were brought in to close her down. They did not succeed, with the result that the poor area around Carrick had one of the most open and competitive secondary-school systems when that kind of education was available only to the well-off or scholastically brilliant.

The Brothers were remarkably liberal for that time, concentrating more on academic excellence and sport than on the world to come, and the lay teachers they employed were in a similar mould. I owe them nothing but gratitude. They considered themselves somewhat superior. A Brother Damien used to address us every summer before we went on holiday with, 'My dear boys, you'll discover the more you enter into life that this country has more than its surfeit of human ignorance, and once it is learned you're attending the Brothers it'll be assumed to be the Christian Brothers. Now, inform these people from me that you are Christian in the sense that you are not pagan, but *in no other sense.*' When I came to teach for the Christian Brothers – I taught for a year in their school in Drogheda – I saw that the two Orders, in attitudes at least, were worlds apart.

All through this schooling there was the pressure to enter the priesthood, not from the decent Brothers but from within oneself. The whole of our general idea of life still came from the Church, clouded by all kinds of adolescent emotions heightened by the sacraments and prayers and ceremonies. Still at the centre was the idea: in my end is my beginning. The attraction was not joy or the joyous altar of God; it was dark, ominous, and mysterious, as befits adolescence and the taking up, voluntarily, of our future death at the very beginning of life, as if sacrificing it to a feared God in order to avert future retribution. There was, too, the comfort of giving all the turmoil and confusion of adolescence into the safekeeping of an idea.

The ordained priest's position could not have been easy either. No matter what their power and influence was they were at that time completely cut off from the people, both by training and their sacred office which placed them on a supernatural plane between the judgement seat and ordinary struggling mortals. Though they were granted power, they were also figures of sacrifice, and, often cynically, they were seen to be men who had been sacrificed.

I went from Carrick to train as a National Teacher in St Patrick's College, Drumcondra, Dublin. Teaching was known then as the second priesthood. Everything that happened during that training pointed to the fact that our function had been already defined by the Church. We were being trained to lead the young into the Church, as we had been led, and to act as a kind of non-commissioned officer to the priests in the running of the parish. In all things we would be second to the priest, including education. They gave us no education to speak of other than some teaching practice. What was under scrutiny at all times was our 'character', not in the true sense of the word but in the sense that we would be religious in observance, obedient and conventional, cogs in an organizational wheel. The scrutiny took place mostly in the first of the two years. *Ní bheidh sibh ar ais* was the dreaded sentence, and every year a number of students were not *ar ais* to complete the second year of the course.

Each college day began with morning Mass and ended with evening Devotions in the chapel. Each meal was served by small boys from the orphanage in Artane in the huge refectory framed by public prayers of blessing and thanksgiving. All the societies in the college were religious. There wasn't a literary or historical or philosophical or, even more surprising, a Gaelic society. A few did attempt to start some kind of intellectual society, but they were hounded mercilessly by other students and dubbed *Oideachas Éireann*. They were seen, in the grand Irish phrase, as getting above themselves. Not to attend daily Mass or evening Devotions was to invite certain expulsion. Not to belong to a religious society in the first year was to put oneself in danger.

As soon as I could I joined the Society of St Vincent de Paul. (Ambrose Bierce's definition of a coward is one who in an emergency thinks with his heels.) I remember well visiting an old woman in a slum off Talbot Street. There was the unmistakable smell of poverty in her room, a photograph of a British soldier in uniform was on the peeling wallpaper. Myself and the other Brother were eighteen years of age. We sat and questioned the woman on the state of her soul. Her answers were properly hypocritical, she got her food tickets, and we solemnly reported on the visit to the Society.

We were allowed to go outside the college on Wednesday and Saturday afternoons and all day on Sundays, but even then we had to be back for meals. The gates were locked at ten. Anybody late had to climb the high barbed-wired wall or enter through the president's house. That required serious explanations. Any whiff of alcohol was guaranteed disgrace and freedom in the morning.

After the Presentation Brothers in Carrick I found the college half barbaric and hid behind a kind of clowning. It is only fair to add that those students who came from the diocesan seminaries found the place quite agreeable by comparison. Seminaries at that time were pointed firmly towards Maynooth, and as ours was the second priesthood it could afford to be less rigorous.

When we left the College, the Dean, a Father Johnston, a strange figure known as the Bat, gave us all a little packet of salt, very like promotional packets of breakfast cereals that are pushed through letter boxes nowadays. I think it was called *Cerberus*. The Bat informed us that while we had our own Catholic country now, nearly all the wealth of the country was controlled by Protestants or Jews. This salt was the one brand owned by a Catholic company. Saxa, the best-selling salt, was in the hands of the Protestants. As we were sent out to lead the little children unto God, we were given the little packets of Cerberus to promote Catholic salt and all things Catholic. At the time when I had acquired the sky above the rushy hill as the image of heaven and all eternity, we were told that if we could manage to place a pinch of salt on a bird's tail we could capture the bird, even in flight, and we threw salt time and time again towards branches where birds sat. The little packets of Cerberus, I am happy to report, proved as ineffectual as the other grains of salt we had scattered so hopefully on the swift birds.

In *The Human Condition* Hannah Arendt describes how Christianity displaced the ancient order:

For the Christian 'glad tidings' of the immortality of individual human life had reversed the ancient relationship between man and world and promoted the most mortal thing, human life, to the position of immortality, which up to then the cosmos held.

In doing so, it made this world subservient to the world to come. The fear of God displaced the fear of death, and this solid world of ours became no more than a testing ground or place of trial for our position in the eternal world to come. Arendt points out that this intrinsic value given to life still remains unchallenged in purely secular modern states long after the reason for it has been lost:

If modern egoism were the ruthless search for pleasure (called happiness) it pretends to be, it would not lack what in all truly hedonistic systems is an indispensable element or argumentation – a radical justification of suicide. This lack alone indicates that in fact we deal here with life philosophy in its most vulgar and least critical form. In the last resort, it is always life itself which is the supreme standard to which everything else is referred, and the interests of the individual as well as the interests of mankind are always equated with individual life or the life of the species as though it were a matter of course that life is the highest good.

In the older civilizations suicide was thought preferable to an intolerable life. Unwanted new-born infants were left by the wayside. A slave would want to commit suicide if he realized his condition.

The spirit of Proust's spire pointing upwards into the sunset – 'where it loses itself so lovingly in the rose-coloured clouds; and which, at first sight, to a stranger alighting in the village, looks somehow better, nobler, more dignified, with more meaning behind it, and with, what we all need, more love' than any other buildings – was the spirit of the Christianity to which the Gothic cathedrals gave such extraordinary architectural expression. The religion was the same for the earlier Romanesque cathedrals, but the preoccupation with sin and the consequence of sin had been transformed into an elevation and emancipation of the soul, of love and light, height and openness.

In Ireland we were left the Romanesque spirit – the low roof, the fortress, the fundamentalists' pulpit-pounding zeal, the darkly ominous and fearful warnings to transgressors. To some extent this can be explained by history, but it was further emphasized when the Church was re-established by Great Britain as a tool of colonial order. The huge nineteenth-century presbyteries all over Ireland for celibates are touching examples of British benevolence.

After independence, Church and State became inseparable, with unhealthy consequences for both. The Church grew even more powerful and authoritarian: it controlled all of education, and, through its control of the hospitals, practically all of health-care too. The right to divorce was taken away from minorities. The special position of the Church was even inserted into the Constitution. Childishness was nurtured and encouraged to last a whole life long. Foolish pedantry took the place of thought and feeling. (When I was young I heard a conversation between a priest and teacher on whether Einstein or de Valera was the greater mathematician. They came down firmly on the side of de Valera.) Faith and obedience were demanded, mostly taking the form of empty outward observances and a busy interest that other people do likewise, which cannot be described as other than coercive.

A kind of utopia was described in the national psyche. It was as if suddenly the heavenly world of all eternity had been placed down on the twenty-six counties, administered by the Church and the new class which had done well out of Independence. Those who managed to stay in this utopia – many of them deep in all kinds of poverty – even managed to think of themselves as superior to those unfortunates who were forced to emigrate into foreign unholiness. Few of our writers would have any truck with this state of grace, and the Church had even less truck with them.

The copy of *Ulysses* which I still possess was bought from under the counter in Brown & Nolan's Bookshop and wrapped in brown paper before it was handed to me. Since I knew it hadn't been banned I enquired why it wasn't on the shelves. The assistant told me courteously that putting it on the shelves would offend the priests from the colleges. School textbooks were the shop's bread and butter.

As well as the substitution of empty observances for reflection, thought or judgement, there was an obsession with morality, especially sexual, which resulted in an almost complete exclusion of the spiritual. I believe that religion and morals are two separate things. Religion is our relationship with our total environment; morals, our relationship with others.

When I came back to Ireland to live as a small farmer in the countryside I discovered that most of the people there had no belief, and they looked cynically on both Church and State.

'Oh, sure,' I was told as if it explained everything and how nothing under the sun is new, 'we had the auld Druids once and now we have this crowd on our backs.'

'Why don't you go to Mass, John?' I was asked by a dear friend and neighbour once.

'I'd like to but I'd feel a hypocrite.'

'Why would you feel that?'

'Because I don't believe.'

'But, sure, none of us believe.'

'Why do *you* go then?'

'We go for the old performance. To see the girls, to see the whole show.' He was completely unfazed by my question, even mimicking the pious prancing of a fashionable woman as she approached and left the communion rail, and laughed out loud: 'We go to see all the other hypocrites!'

Given such a climate, when change happened it was certain to be rapid, and much of the power that the Church had in my youth has now gone in the South. In the North the power and structures have hardly changed at all, held in place by the glue of intertribal hatred and disgust. The changes in the liturgy are just one more example of emptiness – like restaurant owners who redecorate after losing business – as well as a kind of pandering to a tabloid mentality.

After being out of the country for a long time I attended Mass for a social reason and found myself next to a very pretty girl. At a certain point in the ceremony she suddenly turned to me and shook my hand. I was amazed by the gesture until I saw that everybody else was doing the same. I could not resist whispering to her that perhaps it was a good idea, that one good thing could lead to another: whatever had been encouraged by the small act, it was not spiritual.

And that spiritual need will not go away. If it is no longer able to express itself through the Church it will take some other form. A letter that Jung wrote to a colleague in 1933 I find wisely applicable to all the violence that now surrounds the religious in a rapidly changing society:

As you see, I am wholly incorrigible and utterly incapable of coming up with a mixture of theology and science. This was, as you well know, the prerogative of the early Middle Ages and is still the prerogative of the Catholic Church today, which has set the *Summa* of Thomas Aquinas above the whole of science. It has been one of the greatest achievements of Protestantism to have separated the things of God from the things of the world. With our human knowledge we always move in the human sphere, but in the things of God we should keep quiet and not make any arrogant assertions about what is greater than ourselves. Belief as a religious phenomenon cannot be discussed. It seems to me, however, that when belief enters into practical life we are entitled to the opinion that it should be coupled with the Christian virtue of modesty, which does not brag about absoluteness but brings itself to admit the unfathomable ways of God which have nothing to do with the Christian revelation.

In the original letter he wrote to Georges de Lauris in 1903, Proust concluded: 'Ideas and beliefs die out but only when whatever they held of truth and usefulness to society have been corrupted or diminished, and they will do so even in a theocracy.'

God and Me

I grew up in what was a theocracy in all but name. Hell and heaven and purgatory were places real and certain we would go to after death, dependent on the Judgement. Churches in my part of Ireland were so crowded that children and old people who were fasting to receive Communion would regularly pass out in the bad air and have to be carried outside. Not to attend Sunday Mass was to court social ostracism, to be seen as mad or consorting with the devil, or, at best, to be seriously eccentric. I had a genuinely eccentric school-teaching cousin who was fond of declaring that she saw God regularly in the bushes, and this provoked an uncomfortable nodding awe instead of laughter. In those depressed, God-ridden times, laughter was seen as dangerous and highly contagious. The stolidity of the long empty grave face was the height of decorum and profundity. Work stopped each day in shop and office and street and field when the bell for the Angelus rang out, as in the Millet painting. The Rosary, celebrating the Mysteries, closed each day. The story of Christ and how He redeemed us ran through our year as a parallel world to the solid world of our daily lives: the feasts of saints, Lent and Advent, the great festivals of Christmas and Easter, all the week of Whit, when it was dangerous to go out on water; on All Souls' Night, the dead rose and walked as shadows among the living.

Gradually, belief in these sacred stories and mysteries fell away without my noticing, until one day I awoke, like a character in a Gaelic poem, and realized I was no longer dreaming. The way I view that whole world now is expressed in Freud's essay *The Future of an Illusion*. I did not know that the ordinary farming people I grew up among secretly viewed the world in much the same terms. They saw this version of Roman Catholicism as just another ideological habit they were forced to wear like all the others they had worn since the time of the Druids, observing its compulsory rituals cynically, turning to it only in illness or desperation. Yet none of this is simple.

Before the printed word, churches have been described as the Bibles of the poor, and the Church was my first book. In an impoverished time, it was my introduction to ceremony, to grace and sacrament, to symbol and ritual, even to luxury. I remember vividly the plain flat brown cardboard boxes in which tulips for the altar, red and white and yellow, came on the bus in winter when there were no flowers anywhere.

In 1903, Proust wrote to his friend Georges de Lauris:

I can tell you at Illiers, the small community where two days ago my father presided at the awarding of the school prizes, the *curé* is no longer invited to the distribution of the prizes since the passage of the Ferry laws. The pupils are trained to consider the people who associate with him as socially undesirable, and, in their way, quite as much as the other, they are working to split France in two. And when I remember this little village so subject to the miserly earth, itself the foster-mother of miserliness; when I remember the *curé* who taught me Latin and the names of the flowers in his garden; when, above all, I know the mentality of my father's brother-in-law – town magistrate down there and anticlerical; when I think of all this, it doesn't seem to me right that the old *curé* should no longer be invited to the distribution of the prizes, as representative of something in the village more difficult to define than the social function symbolized by the pharmacist, the retired tobacco-inspector, and the optician, but something which is, nevertheless, not unworthy of respect, were it only for the perception of the meaning of the spiritualized beauty of the church spire – pointing upward into the sunset where it loses itself so lovingly in the rose-coloured clouds; and which, all the same, at first sight, to a stranger alighting in the village, looks somehow better, nobler, more dignified, with more meaning behind it, and with, what we all need, more love than the other buildings, however sanctioned they may be under the latest laws.

When a long abuse of power is corrected, it is generally replaced by an opposite violence. In the new dispensations, all that was good in what went before is tarred indiscriminately with the bad. This is, to some extent, what is happening in Ireland. The most dramatic change in my lifetime has been the collapse of the Church's absolute power. This has brought freedom and sanity in certain areas of human behaviour after a long suppression – as well as a new intolerance.

The religious instinct is so ingrained in human nature that it is never likely to disappear, even when it is derided or suppressed. In *The Greeks and the Irrational*, E. R. Dodds proposes this lucid definition and distinction: 'religion grows out of man's relationship to his total environment, morals out of his relation to his fellow-men.'

For many years Dodds was a sceptical member of the British Society for Psychical Research. He distinguishes between two approaches to the occult, though he admits they are often mixed in individual minds. The psychic researcher he describes as wishing to abolish the occult in the clear light of day, while the occultist seeks experience rather than explanation. If the true religious instinct as described by Dodds – our relationship to our total environment – will not go away, neither will its popular equivalent seeking signs and manifestations and help in an uncertain and terrifying world.

Not very many years ago, a particularly wet summer in Ireland became known as the Summer of the Moving Statues. Rumours circulated that statues of the Virgin Mary in grottos all around the country were seen to move and had given signs that they were about to speak. Many of the grottos were constructed during the Marian Year of 1954, when no housing estate or factory was built without a grotto of the Virgin and a blessing by a bishop; and there were also grottos from much older times, often set in a rock-face with dripping water, or by a holy well that was once a place of pilgrimage. Crowds gathered in the rain to stare at the statues. There were pictures on TV, reports on the radio and in the newspapers. The journalist Dick Walsh decided to travel around Ireland to investigate this phenomenon. He saw many small groups gathered in all weathers staring at the statues as if willing them to move and speak. When he returned, he reported that the statues looked steady enough but he was less certain about the people.

Whether it be these humble manifestations or the great soaring spires of the Gothic churches, they both grew out of a human need. This can be alleviated by material ease and scientific advancement but never abolished.

Still sings the ghost, 'What then?'

The Christmas Rose

'My mother told me that the autumn of 1798 was the finest she ever saw. It was like summer all through November, and on Christmas Eve, mother cut a large bunch of roses in the garden at Annadale. But though flowers were unusually plentiful, food was scarce,' wrote Angel Anna Slacke's granddaughter in her memoirs, quoted by Liam Kelly in his introduction to *The Face of Time*, a remarkable collection of photographs taken by Leland Duncan around Annadale in County Leitrim between 1889 and 1894.

Angel Anna's daughter cut roses from the garden at Annadale on Christmas Eve. We gathered holly. It was often difficult to find berried holly on Christmas Eve, and part of the excitement was finding the sprigs with red berries that the birds had missed. The only flowers we saw at Christmas were the tulips that came in flat cardboard boxes for the altar.

Christmas Eve was more fun than Christmas Day. The postman would get a glass of whiskey in some of the houses that day, and our house was the last but three on his rounds. There he would be given a final whiskey and I'd deliver his letters and cards and maybe a parcel to the three remaining houses. Then my father would rope the postman's carrier bicycle to the back of the car and drive him home. There were no breathalysers, but there was a straight line in the barracks people were asked to walk. On Christmas Eve our postman would take some convincing that any line was straight.

The town would be full, with much meeting and greeting as people hurried between the small shops, the air thickly warm with 'Happy Christmas!' At the shop we traded at all year we'd be given a Christmas hamper. The cardboard box could hide a ham, biscuits, raisins, a fruit cake, cigarettes, tea and always the small half-bottle of Redbreast whiskey.

We believed and didn't believe in Santa, and would have sharp eyes for anything being purchased that we might receive from the foot of the chimney early the next morning. There would be a great bustle of excitement around the railway station as the big gates at the end of the town were closed and the little narrow-gauge train puffed past the three stunted fir trees, bringing people home for Christmas.

Eddie McIniff was always on this train. I was very fond of Eddie. He had worked for my mother on a small farm we had during the war. He was agreeable, generous and likeable and came home from England every Christmas. Nobody could ever imagine how he managed to save money. Once home he'd treat everybody he met until all his money was gone, then his friends made a collection with which to send him back to England until the next Christmas.

Coming home from the town the whole mountainside would be sprinkled with lights, the curtains taken away and a single candle set to burn in each window. Candles burned in my grandmother's windows but there was never holly. The whole house shone. Even the table that hung from an iron rail on the wall between mealtimes was freshly scrubbed. That small room had a great sense of space with the white-washed walls, the big hearth at one end facing the open loft above the bedroom and beneath the thatch where the horses' harnesses hung and my uncles used to sleep when they were young.

The plum pudding would have been made weeks before, soaked in whiskey, wrapped in damp gauze, and hidden away in a big biscuit tin.

Christmas Day was a closed day. Everybody stayed within their own house. It was considered bad manners to visit or even to move very far from your own house. The whole day revolved around the Christmas dinner, the kitchen full of delicious smells from late morning on. The tables would be drawn together and set, the huge browned turkey placed in the centre of the table, the golden stuffing spooned from its breast – white, dry breadcrumbs spiced with onion and parsley and pepper – with small roast potatoes and peas: and afterwards the moist whiskey-soaked plum pudding with spoons of cream.

Lemonade was squirted into glasses from siphons with silver tops.

After the meal the rest of the day was hard to get through. There were all kinds of games, cards, puzzles, the old Cossar wireless tuned to Athlone. Long before night and the Rosary we longed to escape the house, to walk the roads or even the fields.

As if to make up for the closing of the house on Christmas Day, all doors were thrown open on St Stephen's Day. People continually trooped between houses, bringing presents or friendly words or just making calls. Then the first wrenboys would come, usually neighbours' children in gaudy carnival rags, wearing masks or warpaint.

Few could dance or sing or play. Usually, they performed a painful parody of all three while they rattled coins vigorously about in a tin canister. Between the little bands of children the real musicians came on the Arigna coal lorry. An accordion would strike up as they swarmed from the lorry towards the house; more accordions, fiddles, fifes and drums. Dancers skipped towards the girls and women and, amid screeches and laughter and hoots and whistles, danced them round and round. Silence might fall in the open day for an old song to be sung. Before they left they'd be given a ten-shilling or a pound note.

All the money they gathered would be spent on barrels of porter and lemonade and whiskey and tea and sandwiches for a big party and dance at Kirkwood's barn that night. The same musicians would play and every house was invited. All would drink and eat and talk and dance out the last of the three big days of Christmas.

In his witty and sour *The Devil's Dictionary*, Ambrose Bierce defines 'genealogy' as 'an account of one's descent from an ancestor who did not particularly care to trace his own'. It is unlikely to be used to entice our newly-found diaspora back to search for their roots. This came to mind because I was invited recently to contribute any memories I might have of talk of the Great Famine heard as a child for a book to be published in America.

I had the luck and privilege of knowing both my grandmothers. Their parents would have lived through the Famine. Never once did I hear them mention it, nor did I hear any talk of it other than in the schoolroom. Was the experience too horrible?

Many who lived through the Famine must have done so at the expense of others. Was there too much shame and guilt? There is a state of mind I have met in the Irish countryside that is often described as the 'Famine mentality', a blind rancour against neighbours coupled with an equally blind grasping after even useless advantages.

I had close relatives who had fought in the War of Independence and the Civil War. I never heard these people speak of the wars or their part in them other than casually or in passing. Innocent people were killed. Old scores were paid off. Was it too compromising to speak about? Did silence confer a glory that speech would have reduced to the common-place? As with the Great Famine, was it politic to be silent, or was the experience too terrible for words? I'm inclined to think not, in both instances.

These people were poor and proud and many were intelligent. They possessed a simple but definite culture based on survival, a proud inde-pendence, together with a generous sense of their fragile interdepend-ence. Leisure and luxury were looked upon suspiciously. They could be shrewd and humorous about human character, but it was a shrewdness based on whether the person was likely to be of use or hindrance. If they had any political thought it was centred on the family. The moment and the day were everything. The past was a cutaway bog or an exhausted coal seam on the mountain. The future belonged with God. Too much talk they saw as unlucky and essentially idle. They left no records. Their presences are now scattered on the mountain air they once breathed.

Very movingly, I was reminded of them, as well as the society of their overlords, by a remarkable collection of photographs taken by Leland Duncan in Leitrim from 1889 to 1894. The collection was discovered by Liam Kelly while researching the history of his own parish of Kiltubrid. He has now published the photographs, with a lucid and fascinating introduction. The photographs are beautifully laid out. There is a learned note by David Davison on the technique of photography at that time.

Like his father, Leland Duncan became a high-ranking English civil servant. He grew up in Lewisham and lived out his whole life there. He was made a member of the Victorian Order for his part in arranging Queen Victoria's funeral, and was awarded the OBE for his service at the War Office. He had a passion for photography, folklore, local history.

The family had high literary connections. His first cousin, John Walter

Cross, married the great writer of *Middlemarch*, George Eliot, and jumped from their bedroom window into the canal below during their Venetian honeymoon. Soon after George Eliot's death, Cross confided to Henry James that he felt like 'a cart horse yoked to a racer' during their brief marriage, and James concluded 'that if she had not died, she would have killed him'. Leland Duncan never married.

His great-grandfather, Leland Crosthwait, had been Governor General of the Bank of Ireland, and Duncan had many Irish relatives, most importantly his aunt, Mrs Slacke, and his first cousins of Annadale House in County Leitrim. The most interesting of the Slackes was Angel Anna Slacke. Not only did she give Annadale her name; as a young woman she developed a taste for Dublin society and the theatre, and she was widely read. Her diary ('this account of my secret feelings') was kept at irregular intervals between 1785 and 1796. The diary and some of her letters survive. On a visit to Dublin, Angel Anna converted to Methodism and transferred her passion for the theatre to Methodism and the Methodist preachers. Among the preachers who stayed at Annadale were James Bredin and John Wesley.

The history of Annadale is a microcosm of the country's history – increasing poverty, land unrest, violence. Angel Anna wrote in her diary: 'I have heard the strokes of the hatchet from ten till two at night, felling some of my husband's timber, some which grew near the house, of which they formed handles for spears, pikes and forks.'

There were early warnings of what was to come: 'My mother told me that the autumn of 1798 was the finest she ever saw. It was like summer all through November, and on Christmas Eve, mother cut a large bunch of roses in the garden at Annadale. But though flowers were unusually plentiful, food was scarce.'

In 1847, when the full force of the Famine struck, the people starved. They died of fevers. Some went to the workhouses. Others, who could, emigrated. An ambitious programme to build a canal between the Shannon and the Erne was started. This gave relief work, but many were too weak to work. Kelly's whole account gives an added poignancy to Duncan's extraordinary photograph of the mud cabin – the boy and the woman, the ducks and the goats, the cured goatskin.

The Annadale estate was almost two hundred years old when the eighteen-year-old Duncan first visited his aunt and cousins in 1880. Annadale House, with its master and mistress at its head, was the focus and centre of the entire community, a complete world of servants, tradesmen, gamekeepers, herdsmen, tenants – all of whom knew their place. He and his sister Carrie continued coming to Annadale through the 1880s, and he came to know the area and its people well.

Duncan seems to have been much more drawn to the life of the poor, the servants and tenants, than to the social life of the gentry. In 1889 he took his first photographs. In 1890 his sister Carrie married her first cousin, James Slacke, and came to live at Annadale. Through the summers of 1892, 1893 and 1894 Duncan continued taking photographs of the people and the area.

They have the fascination of nearly all old photographs. Time that is still our element has already washed over these lives, and they seem to look at us out of a depth of time or waters in fashions that have ceased. What an added pleasure it is to see how unselfconscious these people are. They could not imagine how they would look in a photograph. Their mute presence is more eloquent than any idea of self.

In the Spirit of Christmas

In America, it is Thanksgiving; in Scotland, the New Year; and in Ireland, the great festival is Christmas. We have St Patrick's Day and Easter and Hallowe'en and the big Bank Holidays as well. Irregular carnivals, which we call funerals, go on throughout the year, but all of them appear shadowy beside Christmas. Christmas has always fascinated me.

The fascination is different now from a child's fascination, but it is still powerful, and, like many continuing fascinations, it remains only partly understood. I find myself returning to Christmas again and again in fiction. Perhaps it has to do with the unifying spirit that pervades the festival, a spirit so pervasive and inescapable that it can easily bring about an effect other than that it intends, which is, I believe, why so many people find it the loneliest time in the year. It so depressed the German poet Rilke that he wrote that all compulsory festivals, like Christmas and Easter, should be abolished; there should be only festivals of the spirit. The logical end of such an injunction surely means that these festivals must be celebrated alone – a man or woman suddenly dancing a jig for themselves in some upstairs room.

The very name *Christmas* and the still potent symbols of the festival belong to the story of Christ and to the beginning of Christianity: the journey to Bethlehem, the closed inn, the miracle of the Virgin Birth that will redeem the world, the ox and the ass, the shepherds and kings. Like many people, I believe that the festival is much older than Christianity, and would be with us under a different name if Christ had not come.

Around where we live, as soon as the summer ends and the October days start to shorten visibly, the constant muttering begins against the coming of the long nights, the approaching winter that must be faced and got through: 'How will the time be put round 'till the long days come?' The articulation is so constant and precise that it must have been refined and worn over many years, even generations; and sometimes the words take on an echo of a deeper railing against all of darkness and extinction. Though the phrases themselves never vary, their expression alters much from person to person. For one person it is a simple, deep dread of the winter, the boredom and lack of company during the long nights; for another, the expense of keeping a house warm or having to trudge for months through mud to fodder cattle; and the same words will be found forever in the mouth of the fellow at the bar counter showing off that he is a complete master of cliché.

But the dread of winter that the simple words articulate is suddenly broken up by the prospect of Christmas. The celebration is looked forward to, and it becomes as well a great communal kick at winter and isolation.

The following scene from *Amongst Women* was imagined taking place in the 1950s or early 1960s.* Today, the family might watch television. There might be no Midnight Mass to attend. The wrenboys would not come. The girls would go to a disco instead of to a barn dance, but if the words are right, the spirit they seek out will not have changed.

---

* This brief reflection was written to introduce an extract from *Amongst Women* that was printed in the *Irish Independent* on 15 December 1990. The extract from pages 94–100 of the novel describes the excitement and anticipation of the days leading up to Christmas, the Church appearing 'like an enormous lighted ship in the night' on the way to midnight Mass, the boredom of Christmas Day, the visit of the wrenboys and the prospect of sexual indiscretion that the dance in the Kirkwoods' barn promises to the younger generation of Morans. The situation that is dramatized in this passage of *Amongst Women* is also described by McGahern in some detail in 'The Christmas Rose'.

Life as It Is and Life as It Ought to Be

A very rare event took place here in the early winter. There was a funeral in the little Protestant church in Fenagh. Willie Booth was the dead man's name. He was a prosperous farmer, a widower with a grown family, very interested in all kinds of machinery, in breeds of sheep and cattle, active in the various farming organizations. He was pleasant, outgoing, extremely likeable and he loved to dance, which took him to places of dance for miles around. I did not know him, other than in the casually passing way of town and market and various communal farming chores, until one evening, out of the blue, he telephoned and invited me to his house. He wanted to know if I could advise him on books and papers in his possession. We arranged an evening.

In a room that was lovely in its plainness, he showed me ledgers and papers. They recorded events in the lives of the small Protestant community, now almost extinct. He was the sole curator. He wanted to know how they could be organized into a formal account or history. These local histories have always held more interest than the great figures and affairs of state, but even though I found the papers fascinating, I wasn't able to offer Willie practical help. Before the evening ended, we discussed the possibility of restoring the small Protestant church in Fenagh as a library or museum to house these records. Though its beautiful shape was intact, it was derelict. Windows were broken. Lead had been stolen from the roof. There was woodworm in the timbers. Due almost entirely to Willie's enthusiasm and energy, in a few short years, the church was restored as part of a FÁS scheme. A dance was held in Mohill to pay off the debt. The whole community turned out and each person paid what they could afford. They gave generously. The debt was paid off, and Willie didn't miss a dance during the course of the long, happy night.

The restored church was now ready to hold his funeral service. Years before, we would have laughed if either of us had foreseen such a use. The church was filled to capacity a good hour before the service was due to begin and was bright with flowers. People spilled out among the old Protestant headstones, and the road on either side of the church gate was so crowded with cars and people that traffic had to be diverted. Members of the farming organizations formed a double line of honour as the coffin was carried from the hearse to the church. Everybody waited outside during the hour-long service, chatting to one another in the wintry sunshine, gathering about the grave when the coffin was taken from the church for burial. The open grave was lined with moss and ivy and wild flowers. 'The Protestants do it all in one go and isn't it far more sensible?'

Mourners from the Protestant community came from far and wide, but they were greatly outnumbered by the dead man's Catholic friends and neighbours. A Protestant I had gone to school with in Roscommon was there. I remembered him as a bright, intelligent boy who used to have to wait outside in the school porch during prayers and religious instruction. He had driven twenty miles to attend the funeral.

As everyone scattered to their houses or the village bars, I heard people counting back years to remember if there had ever been a bigger local funeral. 'There's no difference here any more between Protestants and Catholics,' a neighbour said. 'They go to the same bars, play cards, drink together. They all pull and work together. No one passes the least heed. You'd wonder what's wrong with that crowd in the North that they can't be the same.'

I had heard the statement many times before and knew it to be a widely held view. I thought of Chekhov's famous definition of fiction – 'life as it is, life as it ought to be' – and wondered how much of the statement was true and how much communal wishful thinking. Only people like Willie Booth or the man who had stood as a boy in the school porch really knew how true it was, and they would be naturally too courteous and careful to say. Mostly, I suspect, it expressed nothing more or less than how little the people in the South know about the North and how little they know of their own recent history.

When I was a child, the North was the 'Black North'. Protestants were dominant there. Nobody knew anything about it other than those engaged in smuggling or eel fishing. 'They should put up a fukken wall around the place,' an uncle of mine used to say when he was young, and later when bombings or killings were shown on the television, he would repeat 'the wall . . . the wall' in a tone that barred discussion. Granted, certain alcoholic relatives had occasional recourse to a place called 'The Gran' near Enniskillen, where there was a priest who was reputed to have powers to cure the desire for drink; but as these were sociable, spirited people, they generally celebrated their good intentions afterwards in Enniskillen, and their arrival home seldom added to their reputations or that of the North. My uncle disapproved of the drink even more than of the North, but in a way he was right – as he was in his own way about many things: there was a mental wall constructed against the North.

For a country with such a sorry history, it is remarkable how trouble-free this State has been since its foundation. I think that this is because of the presence of Britain on one side and the North on the other. Social unrest and economic failure was avoided by the proximity of Britain and the availability of work there. At the creation of a sectarian state for a Catholic people, Protestant unrest was avoided by the existence of the North, where a majority of Protestants were able to create their own equally sectarian state. Both places closed their eyes and went their own way. If it was necessary, one side could always point to the other to justify their own bigotry. Here, Protestants like Willie Booth remained and prospered, but many, many more were either absorbed by the Catholic marriage laws or emigrated. People I knew went to Canada or the North, and, by and large, unlike many Catholics, they didn't have to emigrate for economic reasons.

Irish became compulsory in schools but it was only useful to the new emerging middle classes, the civil service and the professions, to whom the sectarian state here was primarily addressed. There were many contradictions. No one advocated Irish more strongly than the Church, but they were careful to ensure that all religious instruction took place in English. The sectarian state here has largely disintegrated, probably because of a lack of a serious opposition, and it has been seen, increasingly, as the narrow, bigoted artefact it always was, and lest there be any self-congratulation, in many ways still is.

On a *Late Late Show* that went out from the King's Hall in Belfast in the 1960s, an amusing experience showed me how the South was viewed from the North. I was invited to attack the Catholic Church, and when I declined, separating the Church spiritual, which was the emotional weather of my early life and for which I had nothing but gratitude, from the Church politic, its priests and bishops, the live studio audience would have none of it, seeing it as Jesuitical casuistry, or worse. A man rose, pointing at me, and said: 'There's a fellow whose book has been banned in Dublin and he's been sacked from his job by the Archbishop and he gets up here on his hind legs and praises the Catholic Church. Now, could Moscow do a better job of brainwashing than that?'

When I'm asked about the North, and I'm often asked about it outside the country, because of the violence, I can only say that it wasn't part of my experience, and a person can only speak of what he knows. Even to visit it for a few hours is to realize it is a very different country. To me it is now stranger than France or Britain or the United States, and I live beside the border. That the people are more polite and businesslike than in the South, the Protestant work ethic more prevalent, makes it a more difficult place to get to know. Behind all the surface good manners, I feel much of it is deeply hidden, even aggressively so. All that one hears at first hand or notices seems to emphasize that sense of difference.

A young Catholic priest, a diocesan examiner, told me that to examine a primary school in the South and then to cross the border to examine a Northern school meant travelling only three or four miles to examine the same set of doctrines and morals but to find the respective attitudes to those doctrines forty or fifty years apart. Years ago, in London, a Presbyterian gloomily told me that in Ireland we might be Protestants or Catholics, Unionists or Republicans, but in Britain we are just Irish. Similarly, both Unionists and Nationalists are now seen in the South as Northerners and have more in common with one another than with anyone here.

Not long ago I was talking with an intelligent and attractive young woman in Belfast who had been to university and was making her way in a profession that interested her deeply. She was liberated – though her parish priest would think otherwise. She lived with her boyfriend, took the pill and looked sceptically at most of the Church's teaching on women. 'You can hardly call yourself a Catholic?' I suggested. 'Oh, yes, whether I like it or not I'm defined as a Catholic in the North, and if I get married I'll do so in the Church; to do anything else would be like turning one's back on one's own people.'

Different in age and in attitude was another family from another part of the North. Catholic, middle-aged, conservative, quiet-spoken, devout, enjoying a prosperity that went back at least three generations. Surprisingly, though they couldn't see it happening in their lifetime, they would like to believe that one day there would be a united Ireland. For instance, they always found the police courteous and helpful in all their dealings with them, but they never really felt that they were *their* police. The police represented the other side. In their eyes, as Catholics, they felt they would be done without in an ideal Protestant state. These quiet and intelligent people would be considered to be the conservative bedrock of any community, and to hear them express their separation from the force of law was bizarre. If decent, law-abiding Catholics feel such estrangement in the North, what must similarly decent Protestants feel when confronted with a vision of a united Ireland?

The only way I could relate to their experience was a conversation I had with a Christian Brother in the 1950s. On certain days, classes were doubled for religious instruction which was taught exclusively by the Brothers, thereby giving the lay teachers a free hour. Delighted with the arrangement, I asked the Brother why he should want to take on the extra work. Religious instruction, he told me, was too important to be left to lay teachers, and if vocations could be increased he could see the day when lay teachers could be dispensed with altogether. He was so convinced of the rightness of his vision that he saw no incongruity in communicating it to me even though it meant depriving me of my livelihood.

Such states of mind are the real foreign countries. When I hear 'you'd wonder what's wrong with that crowd in the North that they can't be the same as down here?' I feel like asking people like Willie Booth if it was really so simple to live here. When I think of him and other Protestants

I have known in the South I am reminded of certain Irish people who prosper in England. Unlike their American counterparts, they do not flaunt their Irishness. They join the Rotary Club, vote Conservative, and stir uneasily at every IRA outrage. They know that racism sleeps lightly and is, potentially, all around us.

Rural Ireland's Passing

I saw the mass protests and pickets outside the meat plants as one of those convulsions that occur when something that has endured for long and was deeply embedded in the life is coming to an end and facing extinction. I believe the farmers had right if not the law on their side, and that they acted after long provocation and much manipulation. The meat business has always been a rough trade.

For most of a century Ireland remained largely outside change when wars and social revolution were changing the world. Here, revolution and independence served to reinforce an innately inward-looking conservatism. Mass emigration siphoned away the young, the potential source of disaffection and restlessness. The family farm stood at the heart of society, especially in public claims and utterances, though in practice it got little help and was often laughed at.

What were those farms like and what kind of lives did the people have? Not long ago I met an old man who had grown up on a farm beside where I live. He left for England in the 1950s. He was tall and handsome, one of that generation who are all the more remarkable to look at because they are without consciousness of how they look, like people in early photographs.

I knew the house where he had grown up. It was by the water's edge. The thick round stone piers still remain at the entrance. The stone walls of the house and outhouses are intact, but the roofs have gone. A big ash tree has taken root in the middle of the living room, where food was boiled for fowl and animals, where they also did their own cooking and baking, played cards and chatted and said the Rosary. From the arrangement of the house and the outhouses and the small yard, it is easy to see what a charming place it must have been, sheltered by great oaks and ash on the edge of the lake. It was also a five-cow place, which meant that the family was relatively comfortable. Cherry and apple trees grow wild now in the small gardens close to the house, and hundreds of daffodils and narcissi around the house still greet the spring in a wilderness of crawling blackthorns.

He spoke movingly of the life he had known on this farm, without sentiment or nostalgia. 'We were never bored. That's for sure. There was too much to do. Everybody had to work.' Their life was the life of crops and animals and bog and fowl. Animals, especially cattle, surrounded them. Not a day went by without handling them, and their presence affected every member of the family. Their closeness varied with the seasons; they all had names; some were pets. Before heading out to school the children brought in the cows, and in the evenings went for them again. A huge pot of steaming small potatoes was drained and emptied into a half barrel and pounded into a mash for hens. His sisters gathered the eggs. There was always a search in summer for the nests of hens laying wild. Every week there was churning, the buttermilk either drunk or fed to calves in a mash, the excess butter sold with the eggs.

This was the time of the travelling shop, which sold all kinds of household staples, from soap to thread, to tea and salt, and bought eggs and fowl and butter. The travelling shop and the forge were all a source of news and gossip as were the itinerant tinsmiths. They soldered leaking pots and buckets and sold gallons of shining tin. Flour was bought by the bag. Poor families washed the empty bags and made shirts and housedresses from the white sacking.

Every house kept pigs, and each year a pig was killed. The old man remembered it as a melancholy time. The children would have fed the pig. It was often a pet. The pigsticker would arrive in the morning, and from a bag take out his knives and cleavers. Sometimes after drinking tea in the kitchen he would sharpen the knives. From the pig-house the children could hear the protesting moans of the condemned animal, which was given neither food nor water the evening before. Portions of the ribs, the liver, and little cutlets called *griscíns* – delicious when fried – were made into parcels and given to close neighbours. The favour was returned when they killed their own pig. Fresh pork was as prized a delicacy as wild mushrooms. The pig's bladder was often kept as a football.

In the spring, whole fields were ploughed for potatoes and turnips and mangels and oats. Dropping the potato splits into the ridges was bitter work in the March winds, and there was also the misery of coming from school on a freezing October evening and having to pick all the potatoes dug since morning, hands so blue with cold that they could hardly feel the handles of the buckets of potatoes they dragged to the pit. Nobody complained about the work because the need was so clear. With the animals they were all part of the same living enterprise.

As soon as the potatoes were set, everybody headed for the bog. For vital work the children were kept from school, no matter what the teachers said. There was the stripping of banks, the burning of sedge, the wheeling of heavy barrows out on the spread; and later the back-breaking scattering, the footing, clamping, the small donkeys sinking and struggling in the soft, treacherous passes of the bog as they took the turf out to the road to be carted home. Without it they would have no fire that winter. Like old hay in the shed, old turf was like old gold. The bog was a hungry place, but then the girls would come with sandwiches and bottles of sweetened tea. It was hard to wash the dried mud off hands and feet after a day on the bog; often they had to be washed again in fresh mud.

At that time of year they would all be in their bare feet. They went barefoot from May Day, when primroses were scattered on all the doorsteps, and they didn't put on boots or shoes again until October, other than to go to Mass. They were glad to be rid of them. There was trouble whenever a pair couldn't be resoled and strips of old bicycle tyres were used to protect the leather. To go barefoot was to go free and to kick these anxieties away.

The hay was the most loved work because it was clean and the meadows sweet-smelling, though it had its own anxieties in wet summers. The whole house gathered in the meadows with rakes and pitchforks. In good weather there was a great sense of fun and banter. It was the one work on the farm that men and women shared, and there was a great sense of happiness when the hay was won. Usually a whiskey or a *poitín* bottle and a dozen or two of stout were opened when neighbours gathered for the building of the rick. Pasternak wonderfully captures this time of year in the meadows:

> At first light cart after cart
> Rolls darkly through the fields.
> The day gets out of bed
> With hay in its hair.
> And at noon the ricks are clouds,
> The sky is blue, the earth
> Has body and strength
> Like vodka with aniseed.

The critical time of the year, then as now, was when the cattle were sold. They defined the family's relative wealth. They were the real old gold or the frail defences against the outside winds that blew. They paid the priest, the doctor, the rate collector, the shopkeeper, the gombeen man, the undertaker.

Sometimes a trusted buyer came and bought the cattle on the land. But mostly they were sold at the fair in town. In darkness they would set out with the excited cattle, carrying sticks and weak flashlamps, reaching the town at daybreak if they met with no accidents along the way. During the first miles the children had to run through the fields alongside the cattle to prevent them leaving the road. 'Tanglers' would meet them on the outskirts of the town, hoping to buy below the market price. A whole comical barrier of chairs and ladders and barrels would be set up along the street to try to prevent the small herds of cattle dirtying the doorsteps or shop fronts. This could lead to confrontations with the townspeople throughout the day.

There was the ceremony of buying, of going away insulted, being dragged back by third parties, the seller in turn becoming insulted, the slapping of hands, the splitting of differences, the crucial luck penny. The ritual must be ancient. I saw it recently in a market in Morocco exactly as I remembered it here in all its slow and volatile movements.

I have taken part in all the life the old man had described and could share its emotional truth and accuracy. It must have more or less remained that way for the best part of a hundred years. The great weakness of these places was that, while large families often worked the farm, it could only be handed on to one person, and for the others there was only the train to the night boat then. In spite of the obvious hardship and the unpredictability of weather and prices, he thought it a rich and satisfying life if a living could be won, but didn't want to see his old house or fields on the shore of the lake and said he preferred to remember it as it was. I suspected there could have been trouble over the succession.

Since then everything has changed. Like fishing, it has become an industry. The machines have taken away the hardship and the uncertainty, but larger farms and fewer people are needed to justify their cost and efficiency. Nobody can make a living from the small farms any more unless they have another job, or the wife has, or both have jobs. Young people do not want to have anything to do with these small farms.

There has been gross and short-sighted mismanagement. People have been given grants and encouraged to borrow to increase cattle numbers and to build slatted sheds on shallow lands unable to take slurry, with a devastating effect on the lakes and rivers and even the fields. There are now so many official forms that it is almost necessary to be an accountant in order to run a small farm. I have heard the new cattle registry described as the Book of Kells. And the cattle prices tell their own story.

To move to the other party in the dispute, the results of the Beef Tribunal were more disturbing for what was obfuscated than for what was revealed. During the recent pickets it became known that some of the meat plants have built enormous cattle sheds and may no longer want farms other than as feeding units for those sheds, where cattle will have a life similar to battery hens and pigs.

The spring lake is dead alongside the deserted farm. Once people came to the lake for their buckets of spring water. It was teeming with pike and perch and eels, and there was a pass for otters. More than thirty houses drew water from the lake in a group water scheme. The lake might have been polluted anyhow, but the Agriculture Institute rented ten acres overlooking the lake. They drained and reseeded it at enormous expense, though the same experiment was proved useless years ago in Britain. Tons of nitrates were poured on the reseeded land and drained into the lake. A green scum decorates the shore. The fish are dead. People in the water scheme have to boil their drinking water before use. This is but a microcosm of large parts of the rest of the country.

The ash tree growing in the middle of the living room may well have been a symbol before its time.

Terrible Tales from the Mart

A few weeks ago, in late November, I had young cattle to sell and took them to the mart. The sale was at night. Though it was still daylight when I reached the mart, I discovered that there were already some hundreds of cattle ahead of me and I knew it was going to be a long night. In fact, it was well after midnight by the time the animals were sold.

The mart is a fascinating place. I had been coming here for years and have seen it change owners. The arc-lights high in the steel girders glare down on the bare concrete, the pens, the rings, the huge clocks above the weighing pens that tell the weights in kilos, the semi-circle of wooden seating above the rings, the lowing of the bewildered animals. There is also something disturbing at the heart of the fascination.

Nearly all the owners are small farmers, sometimes very old men. Younger men occasionally have their children with them. Now and again there is a woman, usually wearing a headscarf, as if in church a generation ago.

The big buyers are easy to tell apart, especially the Northern buyers, their yellow cattlemen's boots laced high, the brown or grey overcoat, the hat. Harder, but not impossible to pick out, is that maligned race, the strugglers, an exact word for those men who live by their wits, attempting to pick up animals below their true price and to sell them on at this mart or some other mart, small-time dealers on the floor of a stock exchange. When I was a child and there were fairs instead of marts, they came out to the outskirts of the town to meet the farmers on their way in with their cattle.

There used to be a contagious excitement about the mart, but that night a few weeks ago in late November everything was muted. The auctioneer's voice called out the bids like the recitation of prayers, anxiously searching around the ring and seat – 'Any more? Any more? One last time' – before reluctantly bringing down the hammer.

He tried to drum up some excitement by describing the next beast entering the ring, as his assistant chalked up the weight on the board, but by his tone you could tell that he knew it would have no effect. He was merely going through a routine. The prices were expected to be low, but not as low as they were that night.

A stranger, an old man, caught my eye as we pushed past one another in the narrow passage on the outskirts of the ring. 'They are for pegging away,' he said. The British farmer may be in worse straits, but if the fabled Celtic Tiger was to appear in that November mart, it would be as a poor beast on her way to hamburger heaven at a knockdown price.

I ran into neighbours that night, both small farmers, both with cattle to sell. As we all had hours to wait, we decided to wander out into the town for a drink. There was a time when the bars around the mart used to be packed, but that night they were almost empty. Both men had grown up on the farms they now worked, as had their fathers before them. They are hard-working, quiet, intelligent. Their families are reared. The children of both men are clever. They went to university and work in various professions, mostly in Dublin.

Occasionally on weekends they come home from the city. None of their sons or daughters would have anything to do with farming, and they are keenly aware that a whole way of life that had remained relatively unchanged for generations will disappear when they go. 'Only for the cheque in the post it would all be gone wallop before now,' one of the men remarked as we stood at the counter. They express neither regret nor disappointment. It is a simple fact, the way things are. Far greater opportunities were open to their children than were ever available to them. The children took the opportunities and the parents are not a little proud. They also see that their children are subject to different stresses than ever they had to contend with.

Even as we talked about the low price of cattle, they remarked that people are now incredibly better off materially than they used to be.

Nobody goes hungry. Nobody has to go to England any more. If anything, these men would complain that people have too much money, more money than they can usefully handle. The small towns are full of drugs. There is nothing particularly Irish about this sudden and dramatic change: like the multinationals, it is everywhere.

All this was much in my mind because I was reading a remarkable book in which these and tangential themes are raised to art of a very high order. The book is the collected stories of Alistair MacLeod, *The Lost Salt Gift of Blood*, a dozen stories in all, the concentrated work of a lifetime. No great publicity attended the book; it came my way by word of mouth. All the blurb tells about the author is that he is a native of Cape Breton in Nova Scotia, Canada, that he has worked as a school-teacher, miner and logger and now teaches creative writing at the University of Windsor in Ontario.

The stories are all set in Cape Breton though they extend out from there in time as well as space. The characters are Scotia whose way of life has scarcely changed in hundreds of years since their Highland ancestors were driven there by the Clearances. Gaelic is still spoken in some of the stories. The same sea that washes the Hebrides beats against these granite cliffs. The people work as farmers, fishermen, miners, lighthouse keepers. In nearly all the stories this world is poised on the edge of eclipse or change. They are written in a language of precision and deep eloquence. The concluding story, 'The Tuning of Perfection', is the lightest, and has a very sly humour. The hero is seventy-eight years old and lives in a house on top of the mountain which he built when he was a young man. His people have lived on the same site since his great-grandfather arrived from the Isle of Skye. His wife and he were so devoted to one another that they almost excluded the world.

They used to sing to one another as they worked: 'They were married for five years in an intensity which it seemed could never last, going more and more into each other and excluding most others for the company of themselves.' When she dies in childbirth, leaving him three daughters, he is lost.

In spite of being young and attractive he never remarries and becomes a human repository of the old Gaelic songs and traditions. Over his house the monogamous eagles fly. Fifty years after his wife's death his granddaughter arrives at the house with two phone messages: a man wants to buy his mare and a television producer is coming to audition Gaelic songs for a show in Halifax which will be presented before some members of the royal family and beamed around the world.

She wants to get on the show but has rivals. They sing '*Fear A' Bhata*' together. She has a good voice but sings the lament as if it were a milling song. He then sings for her:

'Do you know what the words mean?' he said when he had finished.

'No,' she said. 'Neither will anybody else. I just make the noises. I've been hearing the things since I was two. I know how they go. I'm not dumb, you know.'

'Who else are they asking?' he said, partially out of interest and partially to change the subject and avoid confrontation.

'I don't know. They said they'd get back to us later. All they wanted to know now was if we were interested. The man about the mare will be up later. I got to go now.'

She was out of the door almost immediately, turning her truck in a spray of gravel that flicked against his house, the small stones pinging against his windowpane. A muddied bumper sticker read: 'If you're horny, honk your horn.'

Her main rival to get the television show, a rough diamond called Carver whose energy the old man admires, arrives with a man from Montreal to buy the mare. He is offered a much higher price for the mare than he ever expected to receive:

'Has she ever had a colt?'

'Why, yes,' said Archibald, puzzled by the question. Usually buyers asked if the horse would work single or double or something about its disposition or its legs or chest. Or if it would work in snow or eat enough to sustain a heavy work schedule.

'Do you think she could have another colt?' he asked.

'Why I suppose,' he said, almost annoyed, 'if she had a stallion.'

'No problem,' said the man.

'But,' said Archibald, driven by his old honesty, 'she has never worked. I have not been in the woods that much lately and I always used the old mare, her mother, before she died. I planned to train her but never got around to it. She's more like a pet. She probably will work, though. They've always worked. It's in the stock. I've had them all my life.' He stopped, almost embarrassed at having to apologise for his horses and for himself.

'Okay,' said the man. 'No problem. She has had a colt, though?'

Later, when Carver returns with a truck to take the mare away, he explains the purpose for which she was bought:

'Nah, she won't work,' said Carver. 'They want her for birth control pills.'

'For what?' said Archibald.

'This guy says, I don't know if it's true, that there's this farm outside of Montreal that's connected to a lab or something. Anyway, they've got all these mares there and they keep them bred all the time and they use their water for birth control pills.'

It seemed so preposterous that Archibald was not sure how to react. He scrutinized Carver's scarred yet open face, looking for a hint, some kind of touch, but he could find nothing.

'Yeah,' said Carver. 'They keep the mares pregnant all the time so the women won't be.'

'What do they do with the colts?' said Archibald, thinking that he might try a question for a change.

In the end, it comes down to Archibald's decision as to whether he is prepared to sing as part of his granddaughter's group which decides whether she or Carver get to Halifax and appear on television. Archibald has 'presence and credibility'. Carver's crowd has energy. The MacKenzies, the best singers, are not considered at all. Their young singers are scattered to places as far away as Calgary. Only old Mrs MacKenzie is on the Cape. She was a cousin of Archibald's:

He was not even sure of the degree of the relationship (although he could work it out later), remembering only the story of the young woman from an earlier generation of his family who had married the young man from the valley of the MacKenzies who was of the 'wrong religion'. There had been great bitterness at the time and the families had refused to speak to one another until all those who knew what the 'right religion' was had died.

She had only a tape recorder with which to impress the man from the television station,

. . . she who was probably the best of them all and who had tried the hardest to impress the man from Halifax. The image of her in the twilight of the valley of the MacKenzies playing the tape-recorded voices of her departed family to a man who did not know the language kept running through his mind. He imagined her now, sitting quietly with her knitting needles in her lap, listening to the ghostly voices which were there without their people.

Everything is right and sure-footed as the story reaches its delicate and inevitable ending.

IV
LITERATURE

A Literature without Qualities

The work of a writer does not define itself in advance, even in the case of a writer who appears to identify and conform perfectly with his own time or when his hope is to be exemplary and right-thinking. If he is a great writer, his work is shaped in the writing itself first of all, and then in successive re-reading and the intervention of specific poetic elements, which bypass ideological notions.

It is known that Sophocles was described by one of his contemporaries as one of the happiest men of his time – a personal friend of Pericles, a skilful and honoured soldier, reaching a serene old age without suffering. The aim of his tragic plays is to show disasters that cause inordinate suffering. Looking more closely, the intention is functional and conservative – that, at least, would be the opinion of any contemporary intellectual. However, in an unexpected way, it is not the dangers of incest that are revealed, for example, but rather the attractions; and as well he tells us that a tragic destiny is made up not only of immoderation but also is the outcome of the compelling importance of objectivity.

A writer's work does not define itself by intentions but by results. I think that what is happening – for economic, political and social reasons – is that the reader is predetermined in advance and that the contents of literature are imposed on the reader by means of things outside of literature. On book jackets, in newspaper articles, through publicity and blackmail of the bestsellers, one passes over the actual text; whatever value it might have is secondary. Consequently, the reader thinks that he knows in advance what he must find in a book, and whether or not he finds it has finally no importance whatsoever. In my opinion it has to do with a plan of a repressive nature, contrived to do away with the aesthetic experience, which is after all an extreme form of liberty.

We are told that when Sophocles presented his work to the Olympiad it was a certain Philocles, nephew of Aeschylus, who won the prize. One can imagine that what was disliked in the trilogy was just that excess or immoderation which the play was supposedly criticizing and which is really the poetic base, thanks to which it has come down to us. Also, Sophocles makes us a bit more aware of our own animality. He saw the world through the eyes of a tragic poet, in spite of the social rules which he sincerely defended and which no doubt were a part of him. Poetry, a kind of act manqué, will in certain respects obey the laws of *lapsus linguae*, the same laws that Freud describes in *Jokes and Their Relationship to the Unconscious*. Searching for the means of intelligible, social speech, the poet risks uncovering, while revealing, unimaginable aspects of himself and the human condition and man's relationship to the world.

The rules of conduct and of thought in contemporary society have become institutionalized. Political power, censorship, journalism, the demand for profit returns, the press and audiovisual agencies supply orders which follow the product so that not only the artist but the consumer as well will conform. As Nathalie Sarraute says, 'We live in an era of suspicion.' Everything must be pre-planned so that nothing, not even aesthetic experience, can escape social control.

Thus it is that certain things which should be merely informative and are of no importance become, by their very existence, aesthetic labels. For example, this is what happens with the label 'Latin American Literature'. This tag, fashionable in the media and with compliant university critics, does not limit itself to giving information on the authors' origins, but is charged with aesthetic judgements. Its use implies various styles and a certain refined rapport of the author to his own society. Latin American literature is credited with energy, elegant insouciance, healthy primitivism, political commitment. Most authors, consciously or not, fall into the trap of this predetermination, acting and writing in conformity to the needs of the public (not to say, more crudely, the market). As in the golden age of colonial exploitation, most

Latin American writers give the European reader certain things which, as the experts claim, are rare commodities in a city – primal matter or tropical fruits which the European climate is unable to produce: spontaneity, freshness, energy, innocence, a return to one's roots. In addition, every product must have a decent Latin American look, and published work a resemblance, so that Latin American literature accomplishes not so much an illuminating praxis but a basic, ideological function.

It goes without saying that the great Latin American writers of the twentieth century – Rubén Darío, César Vallejo, Macedonio Fernández, Vicente Huidobro, Neruda of the 1930s and 1940s, Jorge Luis Borges, Juan L. Ortiz, Felisberto Hernández are all, for the most part, unknown in Europe and hardly read at all on their own continent. As well, in the course of getting to know their work, we discover that not only do they have little or nothing in common but that they passionately conflict with each other. All of them, though, in their work possess something that is to be found only in the great texts of modern literature: the will to create an individual work, a unique expression, endlessly reworked and enriched, until it is pared down to an individual style, to the point that the man behind the work is his work and eventually becomes one with it. All the energy and determination of their personalities, consciously or unconsciously, are united in one constant image of the world, an image which universalizes their personal experience. That commercial society has the illusion of appropriating these important works, making them official, is a phenomenon which deserves careful study; but beforehand we can state that works on this level remain in a certain way hidden and will always escape the game of supply and demand: only love and admiration are allowed to enter their life-giving and generous aura. All that survives does so by acquiring lovers.

For all these reasons I think that a writer in our society, whatever nationality he or she might be, must, as a writer, refuse to represent any kind of ideological interests, any aesthetic or political dogma, even if it marginalizes him or condemns him to obscurity. Every writer has to establish for himself his own aesthetic principles; dogma and pre-judgements must be excluded from his world. The writer must be, using Musil's words, a 'man without qualities'; that is, a man who does not puff himself up like a scarecrow with a handful of acquired certainties or edicts of social convention, but who, *a priori*, rejects all constraints. This applies to every writer of every nationality.

In a world governed by the desire for total control, the writer must be the caretaker of the possible.

The flimsiness of basing anything on conflict such as has taken place in Northern Ireland. This was brutally shown up by the fact that several works – novels, stories, travels – were in danger of being rendered obsolete before they saw the light of publication day because the peace threatened to break out. This is not to say that serious work cannot be written out of a fashionable conflict. It can, but only in so far as it attracts a writer of talent, and given no more or less importance than a comparable talent['s] interest in a woman combing her hair or adjusting or checking the control panel of an [?], someone tending their garden or getting ready to meet their beloved. [. . .]

Mr Joyce and Mr Yeats

Foreword to a *James Joyce Exhibition Catalogue*
at Colgate University

James Joyce, Joyce James, Jim, Jamesy, Stephen, Bloom, Mr Joyce. Who is he? Whatdoyoucolumn?

A lord of language, certainly, though that had to be taken from Lawn Tennyson; and some others would assert that lord of chaos might be drawing closer. The Americans hired James Joyce to ruin the English language, Mr Evelyn Waugh spoke out forthrightly. Svevo slyly noticed that Mr Joyce was not a man whose own works could be read aloud in his presence.

It was a long journey: from the scrupulous clarity of *Dubliners*, where the first shapes are, where the wonderful aural wit first stirs, crux upon crux – out into *Finnegans Wake*, the words now losing their definite line to merge and chime and swim, calling up other words, always changing, always taling, summoned by the incredible energy of that comic genius, always expanding, expounding, playing. Words alone seem certain good. Talk will save us. We have left the world of letters and reached impure sound. *Finnegans Wake* is a work of genius, Mr T. S. Eliot, Joyce's great supporter, suggested, but of such a kind that one such is enough.

There are two lovely old apple trees just below Merrill House, earlier the President's House, and now the Faculty Club of Colgate University. They had been pruned and shaped once and though they grow close together are very different. I fell into the habit of thinking about them as Mr Joyce and Mr Yeats in much the same way, I imagine, as a man once called his two cats Chatto and Windus, after much dealing with that

185

publishing house. Then, in the late spring of 1977, there was a sudden fall of wet snow. It broke power lines, brought down young trees, stripped away branches, damaged roofs.

Suddenly Messrs Joyce and Yeats stood like a pair of weightlifters with the dumbbells shoulder high, crowned by this weight of snow, changed out of all shape. Mr Joyce, in particular, had been brought very low, and split into practically two separate trees, straining away from one another. It struck me that I was seeing for the first time these two great writers beneath the weight of their critics.

I knew that the vision, in some ways, was unfair, a gross caricature. For the best criticism surely grows out of love, the same root as true, original work, love that will survive the inevitable disappearance of even the greatest trees, the most luminous snow; but since that late spring day I have been even more loath than before to add to the weight of snow on these two trees.

When asked to contribute to a special Thomas Hardy number of the *Revue Nouvelle* in 1928, Joyce wrote:

But whatever diversity of judgement may exist about his work (if any does exist), it is none the less evident to all that Hardy demonstrated in his attitude of the poet in relation to his public, an honourable example of integrity and self-esteem of which we other clerks are always a little in need, especially in a period when the reader seems to content himself with less and less of the poor written word and when, in consequence, the writer tends to concern himself more and more with the great questions which, for all that, adjust themselves very well without his aid.

The poor written word . . . we other clerks . . . *la pauvre parole écrite . . . nous autres clercs* . . . I find the statement not only moving but useful. They were uttered by a great clerk. They are even more needed now than then.

Mr Elmer Sheets is of the Colgate class of 1926. Throughout his life he has collected books, and has written: 'Book collectors usually get that way primarily because of a love of books. I bought and kept only what I read.' This love grew into the Lillian and Elmer Sheets Collection of Modern First Editions. He is now bringing the James Joyce part of that collection to the University at which a whole half century ago he studied; and all I want to say is that this most moving act of generous fealty is an occasion for celebration.

Brian Westby

Linton waits for the boy to join him in the car that is to take them to the boat, away from his mother. In its perfect description of suffering this strange, confused, sometimes brilliant and – I say hesitantly – seemingly dishonest work almost redeems itself:

It was twenty minutes to five, and Linton stood at the window looking out. He had paid his bill, his luggage had been brought downstairs, and the boots was now mounting guard over it in the hall. He had tipped the servants, had said good-bye to Miss O'Casey, had put on his coat, was ready to start. And suddenly he felt his whole body was shaking with nervous excitement.

This was stupid; he must control himself; there was no reason to be so agitated . . .

But the car was late . . . Well – no, it wasn't, for he heard it at that moment at the door. Linton left the room and walked quickly down the passage.

His baggage was already being stowed away, and while this was proceeding he told the driver what he wanted him to do. He had told him before, but he told him again. He was the same man who had driven them to Fair Head and assured Linton that he understood: – they were to pick up the young gentleman – young Mr Westby – at the school . . . The boots was holding the door open, and Linton took his seat in the car.

Once they were started he felt better. It had been the interval between packing up and the arrival of the car which had proved so trying. He had found it impossible to do anything except watch the hands of the clock; but now, with the journey actually begun, though his excitement and anxiety had not decreased, he felt the relief that comes from action. He leaned back, not looking out of the window as they drove past the post-office, past the turning down to the railway station, past the shops in the main street, and so on to the end of the town. There close to the side of the road and immediately opposite the school, the car drew up, and Linton looked out eagerly. But nobody was waiting.

Of course nobody *would* be waiting, he told himself; he was much too early. His hand was trembling as he unbuttoned his overcoat and fumbled for his watch, getting it out with some difficulty. Yes, he was eight minutes before his time. Once more he leaned back, and tried to drain his mind of all thought. He would not look out again until he heard footsteps and started up.

It was only an old man carrying a spade over his shoulder. Linton leaned out of the window and gazed back along the straight dusty stretch of road. It was empty and bathed in sunlight. He sat now with his watch before him, his eyes fixed on the tiny hand that marked the seconds and was the only one which appeared to be moving. And then suddenly it seemed to be moving very fast indeed, and he watched it completing circle after circle. Somewhere behind him he heard a clock striking the hour, and directly afterwards the rumble and rattle of an approaching cart. The cart lumbered by. It was carrying a load of wet brown seaweed, and a man was walking at the horse's head, holding the bridle. Two girls passed on bicycles and after that nothing till a yellow cat appeared at the entrance of the school, pausing cautiously for a few seconds before gliding on round the side of the house . . . Linton put away his watch and shut his eyes . . . Brian was late . . .

A long time seemed to elapse before he felt a kind of faintness, and struggled against it. He must not – he must not . . . Two or three drops of sweat trickled down his forehead. He took off his hat and wiped his forehead with his hand-kerchief . . .

The driver had got out some time ago, and now he approached Linton's door. 'How long am I to wait, sir?' he asked. 'It's nearly twenty-past.'

'How long *can* you wait?' Linton said, conscious that the man was looking at him strangely.

'Well – better not cut it *too* fine, sir. Say, a quarter to six at the latest.' But he still lingered by the door, and next moment he added awkwardly, 'What about getting out, sir, while we're waiting? You're looking kind of – not too well; and you'd maybe find it fresher outside. You could sit there on that wall.' Linton followed his advice, though he did not sit down. He stood by the wall, resting his hand on it; and the driver stood by the door of the car and presently lit a cigarette. The clock chimed the half hour.

There was still plenty of time, Linton told himself. After all, even if they missed the boat –

Brian had said he would come by the inland road. Should he go back to meet him? It would be easier than waiting like this. But suppose he missed him! – suppose he came by another way! No, it would be safer to wait on here . . . Only, why *didn't* he come? Surely he must know that this kind of thing was an agony . . .

Again he shut his eyes, but opened them, almost at once, at the sound of an approaching car. It was climbing the long straight hill, and as it drew rapidly nearer both its shape and colour were vaguely familiar to Linton. 'Mr Graham's car, sir,' the driver mentioned, as if reading his thought.

The car was almost abreast of them now. Now it *was* abreast; and now it had gone by – leaving a falling cloud of dust behind it. Linton stood gazing after it, though presently only at the empty road and through a kind of mist. What was he waiting for? There was no longer any need to wait. Yet still he stood there until the driver spoke.

'Wasn't the young gentleman in the car, sir?' he said, and Linton's lips moved though no sound issued from them.

'And he never looked out,' the driver muttered half to himself. 'The young lady – she looked out; but *he* kept his head down . . . Well, I suppose we needn't wait any longer.'

Linton took a step forward. 'No,' he said. 'We can go now.'

'You're not well, sir,' the man exclaimed, catching him by the arm and speaking with a rough friendliness. 'If you ask me, I don't think you're fit for this drive. Best let me take you back to the hotel, and put it off till to-morrow.'

'Yes, I'll go back,' Linton murmured. 'Perhaps – to-morrow morning.'

He got into the car, stumbling clumsily over the step, and the driver followed him. But while they were turning, Linton leaned forward. 'Take me to Mrs Belford's,' he said, 'not to the hotel.'

'All right, sir.' And they started.

At the post-office they branched off, going by the inland road, and when they stopped at Mrs Belford's door Linton got out. 'Perhaps you would take my things on to the hotel for me,' he said, 'and perhaps you would explain to them.'

'Hadn't I better wait for you, sir?' the man asked doubtfully.

'No, thanks; I'll be all right now.' He stood motionless till the car had started: then he walked up to the house and knocked at the door.

Again it was Mrs Belford who answered it, though this time she was prepared for visitors and immediately recognized Linton. 'They've gone, Mr Linton,' she said brightly: 'the whole family's gone. It's too bad you're missing them, for it's hardly a quarter of an hour since they left, with young Mr Graham, who's going to drive them home.'

'Yes – I thought I saw them: I just wanted to know –'

Mrs Belford's face had suddenly altered: she was looking at him now the way the driver had looked. Why should they look at him like this? 'Mr Brian –' he said. 'I called in case he might have left a note for me – a message perhaps –'

He broke off as he saw there was no note, no message. Mrs Belford, indeed, appeared to have been struck dumb. But presently she answered, 'No, Mr Linton. No; he left no message.'

Linton felt himself flushing violently. 'Perhaps – at the hotel –' he stammered.

'Well, perhaps,' Mrs Belford agreed. But he could see, he could hear, that she was only trying to be kind and in fact almost immediately she contradicted herself. 'Mr Brian wasn't out all afternoon,' she said, 'and they didn't drive that way.' Next moment, however, she looked at him with an increased uneasiness, as if conscious that for her hearer these words must hold some deeper and more painful significance than any she could find in them. 'Mr Brian wanted to,' she went on – 'he did his best to persuade them to go home by the coast, but Mr Graham had some reason for taking the back road, and the others wished to go that way too. I'm just telling you in case you'd be thinking maybe they stopped to leave word for you in passing, and be disappointed. It's more likely you'll get a letter in the morning.'

Linton said nothing; but neither did he move; and Mrs Belford, not caring to close the door while he still remained there, after waiting a little while was obliged to speak again. 'Mrs Westby didn't make up her mind to go until two o'clock. Both she and Mr Brian seemed very much upset, and though she didn't say so, I'm sure something unexpected must have happened. She only told me it would be necessary for them to get home to-day. Maybe it was young Mr Graham who brought the message, for he was the only one that called, and I know there was no telegrams or letters. It was decided all in a hurry, you might say; and I don't think they can have been expecting you.'

'Thank you,' Linton murmured.

The sun was hurting his eyes, and he pulled his hat lower. For a few seconds he shut his eyes. It was this glare, this heat . . . Then he turned again to the house, but Mrs Belford was gone and the door closed: the house itself, in fact, was several yards away. He didn't remember her shutting the door . . . Perhaps – Anyhow he must not stand here, and he began to descend the hill.

When he reached the hotel he turned to the left and went down to the shore. He found the place where they had sat that morning making their plans. But the tide was farther out now: there was a broad strip of uncovered yellow sand between the rocks and the sea.

It is as beautifully calm as Henry James's, one of Forrest Reid's masters, ending of *Washington Square*: 'Catherine, meanwhile in the parlour, picking up her morsel of fancywork, had seated herself with it again – for life, as it were.' It has, above all, which Reid always has, often when not even writing well, the same gloved sureness and mastery of prose rhythm. I print it in full, not only for its beauty, but because it is not in print and should be. It is, perhaps, the finest single chapter Reid ever wrote.

The plot is improbable enough, Reid choosing to limp along with the conventions that he is plainly unhappy in. Linton has had a near fatal illness. When his doctor had suggested somewhere quiet by the sea to complete his recovery, Ballycastle was instantly in his mind like a vision, and he yielded to it, and came – though he had hardly thought of the place more than twice since he'd last visited it more than twenty years before. As for Stella, with whom he had first visited the place, he had not heard of her since their separation and divorce, other than she had wanted the divorce to marry Westby; and he had no reason to believe he was less or more likely to meet her in Ballycastle than anywhere else. He has just come to this quiet place by the sea to complete his recovery, and not to write – but the trouble was that with the drying up of his creative faculty he has nothing to live for.

As he strolls across the golf links on his first morning in Ballycastle, he feels his life has failed, and he sees where it has failed:

Happiness is only made by affection. Nothing else in the long run matters. The responsibilities and anxieties that accompany affection are in themselves blessings. He had no responsibilities, no anxieties, and he felt that he had lived long enough . . .

Yet he feels beauty endlessly flow by him, but he is powerless to arrest it, through some moral or spiritual disintegration: 'For there was no such thing as beauty apart from a human interpretation of it.' Then he comes on the boy, and recognizes his own first novel by its cover on the dry grass beside him. Linton pauses as the boy looks briefly up but, as he does not look up again, after a hesitation he passes on, but his whole mood has dramatically changed. Everything seems closer to him, acquires a new value. 'The whole scene [has] acquired an *interest*.'

On his way back he engages the boy in conversation about his own first novel, pretending to be a friend of Linton. This arouses the boy's curiosity – his housemaster had loaned him the novel – as to what sort of person Linton is. This, in turn, leads to a discussion about writing in general, and to the boy's confession that he is engaged in writing a novel. As he listens to the boy's description of what he is writing, Linton realizes with dismay, for already he is extraordinarily attracted to the boy – Brian Westby – that it is unlikely to be his kind of novel: but finds consolation in the knowledge 'that if there is one quality which the writings of the very young rarely or never express, it is the spirit of youth', Brian's very attraction for him; and anyhow he regards precocity as being of all the qualities the least promising. They part after Brian promises to bring Linton part of his novel to read.

In alternating chapters, through Brian's eyes and then Linton's, and later still it will be through Linton and Brian together, the scene unfolds, Jamesian lamps playing on the dark central object. It is even coyly played with:

'Don't you think the weather might account for it?' Linton said. 'The sunshine – or possibly the view? The view, as a matter of fact, I'm sure had something to do with it.'

'What view?'

'*My* view . . . You needn't look,' he went on: 'you won't be able to see it, because you're part of it . . .'

There is play, too, throughout the whole work on the words *interest* and *sympathy*, without which Life or Beauty hardly live at all; and they both serve to illumine and veil the paedophilic nature of Linton's love, as the superficial plot improbably reveals that the boy isn't Brian Westby but Brian Linton, Linton's own son, and that he is here for the season in Ballycastle with his mother and half-sister. An accident has conveniently kept the mother indoors until now. For a time, and especially since this first part is prefaced by, 'As in water face answereth to face, so the heart of man to man', it appears that Reid may be using the plot's device to have the writer at the end of his career meet with himself when he was taking the first crude steps in his art; to have set, in fact, his drama firmly in the well of Narcissus. Here, it has some affinity with Hardy's

The Well-Beloved, and this current does flow among the other confused currents throughout most of the work.

In 'The Day-Spring', the novel's second part rung in by Wordsworth's 'Our souls have sight of that immortal sea . . .', Linton's sense of Stella's perfidy in concealing his son's existence from him at their separation and divorce justifies him in continuing to conceal his own true identity. Time had meant everything to him – time which had permitted the boy to get to know him, to get to like him, to form his own impression of him. As in the first part, when the sight of Brian drew him closer to the whole natural scenery, he now determines to use the time to draw closer to the essential in the boy's personality, to reach past his changing or hostile moods, to what Linton feels to be constant, 'when he is responsive, affectionate, sympathetic . . .' The boy now becomes an echo of the artist's traditional relationship with the Muse:

Moreover, he was not only aware of this spirit intellectually, he could actually see it – see it as clearly as he could see the boy's body. And he had a feeling that if he should ever really offend or distress it he would never see it again.

At Linton's suggestion, they begin to collaborate on a story. There is much talk of writing. Reid, through Linton's works, states his own true vision of the activity:

'. . . It's true, Brian, you know, one *can* have such a vision: – something which remains ever afterwards as an influence – which creates an ideal – and a longing that it may come again . . . You don't want to write the kind of stuff which can't be read a second time until the first reading is forgotten – which depends on mere surprise for its interest. There must be something behind – or rather all *through* your work – a spiritual atmosphere. It seems to me that this alone can give it richness. Art isn't just life in the raw: it is a selection from life: it *is* a vision: – life seen through a temperament, as Zola said. And its quality depends on the quality of that temperament far more than on the material out of which the actual pattern is woven.'

But it is here, in this literary hothouse, that the novel is at its worst, Winter coyly hiding its desire for Spring's young body beneath the cloak of Instruction. Side by side with this 'spiritual drawing closer', the 'plot' is pushed uncertainly along. So much artificiality and subterfuge have had to be resorted to that when the prose reaches for what only has interested it from the beginning of 'The Day-Spring', the revelation of the eternal or spiritual in the mortal – the beautiful as it is in itself – has, because of the insincerity and pure embarrassment of much that has led up to it, been drained of much of its credibility. It is as if Proust, while gazing on the sleeping Albertine, should be writing of the death of Bergotte:

The accumulated affection of years had found at last an outlet, and in this passion of protective tenderness which filled him, his life acquired a new meaning and usefulness. Had there not been, in the very fact of their meeting, something which suggested intention, beneficence, a conscious providence? It so easily might not have happened, and that it should have happened made so wonderful a difference! Surely if there were any spiritual reality at all, an emotion which aroused and encouraged all that was best and least selfish in him could not be wasted? And it would be wasted if, to the object of it, it might as well never have been; if it awakened no response, if it did no good, if it lived and died only in itself. For it was primarily an impulse to give, an impulse to share – not only material things, but the beauty of this summer day for instance – the beauty that has been achieved by the spirit and genius of mankind working on, age by age, in poetry and stone and music – the beauty that is goodness. And it was an impulse to protect – to protect from what is hurtful and unclean and evil. And it was an impulse to strengthen and encourage and arm, to implant wisdom and independence, to quicken generosity, admiration, and compassion . . .

Early in 'The Choice', the third and final part, prefaced again by Wordsworth's lines from one of the late sonnets,

> Speak! – though this soft warm heart, once free to hold
> A thousand tender pleasures, thine and mine,
> Be left more desolate, more dreary cold
> Than a forsaken bird's-nest . . .
> Speak, that my torturing doubts their end may know!

the work begins to recover much of its dignity. Yet, since Linton cannot be seen to be conscious of his true feelings, a degree of tact and maturity is thrust on to the boy that his character can hardly credibly support. But when Linton discloses his true identity to the boy on Fair Head, it is with almost physical relief that the prose casts off its dependence on the conventions. (In the light of Stanislaus Joyce's statement on the different position compared to his English counterpart the Irish writer's lack of a tradition immediately places him in, it is interesting that the attempt of Forrest Reid's friend, E. M. Forster, to write outside the conventions in *Maurice* was to prove at least as disastrous as Reid's inability to dispense with them in *Brian Westby*.)

Now that Linton is declared the boy's father, there is no longer need of deceit and subterfuge. It is ironic that one of Linton's first criticisms of his own early work should be: 'In fact it's worse than feeble, it's insincere; and I hate insincerity. I hate it in life; and in art, of course, it's fatal.' Freed finally of the need of insincerity by declaring himself openly the boy's father, the guilty love is legitimized. Clear as the words of Wordsworth the prose rings out that it is speaking of what Proust calls that carnal attraction of any profundity, carrying always within it the possibility of calamity, that men call love:

Presently he was sure it was; and as he sat there, he saw his dream fading, dying, and a grey desolation stretching out in its place. The sudden collapse of what had been more than hope brought with it a kind of physical sickness, as if all that was vital in him had been drained away, leaving a feeling of emptiness, weakness, and exhaustion. 'I'm sorry,' he muttered.

The prose can now cry out in the naked language of love:

It was as instinctive in a human soul to reach after happiness as it was in a plant to turn to the sun, and it would be the veriest hypocrisy to pretend that the knowledge that Brian was happy would in itself be sufficient, should he never see him again, to make *him* happy. It wouldn't. Nor could he now, he thought, find courage to face the existence which had been tolerable a few weeks ago, because, even to reach *that* apathetic state, he would first have to become indifferent, have to forget. And in a sudden final flash of self-knowledge he spoke aloud the truth: 'I cannot live without him.'

I cannot live without him. The heart is caged:

Then the question would come – half shyly, half confidently – 'When do you want me again?' It was extraordinary how those simple words could give him so much pleasure – so much pleasure at the time, so much pleasure afterwards in recollection. A word, an intonation, a passing change of expression, a sudden smile – what was there in things like these which seemed to twine them around one's very heart, so that never afterwards could they be forgotten? ...

Fragments of talk – scenes – pictures – arose before Linton in the golden light: – all the hours that had been happiest and pleasantest . . . And it seemed to him now, that in comparison, nothing else in his life had ever been worth while . . .

As Linton stands unaware of the rain, devouring the sight of the boy in the lighted room, and as the light suddenly goes out, there is the premonition of disaster:

Suddenly, without even a warning flicker, the light upon which Linton's eyes were fixed went out, and he found himself alone in the darkness. So abruptly it happened that he had the sense of a physical shock, violent and brutal. Instantly the empty dreary night was there, and he became conscious of the rain and the cold – and of his own body chilled and cramped and wet, while far down below, on the desolate shore at the cliff's edge, he heard the remote, unresting crying of the sea. Yet the shock was less physical than spiritual. It was like a callous and cruel awakening. Until now, through all his long vigil, he had had the feeling that Brian was with him. The river of light flowing between them had been a bond. Now this bond was broken, and in the darkness Linton knew he was alone. And his loneliness aroused in him an intense desire to attract the boy's attention – to call to him, to throw a handful of gravel at his window – a desire none the less acute because he never for a moment dreamed of yielding to it.

Brian gravely counterpoints it:

As for himself, happiness – lasting happiness – he thought was impossible. He didn't feel that there was anything to be happy about – either in the past, the present, or the future. You were happy in the beginning perhaps, as a puppy or a kitten is happy, but once that brief period was ended, once you came in contact with reality and began to think, the world grew steadily darker . . . He remembered a remark Mr Martin had once made, that life, even at its worst, will always seem to be worth living if there is somebody for whom you care sufficiently. Some one – or some thing . . . But suppose there wasn't? All that remained then was the feeling that there are certain duties which you must do your best to fulfil, though even where *that* feeling came from, or why you had it, you did not know. Only there was nothing else – and the sooner you had done your task the better . . .

The struggle with the mother for the boy's affection is no longer caught in the toils of the plot, has only superficial relevance – as love's sickness feeds on poisonous hope:

It took shape and colour in his imagination – a dream of renewed life and happiness. It grew brighter and brighter, more and more tempting – a dream of their life together – of work and of leisure, of sympathy and friendship, of shared thoughts and feelings and plans, of the long intimacy of firelit winter evenings, of summer holidays, of watching Brian's career, of helping in it, of being present when he had his first success. The dream rose before his inward gaze, like a summer-morning sun over a lonely world, filling the sky and drenching the earth with its light and warmth and blessing. And from a dream it could so easily pass into reality! There would be plenty of time later to discuss details – to plan and to settle. Plenty of time – an enchanted river, cool and fresh and clear, flowing on and on to an unknown sea . . .

But in the last perfect chapter about suffering Forrest Reid was not wrong: 'But the tide was farther out now: there was a broad strip of uncovered yellow sand between the rocks and the sea.'

I think of two other works alongside *Brian Westby*. They are far more truly realized and both German, Mann's *Death in Venice* and Hesse's *Demian*. They are both romantic and written within an established tradition. This Forrest Reid did not have. Linton seems to realize that he has hardly the means to be a novelist at all:

I mean, he's got an ideal; and each of his books is an attempt to express it. So far as it *is* his book, that is to say, for the subject sometimes won't allow it to be. That's what I meant when I said he chose the wrong subjects. There's only the faintest glimmer of what he's really after in op. one, for instance; and in none even of his latest books, perhaps, is it there all the time.

Yet, Forrest Reid has what is more in this ideal, never far and never lost in the beautiful rhythmical prose, a true and permanent voice. And for all its flaws as a work, this voice rings out more powerfully and poignantly in parts of *Brian Westby* than perhaps anywhere else in Reid's many books.

There is a letter of Proust's, where he protests at the exclusion of the village *curé* from the school committee, saying that he should be there with the tobacconist and newsagent and tax collector if for nothing else but the spire of his church, which lifts men's eyes from the avaricious earth. Such a spire is still at the heart of *Brian Westby* and all Reid's work.

That spire is but a symbol of what Reid himself has beautifully called a moral fragrance.

Rich as his best work is in its echoes of great pastoral poetry, as well as the prose rhythms of Henry James and Jane Austen in the delicate sense of timing, the voice might never have become individual without the tension of being Irish, of being outside the tradition he knew and loved; and he might have become just another English writer of no very great distinction. Or, freed of the tension by being born within the tradition, his work might have been more fully realized, less warped. We cannot know. What we do know, a hundred years after his birth, is that he has a firm place, private and a little apart, in a younger tradition, and he is as necessary there as Proust's *curé* should have been if for nothing else but that he wrote uncommonly well.

Dubliners

Dubliners has often been compared to *The Untilled Field*; Moore's stories are seen to have foreshadowed Joyce's, and they are linked in trying to establish a tradition for that dubious enterprise, The Irish Short Story. I do not use 'dubious' in the pejorative sense, other than the absurdity of trying to tout one race or literary form above any other. Remarkable work in the short story has come continually out of Ireland, but it is likely that its very strength is due to the absence of a strong central tradition. Stanislaus Joyce is most persuasive in his articulation of this problem for the Irish writer, if problem it be; for to live here is to come into daily contact with a rampant individualism and localism dominating a vague, fragmented, often purely time-serving, national identity. James Joyce's remark about the citizens of Trieste – 'They are all for the country when they know which country it is'* – could be equally true of his own countrymen. Moore expressed this rowdy individualism, and in some respects he personified it, as did Patrick Kavanagh later, but it is not applicable to Joyce.

The author of *The Lake, A Drama in Muslin, Hail and Farewell* was a writer of genius. The stories in *The Untilled Field* are as fresh on the page today as when Moore wrote them to be translated into Irish in 1900. That he wrote them for translation may have much to do with their

---

* McGahern misquotes Joyce here, probably because he is citing from memory. Compare: James Joyce, *Giacomo Joyce* (London: Faber and Faber, 1968), p. 9. See also McGahern's review of Leonardo Sciascia.

freshness and energy. Moore's artistic insecurity was as great as Kavanagh's. That he was writing the stories for translation probably freed him from a crippling responsibility: he did not have to protect himself with an imposed formality; above all, he did not feel called upon to ruin them with 'style'. In his forthright way Joyce described these stories as 'stupid', but the social inaccuracy he pinpointed we do not notice today. Moore was not so scathing about *Dubliners*, though his reaction was almost as unsympathetic. Given the disparity in temperaments, backgrounds, and upbringings, it could hardly have been otherwise, and it makes the attempt to force the two books into the same tradition extraordinarily misplaced. Moore's genius was erratic and individualistic. Joyce's temperament was essentially classical, and he knew what he was attempting in *Dubliners*:

As for my part and share in the book I have already told all I have to tell. My intention was to write a chapter of the moral history of my country and I chose Dublin for the scene because that city seemed to me the centre of paralysis. I have tried to present it to the indifferent public under four of its aspects: childhood, adolescence, maturity and public life. The stories are arranged in this order. I have written it for the most part in a style of scrupulous meanness and with the conviction that he is a very bold man who dares to alter in the presentment, still more to deform, whatever he has seen and heard. I cannot do any more than this. I cannot alter what I have written. All these objections of which the printer is now the mouthpiece arose in my mind when I was writing the book, both as to the themes of the stories and their manner of treatment. Had I listened to them I would not have written the book.

The authority and plain sense suggests that Joyce was well aware that he was working within a clearly defined tradition. To look towards Moore for any tradition is not useful. All of Moore is self-expression: he constantly substitutes candour for truth. In *Dubliners* there is no self-expression; its truth is in every phrase. 'The author is like God in nature, present everywhere but nowhere visible.'*

I do not think we have to look further than Flaubert and the group of

---

* McGahern misquotes Flaubert's famous aphorism, but without changing its meaning. Compare: *The Letters of Gustave Flaubert 1830–1857*, translated and edited by Francis Steegmuller (London: Faber and Faber, 1981), pp. 173 and 230.

writers close to him who wrote in France at the height of the nineteenth century. The early Joyce, aesthetically at least, would have fitted perfectly into this portrait of the group Henry James wrote to William Dean Howells:

What was discussed in that little smoke-clouded room was chiefly questions of taste, questions of art and form, and the speakers, for the most part, were in aesthetic matter, radicals of the deepest dye. It would have been late in the day to propose among them any discussion of the relation of art to morality, any question as to the degree in which a novel might or might not concern itself with the teaching of a lesson. They had settled these preliminaries long ago, and it would have been primitive and incongruous to recur to them. The conviction that held them together was the conviction that art and morality are two perfectly different things, and that the former has no more to do with the latter than it has with astronomy or embryology. The only duty of a novel was to be well written; that merit included every other of which it was capable.

The first reactions to *Dubliners* were not unlike the criticism Flaubert had to confront until the end of his life: that the work was depressing, with no uplifting message, too withdrawn and cold; and, though all too accurate, lacking in feeling and compassion.

In the light of Joyce's statement – 'I have written it for the most part in a style of scrupulous meanness and with the conviction that he is a very bold man who dares to alter in the presentment, still more to deform, whatever he has seen and heard' – it is interesting to look at the following paragraph from a letter George Sand wrote to Flaubert in 1876:

This wish to portray things as they are, the adventures of life as they present themselves to the eye, is not well thought out, in my opinion. It's all the same to me whether one depicts inert things as a realist or as a poet; but when one touches on the emotions of the human heart, it's a different matter. You cannot detach yourself from this consideration; for you are a human being, and your readers are mankind. Your story is inevitably a conversation between you and the reader. If you show him evil coldly, without ever showing him good, he's angry. He wonders whether he is the villain, or you. What you wanted to do, however, was to rouse him and maintain his interest; and you will never succeed if you are not roused yourself, or if you conceal your emotion so effectively that he thinks you indifferent. He's right: supreme impartiality is antihuman, and a novel must above all be human. If it isn't, the public cares nothing for its being well written, well composed and well observed in every detail. The essential quality – interest – is lacking.

In the same letter she also writes:

I have already challenged your favourite heresy, which is that one writes for twenty intelligent people and doesn't care a fig for the rest. That is not true, since you yourself are irritated and troubled by lack of success . . . One must write for all those who have a thirst to read and can profit from good reading. Then the writer must exhibit his own highest moral principles, and not make a mystery of the moral and beneficent meaning of his book. In *Madame Bovary*, people perceived what that was. If one part of the public cried scandal, the healthier and more numerous part saw in it a severe lesson given to a woman without conscience or faith – a striking lesson to vanity, to ambition, to irrationality. They pitied her: art required that; but the lesson was clear, and it would have been more so, it would have been so for *everybody*, if you had wished it to be, if you had shown more clearly the opinion that you held, and that the public should have held, about the heroine, her husband, and her lovers.

In all of Flaubert's long and rich correspondence, nowhere is his position stated more lucidly than in his reply; despite his obvious affection for George Sand, he is uncompromising:

And now, chère maître – and this is in reply to your last letter – here, I think, is the essential difference between us. You, always, in whatever you do, begin with a great leap toward heaven, and then you return to earth. You start from the *a priori*, from theory, from the ideal. Hence your forbearing attitude toward life, your serenity, your – to use the only word for it – your greatness. I, poor wretch, remain glued to the earth, as though the soles of my shoes were made of lead: everything moves me, everything lacerates and ravages me, and I make every effort to soar. If I tried to assume your way of looking at the world as a whole, I'd become a mere laughingstock. For no matter what you preach to me, I can have no temperament other than my own. Nor any aesthetic other than the one that proceeds from it. You accuse me of 'not letting myself go' naturally. But what about discipline? What about excellence? What do we do with those? I admire Monsieur de Buffon for putting on lace cuffs before sitting down to write. That bit of elegance is a symbol. And, lastly, I try, naively, to have the widest possible sympathies. What more can be asked of anyone?

As for revealing my private opinion of the people I bring on stage, no, no! a thousand times no! I do not recognize my *right* to do so. If the reader doesn't draw from a book the moral it implies, either the reader is an imbecile or the book is false because it lacks exactitude. For the moment a thing is True, it is good. Even obscene books are immoral only if they lack truth . . .

And please note that I execrate what is commonly called 'realism,' even though I'm regarded as one of its high priests.

Make what you can of all that.

To try to please readers seems to me absolutely chimerical. I defy anyone to tell me how one 'pleases.' Success is a result; it must not be a goal. I have never sought it (though I desire it), and I seek it less and less.

In reply George Sand wrote:

You no longer look for anything but the well-turned sentence. That is something, but only something – it isn't the whole of art, it isn't even half of it; it's a quarter at most, and when the three other quarters are fine one does without the one that is not.

He is, if anything, even more forthright:

You make me a little sad, chère maître, when you ascribe to me aesthetic opinions that are not mine. I think that rounding out a sentence is nothing. But that *to write well* is everything. Because: 'Good writing implies strong feeling, accurate thinking, and effective expression.' (Buffon.)

The last term is thus dependent on the two others, since it is necessary to feel strongly in order to think, and to think in order to express. Every bourgeois can have heart and delicacy, be full of the best feelings and the greatest virtues, without for that reason becoming an artist. And finally, I believe Form and Matter to be two abstractions, two entities, neither of which ever exists without the other.

The concern for external Beauty you reproach in me is for me a *method*. When I come upon a bad assonance or a repetition in one of my sentences, I'm sure I'm floundering in the False. By dint of searching, I find the proper expression, which was always the *only* one, and which is, at the same time, harmonious. The word is never lacking when one possesses the idea.

'The concern for external Beauty you reproach me with is for me a *method.*' The method in *Dubliners* is that people, events, and places invariably find their true expression. This is so self-evident that comment becomes superfluous. Everything is important in *Dubliners* because it is there and everything there is held in equal importance.

In 'The Sisters', a priest's madness is toned down to the banal, to social sanity and acceptance: 'Wide-awake and laughing-like to himself . . . So then, of course, when they saw that, that made them think that there was something gone wrong with him . . .' A simple walk through Westmoreland Street in 'Counterparts' is seen through a vain and weak man raising himself in his own eyes:

He came out of the pawn-office joyfully, making a little cylinder of the coins between his thumb and fingers. In Westmoreland Street the footpaths were crowded with young men and women returning from business and ragged urchins ran here and there yelling out the names of the evening editions. The man passed through the crowd, looking on the spectacle generally with proud satisfaction and staring masterfully at the office-girls. His head was full of the noises of tram-gongs and swishing trolleys and his nose already sniffed the curling fumes of punch.

The whole of the Roman Church in the figure of the silenced priest is completely redeemed into the company of the little Dubliners engaged with themselves and the ward elections in 'Ivy Day in the Committee Room':

—Tell me, John, said Mr O'Connor, lighting his cigarette with another pasteboard card.

—Hm?

—What is he exactly?

—Ask me an easier one, said Mr Henchy.

—Fanning and himself seem to me very thick. They're often in Kavanagh's together. Is he a priest at all?

—Mmmyes, I believe so . . . I think he's what you call a black sheep. We haven't many of them, thank God! but we have a few . . . He's an unfortunate man of some kind . . .

—And how does he knock it out? asked Mr O'Connor.

—That's another mystery.

—Is he attached to any chapel or church or institution or –

—No, said Mr Henchy, I think he's travelling on his own account . . . God forgive me, he added, I thought he was the dozen of stout.

The rich local humour is never allowed to stray out of character. It generally consists of badly digested scraps of misinformation which are adhered to like articles of faith once they are possessed, and used like weapons to advance their owner's sense of self-importance, or to belabour that of others. It could have been a happy evening in 'Grace' but they 'vituperated' one another:

—Pope Leo XIII., said Mr Cunningham, was one of the lights of the age. His great idea, you know, was the union of the Latin and Greek Churches. That was the aim of his life.

—I often heard he was one of the most intellectual men in Europe, said Mr Power. I mean apart from his being Pope.

—So he was, said Mr Cunningham, if not *the* most so. His motto, you know, as Pope, was *Lux upon Lux – Light upon Light*.

—No, no, said Mr Fogarty eagerly. I think you're wrong there. It was *Lux in Tenebris*, I think – *Light in Darkness*.

—O yes, said Mr M'Coy, *Tenebrae*.

—Allow me, said Mr Cunningham positively, it was *Lux upon Lux*. And Pius IX. his predecessor's motto was *Crux upon Crux* – that is, *Cross upon Cross* – to show the difference between their two pontificates.

The inference was allowed. Mr Cunningham continued.

—Pope Leo, you know, was a great scholar and a poet.

—He had a strong face, said Mr Kernan.

—Yes, said Mr Cunningham. He wrote Latin poetry.

—Is that so? said Mr Fogarty.

Mr M'Coy tasted his whiskey contentedly and shook his head with a double intention, saying:

—That's no joke, I can tell you.

While Maria in 'Clay' is disturbed and confused and sings the first verse of her song twice over, the prose is never any of these things and remains wonderfully alert and balanced:

But no one tried to show her her mistake; and when she had ended her song Joe was very much moved. He said that there was no time like the long ago and no music for him like poor old Balfe, whatever other people might say; and his eyes filled up so much with tears that he could not find what he was looking for and in the end he had to ask his wife to tell him where the corkscrew was.

Particularly in 'The Boarding House', 'Grace' and 'The Dead', pun, co-incidence, and echo are used as a writer of verse would use the formality of rhyme, deepening the sense of the lives of these mortal-immortal Dubliners, drawing together the related instincts of the religious, the poetic, and the superstitious.

The prose never draws attention to itself except at the end of 'The Dead', and by then it has been earned: throughout, it enters our imaginations as stealthily as the evening invading the avenue in 'Eveline'. Its classical balance allows no room for self-expression: all the seas of the world may be tumbling in Eveline's heart, but her eyes give no sign of love or farewell or recognition.

Joyce does not judge. His characters live within the human constraints in space and time and within their own city. The quality of the language is more important than any system of ethics or aesthetics. Material and form are inseparable. So happy is the union of subject and object that they never become statements of any kind, but in their richness and truth are representations of particular lives – and all of life.

I do not see *Dubliners* as a book of separate stories. The whole work has more the unity and completeness of a novel. Only in the great passages of *Ulysses* was Joyce able to surpass the art of *Dubliners*. In many of these, like the Hades episode, his imagination returns again and again to his first characters, his original material.

The Stories of Alistair MacLeod

Alistair MacLeod's stories have a uniqueness that is rare in the writing of any time. This quality is easily recognizable but is almost impossible to describe.

A different kind of genius marks every magical page of *The Great Gatsby* and 'The Rich Boy' and stories like 'May Day', yet in much of Scott Fitzgerald's other work, where this rare quality is missing, the writing never rises above the level of a competent journeyman, in spite of its unfailing good manners and charm. In true work we see a talent dramatizing a particular area of human experience within a recognizable social setting. Once the talent moves outside these limitations we see it begin to fail, or to work at a less exciting level.

MacLeod's careful work never appears to stray outside what quickens it, and his uniqueness is present in every weighted sentence and the smallest of gestures. He writes about people and a way of life on Cape Breton, Nova Scotia, that has continued relatively unchanged for several generations, since the first settlers went there from Scotland at the time of the Clearances. They work as fishermen, miners, smallholders, loggers, lighthouse keepers, migrant workers. They live in a dramatically beautiful setting provided mostly by nature and hostile to much human endeavour. Animals too have their own place within this proud and fragile interdependence and are part of a fierce and unsentimental tribal affection. The poetic, the religious and the superstitious instincts are always close. As we come to know this world, it is poised on the edge of extinction, like the bald eagles MacLeod writes about so well:

He looked up to the sound of the whooshing eagles' wings. They were flying up the mountain, almost wavering in their flight. Like weary commuters trying to make it home. He had watched them through the long winter as they were forced to fly farther and farther in search of food and open water. He had noticed the dullness of their feathers and the dimming lustre in their intense green eyes. Now, and he was not sure if perhaps it was his eyesight or his angle of vision, the female's wing tips seemed almost to graze the bare branches of the trees as if she might falter and fall.

The eagles had known other seasons and circumstances when their universe was unthreatened:

He had seen the male seize a branch in his powerful talons and soar towards the sky in the sheer exuberance of his power and strength; had seen him snap the branch in two (in a way a strong man might snap a kindling across his knee), letting the two sections fall towards the earth before plummeting after one or the other and snatching it from the air; wheeling and somersaulting and flipping the branch in front of him and swooping under it again and again until, tired of the game, he let it fall to earth.

And he had seen them in the aerial courtship of their mating; had seen them feinting and swerving high above the mountain, outlined against the sky. Had seen them come together, and with talons locked, fall cartwheeling over and over for what seemed like hundreds of feet down towards the land. Separating and braking, like lucky parachutists, at the last minute and gliding individually and parallel to the earth before starting their ascent once more.

MacLeod's world is masculine, in its strengths and its vulnerabilities. The men and women of the stories inhabit separate worlds. They are drawn together for love or procreation, and then part, withdrawing further and further into their own separate world:

Now my wife seems to have gone permanently into a world of avocado appliances and household cleanliness and vicarious experiences provided by the interminable soap operas that fill her television afternoons. She has perhaps gone as deeply into that life as I have into the life of the shafts . . . Yet we are not surprised or critical of each other for she, too, is from a mining family and grew up largely on funds sent home by an absentee father. Perhaps we are but becoming our previous generation.

Sometimes they drift apart naturally through absence, as in the case of the migrant workers – through silence, or the inability to communicate, or through sudden death. This is stated with gentleness and sympathy and palpable regret, but it is also seen to be as unavoidable as fate. In the moving and beautiful 'In the Fall', it is the actual violence that their conflict engenders in the child that draws the man and the woman together:

My father puts his arms around my mother's waist and she does not remove them as I have always seen her do. Instead she reaches up and removes the comb of coral from the heaviness of her hair. I have never seen her hair in all its length before and it stretches out now almost parallel to the earth, its shining black-ness whipped by the wind and glistening like the snow that settles and melts upon it. It surrounds and engulfs my father's head and he buries his face within its heavy darkness, and draws my mother closer toward him.

It is no accident that the man and the woman work together, against all the conventions, in the building of their house, and sing together as they work in the one pure love the stories detail:

On clear still days all of the people living down along the mountain's side and even below in the valley could hear the banging of their hammers and the youthful power of their voices . . . They were married for five years in an inten-sity which it seemed could never last, going more and more into each other and excluding most others for the company of themselves.

Such is the purity and perfection that it can only endure finally in song:

Every note was perfect, as perfect and clear as the waiting water droplet hanging on the fragile leaf or the high suspended eagle outlined against the sky at the apex of its arc. She sang to him until four in the morning, when the first rays of light began to touch the mountain top. And then she was gone.

Often the men need dangerous work for their own physical self-expression. Sometimes they are like gladiators, where women have no place:

For we are always expanding the perimeters of our seeming incarceration. We are always moving downward or inward or forward or, in the driving of our raises, even upward. We are big men engaged in perhaps the most violent of occupations and we have chosen as our adversary walls and faces of massive stone. It is as if the stone of the spherical earth has challenged us to move its weight and find its treasure and we have accepted the challenge and responded with drill and steel and powder and strength and all our ingenuity. In the chill and damp we have given ourselves to the breaking down of walls and barriers. We have sentenced ourselves to enclosures so that we might taste the giddy joy of breaking through. Always hopeful of breaking through, though we know we will never break free.

The miners can be seen in their enclosures as a metaphor for MacLeod's sophisticated yet simple, his sensuous and very supple art:

I have always wished that my children could see me at my work. That they might journey down with me in the dripping cage to the shaft's bottom or walk the eerie tunnels of the drifts that end in walls of staring stone. And that they might see how articulate we are in the accomplishment of what we do . . .

I would like to show them how professional we are and how, in spite of the chill and the water and the dark and the danger, there is perhaps a certain eloquent beauty to be found in what we do. Not the beauty of stillness to be found in gleaming crystal or in the polished hardwood floors to which my wife devotes such care but rather the beauty of motion on the edge of violence, which by its very nature can never long endure.

Running through the work is the deep irony that it is human ingenuity that is bringing to an end this ancient, traditional world just as MacLeod is bringing it to such vivid life. Often this is faced with grim humour, as when Archibald sells his young mare from a breed he has worked with all his life:

'This guy says, I don't know if it's true, that there's this farm outside of Montreal that's connected to a lab or something. Anyway, they've got all these mares there and they keep them bred all the time and they use their water for birth control pills.'

It seemed so preposterous that Archibald was not sure how to react. He scrutinized Carver's scarred yet open face, looking for a hint, some kind of touch, but he could find nothing.

'Yeah,' said Carver. 'They keep the mares pregnant all the time so the women won't be.'

'What do they do with the colts?' said Archibald, thinking that he might try a question for a change.

In the largeness of the vision, even differences are viewed with the same deep sympathy and understanding as likenesses:

She was out of the door almost immediately, turning her truck in a spray of gravel that flicked against his house, the small stones pinging against his windowpane. A muddied bumper sticker read: 'If you're horny, honk your horn.'

He was reminded, as he often was, of Cora, who had been dead now for some fifteen years and who had married another man within a year of her visit to him with her open proposal. And he was touched that his granddaughter should seem so much like his brother's wife instead of like his own.

I think of the novel as the most social of all the art forms, the most closely linked to an idea of society, a shared leisure and a system of manners. The short story does not generally flourish in such a society but comes into its own like song or prayer or superstition in poorer more fragmented communities where individualism and tradition and family and localities and chance or luck are dominant. This appears to be particularly true of Alistair MacLeod's imagined world. The form is inseparable from his material, and his sure talent is happy and at one with them both; it is as if he was sentenced to these small enclosures and made of them his plough. He has turned them into a strength and a glory: the effect is the very opposite of confinement.

The work has a largeness, of feeling, of intellect, of vision, a great openness and generosity, even an old-fashioned courtliness. The stories stand securely outside of fashion while reflecting deep change. In imagination they can move with naturalness across several generations as if they all shared the same eternal day. The small world on Cape Breton opens out to the vast spaces and distances of Canada and the oceans that surround its granite coasts and their people, returning in the summer, or at Christmas, for weddings or bereavements, bringing these vast distances home. In their surefootedness and the slow, sensuous unfolding, the stories gradually acquire the richness and unity of an epic poem or an important novel. Unwittingly, or through that high art that conceals itself, we have been introduced into a complete representation of existence, and the stories take on the truth of the Gaelic songs their people sing. In the mystery of their art they take joy from that very oblivion of which they so movingly sing.

Knowledge of the World:
John Williams's *Augustus*

Augustus was John Williams's most successful novel, winning the National Book Award in 1973, and has appeared in America in four editions since then. Using the epistolary form – fictional memoirs, dispatches, letters – it tells the story of Octavius, a sensitive and scholarly nineteen-year-old, who on the death of his great-uncle Julius Caesar finds himself heir to the vast power of the Roman Empire, now plunged in civil strife by Caesar's murder. Gradually, through a combination of luck, guile, ruthlessness and intelligence, he succeeds in bringing what was then most of the civilized world under the rule of law, giving Rome an unprecedented period of peace and prosperity. He became the first Roman emperor, Augustus Caesar (63 BC–AD 14).

To achieve this, he had to overcome many obstacles, not least his own nature, in order to put down the challenges of such men as Cicero, Brutus, Cassius and finally Mark Antony. Late in his life he imprisoned and exiled his daughter Julia to a remote island under a law he had enacted for adultery, a daughter he was so devoted to that he supervised her education at a time when it was unusual for a woman to be given any schooling. What emerges from the brilliant play of lights that the fictional epistles become is a fascinating portrait in an extraordinary time of a complicated private and public man. Amidst his family, friends and enemies, he deals with the exactitudes that the use and retention of power imposes, and all is brought to such immediate life that it feels as present as Washington today. This is a man who shaped himself in order to shape the world, who put as much faith in superstition as in his intelligence, who loved to gamble on the races and in private to play the dice, preferring the rigours of the battlefield and the solitude of the study to the luxury and pomp of office. As a friend of Virgil and Horace he wanted nothing more than to be a scholar/writer in his youth. He played, in his time, so many roles that at the end he was able to come into the knowledge of the contrariness hidden at the heart of all experience and the ultimate futility of power:

It was more nearly an instinct than knowledge, however, that made me understand that if it is one's destiny to change the world, it is his necessity first to change himself. If he is to obey his destiny, he must find or invent within himself some hard and secret part that is indifferent to himself, to others, and even to the world that he is destined to remake, not to his own desire, but to a nature that he will discover in the process of remaking.

John Williams's four novels are so different from one another in subject matter, setting and time that it has been said that they could pass for the work of four different writers. This is at once both true and untrue. Williams himself discounted his first novel *Nothing But the Night*, and while the talent is obvious it is fair to say that it is less achieved than his other novels. In the powerful and savage *Butcher's Crossing*, he turns to three men who ride into Colorado to hunt for buffalo. At a time when buffalo herds were hunted to extinction they get wind of an undiscovered valley filled with buffalo in the high Rockies. They find this Eden of woods and streams and lush grass with a great herd grazing at peace. The leader of the gang is Miller, an experienced hunter, and they are all betrayed by Miller's obsession to kill every head in the herd while the worsening weather cuts off their retreat. In this anti-Western there are no heroes and no villains. At times the raw power of the writing is almost unbearable as the story unfolds against all the easy myths Hollywood and the East invented for the West.

Stoner followed, the finest novel I know of university life, and it is the single work that most closely shadows Williams's own life and career, though it is set a generation back, in the first half of the twentieth century. Williams grew up poor in Texas during the Depression. His grandparents were dirt farmers, his stepfather a janitor in the post office. Before the Second World War he worked as an announcer at small Texas radio stations. In the war he served in the Army Air Force as a radio operator on aircraft transporting supplies and troops in India, Burma and China, and during breaks in these missions wrote *Nothing But the Night*. At a loose end after the war, he rewrote the novel several times. It was accepted by Swallow Press in Denver, which was run by Allen Swallow, who had revitalized the reputations of Yvor Winters and Allen Tate. Swallow encouraged Williams to go to college on the GI Bill and get a teaching degree. Not unlike Stoner, he received his BA and MA from the University of Denver, his PhD from the University of Missouri, and began his teaching career.

The transition from a buffalo hunt to *Stoner* is dramatic enough by any standard, but the leap from Stoner to Augustus Caesar, from an unregarded academic to the most powerful man on earth in his time, is even more so. In a rare and fascinating interview Williams gave to Bryan Woolley in 1985,* he argues that the transition from *Stoner* to *Augustus* wasn't as great as it might appear:

I was dealing with governance in both instances, and individual responsibilities, and enmities and friendships . . . In a university, professors and others are always vying for power, and there's really no power there. If you have any power at all, it's a nothing. It's really odd that these things would happen in a university, but they do. Except in scale, the machinations for power are about the same in a university as in the Roman Empire or Washington.

Many years before, after *Butcher's Crossing* and before starting work on *Stoner*, a writer Williams knew, Morton Hunt, showed him the page proofs of a book he had written, *A Natural History of Love*, which was a popular history of various attitudes to love from Greek times to the present. While they were talking casually about the book, Hunt told him the story of Augustus, who had a daughter, Julia, whom he loved, but he exiled and imprisoned her in order to save the State because she had broken the laws on adultery that he had enacted. This fascinated Williams and he started to read about it. Discovering that Julia had been effectively written out of the histories, the more he read the more he was

---

* The interview with Bryan Woolley to which McGahern refers both here and in his introduction to *Stoner* is: 'An Interview with John Williams', *Denver Quarterly* 20.3 (Winter 1986): 11–31.

engaged by what he describes as 'the ambivalence between the public necessity and the private want or need' which is at the novel's core. By the time he came to write the novel, he was steeped in that Roman world. In the interview with Woolley he gave his reasons for deciding on the epistolary form. Williams held to the belief that to read anything without joy or pleasure was stupid, that a novel or poem was there to be *experienced* rather than to be understood or explicated:

I didn't think I could handle it in a straight narrative style without making it sound like a Cecil B. DeMille movie or a historical romance. And I didn't want it to sound historical. Those people were very real and contemporaneous to me. I wanted a kind of immediacy in it, but I couldn't figure out how to do it. I also knew that all educated Romans were great letter-writers. Cicero would write eight, ten, twelve letters a day. And the Roman postal service was probably as good as our postal service is today . . . I wanted the characters to present themselves. I didn't want to try to explain them myself. I didn't want to have a twentieth-century vision of the Roman times. So the epistolary form lets the people speak for themselves . . . This provincial notion of how much more advanced *we* are – that's nonsense!

The novel is a triumphant vindication. The world of the Roman Empire is brought as close to us as our own lives.

Any serious reading of *Augustus* and the other novels soon dispels the notion that all of Williams's novels are so diverse as to be the work of so many different writers. In *Augustus* Williams has Gaius Cilnius Maecenas write to Titus Livius (12 BC):

No, it is what I perceive in the tenor of your question that begins to give me offense; for I think (I hope I am wrong) I detect the odor of a moralist. And it seems to me that the moralist is the most useless and contemptible of creatures. He is useless in that he would expend his energies upon making judgments rather than upon gaining knowledge, for the reason that judgment is easy and knowledge is difficult. He is contemptible in that his judgments reflect a vision of himself which in his ignorance and pride he would impose upon the world. I implore you, do not become a moralist; you will destroy your art and your mind. And it would be a heavy burden for even the deepest friendship to bear.

As I have said, we lied; and if I give the reasons for the lie, I do not explain in order to defend. I explain to enlarge your understanding and your knowledge of the world.

Judgement is easy. Knowledge, since it involves an act of the imagination on behalf of others and their situations in the exigencies of the world, is difficult. The diversity of all Williams's novels is for him a method. In order to render the experience of the world, he chooses first to go by the more difficult paths of the Other before entering the closed world of the Self. The same can be said of Williams's prose as what he wrote of Ben Jonson in the preface to his edition of *English Renaissance Poetry*: 'It is, finally, a language that has passed from the starkness and bareness of outer reality through the dark, luxuriant jungle of the self and has emerged from that journey entire and powerful.' This may be the reason he is able to write so faultlessly of that most difficult subject, sex and sexual love. The love scenes from *Stoner* are repeated in a lighter, less intense way in *Augustus*, but they are no less pure. In the letter from Octavius Caesar to Nicholaus of Damascus (AD 14) that closes the novel, Augustus writes:

. . . [I]t is difficult for me to realize that once this body sought release from itself in that of another; and that another sought the same from it. To that instant of pleasure some dedicate all their lives, and become embittered and empty when the body fails, as the body must. They are embittered and empty because they have known only the pleasure, and do not know what that pleasure has meant. For contrary to what we may believe, erotic love is the most unselfish of all the varieties; it seeks to become one with another, and hence to escape the self. This kind of love is the first to die, of course, failing as the body that carries it fails; and for that reason, no doubt, it has been thought by many to be the basest of the varieties. But the fact that it will die, and that we know it will die, makes it more precious; and once we have known it, we are no longer irretrievably trapped and exiled within the self.

Yet it alone is not enough.

And in her island-prison, Augustus's daughter Julia confides to her journal:

To one who has not become adept at the game, the steps of a seduction may appear ludicrous; but they are no more so than the steps of a dance. The dancers dance, and their skill is their pleasure. All is ordained, from the first exchange of glances until the final coupling. And the mutual pretense of both participants is an important part of the elaborate game – each pretends helplessness beneath the weight of passion, and each advance and withdrawal, each consent and refusal, is necessary to the successful consummation of the game. And yet the woman in such a game is always the victor; and I believe she must have a little contempt for her antagonist; for he is conquered and used, as he believes that he is conqueror and user.

When writing about *Stoner*, I found that the material was next to impossible to paraphrase, since the prose had already been so distilled. Similarly, the world of *Augustus* is so various in the brilliant play of lights the different epistles become that selective quotes seem to diminish the richness the whole lights reveal. Neither *Stoner* nor *Augustus* is any less or more achieved than the other: they are simply different works by a remarkable writer working at the very height of his powers.

A Matter of Love: John Williams's *Stoner*

On the opening page of this classic novel of university life, and the life of the heart and the mind, John Williams states bluntly the mark Stoner left behind:

Stoner's colleagues, who held him in no particular esteem when he was alive, speak of him rarely now; to the older ones, his name is a reminder of the end that awaits them all, and to the younger ones it is merely a sound which evokes no sense of the past and no identity with which they can associate themselves or their careers.

In plain prose, which seems able to reflect effortlessly every shade of thought and feeling, Williams proceeds to subvert that familiar worldly judgement by bringing Stoner, and everything linked to him – the time, the place, the people – vividly to life, the passion of the writing masked by coolness and clarity of intelligence.

Stoner's origins were as humble as the earth his parents worked. In the beginning they are shown as hardly more animate than their own clay, but in vivid scenes, such as their attendance at Stoner's wedding to a banker's daughter, their innate dignity and gentleness contradict that easy judgement, and towards the novel's end Stoner himself seems to acquire their mute, patient strength.

Stoner was an only child, and though good at school had no other expectation than to one day take over the fields he was already helping to work. One evening after the day's toil his father said, 'Country agent come by last week . . . Says they have a new school at the University in Columbia. They call it a College of Agriculture. Says he thinks you ought to go.'

At the university he earns his bed and board by working on a nearby farm owned by a first cousin of his mother. This is bare board and hard, brutal work, but he gets through it stoically, in much the same way as he gets through the science courses at the university. 'The course in soil chemistry caught his interest in a general way ... But the required survey of English literature troubled and disquieted him in a way nothing had ever done before.'

The instructor Archer Sloane changes his life. He abandons science to study literature. At the prompting of his mentor, he stays on at the university, labouring on the cousin's farm while obtaining his Master of Arts. At his graduation he tries to tell his parents that he will not be returning to their farm when they come to attend the degree ceremony. 'If you think you ought to stay here and study your books, then that's what you ought to do,' his father concludes towards the end of that moving scene.

The novel then details the outwardly undistinguished career of an assistant professor of English within the walls of the university: his teaching, his reading and his writing, his friendships, his falling in love with an idealized woman, his slow and bitter discovery of that person once they marry, and how their gentle, pliable daughter becomes the wife's chosen battleground. Outside the marriage, Stoner's affair with a young teacher becomes entwined in bitter, vindictive university politics.

This love affair between two intelligent people is brought to life with a rare delicacy. A healthy sensuality is set against their vulnerability as they discover the glory of the first day of the world: 'The life they had together was one that neither of them had really imagined. They grew from passion to lust to a deep sensuality that renewed itself from moment to moment.' They study, they converse, they play. 'They learned to be together without speaking, and they got the habit of repose.' Not only did they find pleasure in one another but meaning, which is drawn with playful, affectionate irony: 'Like all lovers, they spoke much of themselves, as if they might thereby understand the world which made them possible.'

Integral as it is to the plot, the love affair serves more importantly in the overall vision as a source of light in the darkness of Stoner's marriage, a powerful suggestion of the happiness that might have been.

Stoner's wife is a type that can be glimpsed in much American writing, through such different sensibilities as O'Neill, Tennessee Williams, Faulkner, Scott Fitzgerald – beautiful, unstable, educated to observe the surfaces of a privileged and protected society – but never can that type of wife have been revealed as remorselessly as here:

She was educated upon the premise that she would be protected from the gross events that life might thrust in her way, and upon the premise that she had no other duty than to be a graceful and accomplished accessory to that protection, since she belonged to a social and economic class to which protection was an almost sacred obligation . . .

Her moral training, both at the schools she attended and at home, was negative in nature, prohibitive in intent, and almost entirely sexual. The sexuality, however, was indirect and unacknowledged; therefore it suffused every other part of her education, which received most of its energy from that recessive and unspoken moral force. She learned that she would have duties towards her husband and family and that she must fulfil them.

. . . Her needlepoint was delicate and useless, she painted misty landscapes of thin water-color washes, and she played the piano with a forceless but precise hand; yet she was ignorant of her own bodily functions, she had never been alone to care for her own self one day of her life, nor could it ever have occurred to her that she might become responsible for the well-being of another . . .

Upon that inner privacy William Stoner now intruded.

They marry without knowledge of one another and with nothing in common but desire. Their sexual incompatibility is described with the same chasteness as the deep sensuality of the lovers:

When he returned, Edith was in bed with the covers pulled to her chin, her face turned upward, her eyes closed, a thin frown creasing her forehead. Silently, as if she were asleep, Stoner undressed and got into bed beside her. For several moments he lay with his desire, which had become an impersonal thing, belonging to himself alone. He spoke to Edith, as if to find a haven for what he felt; she did not answer. He put his hand upon her and felt beneath the thin cloth of her nightgown the flesh he had longed for. He moved his hand upon her; she did not stir; her frown deepened. Again he spoke, saying her name to silence; then he moved his body upon her, gentle in his clumsiness. When he touched the softness of her thighs she turned her head sharply away and lifted her arm to cover her eyes. She made no sound.

Her sexuality then changes violently when she decides she wants a child and ceases completely as soon as she is pregnant. Soon after their daughter is born, the child becomes the focus of the mother's inner turmoil, her unresolved hatred of Stoner. If the portrait has a flaw, it is in its remorselessness, yet such is the clarity of the understanding that we come to accept it simply as the way things are, in the same way as the love affair becomes the way things ought to have been.

In the many minor portraits the touch is equally sure and psychologically astute: 'Like many men who consider their success incomplete, he was extraordinarily vain and consumed with a sense of his own importance. Every ten or fifteen minutes he removed a large gold watch from his vest pocket, looked at it, and nodded to himself.' There are Stoner's friends: the brilliant David Masters, who gives voice to some of John Williams's own views on the nature of a university, goes to the war and is killed in France; the worldly Gordon Finch who returns from the war with military honours to the university, where he rises to be dean of the faculty. Finch remains Stoner's loyal if sometimes exasperated ally and protector within the university, and his uncomplicated friendship is there for the whole of Stoner's life. We witness, too, the slow decline of Stoner's mentor, Archer Sloane, and the rise of his replacement, Hollis Lomax, who becomes Stoner's implacable enemy. In a novel of brilliant portraits, that of Hollis Lomax is the most complex. Some of the scenes of conflict are almost unbearable in their intensity.

Stoner is also a book about work: the hard unyielding work of the farms; the work of living within a destructive marriage and bringing up a daughter with patient mutability in a poisoned household; the work of teaching literature to mostly unresponsive students. How Williams manages to dramatize this almost impossible material is itself a small miracle.

In a rare interview given late in life, John Williams says of Stoner:

I think he's a *real* hero. A lot of people who have read the novel think that Stoner had such a sad and bad life. I think he had a very good life. He had a better life than most people do, certainly. He was doing what he wanted to do, he had some feeling for what he was doing, he had some sense of the importance of the job he was doing. He was a witness to values that are important . . . The important thing in the novel to me is Stoner's sense of a *job*. Teaching to him is a job

– a job in the good and honorable sense of the word. His job gave him a partic-ular kind of identity and made him what he was . . . [I]t's the love of the thing that's essential. And if you love something, you're going to understand it. And if you understand it, you're going to learn a lot . . . The lack of that love defines a bad teacher . . . You never know all the results of what you do. I think it all boils down to what I was trying to get at in *Stoner*. You've got to keep the faith. The important thing is to keep the tradition going, because the tradition is civilization.

John Williams is best known for his novels, *Nothing But the Night*, *Stoner*, *Butcher's Crossing* and *Augustus*, for which he won the National Book Award in 1973. He also published two volumes of verse and edited a classic anthology of English Renaissance poetry. The novels are not only remarkable for their style but also for the diversity of their settings. No two novels are alike except for the clarity of the prose; they could easily pass for the work of four different writers. In the course of the long and fascinating interview that Williams gave to Bryan Woolley from which I have quoted his remarks about Stoner, it grows clear that of the four novels *Stoner* is the most personal, in that it is closely linked to John Williams's own life and career, without in any way being auto-biographical. The interview was given in 1985, the year Williams retired as Professor of English from the University of Denver where he had taught for thirty years. Pressed towards the end of the interview he complains about the change away from pure study within the universities, the results of which cannot be predicted, towards a purely utilitarian, problem-solving way of doing things more efficiently, both in the arts and sciences, all of which can be predicted and measured. Then, more specifically, Williams complains about the changes in the teaching of literature and the attitude to the text 'as if a novel or a poem is something to be *studied* and *understood*, rather than *experienced*.' Woolley then suggests playfully, 'It's to be exegeted, in other words.' 'Yes! As if it were a kind of puzzle.' 'And literature is written to be entertaining,' Woolley suggests again. 'Absolutely. My God, to read something without joy is stupid.'

There is entertainment of a very high order to be found in *Stoner*, what Williams himself describes as 'an escape into reality' as well as pain and joy. The clarity of the prose is in itself an unadulterated joy. Set a generation back from Williams's own, the novel is distanced not only by this clarity and intelligence but by the way the often unpromising material is so coolly dramatized. The small world of the university opens out to war and politics, to the years of the Depression and the millions who 'once walked erect in their own identities', and then to the whole of life.

If the novel can be said to have one central idea, it is surely that of love, the many forms love takes and all the forces that oppose it. 'It [love] was a passion neither of the mind nor of the flesh; rather, it was a force that comprehended them both, as if they were but the matter of love, its specific substance.'

The Letters of John Butler Yeats

John Butler Yeats was born in County Down in the north of Ireland in 1839. Both his father and grandfather were Church of Ireland rectors. The Yeatses had been Dublin linen merchants. Butler was added to the name when Benjamin Yeats married Mary Butler. This brought an increase in social standing and later some property. When their son, 'Parson' John, married Alice Taylor they became connected to the powerful officials who ran Ireland from Dublin Castle. John Butler Yeats's father, William, was born in a room in the Castle in 1806.

'Parson' John and his son William were easy-going, sociable, affectionate men. As rector of Drumcliffe in County Sligo, Parson John was loved by the whole countryside, by Catholics and Protestants. It was said that when he was about to enter a room in the Drumcliffe Rectory he used to rattle his keys in case he would find servants of the opposite sex in compromising circumstances. He had also a secret drawer constructed in the rectory where he hid liquor from his wife, and when he died he left a large liquor bill which his son William promptly paid.

The son was very like the father. Once, on a visit home to Drumcliffe from Dublin, he saw a favourite horse he had hunted with in his youth reduced to drawing turf to the rectory; he, grown man that he was, sat down by the side of the road and wept. Especially in the letters written late in his life, John Butler Yeats was fond of extolling 'the virtues of the gentle, affectionate Yeatses', his father and grandfather. When William married Jane Corbet, another distinguished, landowning military Anglo-Irish family was added to the name.

For many years John Butler Yeats was the only child of his parents, their chief source of interest and delight, and he took away from these years a very un-Irish quality: a fundamental belief that was to sustain him throughout his long life in the goodness and kindness of people. From an early age he showed a talent for drawing, which his father encouraged. He was hardly ever scolded. 'In those days it was considered bad manners for parents to speak crossly to their children,' he later recalled, 'and so we grew up in what I may call the discipline of good manners as contrasted with the discipline of good morals.'

The father appears to have been charming, scholarly, intelligent, lovable; he had the power, which his son inherited in rich measure, to make people feel better about themselves. Part of this selflessness came from the belief that the Anglo-Irish were socially the equals or the superiors of most other people, and 'that there were no gentlemen in England'. The Church of Ireland in which his father and grandfather served was the church of the oldest Anglo-Irish settlers. It was also the church of Jonathan Swift, Oliver Goldsmith and Laurence Sterne. While the Yeatses always had good relations with their Catholic neighbours – the theoretical enemy – they remained unacquainted with the dour Presbyterian ministers, the recent arrivals in Ireland. They also held the English virtue of 'getting on' in contempt. If John Butler Yeats inherited in rich measure the family gift of making people feel better about themselves, it can also be said that he inherited to the point of disablement their contempt for getting on in the world: he was never to succeed in making a living.

Prior to following his father and grandfather into Trinity College, he was sent to public schools at Seaforth outside Liverpool, and then to the Atholl Academy on the Isle of Man. The puritanical climate of these schools, enforced with constant floggings, was a severe shock after the easy-going Christianity of the Yeatses, but he adapted quickly, remained cheerful and soon was popular with the masters as well as the boys. Attending the Atholl Academy were two brothers from Sligo, Charles and George Pollexfen. Being slow and sullen, they were not popular, but they had a certain animal authority. Even the masters left them alone. 'They were not the sort to be interfered with.' Their father, Charles Pollexfen, was a flour miller and shipper of grain whose sole interest was the accumulation of wealth and the social advancement of his family.

The two families would not have met in Sligo. The Yeatses and their relatives were civil, military and ecclesiastical powers; the Pollexfen sphere was commercial. In a school on the Isle of Man it was natural that the boys were drawn together because of their shared locality, but it was unusual that such markedly different people as Charles Pollexfen and John Butler Yeats would become such close friends. The Yeatses were used to charming people easily. The Pollexfens could not be charmed, and Charles Pollexfen continued to exercise a fascination over John Butler Yeats for the rest of his life. The friendship was to lead to his marriage to Charles's sister, Susan.

Freed from the Atholl Academy, because of his father's social position he was able to move among the best society in Dublin. With his parents he often dined at the home of Sir William Wilde, as his son, W. B. Yeats, was to dine years later at the London home of their son, Oscar Wilde. Both families were friends of the brilliant and rising politician Isaac Butt. J.B.Y. was able to read freely and widely while preparing to enter Trinity College. During those years he lived with his Uncle Robert Corbet at his comfortable home, Sandymount Castle, partly to save on rooms in Trinity. His parents had a large and late increase in children, and the income from the already mortgaged properties was no longer able to take care of the whole family, a common Anglo-Irish dilemma. J.B.Y. didn't take much to Trinity, which was an arm of the British establishment in Ireland, nor did Trinity to him, but while he was there he succeeded in attracting the best minds in the College. They all remained his friends and often tried, unavailingly, to help him in later life.

Over the years he had often discussed theology with his father. Now, under the influence of Auguste Comte, Darwin and John Stuart Mill – 'that man who wore no peacock's feathers' – he asked his father the grounds of his faith. When his father responded that he had found all the proof he needed in Bishop Joseph Butler's *The Analogy of Religion*, his son was fascinated that one book could exercise such power, especially over such an intelligent and unprejudiced man. He came away from his own reading of the book convinced that it proved Christianity to be nothing more than 'myth and fable'. As he was to put it decades later, 'I came in time to recognize natural law, and then lost all interest in a personal god, which seemed merely a myth of the frightened imagination.' This precluded him from following his father, or his Trinity friend John Dowden, into the Church. Dowden was to go on to become Bishop of Edinburgh.

After his final examination J.B.Y. was urged by his teachers to continue his studies in metaphysics and logic, but he was determined to become a barrister, for which profession he was totally unsuited, apart from his eloquence and persuasiveness in argument. This instinct to go against the grain of his own best interests was to remain with him all his life, and at this time it may also have owed something to his sudden engagement to Susan Pollexfen.

On a visit to Sligo in September 1862 to see Charles Pollexfen he was charmed by both the beauty of the place and at finding his old school friend unusually talkative and happy. There he met Susan, and they became engaged after two weeks. She was extremely pretty but taciturn, withdrawn and gloomy like all the Pollexfens. Apart from natural sexual attraction, it was as unlikely an alliance as the friendship with her brother. The Pollexfens despised literature and art but were impressed enough by the Yeats family and the young man's prospects to approve the engagement.

Back in Dublin he began his law studies at the King's Inns but continued sketching and spending more time with his old friends at Trinity than with his law books, when the sudden death of his father made him head of the family and the landlord of mortgaged property. He took no interest then or later in his properties, passing the collection of rents and management of the estate to others, until he was to lose it all.

The following September, a year after they had first met, he married Susan Pollexfen at St John's Church in Sligo. The newlyweds set up house in Dublin. J.B.Y. worked hard at his legal studies, was elected Auditor of the Student Society, and in that capacity made a brilliant speech on 'The True Purpose of a Debating Society' (to discover truth) in the presence of the Lord Chancellor and the most distinguished judges and barristers. So graceful was the speech, diplomatically kept impersonal, and delivered with such charm as well as passion, that the subversive nature of its content (an all-out attack on the basic principles of the Law Society and, by implication, the whole business of the Law) went unnoticed. The speech won approval in the most influential circles.

When he gained entrance to the Bar two months later, it seemed that a distinguished and comfortable career lay just ahead. Nothing could have been further away. He was completely disillusioned with the law. Though he and Susan had by now two children, the future poet W. B. Yeats and his sister Lily, he spent his time sketching at the law courts instead of looking for remunerative legal work. He continued to see his old intellectual circle at Trinity, people Susan instinctively disliked.

Then, in 1867, against the open hostility of his wife and her family, he gave up the house in Dublin, deposited Susan and their children with her parents in Sligo until he was in a position to send for them, and set out for London to enrol at Heatherley's Art School to study drawing.

He enjoyed studying at Heatherley's. His apprenticeship there was long and would have been longer had he not been under pressure from his wife's family in Sligo to show that art could be profitable. He felt he could have acquired real technique and skill had he not had the need to earn money. This was a sentiment he was to continue expressing decades later in New York. In the most fundamental way he felt himself always a beginner throughout the whole length of his long life. He much preferred drawing and studying at Heatherley's with like-minded companions to seeking commissions. He studied with Samuel Butler and became close friends with Nettleship, Ellis, George Wilson, remarkable but unsuccessful men. With Nettleship, Wilson and Ellis he founded a society named the Brotherhood, dedicated to vague, high artistic ideals.

When he took a lease on a house in Fitzroy Road, his wife joined him with their two children and a younger sister for help and companionship. Susan was already expecting a third child, and during those London years the family was to increase to five – another daughter, Lollie (a son, Robert, who was to die young), and the youngest, the future painter Jack Yeats. Susan Yeats missed Sligo and the sea, hated London and her husband's intellectual friends. She appears to have had as little training or skill in the management of a house as her husband had in the management of his career and estates, and increasingly she withdrew into herself. Several months of each year she spent with the children in Sligo. There were many servants and younger aunts to fuss over the children in Sligo, and it became an important influence on all their lives. At this time, J.B.Y. went on a tour of the Dutch galleries with his old Trinity friend John Dowden, the future bishop. In Holland, with his sallow skin and dark good looks, he was taken for an Italian.

When the lease expired on the house in Fitzroy Road, he moved to a house in North End and then to Bedford Park where there was a community of artists and bohemians. It was there that he commenced the education of his eldest son, which became a long battle of minds and formidable wills that was to last his lifetime; and he turned from the romantic pre-Raphaelite influences of his early work to paint and draw what he saw in front of him. His career made little progress. This was almost entirely due to his own character.

When his work was shown it attracted powerful and influential people. Robert Browning and Rossetti called, but for some inexplicable reason, which even he couldn't explain, he failed to return their calls. Temperamentally, he was incapable of finishing a painting. He would work and rework one canvas until it was ruined. His son recollected in *Reveries over Childhood and Youth* how he became known as the son of the painter who scraped out each day the work he had done the day before.

He was fond of drawing out the personalities of the people who sat for his portraits – he was a very sympathetic listener – and would only paint or draw people he liked. He also gave portraits away to these people and could never bring himself to charge enough for finished commissions. This, plainly, exasperated Edward Dowden, his old classmate at Trinity. By this time Dowden was Professor of English at Trinity, a poet and biographer of Shelley. He commissioned a painting for £100, and when Yeats attempted to give it to him for less, Dowden wrote: 'I must object to the ignorance both you and I display of the true relation of buyer and seller. Let me tell you that the seller always looks for a high price, and the highest he can get; and the buyer, then, tries to cut him down to the lowest possible. You and I seem likely to take just the opposite view.' These unbusinesslike traits were to grow more rooted.

There was no reason the family could not with more prudence have lived comfortably on the income the estates brought in, but there was nothing provident about J.B.Y. When suddenly he decided to return to Dublin in 1882, a city he had left for London with such high hopes fifteen years before, his income had been much reduced by further mortgages. Another result of his long London stay was that he returned to Dublin a committed Irish nationalist, with a violent dislike of the whole English class system, especially what he described as the 'sneer of superiority'.

The family took a house in Howth, near the sea, where Susan Yeats was happier. At first J.B.Y. had a studio in an eighteenth-century house on York Street, which quickly became the centre of art and philosophy in Dublin. He later moved to another studio on Stephen's Green. On weekdays the father and W.B. would take the train to Dublin from Howth and have breakfast together in the studio before the son would go to school, all the time talking of Shakespeare and Blake and Balzac, the nature of poetry and poets, and all the things J.B.Y. distrusted: facile beliefs, the art or poetry of ideas, achievements of the logician. Many of the son's central ideas came from the father, some by the path of opposition. This can be richly discerned in the letters when the son's interests turned to mysticism and religion.

During this time he painted a small masterpiece, *The Bird Market*. In cold weather it was said that he used to bring the newspaper boys in from the street to sit for him by the fire while he painted at the far end of the studio. All the time he worked hard but as usual had little to show. He did many portraits but gained no wide reputation, partly because of the absurdly low prices he charged. Also, his free-ranging conversation tended to unsettle his wealthier and more conventional sitters, Catholic and Protestant alike. He thought the Roman Catholic Church 'good for the heart [but] bad for the brain'. Like many Irishmen of his class, he believed that 'had the Irish been Protestants they would have thrown off long ago the English tyranny'. He considered the Catholic religion to be a 'fraud – but it is a beautiful fraud, prepared and written out by the most intellectual and noblest men of their time'; by contrast, the Protestant religion is 'broad but stupid' but has the advantage of encouraging 'freedom of thought and honest thinking'.

Among other artists his reputation stood high. Some, like Sarah Purser, whose work he admired and whose conversation he enjoyed – sometimes they grilled herrings together on a poker over his studio fire – tried to help, but to no avail. He admitted that the trouble ran deeper than mere practicalities: 'The weakness in my character is a distrust of any kind of personal success. It is a very serious fault, and though I constantly deplore it I cannot overcome it.'

The family moved from the house in Howth to a small house in Rathgar that none of them liked. There was less help available from the heavily mortgaged estates. He concluded that it wasn't possible to make a living as a portrait painter in Dublin, and in the summer of 1887 he set out again for London. This time he met with no opposition from his family. All high ideals and hopes had been temporarily set aside. In London he would take whatever hack work he could find in order to support his family.

The years that followed must have been the most difficult in the whole of his experience, and the pain is clearly visible in the letters written towards the end of his life. He did get work, such as black-and-white drawings for illustrated editions of Defoe, work of which he was ashamed, but not enough work to make any financial difference. Soon after the move back to London, Susan Yeats had her first stroke, and she remained an invalid until her death in 1900. 'My mother was so long ill, so long fading out of life, that the last fading out of all made no noticeable change in our lives,' her son wrote. J.B.Y. continued to paint and draw, but those who sat for him had little money. For one portrait he was rewarded with the gift of an old bicycle. Often the family had to resort to many of the subterfuges of the genteel poor to get by, while the father was beginning to be surpassed in artistic reputation by both his sons. Not surprisingly, with such an example so close to them in their formative years, they both proved astute and hardheaded businessmen in the pursuit of their own careers.

There were consolations. J.B.Y. was able to renew old friendships. In spite of his worldly failure, his personality continued to attract new and stimulating people. All the accounts of the hours passed in Bedford Park speak of the cheerfulness of its atmosphere, the quality of the conversation, the intellectual debate and the great charm; but what was hidden had to be very different. Lily worked in the embroidery workshop run by the disturbed and demanding daughter of William Morris, May Morris. For the first six months after she left this employment, Lily had difficulty believing that every day wasn't a Saturday and Sunday. The energetic but troubled Lollie earned money by teaching brushwork painting. She also wrote a number of books on the subject which were both well received and made money.

Watching his daughters work and struggle, J.B.Y. felt his own lacks even more keenly. In a quarrel with Willie late in his life he articulated bitterly his feelings that the normal expectations they should have enjoyed for young women of their rank and talent had been sacrificed on the altars of their brothers' early careers and his own woeful ineffectiveness. Not dissimilar are the same self-recriminations on the life he had provided for Susan Yeats, her withdrawal into illness and early death. 'Had I had money your mother would never have been ill and would be alive now – that is the thought always with me – *and I would have done anything to get it for her* – but had not the art.'

Soon after her death his estates were sold, leaving him the astonishing sum of £869 after the mortgages were paid. 'Any other man would have known it was coming,' his daughter Lily recorded his astonishment on receiving the lawyer's letter. 'My father has paid off all his debts,' his poet-son wrote, adding enigmatically, 'and must feel very unlike his old self.' What was left over he spent on a two-week visit to Paris; nobody begrudged him that.

When J.B.Y. was close to sixty he acquired the first of his important patrons. Lady Gregory had taken up the cause of W.B.Y. and commissioned the father to do a sketch of his son. She was impressed by the drawing and gave him further commissions for pencil sketches of prominent figures in the Irish Literary Revival. Lady Gregory saw that his skill lay in the pencil sketch, done in a single sitting and not easy to revise and, in his case, eventually to ruin. Also, it allowed him to concentrate purely on the face, which was his chief interest. At a single stroke she gave him self-respect and an income, and a pattern was set that would be continued by her nephew, Hugh Lane, and the distinguished American lawyer and patron John Quinn. The result was a whole gallery of brilliant pencil sketches.

A visit to Lady Gregory's house in Coole Park was less successful. As usual, he enjoyed himself hugely, wandering far and wide about the area, ignoring mealtimes and all other arrangements. 'I think him the most trying visitor possible to a house,' Lady Gregory told John Quinn, with whom she had a brief affair years later in New York. 'Space and time

mean nothing to him, he goes his own way, spoiling portraits as hopefully as he begins them, and always on the verge of a great future.' Her
opinion was not improved by his domestic habits. He was careless of his
laundry and socks, which he dropped anywhere, and was neat only with
his brushes, oils and palette.

In Dublin Sarah Purser had long been angered by the neglect shown
to the work of her old friend and his own ineffectiveness. She urged him
to submit portraits for the Royal Hibernian Academy Exhibition of 1901.
When they were rejected she was furious. Her formidable energies were
roused to organize and put on at her own expense a major exhibition of
his work and that of another neglected painter she admired, Nathaniel
Hone. Miss Purser worked round the clock: she persuaded owners of
J.B.Y.'s sketches, portraits, watercolours, pastels, chalks and oils to lend
them for the exhibition, forty-four in all. J.B.Y. gave her no help. He
almost didn't attend the exhibition, only leaving London for Dublin at
the last minute. All his other moves had been made on impulse and with
insufficient planning. This move was made without any planning. He
was never to see his house in Bedford Park again.

The exhibition was a huge success, not only in the number but in the
quality of the visitors it attracted. The reviews were glowing. At the age
of sixty-two he was for the first time established and famous. From such
a position a different man could have gone on without much difficulty
to a comfortable and honoured old age. He remained as poor as ever.
Hugh Lane, the successful art dealer after whom Dublin's Municipal
Gallery is named and whose early death on the *Lusitania* was to lead to
much friction between London and Dublin over what became known as
the Lane Bequest, provided J.B.Y. with as many portrait commissions as
he wanted. Eventually Lane was forced to withdraw the offer for all the
old reasons, particularly the spoiling of canvases through relentless
reworking and J.B.Y.'s exorbitant demands on the time of his rich and
often busy sitters. Reports of the exhibition reached John Quinn in New
York, and he wrote to the painter with an offer for commissions. Quinn
was to remain a source of all sorts of help for the rest of J.B.Y.'s life.

Dublin was now entering the most exciting and interesting period of
its artistic life. His two daughters moved from London to Dublin to set
up the Dun Emer embroidery and printing works (later the Cuala

Press). The National Theatre was founded by his son. In all these artistic activities J.B.Y. was to play a full part, not only with his sketches of the dramatis personae but even confronting the protesters from the Abbey stage during the *Playboy* riots. In 'Beautiful Lofty Things' W.B.Y. was to recall:

> Beautiful lofty things; O'Leary's noble head;
> My father upon the Abbey stage, before him a raging crowd.
> 'This Land of Saints', and then as the applause died out,
> 'Of plaster Saints'; his beautiful mischievous head thrown back.

In the letters, J.B.Y. recounts what actually happened and how everything had been altered for artistic purposes.

On a more domestic note, the family set up house again, this time in Terenure, and the painter and Lollie used to walk the five miles from the house to the studio in Stephen's Green. Lollie was highly strung and argumentative. She had been disappointed in love, and her father found her intense, painful conversation as trying as did the rest of the family. They would always start out together, but on the way would begin to argue over the shortest route to the studio. They would disagree and separate. He was always the first to arrive. It was said that he ran most of the way.

Then in 1907, in his sixty-eighth year, J.B.Y. left Dublin for ever in much the same way as he had left London. He had never visited Italy, and Hugh Lane had the idea of creating a bursary to send him there. Money was contributed cheerfully. J.B.Y., however, disliked being forced to do what other people planned, no matter how agreeable. At the same time, Lily was about to go to New York to represent Dun Emer at the Trade Fair, and he decided to use the Italian bursary to travel with her to New York. Quinn and other people he had met were in New York. There was a possibility of commissions and a world of other opportunities opening up in a wonderful late flowering.

Quinn was angry when he heard the news, and wrote to the painter to berate him for choosing the worst possible time to appear in New York. The warning had no effect. In his studio he left his unfinished paintings with the text of his unfinished play, his brushes and paints carefully put away and ready for use. He didn't postpone a speech he was to deliver on

4 March in Dublin because he said he would be back in time for its delivery. At Liverpool he was seen off by his old friend Oliver Elton, Professor of English at the University there:

In December 1907, accompanied by Miss Yeats, he stayed with us in Liverpool, in high spirits, for they had taken tickets to New York; yet somewhat distraught. There had been many efforts to keep him back; and afterwards he was often pressed, and even tempted, to return, but in the end he always resisted, refusing, unlike the birds, to change his mind. I think he was impelled, first of all, by the racial instinct, *vis a tergo*, to quit the homeland, still under alien rule, blistered with internal strife and evil memories, and ever oppressed by the difficulty of living. Another impulse, *vis a fronte*, was, I judge, his inextinguishable curiosity; the passion for a new life that would provide a new spectacle of men and women and manners; and perhaps a new hope, perhaps a living for the artist. The hope, as all his letters show, was more than realised ... As he and his daughter sailed, we watched them from the landing-stage, and my wife said 'He will never come back'. His soft hat and white beard vanished slowly as they waved to us. He too watched, and he wrote a few years later: 'I hope Mrs Elton is quite well. The last thing to disappear in the mist of distance at Liverpool was the tuft that ornamented her hat . . .'

Quinn met them at the pier. Despite his attempt to dissuade J.B.Y. from travelling to New York, he showed them wonderful hospitality over the following weeks. They were among the happiest of J.B.Y.'s life. While Lily sold goods each day at the Irish Exhibition in Madison Square Garden, her father sought commissions. Again he was convinced that fortune awaited him and again he was more sought after for his conversation than his art. As usual, he did not help his own case. Quinn discovered that he was up to his old tricks of giving sketches away for nothing to people he liked. 'Of course if that gets out,' Quinn wrote censoriously, 'other people will expect to have their sketches made on the same basis.' Lily had sold all the Dun Emer goods at a handsome profit. She wanted to go home, but her father refused to return. She kept postponing their sailing date in the hope he would tire of New York. It was a forlorn hope. 'To leave New York is to leave a huge fair where at any moment I might meet with some huge bit of luck.' Eventually, on 6 June, after many postponements, she was forced to sail without him. They would not see one another again. She was never to return to New York and his 'Italian' holiday was to last fourteen more years. It is primarily to this separation from his family and friends that we owe the wealth of these letters.

J.B.Y. never quite fell out of love with New York, but the old perplexity of an empty purse proved as durable a companion as before. He did get paid for sketches and portraits, for giving lectures and talks to various societies, for writing on all kinds of subjects for different magazines, but it was never sufficient. Gradually, as he discovered his own circle of friends, he moved away from the rich houses he was introduced to by John Quinn, and, after being evicted from his studio on 44th Street, settled in a boarding house on West 29th Street that was run by three Breton sisters named Petitpas. They had built a reputation for good food and fierce honesty. People who disputed their bills were accused of impugning their honour and not permitted to return. The sisters agreed to his becoming a lodger in one of their upstairs rooms. He had been dining regularly in the restaurant for about a year, and they knew that no matter how high his account rose, the rich lawyer, 'Mistaire Quinn', would stand behind their client. His needs were simple – pea soup, red wine and talk: 'It is as natural for man to talk as it is for birds to sing.' Among the writers and intellectuals drawn to him were two American painters, Robert Henri, a founder of the Ashcan School, and John Sloan, who became a close friend.

In spite of J.B.Y.'s own claims, he had rich opportunities to succeed, and the reasons for his continuing failure – if it can be described as such – lay, as before, deep in his own character. Quinn told J.B.Y. that he was considering asking President Roosevelt to sit for a portrait (he had persuaded the President to attend the influential Armory Show in February 1913, thus lending it respectability, though Roosevelt loathed much of what was on view, particularly the work of Marcel Duchamp). Quinn felt that if J.B.Y. could manage a successful portrait of the President, all sorts of lucrative doors would be thrown open to the old artist; but the idea was dropped when Quinn watched J.B.Y. do a fine portrait of Dorothy Coates, Quinn's mistress at the time, and proceed to ruin it with alterations after the portrait was paid for and signed. So enraged was Quinn that he almost seized the brush from the meddling painter's hand, and J.B.Y. was equally enraged by Quinn's conduct. What we can be fairly certain of is that even if he had managed to paint a successful portrait of the President, he would have contrived to make as little of it as he had made of the great success of the Dublin exhibition Sarah Purser had organized.

In New York, as everywhere else, he went his own sweet way. He sketched and painted. Every day he went for long walks. He had special pocket editions of Shakespeare made to take with him on those walks. Often on impulse he boarded a ferry, allowing it to carry him where it would. With the painter John Sloan he attended baseball games. Occasionally in the evenings he gave talks for small fees, but nearly every evening he dined with his circle of friends at the Petitpas restaurant. Attempts were made from time to time to get him to return to Dublin. Sometimes he even hinted that he had it in mind to return: to make a firm decision to settle in New York would be going too far; but by allowing that he was on an extended holiday that would one day end he retained total freedom. Each day proved sufficient unto itself, and in the mean time he was in the middle of a great carnival.

By this time, John Quinn and W. B. Yeats had become estranged over the same Dorothy Coates whose portrait J.B.Y. had continued to improve until it was ruined, and it was Lily Yeats who agreed with Quinn that it would be useless to give her father any large sum of money. It would be gone in a few weeks and things would be back to where they were. Quinn decided on a subtle plan that would both buttress the old artist's pride and allow him to pay off his debts, leaving him enough to purchase his passage back to Dublin and to live for a time in some ease and comfort there. On the night of 3 February 1911, eleven years to the day before his death, J.B.Y. was given a commission by Quinn in the presence of John Sloan for a self-portrait in oils, for which Quinn would pay whatever the artist asked. J.B.Y. was overjoyed. Though it was specified that it be of a head only, before too long it grew to a full-length, life-sized portrait. Glimpses of its progress are given in the letters, the history of which must stand as one of the longest in commissioned art as well as a monument to J.B.Y.'s lifelong belief that as things constantly change, nothing is ever really finished.

As J.B.Y.'s financial circumstances worsened he was forced to turn to his poet-son for support. The son's patronage was harsh if understandable. Exaggerated rumours of the old man's straitened circumstances had started to circulate in Dublin. In 1914, W. B. Yeats was in New York at the start of one of his American lecture tours, and Dolly Sloan, the goodhearted but alcoholic wife of John Sloan, decided to confront their friend's son. She knocked at the door of his hotel room, and, when he allowed her to enter, complained that his father was in poor health, without money, and that it was his duty to help. He didn't reply. Looking down at the small woman from his great height, he was said to have bowed her to the door with the one phrase, 'Good day, Madam.'

The visit must have jolted the poet. His attitude to his father changed noticeably. J.B.Y. was intensely relieved by this unexpected change and did not want to risk a reversal by bringing up the disagreeable matter of his debts; as usual, he just wanted to enjoy this new good weather. He attended a talk W.B.Y. gave to the Poetry Society accompanied by his great friend Jeanne Robert Forster. Later, Willie spent three evenings at the Petitpas restaurant, where some of the ladies tried to teach him to dance. The sight of the tall, aristocratic, tone-deaf poet attempting to dance must have been quite a spectacle. Not until W.B.Y. was well launched on the tour had the father the courage to write to him about his debts. W.B.Y. responded at once with a cheque to cover most of the debt owed to the Petitpas. In the mean time, he and Quinn patched up their quarrel, and when the poet returned to New York they came to an agreement on how to care for the father.

For many years Quinn had been collecting literary manuscripts as well as paintings. Now he agreed to purchase all of W.B.Y.'s manuscripts and to deposit the monies in a trust account. J.B.Y. would not get to handle any of this money. His debts with the Petitpas sisters would be allowed to accumulate and then be reduced from time to time. In this way it was hoped that J.B.Y. could be kept in contact with the realities of his board and lodgings. When W.B. returned to Dublin he wrote to his father offering to pay off all his debts and to purchase an ocean voyage. He promised that after a season in Dublin J.B.Y. would be free to return to New York if he so wished. The old fox was not about to be trapped. He refused: 'No. When I go home it will be for good.'

Quinn continued to commission sketches from J.B.Y., which he paid for in cash. He also continued to value his company, inviting him to dinners and weekends. On one of these weekends he gave him James

Joyce's *Dubliners* to read. J.B.Y. read half the stories. 'Good God, how depressing. One always knew there were such persons and places in Dublin, but one never wanted to see them,' he said as he returned the book, but conceded that it was 'a great book'. In 1915 he was knocked down by a cart on 6th Avenue while, as Quinn put it, 'strolling like an emperor in his garden'. Typically, he made light of his injuries, but they were worse than he pretended to the Petitpas sisters. As if to underscore the wisdom of not allowing him to handle money, J.B.Y. wrote expansively to his daughter that he ordered fancy drinks for all his friends in the restaurant and had three Scotches himself on learning that his boarding bill had been paid: 'Prosperity opens the heart and loosens the tongue.'

He was under a great deal of pressure to write his memoirs, but instead finished a play nobody wanted. Meanwhile the work on the self-portrait continued. 'This portrait will last my lifetime and get better and better and never be finished,' he boasted, well away from Quinn's hearing. Two months later he was saying that he had begun it 'afresh'.

W.B.Y.'s late marriage to George Hyde-Lees delighted him. When the couple visited New York, he was charmed by the intelligent young wife the poet had won, and was delighted again by the birth of his grandchildren. All his life he adored weddings and the idea of large, happy families.

At the end of 1918, when all America was celebrating the Armistice, he almost died of pneumonia in his room. As soon as Quinn got news of the illness he sent one of his own doctors to the boarding house with orders to have the patient transferred to hospital accompanied by a special nurse. There was no sign of indecision or weakness once the seventy-nine-year-old artist's freedom was threatened. He refused to go to hospital. Quinn then hired a nurse, a Miss Finch-Smith. He found the boarding house so unpleasant that after one visit he never returned, but knowing that Jeanne Robert Forster was a special friend of the old man wrote asking her to oversee the illness. Because of the battle between the nurse and the stubborn painter, the illness had its hilarious moments. He persistently referred to the nurse as the orang-utan. He often locked the door when she left the room and refused to allow her back in. She proved to be as tough as he was, and beat him when he dried his hands on the sheet instead of on the towel she had pinned to the sheet for that purpose. Quinn's sympathies were with the nurse. When the patient was well on the way to recovery he proposed that J.B.Y. go to the country for a time of convalescence with Nurse Finch-Smith. J.B.Y. responded that he would as soon travel with an orang-utan as that dragon. Quinn replied:

Of course, if you have some soubrette in mind who is willing to go with you, or some ex-cabaret dancer or some other sort of ex-parlor entertainer who has the qualities that you apparently looked for in your nurse, and if such a female is willing to go with you, either at no wages, which would mean going with you for love, or at wages not to exceed that of the nurse, which is $35 a week, and if that female can supply me with a reasonably satisfactory certificate of hygienic purity and competence, I am willing to agree to have her go with you.

But somehow cleanliness and cabaret entertainers do not seem to go together. Hygiene and chorus girls do not seem to me to be synonymous. Knowledge of nursing and verbal pyrotechnics do not always exist in the same female uniform.

J.B.Y. admitted that the letter was amusing and had made him laugh but still refused to go to the country. Even more interesting might be Quinn's response to a report he received in May 1921 on the portrait he had commissioned more than ten years before:

It fills my life. I have never an idle moment or idle thought. It is a long revel, just as satisfying to me as Gibbon's *Decline and Fall of the Roman Empire*, and I think I have been at it almost as many years. This morning I scraped away all the paint, but now it looks very promising.

J.B.Y.'s health was failing fast though his mind remained as sharp as ever. The closing letters are filled with awareness of his fast approaching end. His sense of good manners would never have allowed him to state it openly or to complain. Quinn chose not to write of his true condition to the Yeats family until after J.B.Y.'s death when he sent this graphic and moving account:

When he was in my apartment one Sunday, I witnessed a tragic thing . . . I had gone to the room in my apartment where the telephone is to answer a telephone call. While I was talking on the telephone he passed down the corridor to the end of the hall and into my bath-room. Just as I had finished talking I met him in the hallway coming back. His lips were red. I thought that he had a fever, then I got the odor of creosote which I realized that he had taken . . . I saw that he had had a great shock but the kind thing was to say nothing. He said, 'Well, Quinn, I think I will be going now.' But I asked him to sit down for a little while and kept him talking, not wanting him to leave in that shocked condition. So we smoked and talked for an hour or longer . . .

When I came back to my bathroom afterwards I found traces of blood on the toilet seat. He had wiped most of it off but there were traces of a hemorrhage. It was a tragic thing and very brave of him not to speak of it. I knew what that hemorrhage meant.

Had he died then it would probably have been merciful. He would have escaped the publication of one of his son's autobiographies, *Four Years*, an account of those years in Bedford Park that probably marked the low point of the father's life and career. He was deeply wounded. Bitter memories were revived – of his own sense of inadequacy and failure, of an aloof and imperious son who looked down on him, considering him a failure as a man and artist. He felt especially keenly the sacrifices that had been forced on his daughters. Years of restraint were cast aside when he wrote to Willic:

As to Lily and Lollie, they were too busy to be 'enraged' about anything, Lily working all day at the Morrises, and Lollie dashing about giving lectures on picture painting and earning close on 300 pounds a year, and one year more than 300, while both gave all their earnings to the house. And besides all this work, of course, they did the housekeeping, and had to contrive things and see to things for their invalid mother – and all this when quite young girls, and cut off from living like other young ladies of their age and standing. They paid the penalty for having a father who did not earn enough and was besides an Irish landlord. I am sure that 'enraged family' was a slip of the pen. I fancy you yourself did regard us as having the brand of inferiority, but they didn't mind. What woman does?*

---

* This letter, written on 24 June 1921, was not included in McGahern's edition of John Butler Yeats's letters, nor in Joseph Hone's original 1944 edition on which McGahern's selection was based. McGahern had probably read it in William M. Murphy's *Prodigal Father: The Life of John Butler Yeats (1839–1922)* (Ithaca and London: Cornell University Press, 1978), pp. 528–9, of which he owned a copy and to which he refers elsewhere in this essay.

Willie was unmoved and J.B.Y. had to resist a new attempt to force him to return to Dublin, more concerted and determined than anything tried previously. In a letter W.B.Y. wrote to Quinn his exasperation with his father surfaced clearly, sharpened by the most recent quarrel and his part in the futile attempts to force him to return:

It is this infirmity of will which has prevented him from finishing his pictures and ruined his career. He even hates the sign of will in others. It used to cause quarrels between me and him, for the qualities which I thought necessary to success in art or in life seemed to him 'egotism' or 'selfishness' or 'brutality'. I had to escape this family drifting, innocent and helpless, and the need for that drew me to dominating men like Henley and Morris and estranged me from his friends, even from sympathetic unique York Powell. I find even from letters written in the last few months that he has not quite forgiven me.

The differences were essentially irreconcilable since they were rooted in character and conflicting visions of life. To J.B.Y. 'infirmity of the will' would be an insulting expression of his refusal to attempt to climb the greasy pole of success, yielding up all that he held dear in life to the English and Pollexfen principle of 'getting on'. To W. B. Yeats, the idea of a purely private artist was unthinkable. His finest verse play, *Purgatory*, has only a father and son on stage, their natural roles subverted. In its starkness of symbol and setting it presages *Waiting for Godot*. Based on a Sligo ghost story, *Purgatory* contains many of Yeats's recurring ideas. A play as powerful and rich will act as many mirrors, and it has always fascinated me that every line of *Purgatory* is filled with the drama of opposites.

Despite all the pressure put on him to return to Dublin, J.B.Y. remained unbudgeable. Quinn's words to W.B.Y. on their last attempt to get him to go home can only make one smile in the light of the previous correspondence: 'It was not infirmity of the will that made his decision this time. It was strength of will, sheer stubbornness.' J.B.Y. put it more agreeably when he said that it was his 'energy' that kept him in New York.

He continued to sketch, to read, to write letters, to see people, though keeping more than usual to his room. The only person he avoided was Quinn, perhaps fearing a lecture or, worse, being hauled off to a doctor.

He made a final attempt to catch the essence of Jeanne Robert Forster: 'Give me another chance to save my soul and your face. Both are for eternity.' He had always tried to engage his sitters in conversation. Now he carried on a spiritual dialogue with Mrs Forster as he sketched:

He asked whether she thought one could know what was going on shortly after one died. She replied that although she didn't think much about the subject, she felt 'sure' that *she* would know. 'Willie would have a good deal to say about it, I daresay,' he responded. Then, after some seconds he added, 'By Jove, I'd like to believe it.' 'Why?' she asked. 'Because I would enjoy going to my own funeral,' he replied, and then continued 'with great animation': 'Yes, I'd enjoy seeing all the strangeness, looking at myself, watching the people, hearing what they said. I'd like to go through it all with my sketchbook. Think of what a sketchbook a man would have! Sketches of his friends at his own funeral! And I'd have such a curiosity about everything. By Jove! I would be interested. I might even do a sketch of myself.'

When he died days later in the upstairs room of the Petitpas boarding house, the self-portrait that had been commissioned eleven years before to the very day stared down from the wall at the lifeless body. In the light of his belief that nothing is ever finished since everything is continually changing, it could not be said to be finished or unfinished. On 3 February 1922, the artist and his portrait had both just 'stopped'.

J.B.Y. loved letters. Along with the works of Shakespeare and Montaigne, the letters of Lamb and Keats were always by his side during the New York years. Keats's idea of 'negative capability' – 'When man is capable of being in uncertainties, mysteries, doubts without any irritable reaching after fact and reason' – must have exercised particular fascination. Two selections of his own letters were published in his lifetime. They gave him enormous pleasure and some trepidation. The first was by Ezra Pound in 1917 and was an immediate success. Needless to say, the author himself provided nothing but the material: he didn't even bother to read the proofs, waiting until he had the printed copy in his hands before regis-tering a complaint over a misprint caused by Pound's cavalier editing. The selection has a didactic tone that is closer to Pound's personality than to J.B.Y.'s, and was brought about to some extent by the choosing of short extracts from the letters. It is fair to add that Pound was constrained in his selection by J.B.Y.'s inordinate fear of giving offence, and nothing could be more modest than Pound's extraordinarily charming introduction. Also, it is very unlikely that the letters would have been a success without Pound's genius for publicity. The then relatively unknown T. S. Eliot was persuaded to write about them in the *Egoist*:

Mr J. B. Yeats is a highly civilized man; and he has the kingdom of leisure within him. Leisure for Mr Yeats means writing well even when not writing for publication: writing with dignity and ease and reserve. And letter-writing for him means the grace and urbanity of the talker and the depth of the solitary; it means a resolute return to a few important issues, not ceaseless loquacity about novelties . . .

Perhaps New York, encircling the writer with loneliness, has done him a service. Mr Yeats could do New York a service, if New York would listen, but America will probably succeed in shutting its ears . . .

Mr Yeats understands poetry better than any one I have ever known who was not a poet, and better than most of those who have the reputation of poets.

In 1920 a second selection was made by Lennox Robinson, the playwright and manager of the Abbey Theatre. It was much less narrow than the Pound selection, and because it included whole letters or large chunks of letters it had much more the full flavour of J.B.Y.'s personality. The book was more readable than Pound's, and it quickly sold out. 'I am foolish over my own book,' J.B.Y. wrote to his daughter. 'I have a copy which I constantly read and find very illuminating. Swift confesses to something of the sort with his own compositions.' At the Petitpas restaurant he did little sketches on the flyleaf of the copies his friends brought to him for his signature.

The letters did not appear again until 1944 when Faber and Faber (T. S. Eliot was then an Editorial Director) brought out a more comprehensive selection, edited and with a memoir by Joseph Hone, the distinguished biographer of W. B. Yeats, Moore and Tonks, and including a preface by J.B.Y.'s friend, Oliver Elton. It is from this edition that the present selection is drawn. I was tempted to include some letters from *Letters from Bedford Park*, edited by William M. Murphy, particularly two letters to Sarah Purser, but felt that they would only illuminate more poignantly what is already sufficiently evident. For my own attempt to provide a rough, short sketch of the life as a background to the letters I am particularly indebted to William M. Murphy's rich and sympathetic biography of John Butler Yeats, *Prodigal Father*.

J.B.Y. was a well-remembered presence in Dublin when I was young, sometime referred to affectionately as 'the old man who ran away from home and made good.' There were still people alive then who could recall his brilliant conversation. Occasionally fragments of his speech would be heard quoted, one of which – 'Those people who complain about Willie's high style should remember that when he sits down to write his verses Willie always puts on his top hat' – I have never been able to discover anywhere in print, though a more polite elaboration of the same thought can be found in a letter to the practitioner dated 30 June 1921. I suspect that, like most of his life, it was scattered with an open hand on to the living air, no thought being given to its furtherance or preservation until it was articulated again as a new, exciting fresh thought. At that time, while his admired portraits hung in the National and Municipal Galleries and the marvellous letters could be found in libraries and rare bookshops, it was thought that his genius was something more than he had ever managed to get down on canvas or in print. He can never be accused of that exhibitionism when the means of expression is in excess of what is being said.

The letters have given me pleasure for many years. They can be gossipy, profound, irascible, charming, prejudiced, humorous, intelligent, naive, contradictory, passionate. They are always immediate. Never far away from the absorbing questions of the day is an infinite curiosity about those questions that are concerned with the nature of art and thought: What is the Good and the nature of what is good, and what, above all, is the *summum bonum* or the *primum mobile*?

I think it can be seen how intimately the charm of the letters is linked to the qualities that were to prove so disastrous to the career of this man of genius. The facts are always situated in a dream of becoming, never in mere being:

My theory is that we are always dreaming – chairs, tables, women and children, our wives and sweethearts, the people in the streets, all in various ways and with various powers are the starting points of dreams ... Sleep is dreaming away from the facts and wakefulness dreaming in close contact with the facts, and *since facts excite our dreams and feed them we get as close as possible to the facts if we have the cunning and the genius of poignant feeling* ...

And affection springs straight out of memory:

Now, a most powerful and complex part of the personality is *affection* and affection *springs straight out of the memory*. For that reason what is new whether in the world of ideas or of fact cannot be subject for poetry, tho' you can be as rhetorical about it as you please – rhetoric expresses other peoples [sic] feelings, poetry one's own.

In abolishing time and establishing memory, the letters of John Butler Yeats go straight to the very heart of affection.

When Bertrand Fillaudeau of José Corti invited me to introduce a work in my own literature that was not already known to French readers, I chose these letters for reasons I hope the introduction manages to make clear. As John Butler Yeats is completely unknown in France, other than to specialists, I kept only those letters from the Hone edition that I thought the most striking or interesting or relevant. When it was decided to publish this English edition, I saw no reason to alter the selection, because John Butler Yeats is now almost equally unknown here. I want to recall with gratitude the late Professor Donald (D.J.) Gordon, of Reading University, for his patronage and brilliant conversation on these letters, and other subjects, in his house in Reading, where J.B.Y.'s drawing of Synge, which he had bought from Daniel Corkery for £25, hung in the hallway. [...]

In Pursuit of a Single Flame:
Ernie O'Malley

When I was teaching in Clontarf in the late 1950s I had an O'Malley boy in my class. He was an attractive child with black hair and very pale skin. I became aware that he was a nephew of Ernie O'Malley when, soon after his death, correcting exercises one morning, I discovered that the boy was doing his sums on the blank pages of a large notebook filled with O'Malley's writing. Like many writers, O'Malley wrote on only one side of the page. The clear writing described the experience of listening to music and looking at certain paintings.

A few months before, when Ernie O'Malley died in 1957, he was given a State funeral attended by the President of Ireland and the Taoiseach, both Houses of the Oireachtas, the judiciary and all the paraphernalia of State. The crowds that lined the Dublin footpaths to watch the cortège were honouring the Revolutionary soldier. His one published book had been long out of print, its importance known only to the very few. O'Malley the soldier was being honoured that day, and the notebook his nephew used for his sums has stood for me ever since as a symbol of the disregard shown to the writer.

He was born in 1897, the second of eleven children, into the comfortable Catholic middle classes that identified with the British administration in Ireland. His mother, Marion Kearney, came from a farm near Castlerea in County Roscommon and was a trainee nurse in Dublin before her marriage. Luke Malley was born close to Castlebar, and at the time of his marriage was managing clerk for Luke Kelly, the Crown Solicitor for Mayo. *On Another Man's Wound* is O'Malley's account of that upbringing and his part in the war that led to the foundation of the

Irish State. The Malleys already belonged within the caste system of the Empire. Their house in Castlebar faced the barracks of the Royal Irish Constabulary, who 'touched their caps to father'. In this world all Protestants were rich and respectable. The Protestant minister invited the Malley children to cinematographic shows in his house, but he does not appear as a visitor in their home. Priests came to their house for dinner:

They were hearty men who drank their whiskeys and sodas with father or sat at the fire sipping at sweet-smelling punch; but why did they screw up their faces after a long drink if it was not pleasant? One of them always called the 'pope's nose' on a bird 'the ecclesiastical part'; that meant a laugh at table.

At this time, the Irish cultural revival was at its height. The folklore and legends of a lost Gaelic past had been unearthed and popularized, the long history of dispossession traced. With the fall of Parnell, constitutional nationalism was seen to have failed, and romantic nationalism at last had a free field. Violence was advocated openly as a legitimate means of obtaining political ends. The myths and legends, the whole romantic climate, reached the Malley children through the stories told to them by their servants. The stories gave glamour to the country people who came into Castlebar on market days – their talk and laughter, their hot-blooded blows – and to the wild country outside the town, the mountains and ocean. In his book O'Malley exaggerates this influence in order to provide a heroic backcloth to the struggle that was to lead to Independence, which is the principal focus of the autobiography, but it was also very much in the air at the time. O'Malley eventually had to live too close to the people during the course of the war for this romanticism to be sustained, but landscape is seen in a romantic light throughout the book, and it is often a source of solace and of healing.

In 1906, Luke Malley, Ernie's father, moved to Dublin to begin work as a civil servant in the Congested Districts Board. The family settled in the comfortable suburb of Glasnevin and the boys attended the O'Connell School run by the Christian Brothers. The Christian Brothers had been set up by the Catholic hierarchy to counteract attempts by the British, under the Whig ministry of Earl Grey, to establish a non-religious system of education in Ireland. They were more nationalistic than other schools (set up against the godless English, their textbooks glorified nationalist violence in the past) and they were to provide much of the future IRA leadership. At home, there were social strictures about the class of people the Malleys could mix with, but 'At school there was no stress on relative wealth; brains were shared equally by rich and poor'.

O'Malley vividly records the ferment of Dublin at the time: the great lockout of the Dublin workers in 1913, the ceremonial nationalist funerals, the public speeches, the gun-running at Howth, the marching and drilling in the streets and in the Dublin Mountains, the outbreak of the First World War.

The Malley household was as staunchly British as it was Catholic. The nationalist displays were no more than amusing topics to be discussed at dinner. Frank, the eldest son, joined the British Army as a cadet. Ernie won a Dublin Corporation Scholarship and enrolled as a medical student in the National University. By the time of the 1916 Easter Uprising, he was thinking of joining his brother in the forces.

The atmosphere of that Easter Monday is beautifully caught – the good weather, watching the ducks and gulls in St Stephen's Green, people on their way to the races or to the mountains, the sense of holiday. Walking into the city, he suddenly discovers that O'Connell Street had changed:

From the flagstaff on top of the General Post Office, the GPO, floated a new flag, a tricoloured one of green, white and orange, the colours running out from the mast . . .

I walked up the street. Behind Nelson's Pillar lay dead horses, some with their feet in the air, others lying flat. 'The Lancers' horses,' an old man said, although I had not spoken . . . Seated on a dead horse was a woman, a shawl around her head, untidy wisps of hair straggled across her dirty face. She swayed slowly, drunk, singing:

> Boys in Khaki, Boys in Blue
> Here's the best of Jolly Good Luck to You.

On the base of the Pillar was a white poster . . . I began to read it with a smile, but my smile ceased as I read.

The signatories of the Proclamation – Clarke, Pearse, Connolly, MacDonagh, Plunkett – did not mean much to him. They were only names. He describes the aftermath of the Rebellion, the looting and general breakdown of order:

People from the slums, the crowded, dilapidated tenements of the eighteenth-century grandees, had looted some of the shops. Boys walked around with a bright yellow shoe on one foot, the other bare. Women carried apronsful of footwear, stopping at intervals to sit on the curb and try on a pair of satin shoes; then, dissatisfied, fling them away and fit on another and different variety. Boys wore silk hats perched on their noses or backwards at a drunken angle.

The Uprising was as decisive for O'Malley as it was for many others. When the Rebellion was followed by the execution of the leaders, he joined the First Dublin Battalion of the Volunteers and began to drill with broom handles in halls that were used for classes in Irish and dancing, mixing with workmen as well as intellectuals, paying a few pence each week towards the purchase of a weapon. When he received his rifle, he had to hide it beneath the floorboards of his room. A theatrical daring or foolhardiness that manifests itself throughout his memoir, showed itself early, when he borrowed his brother's British officer's uniform and presented himself in the Provost Marshal's office in Dublin Castle to obtain a permit to buy a revolver and ammunition. Later he was sent by Michael Collins to impersonate a British officer on missions to Liverpool and London. As O'Malley's involvement in the movement increased, it became more difficult to account for his activities at home, and once his secret was in the open he reacted with typical decisiveness.

He volunteered for full-time duty and was sent north, where he was given command of the Coalisland Company with the rank of second lieutenant. He gained rapid promotion, and in the remaining years of the war against British forces in Ireland he was sent all over the country to organize, train and command the companies and brigades of several areas. *On Another Man's Wound* becomes the story of that war through O'Malley's eyes. What emerges is a picture of a brave, daring, headstrong young leader, without gifts of tact or patience, too dedicated to military theory and textbook strategy, in a countryside that had little use for anything but the immediate and the practical. Upbringing had combined with temperament to make him half an alien among his own people. A quixotic code of honour was brought to what was, mostly, a mean struggle. In Galway he was confronted by a sergeant and a constable with a warrant for his arrest:

I drew my revolver. As we looked at each other the sergeant said, 'Draw.' The constable drew his Webley. The sergeant had a fair moustache, red hair showed at the sides of his soft service cap; we had met in the demesne.

'Fire,' shouted the sergeant. I had a mixture of respect for law and the idea the other fellow should fire first. I felt a sharp thrust in my wrist as I half turned to fire twice at the constable who had run to a doorway. I pointed my gun at the sergeant; he did not move nor did he put up his hands. He shouted orders; police rushed out from the barracks. I threw my useless bicycle to the ground . . . I took the first corner at racing speed and dashed at an impossibly thick hedge of thorns and brambles. I got through. I ran through the fields till I was tired. I came back to the road, crossed it and lay down. My wounds began to pain now.

In Clare he allowed a police patrol to go by unharmed:

I could not give the order; shooting like that did not seem fair. There was no moral element in my thoughts. We waited until the patrol repassed, and again I let them go, cursing myself for the second irresolution. 'We'll leave them be,' I said, in gloomy silence. The men went as far as the house I was to sleep in. I did not explain to them; but I knew they were disgusted.

Often when a carefully planned operation failed, either through enemy preparedness or their own indecision, O'Malley admits he was 'at heart relieved'. He feared failure, but once the fighting began he never worried about the result. There are vivid accounts of the seizing of arms, the taking of military barracks in the towns, the constant fear of being surprised by the enemy during training sessions or in the safe houses where they slept. They had to fight their way out of these houses in the darkness. Occasionally, danger came from within the house, as when a girl entered a room where he was writing and lifted his revolver from the desk, thinking it wasn't loaded, and in play blew out the glass of the lamp behind his head.

When a provisional government was set up in opposition to the British civil administration, O'Malley found himself the first president of a land court in Tipperary, at little more than twenty years of age, presiding over hearings held in people's houses.

Soon afterwards he was captured, surprised by British soldiers in a safe house. He was interrogated, tortured, tied with ropes and thrown into freezing cells, taken out for further interrogation, threatened with summary execution, his bare feet stamped on, but he did not break or yield his identity. In the morning, he was brought outside: 'This is your last look at the sky'. Blindfolded, put on a lorry and taken to the house he was captured in, which has since been razed to the ground, he prepared himself to face execution by the roadside. I know of no more powerful expression of that spirit which turns revolt into revolution, and, once established, will prevail over almost impossible odds and far greater military force:

My lips were dry; they were of rough leather. I had been trying to say some prayers, but could not. My thoughts ran on ahead, crossed and recrossed. I was not afraid of death now. Faces I knew came up, my brother Frank's, Seán Treacy's; then I felt at peace. It was hard to pin anything down, to think I was going to die on the roadside. I would tell them that they were fools, that they could not win; dead men would help to beat them in the end.

And there are flashes of grim humour. After the capture of the military barracks in Mallow, they come upon an unfinished letter on an officer's desk: 'Mallow is a very quiet town; nothing ever happens here . . .'

O'Malley is alert to how the character and spirit of the people can change from area to area within the space of a few miles. The cooking he learned to dread:

The food was good, but rough and badly cooked. Bulk seemed to matter most. Tea, eggs, bacon, stirabout, potatoes and cabbage were the usual food; tomatoes, lettuce, celery, beans, and fruit in general were unknown. The lack of green vegetables was said to be due to the famine years when the people ate nettles and grass. Mangels and turnips went to the horses, pigs and cattle; they bubbled and smelled with cabbage in cast-iron cauldrons. Herbs – tansy, mint and wild garlic – were used sparingly. I gave a tomato to a man I knew at a fair. He eyed the shining scarlet. 'What kind of a thing is this?' He bit into it, then spat out the pulp in disgust. 'Man dear, do you want to poison me?'

Throughout the book are descriptions of the countryside in its different seasons and weathers. There are passages on which the dead hand of English composition lies heavily, but these are, fortunately, rare. The observation is usually close and excitingly accurate, especially when action is linked to landscape:

We got down off the horse, walked a little, then lay down behind a hedge and waited for dawn. I was cold and stiff. The dew was deep on the long grass of the meadows. We saw the few stars go out and the light drop slowly on to the country, a cold light that took the colour out of the land.

He learnt to judge men by a look, bearing, intensity or deliberateness of speech. Often his own life and the lives of his men were dependent on these judgements. There are memorable portraits of leaders, such as Collins, de Valera, Cathal Brugha, and intellectuals like Darrell Figgis; but the most affectionate portrait is of Paddy Moran, who was in a cell close to O'Malley's in Kilmainham:

Of stocky build, but sinewy; fuzzy thick hair, showing two moons on his broad forehead. He had a strong, pleasant face. He knew Collins and Mulcahy, and he spoke of himself as 'the old gunner'; he was captain of a Dublin company and had been, I was told, second in command of the GPO during Easter Week.

To keep up their spirits in the jail, he and Moran used to retrace in their minds the walk down the right bank of the Shannon from Lough Allen to Carrick, and in the evening come back up the opposite bank, each time adding fresh details along the way. At exercise time, they kept close to one another in the prison yard. 'Do you remember the colour of the Curlews after rain?'

O'Malley was constantly interrogated, tortured, beaten up and threatened with execution:

Many things could happen; they could do us in quietly, or torture us, or keep us in suspense. I had not expected anything but death to end my part in the struggle; we had seen the grey face of death too often not to be able to know his shadow as we wandered. We did not expect to live through the war; there were too many risks to be taken, but we did feel that our cause would win. However mean and petty our individual lives and thoughts were, there was something in us now, bigger than ourselves, and that could make up for a certain futility when we looked too closely into our thoughts.

His presence in jail became known to Collins and the leadership. A revolver and bolt-cutters were smuggled in. An auxiliary who had secretly gone over to the Volunteer side aided his escape. Paddy Moran refused to join them at the last minute. He believed his innocence would be proved at his trial (for shooting British undercover agents), and he did not want to let down his witnesses. A few months later he was hanged.

After his escape, O'Malley was given the command of the Second Southern Division and started preparing his men for the long struggle he was certain they would win; but already the war was winding down. One of his last duties was to oversee the execution of three British officers. At the time, captured British officers were shot as reprisals for the execution of Republican prisoners. This melancholy duty he carried out with his usual punctiliousness:

We walked into the closing-in darkness, riflemen in front and behind the trap, until we were a distance from where the officers had been captured . . . Sentries were posted. The girls and women of the house got ready supper; they did not ask any questions. A fire was lighted in the room where the officers were. After supper I went into the room. The blinds were drawn so that they could not look out. It was a large room. They were seated at a table. One had his head in his hands.

'Would you like to see a clergyman of your own religion?'

'No,' said one. The others shook their heads.

'Would you like a civilian, an imperialist, to stay with you?'

'No.' They did not need anyone.

'Here's writing paper and envelopes. You can write to anyone you wish. If you give me your words of honour that you won't mention anything of military importance, you can seal the envelopes yourself.'

Each gave me his word. There were beds for them to sleep on.

I sat in the kitchen by the fire. The women of the house had gone to bed quietly. None of us spoke for a long time. I was putting myself in the place of the men inside.

My turn might come, too, and soon. It seemed easier to face one's own execution than to have to shoot others.

As he prepared to abandon a war he felt should be pursued to the end no matter what the cost, there is a passage that is like a valediction:

I felt I understood the country better now. I had sloughed off some conventional skins, and the layer of the importance of bookish reading which had prevented a closer contact with the life about me. The people had, essentially, warmth, feeling and heart, and they knew of life through living. I had been sponsored by the movement and nurtured by the people. They softened down actuality.

O'Malley saw the Treaty as a compromise and joined the Anti-Treaty side in the Civil War. His account of that war, *The Singing Flame*, was published posthumously in 1962, edited by Frances-Mary Blake. While the book contains vivid and fascinating passages, it has neither the spirit nor the coherence of *On Another Man's Wound*. There is a pervasive longing throughout for action, as if action in itself could bring clarity to the confusion and futility as friends and former comrades fought one another. He commanded the capture and defence of the Four Courts, and was even more severely wounded than in the War of Independence. For long periods he was close to death, and much of the book is spent in prison and prison hospitals. The severity of his wounds was probably all that saved him from execution. On his release in 1924, at the age of twenty-seven, he was in poor health. While in prison he had been elected to the Dáil, but because the Oath of Allegiance was a step too far, he never took his seat. After a spell of wandering on the Continent, he enrolled again as a medical student. He spent much of his time in college with the literary and dramatic societies, wrote poetry, and failed his medical exams. In 1928, he embarked for the United States with Frank Aiken to raise money for the proposed *Irish Press*, and when Aiken returned to Ireland at the end of the long fund-raising tour, O'Malley stayed behind. During the next five years he moved around California, Taos, New Mexico and Mexico, mingling with the artistic communities, and he began the book that was to become *On Another Man's Wound*. Among the friends he made were the poet Hart Crane and the photographer Paul Strand, who was to remain a friend all his life. In a letter dated June 1931, to Malcolm Cowley, Crane set down this impression of O'Malley:

I have my most pleasant literary moments with an Irish revolutionary, a red haired friend of Liam O'Flaherty . . . shot (and not missed) seventeen times in one conflict and another; the most quietly sincere and appreciative person, in many ways, whom I've ever met. It's a big regret that he's Dublin bound again after three years from home, in a few weeks. Ernest O'Malley by name. And we drink a lot together – look at frescos – and agree!

Crane committed suicide the following year, but O'Malley was not yet Dublin-bound. In New York, he met Helen Hooker, of the wealthy Huntington-Hooker family of Greenwich, Connecticut. Despite her father's hostility, they were married in London in September 1935.

In 1932 de Valera came to power, and those as prominent as O'Malley had been on the Republican side in the Civil War were attaining high position. Such positions never held much attraction for O'Malley, but in 1935 he completed his book and returned home. Under the 1934 Pension Act he was entitled to a general's pension. Returning to Dublin, O'Malley resumed his medical studies in deference to the family's expectations. More than twenty years had passed since he had first taken up these studies, and he found he could no longer drum up enough interest to acquire the knowledge necessary to face the examinations. His age and military fame must also have created difficulties. *On Another Man's Wound* was accepted by a London and a Boston publisher that same year, was serialized in the *Irish Press*, and was an immediate success.

The O'Malleys were a wealthy and glamorous couple in the poverty of de Valera's Ireland. They first rented and then bought Burrishole Lodge and lands by the ocean near Newport in Mayo, and started to restore the house, to work the land and buy more of it. (Neither had any experience of land or farm work, but it was in keeping with the romanticism of the time.) The couple had three children. 'Here, nobody is interested in creative work. I have nobody to speak the language of books, literature or criticism,' O'Malley wrote from Newport. For intellectual company, they had to go to Dublin, where they had a house. Helen exhibited her sculpture and became involved in designing stage sets for the Players' Theatre, a breakaway group from the Abbey.

O'Malley wrote about painting and organized exhibitions – among the artists he supported was Jack Yeats, and they became friends. The couple travelled abroad, Helen's wealth allowing them to become serious art collectors; but they were not happy together for long. Helen sought divorce and custody of the children, eventually kidnapping the two eldest from their school and taking them to America. The youngest child remained in Ireland with his father.

In these last years, the care and upbringing of his young son became O'Malley's principal concern. He did radio broadcasts about the war and wrote articles for the *Sunday Press* that were collected after his death in *Raids and Rallies*. He worked as an adviser for his friend John Ford on the filming of *The Quiet Man* and *The Rising of the Moon*, and went with his son to visit another old friend, Samuel Beckett, in Paris. By the time of his death, despite the State funeral, he had become a marginal, isolated figure in a country he had helped to bring into being. As with many of the Revolutionaries, what had emerged was not much to his liking. The class that came to power with the Church was as unadventurous as it was sanctimonious. Even as far back as 1936, we find O'Malley chairing a meeting of anti-Franco Republicans, when the Catholic hierarchy and most of the country were all for Franco. He sent his children to school at Ampleforth in England.

There are certain writers who probably would never have written but for a single defining experience. The war for Irish Independence was the most intense experience of O'Malley's life, an experience he did not expect to survive. His intelligence, his cultivation, his life among writers and artists during the years he spent wandering in America and Mexico gave distance and a different focus to the experience when he came to put it into words, and, largely, he got the words right. That is not given to many, but once the work was done, in a certain way his life was over, though he still had more than twenty years to live.

On Another Man's Wound was highly praised, both here and in the US, but ran into immediate bad luck. Derry-born Joseph O'Doherty, a barrister and a Fianna Fáil TD for Donegal, claimed he had been presented in a cowardly and dishonourable light in the book, and the libel case came to trial in Dublin in 1937. O'Malley's defence was that the words in question did not refer to O'Doherty and that the facts were true and were expressed in good faith. 'I had to stand over what I had honestly remembered and sincerely written,' he said. Counsel for O'Doherty presented the book as a self-glorifying, unreliable work. The High Court found against O'Malley, and he had to borrow £400 to pay his share of the damages. The book was withdrawn. Many historians have since sided with the counsel's view of the book, while acknowledging the high quality of its writing.

I cannot answer the accusation that O'Malley altered historical fact for his own purposes, but I know that the few short sections of the material with which I am well acquainted – the area around Lough Key and the portrait of Paddy Moran – are accurate. The work as a whole has imaginative truth. What is so extraordinary is not the material itself but that most of it is so well written. For far too long its right to a permanent and honoured place in our literature has been denied. It is probably true that O'Malley had little sense of the complications of history, the necessary compromises and accommodations. At the libel trial, he was particularly hurt that people who could verify privately facts and incidents would not appear as witnesses in court. When young, he had absorbed a myth and was prepared to follow it, like a single flame, no matter what the cost was to himself or to others.

Not only did O'Malley write well about the war but he was also a conscious intellectual interested in the ideas and strategies of revolution. Like W. B. Yeats, whom he detested, he held democracy in contempt. He believed that the people should be led and coerced if necessary. A small band of committed militants could bring about the condition of revolution through isolated military actions designed to show the authority as ineffective. The people could then be manipulated by way of a process O'Malley defined as inspiration, intimidation and provocation. The romantic myth of an Irish identity was already fashioned. All it needed was to be reawakened, and as long as the myth worked it did not matter that its authenticity was questionable. Once awakened, it could be manipulated through calculated acts of violence. Whenever this failed, the people could be intimidated into acquiescence. Inspiration and intimidation were complemented by provoking the State into action that was counter-productive in its harshness. The rule of law was crucial to the British administration. To provoke them into breaking their own laws was to subvert their most powerful weapon. Guerrilla activity would ensure that the cost in life and property would be too heavy for the British administration to carry. Ernie O'Malley was more candid than his later successors about these tactics. *On Another Man's Wound* is the one book of high literary quality permanently on display in Sinn Féin windows during recent decades, and the one classic work to have emerged directly from the violence that led to the founding of the Irish Free State.

What Is My Language?

In James Joyce's 'The Dead', Gabriel Conroy and Miss Ivors have this confrontation:

—And why do you go to France and Belgium, said Miss Ivors, instead of visiting your own land?

—Well, said Gabriel, it's partly to keep in touch with the languages and partly for a change.

—And haven't you your own language to keep in touch with – Irish? asked Miss Ivors.

—Well, said Gabriel, if it comes to that, you know, Irish is not my language.

What Miss Ivors is reflecting is Irish cultural nationalism, a movement fashioned by many hands throughout the second half of the nineteenth century. With the fall of Parnell, it was given a free field, and by the time of 'The Dead' must have been everywhere in the air and as solidly on the ground as Miss Ivors. This can be recognized in many sources, but nowhere is it rendered more vividly than in Ernie O'Malley's *On Another Man's Wound*. It probably found its most pure artistic expression in Synge's *The Aran Islands* and its most virile legacy in the GAA. There are also interesting aspects of the same debate in Kate O'Brien's fine novel *The Ante-Room*, and George Moore took a part in the movement when he wrote *The Untilled Field* for translation into Irish. What Gabriel Conroy is probably reflecting is a version of Joyce's own position at the time. If Irish was not his language, neither, it would appear, was English fully his language, his eyes turned to Europe. This is further advanced in the verbal play with the Dean of Studies in *A Portrait of the Artist as a Young Man* over the words 'funnel' and 'tundish': 'It is called a tundish in

Lower Drumcondra, said Stephen laughing, where they speak the best English.' To Stephen's own reflection: 'The language in which we are speaking is his before it is mine. How different are the words *home, Christ, ale, master*, on his lips and on mine!' Stephen is forced to acknowledge, 'I cannot speak or write these words without unrest of spirit. His language, so familiar and so foreign, will always be for me an acquired speech.'

In Beckett, where language itself is a character and a presence, comically and sometimes even tragically aware of itself, we find the same dilemma appearing in an altered context. In the play for radio *All That Fall* there is this exchange:

MR ROONEY: . . . Do you know, Maddy, sometimes one would think you were struggling with a dead language.

MRS ROONEY: Yes indeed, Dan, I know full well what you mean, I often have that feeling, it is unspeakably excruciating.

MR ROONEY: I confess I have it sometimes myself, when I happen to overhear what I am saying.

MRS ROONEY: Well, you know, it will be dead in time, just like our own poor dear Gaelic, there is that to be said.

[*Urgent baa*]

In Beckett it is not only necessary to be dead but to be forgotten as well, the awareness of nuance so intense that the words seem to be turning in on themselves: among the many echoes and intonations it brings to mind is the father in Pirandello's *Six Characters in Search of an Author*:

But don't you see the whole trouble lies here in words, words. Each one of us has within him a whole world of things, each one of us his own special world. And how can we ever come to an understanding if I put in the words I utter the sense and value of things as I see them; while you who listen to me must inevitably translate them according to the conception of things each one of you has within himself. We think we understand each other, but we never really do.

It also brings to mind Bergson's essay on *Laughter*, which brilliantly analyses laughter in its various forms and laws, until, at the very end, Bergson is forced to rest his case on the intuition that its source lies close to a darkness at the bitter heart of the human condition.

I have set down these examples to show the awareness and the presence of the older language in our literature in English, and there are many different examples that could as easily have been chosen. The references to Bergson and Pirandello through Beckett point to a difficulty beyond language, where silence becomes a part of speech, but, as Beckett suggested, silence – especially the silence of writers – cannot be measured. What can be measured, even with half an ear, is the presence of the older language in the English we speak and use in Ireland, in many speech constructions, in its rhythms and its silences, and in those words withheld deliberately or left unspoken. This is the very opposite of that pseudo Irish/English language we have from time to time been afflicted with – 'The mists that do be travelling on the bog', 'Those bright scarves of our laughter', in which local colour is purveyed as art to an ignorant audience. I would exempt most of Synge and especially *The Playboy of the Western World*, which I view as a great farce, though I can understand Philip Larkin's reaction to the first half when he decided to remain on in the theatre bar after the interval, leisurely finishing his drink, and then, when the play had resumed, walked out into the fine English evening. *The Playboy* conforms to all the Bergsonian laws of farce, in that an artificial language is used to reflect the unreal or unnatural happenings. If a natural or living language is used in farce, Bergson argues, emotion or recognition will inevitably filter through to render the unbelievable happenings no longer either funny or enjoyable, and the great liberating kick farce takes at reality becomes ineffectual because the farcical events aren't hermetically sealed in an equally artificial language.

I turn to a work that has no obvious artifice, and was written in Irish, Tomás Ó Criomhthain's *An tOileánach*, translated into English by Robin Flower. When I first became interested in *The Islandman*, and I had read it a number of times – easily and quickly in English, but slowly in the original, as my Irish is far from fluent – I was puzzled by the difference between the original and the translation. In that lazy fashion when faced with difficulty, when it is easier to substitute judgement for understanding, I was inclined to blame this on the literalness of Flower's translation; but when I tried to translate parts of it myself* I came to realize how

* A fragment of McGahern's own translation of *An tOileánach* was published under the title 'Springtime Comes to the Turf Bog', *Irish Times* 2 November 1991: Weekend 8.

good a translation Robin Flower's is and that the difficulty was deep in the language itself, in the style.

If we think of the style as the person, the revelation of personality in language, and that the quality of the personality is more important than the material out of which the actual pattern is shaped, then the opposite can be argued: style itself must be the outcome of a view of reality.

Ó Criomhthain has a definite style, in the sense that a persistent way of seeing and thinking falls naturally into an equally persistent form of expression. This is further reinforced by the fact that his view of reality is at no time a personal view and is never at variance with the values of his society as a whole. We find him boasting that never once in a whole lifetime did he infringe custom, and custom was the law of that civilization. There are people in the book who disagree with Ó Criomhthain, who do not respect custom, and he always looks on them as degenerate.

Nowhere in the work does he attempt to describe the little island he lives on. Flower draws attention to this in the introduction to his translation, and he goes on to describe for the benefit of his readers the island group of the Blaskets, a benefit it never occurs to Ó Criomhthain to confer, though he is continually addressing himself directly to the reader. I believe this fact to be linked with Ó Criomhthain's view of his world, his view of reality. Within that view such a description would be pointless. The island is simply there as a human habitation, a bare foundation of earth on which people live and move. The scenery furnishes the necessary frame and sustenance for life. Places are seen in their essential outline, which is inseparable from their use or function. Sometimes a place is seen as friendly to whatever action is happening, more often it is hostile, but place and action are always inseparable. One cannot subsist without the other. There are no idle stretches to be filled with contemplation of the daffodil. A mountain is there to be climbed, turf has to be cut and won and creeled home. It is remarkable that no description is ever given of the turfcutting, other than what helps or, more often, hinders it. There are no 'turf banks stripped for victory', as in Kavanagh, no scattering, footing, clamping. All we are told is how well he is working, how much he has succeeded in getting done by a certain time of day. Movingly, we are told that his mother brought home the turf so that he could attend school; otherwise the book we are now reading would never have been written. A field is described only as it is reclaimed and cultivated; a strand is there to be crossed, a sea to be fished, a town to be reached, a shore to be gained, walked upon, lived upon. These are all near and concrete realities but so stripped down to their essences because of the necessities of the action as to seem free of all local characteristics. One conditions the other to the same simplicity of form. So elemental is the vision that it can only be rendered into the English we now possess in a weakened half-light.

In a famous but not quite accurate remark, Borges argues that a proof of the authenticity of the Koran is that you can find no camels in its pages; they were so taken for granted that there was no need for them to be mentioned. Borges was arguing slyly against the substitution of local colour for reality in South American writing, but even on this small count Ó Criomhthain is constant. There were donkeys on the island, but they are only mentioned twice and would not have appeared at all had not a creel been blown out to sea off one of the donkeys when drawing home the turf; and when the bailiffs came to seize property, all they could find was an old donkey at the other end of the island with nothing alive but the two eyes in his head. Such is the simplicity of the vision that sometimes even people and the elements are equated, as the drunkards are with the spent storms in Dingle. In full cry they had both converged to prevent him from concluding his business in the town and returning to the island.

So free is the action of everything that is not essential that it could as easily have taken place on the shores of Brittany or Greece as on the Dingle Peninsula. In a very different fashion, coming as he did at the end of the great modernist movement and having worked his way through its many allusions and complications, Beckett, too, can be said to have reached an elemental spareness that was equally shorn of local characteristics.

There is a haunting phrase that echoes like a refrain throughout, *lá dár saol*. Flower translates it simply as 'a day of our lives', but it is probably untranslatable. The phrase conveys the whole life of a person as being formed by a succession of single days. When he apologizes for the waste of a day in Dingle, in relief of hardship through drunkenness, there is the physical sense of the day being taken out of the succession of days and squandered like money. Throughout the book the basic unit of time is the day.

If the interdependence of scene and action serves to reduce one another to bare essentials, the sense of timelessness that the book has – of being outside time – comes from the day, a single day breaking continually over the scene and the action. This law conditions even mealtimes. There are only two meals, the morning and evening meal. They eat enough in the morning to get through the day, and restore themselves again at its end. There is a continual setting out and a return-ing. The concerns are immediate: a boon to be won or lost, a constant alertness to take advantage of any sudden windfall – copper bolts from a wrecked ship, barrels of oil, chests of tea; the same alertness to thwart danger – the sudden shock of the shark in the net, the storms, the constant danger of the sea. No two days or two persons are alike. There is no way to foretell what the day may bring. To plan ahead is as useless as to look back in regret. Certainly, there are disappointments, but they are always greeted in the same way. Events, we are told laconically, often turn out differently from what people expect, which is as applicable to misfortune or death as it is to good fortune. There seems to be a super-stitious fear of predicting events, as if the very human attempt itself may be enough to incur the wrath of nature. Motives are of no importance. Ó Criomhthain never examines why people behave in such and such a manner, why an event turns out one way and not another. What happens is all. The same view is taken of the spending of money:

If we had been as careful of the pounds in those days as we have been for some years past, it is my belief that poverty wouldn't have come upon us so soon . . .

People say that the wheel is always turning, and that's a true saying, for in the part of the world that I have known it has turned many times; and if the world improved a bit round the Blaskets at that time, and God gave us that much good fortune, I fancy we didn't take the care we should have done of it, for 'easy come, easy go' is always the way.

What comes through is that when they had plenty they spent it grate-fully and joyously, without thought for the morrow they might never see. When they had to go without, they tried as best they could to endure.

If the strong sense of the day, the endlessly recurring day, gives to the work its timeless quality, it is deepened still more by the fact that people and place seem to stand outside history. There is no sense of national pride. The rumblings of a new Ireland are brushed aside as distant noise, O'Malley's Ireland, or Parnell's or Redmond's or Yeats's or Pearse's:

Just at the time that these companies were sending their boats to us, the talk was beginning throughout Ireland about self-government, or Home Rule, as it is called in another language. I often told the fishermen that Home Rule had come to the Irish without their knowing it, and that the first beginning of it had been made in the Blaskets now that the yellow gold of England and France was coming to our thresholds to purchase our fish, and we didn't give a curse for anybody.

The same harsh independent materialism is reserved for the language he writes and speaks: 'I hear many an idle fellow saying that there's no use in our native tongue; but that hasn't been my experience. Only for it I should have been begging my bread!'

They pay no taxes. They'll let the boats rot in Dingle before they'll pay rent. A woman in her madness to prevent the bailiffs coming ashore will lift her own child to hurl when she cannot lay hands on a rock. The State cannot punish or reward. They can hope for little fame. Fame is literally the news that sticks to any remarkable event, insofar as it happened and was witnessed:

. . . a woman of the Manning family, a marvellous woman. She it was who finished the bailiffs and the drivers who used to come here day after day ruining the poor, who had nothing to live on but famine. A bailiff climbed on to the roof of her house and started knocking it down on her and on to her flock of feeble children. She seized a pair of new shears and opened them – one point this way, the other that. A stout woman and a mad woman! The bailiff never noticed anything till he felt the point of the shears stuck right into his behind. It wasn't the roof of the house that came in through the hole this time, but a spurt of his blood. That's the last bailiff we've seen.

Even the boon of the pension is viewed with deep suspicion: 'I have only two months to go till that date – a date I have no fancy for. In my eyes it is a warning that death is coming, though there are many people who would rather be old with the pension than young without it.'

Such far-flung places as Dingle and America are brought in and ruth-lessly reduced to the simplicities of the island frame. America is the land of sweat, *deor allais*. His sister had been there and could live where a rabbit could, like all the rest who had spent time in America. His brother had been there. We see how it has changed him as they fish for lobsters:

'. . . how I should have had to sweat in America to make two shillings, and all I have to do here is to pull up a pot through two fathoms of water! . . . there are people in America who, if they could come by money as easily as this, would never slumber or sleep. They'd be pulling up all the time.'

We see Ó Criomhthain's wariness, and how America too is etched into the island frame: 'I believed him well enough so far as that went, though he blethered a lot generally, and I often had some difficulty in believing him. I wasn't so ignorant that I couldn't understand how it was in coun-tries overseas – hard work, and the ganger spying on you, two of them sometimes.'

America coarsens manners and, with the emphasis on self-seeking, endangers custom, and custom is their only law, the guardian of their delicate and fragile interdependence. We hear the clear tone of exasper-ation. This makes no human or island sense: 'You might think there was something in what he said. Still you have to consider that a poor sinner can't keep at it night and day alike.'

Pats, the brother, brings no respect to the table of strangers. He is dirty and does not care. We see the difference:

I was rather shy, being so smudgy and dirty in a place like that, but the other chap never gave it a thought; all he wanted was to fill his belly; he'd left all the shyness and nervousness of his early days in foreign lands, and he told me, too, that if I'd been away from home a bit, I wouldn't have cared what sort of a place I got food to eat in.

I have attempted to show how the individual is left very much to his own devices in a setting provided mostly by nature. His concerns are always near, a living to be won or lost, some small advantage to be gained. They live hardly differently to beasts, always at the mercy of what the day might bring; but custom brings in the social, and here again we find the same view of reality, the same simplicity of form conditioned by the same necessity. As the day is the unit of time, the family is the moral unit. E. R. Dodds generalizes with beautiful simplicity in *The Greeks and the Irrational,* when he writes that 'religion grows out of man's relationship to his total environment, morals out of his relation to his fellowmen'.

In the moral unit of the family, the parents come first and are inviolate. When Pats's sons disappear into America, abandoning their father, Ó Criomhthain's shock at the impiety is palpable. This is the worst possible offence, since a son's life is seen as a continuation of the father's. Brothers and sisters come next in the moral unit, which extends to blood relations and to those linked to the family through marriage, and finally to good neighbours: 'I was terrified for the boat that had left me and no wonder for some others of my kin were in her and besides even if I had no relation on board a man is often worried about good neighbours.' The sexual instinct, too, is subordinate to the family. It is a healthy instinct. We see it so in the nights of dancing, the uninhibited encounter with the girls on the mountain, and Ó Criomhthain boasts that in all his years on the island, in spite of health and youth and the long nights, not once did a sexual irregularity occur. As an observant outsider, Synge notes about the Aran Islanders:

The direct sexual instincts are not weak on the island, but they are so subordinated to the instincts of the family that they rarely lead to irregularity. The life here is still at an almost patriarchal stage, and the people are nearly as far from the romantic moods of love as they are from the impulsive life of the savage.

Ó Criomhthain's own marriage is made in an identical mode. He was in love, if we can call it such in this context. It is with a sense of inevitability that he turns away from the girl of his heart ('The most lovely girl on blessed earth at that time') and watches his marriage being arranged as if he were observing a separate person, a person in a drama. What interests him most is the pull and tug of the different family factions as they battle to decide which girl will get him, in the hope that the house will be more useful to them if they can install their own favourite. His sister wins. She persuades the parents that the family of the 'most lovely girl on blessed earth' lives too far away. They live on Inishvickillaun, an island a few miles to the south, an eternity away in an emergency. She argues that anybody making an alliance with such a family was taking on a great responsibility as they would never be in a position to lend much of a hand. She herself had picked an excellent, knowledgeable girl whose people lived in the village and could be relied upon when needed. Once it was arranged, we hear no more about the marriage; it is tombstone writ: 'A week from that day we were married – Tomás Ó Criomhthain and Máire Keane – the last week of Shrove in the year 1878.' All we hear afterwards of the marriage is a catalogue of troubles, his wife's failing health and death, the deaths of their children.

In the same way as *lá dár saol*, another equally haunting phrase – *rithe mo laethse* or *rithe mo bhearthain* – runs throughout the book. 'In the running of my days' is Flower's literal translation, but it has more the sense of a great tide, filling the strand with the vigour and glory of youth coming to a fullness, and then gradually and weakly withdrawing. He goes to extraordinary care, as if it were a religious rite, to point out the time in his life when the tide turned. It seems to me that it is here that the religious, the poetic and the superstitious instincts are very close. He marks the point between the day the poet kept him from cutting the turf and the girls fell upon him on the mountain: 'From the day out, for the one day that went with me six went against me.'* Up to that time the strand was filling, there was the great heart and the fun, *mórchroí agus scléip*, but from that marked time on, we are in the ebb tide, and there

---

* This quotation is substantially different from Robin Flower's standard English translation of *An tOileánach* (which reads: 'for the fact is, for one day that went well with me, five would go wrong for me from that day out'), as are the quotations in the rest of this paragraph and that of the book's final words (about his mother) a few pages later in this essay. Compare: Tomás O'Crohan, *The Islandman*, translated by Robin Flower (Oxford: Oxford University Press, 2000), pp. 87, 186 and 245 respectively. For the largest part of this essay McGahern appears to be citing from Flower's translation (though with occasional minor silent changes: like the reinstating of names in their original Irish forms, or the substitution of 'to her own people' for Flower's more prosaic 'home'), but in these diverging passages the English translations are probably his own. McGahern draws attention elsewhere in this essay to his unease with Flower's translation, and the only published excerpt from McGahern's own translation of *An tOileánach* (see previous note) also differs significantly from Flower's standard translation.

was much he had to endure in that withdrawal. He found solace where he could. Of his son's death: 'We had only one comfort, there was no wound or blemish anywhere on his body though it was a steep fall from a cliff, and we had to put up with it and plough on and be satisfied'; and he leans on the old constant truisms, 'Those that pass away cannot sustain the people who remain', and 'We too had to put our oars out and drive on.' *A bheith ag treabhadh linn.*

It is no different when his wife dies, or when his son dies trying to rescue the Dublin girl from the sea. All that concerns him is that the girl's parents shouldn't think him stupid enough to feel enmity towards them because his son died trying to save their daughter, because he understood well that his son had to die sometime anyhow and the occasion was not important since it could not have been foreseen. Death is like a roll call. There is nothing for it but to endure and go on. Each new day will break on the world with its own claims, demands that care nothing for sorrow. Sorrow, because it blinds and weakens us, is an impairment, and the action required by the new day will demand all our faculties and our strength. Here the family unit brings help once more. Each night Uncle Diarmuid calls to the house in an attempt to lighten trouble with news of worse – a ship lost at sea with hundreds on board, a wall of rock falling on all the workers of a mine – to put heart in them and to renew their courage.

The only thing they seem unable to deal with is madness. Death is a fine thing, Ó Criomhthain says, besides certain things that hang over poor sinners. When Diarmuid's son goes mad, the community appears to be afraid to help or touch the insane person. Ó Criomhthain, who is usually so boastful of his readiness to give help, when asked to make up a crew to take the boy to Dingle, says mournfully that at such moments all one can do is to stand up and be counted. When the boy drowns himself and they find the body and bring it ashore, it is with a tentativeness, haste and deep unease that he is left with God in Castlepoint.

In Ó Criomhthain's world all things are reduced to their essentials and are immediate and concrete. Place only exists in so far as it is necessary to the action. All mysterious and far-flung places are brought in and reduced to the island frame. The single day breaks over this world to bring light for the action. This immediate action, its hope and its fears, its stresses, its ebb and flow, fill the one day without regard to what went before or will come after. Everything runs to its conclusion in that single frame. Actions that require months or years are so reduced that they seem to take on the rhythm of the day. The following passage could be the material of a novel or a long story running to many pages, by George Moore, say:

Martin lived only a year after his marriage, and then my sister had to return to her own people, for one of Martin's brothers came back to live with the old people. They wouldn't give Máire anything, although Martin left a boy child. Máire left the boy with us and went off to America. After three years there she came back home again. She had the law on them, and got the father's share for the son.

The shape and rhythm of the story are that of a single day. People, too, are presented only in their essential outline, and that is only in so far as their striking identities are visible to the eyes of those around them. What emerges finally is a simple, heroic poetry, not in the sense of any striking metaphor or image; on the contrary, when we come on such an image towards the end of the book – the 'crag in the midst of the great sea, and again and again the blown surf drives right over it' – we are almost inclined to suspend belief, at least to become suspicious, since it is so out of character with the style. The poetry, rather, seeps through the book as a whole, like water or the sea air round the place itself; so persistent is the form of seeing and thinking that it seems always to find its right expression: unwittingly, through the island frame, we have been introduced into a complete representation of existence.

At the end, he speaks of the actual writing of the book. He has, he says, rescued the days from forgetfulness, those days he has seen with his own eyes and whose burden he has borne, *a rabhas ag broc leis*, another phrase that cannot be properly rendered into English. Then he looks forward to a dream of eternity, when all this will have vanished, and all that will be left is his account of his own life and the lives of his neighbours, without a bitter word ever having passed between them.

An uninhibited boasting runs through the book. The conclusion must have disturbed the original editors. Much of it has been either toned down or edited out. This can be seen in Flower's translation, which is based on the version that the *Seabhac* put together. In the 1929 edition, Ó Criomhthain says, 'I am proud to set down my story and the story of my neighbours.' But the original text is: 'One other thing' – a characteristic addition: 'There's not a country or neighbourhood or nation in which one person doesn't triumph above all others! *Tugann an craobh leis.*' He continues: 'Now, from the first time the fire was lit on this island no one has written about its life or its people. That leaves the *craobh* or the branch of victory with the person who did it.' And that is, namely, *an t-uasal* Ó Criomhthain. Then, at the conclusion, with that sure instinct which I find throughout the book, a persistent way of thinking and feeling finding the right expression, he returns to the final dream of eternity, and the last sentence gathers in all the primary characteristics:

My mother used to go drawing turf when I was eight years old, so that she could have me at school. I hope that she and my father [the two inviolates] will inherit the blessed kingdom and that I and every single person that will read this book will meet up with them again in the island of paradise.

I believe that this island lies closer to Mount Olympus than it does to the Roman gate of heaven that we used to pray to in our youth.

I have dwelt on this work written in Irish because I believe it to be a true work. Such books always cast their own light, reflecting outwards. Besides, more than any single work in English it reflected the reality of the lives of the people I grew up among and who brought me up. One of the marks of that society was that when people were removed from the necessities of the landscape, like Ó Criomhthain's brother Pats, and the unwritten laws of the civilization were no longer enforced by church and custom, in places like England and America, those old manners and morals and beliefs quickly degenerated. In our new world of sudden prosperity, something similar appears to be happening in Ireland.

I have taken the original argument – that style itself must be the outcome of a view of reality – from Paolo Vivante's great work, *The Homeric Imagination*. Ó Criomhthain's style is such an outcome, and while it would be foolish to compare him to Homer, he did give vivid utterance to a society brought to refinement by the conditions of an unchanging reality over many days and generations.

What, then, is my language?

I will not resort to the very Irish strategy of arguing that since there are no answers to any really profound questions, all we can do is rephrase the question differently. That, in some way, I have already done – I hope not too evasively or at too great a length.

The speech my mother gave me was the English spoken on the Iron Mountains. That language still contained within it at least the ghost of the Irish language. It was a slow, careful, humorous speech, grounded and practical, with a strong Northern accent, its rhythms almost entirely Gaelic, and Gaelic words were retained in the English usage. Her speech was not as earthen as her mother's speech or that of her brothers and sisters; it was refined by years of schooling with the nuns and girls from rich families in the Marist Convent in Carrick-on-Shannon and in the training schools of Trinity College. Many of the families from the mountain had been weavers in Armagh and Fermanagh, undercutting the established Protestant weavers. In an uprising in Armagh towards the end of the eighteenth century, their homes had been pillaged, their webs and looms broken, and they fled west and south. Though low-grade seams of coal and iron had been mined on the Iron Mountains for generations, nobody thought a living could be won from the slopes until those Northern families came and settled there. It was the realities of their precarious existence I found reflected in *An tOileánach*. Naturally there were differences as well. They were careful with money, had a horror of display or extravagance, and were extremely political. Motives and character came at all times under intense scrutiny. The localities I grew up in were all within sight of these mountains. The speech in these places was not greatly different but was softened and obscured by the gentler influences of the West. As my mother's speech was refined by education, my speech was probably tempered in turn by an indiscriminate reading of books in English and by the prayers and ceremonies of the Catholic Church. If I have used that language in any way well, it will in its turn have used me.

I think of the aged Tolstoy being driven past great Russian estates and asking, 'Who owns these woods, that river, those fields, that walled estate?' On being told the names of the landowners, he replied, 'They don't own them. God does.' Or do the people who have power and dominion own them – those people who write our histories and absorb our languages and who, in time, will fall prey to the laws of change and decay and be appropriated into some other form or language? Or does language belong to all who use it, in both its great and humble manifestations, and in turn use us as it grows and dies and is renewed?

V

PREFACES AND INTRODUCTIONS

Preface to the Second Edition of
The Leavetaking

The Leavetaking was written as a love story, its two parts deliberately different in style. It was an attempt to reflect the purity of feeling with which all the remembered 'I' comes to us, the banal and the precious alike; and yet how that more than 'I' – the beloved, the 'otherest', the most trusted moments of that life – stumbles continually away from us as poor reportage, and to see if these disparates could in any way be made true to one another.

Short stories are often rewritten many times after their first publication, novels hardly ever. This obviously has to do with length, economics, the hospitality of magazines and anthologies to stories, perhaps even convention: and I believe it to be, as well, part of the excitement of the novel. The novel has to stand or fall alone. Any single story in a collection of stories can lean on the variety and difference of the others, receiving as well as casting light.

That the second part of this edition of *The Leavetaking* came to be reformed is in part an accident. Several years after its first publication, I found myself working through it again with its French translator, the poet Alain Delahaye. The more I saw of it the more sure I was that it had to be changed. The crudity I was attempting to portray, the irredeemable imprisonment of the beloved in reportage, had itself become blatant. I had been too close to the 'Idea', and the work lacked that distance, that inner formality or calm, that all writing, no matter what it is attempting, must possess.

What is certain is that this luck of a second chance is undeserved.

It should have been written right the first time. What is still uncertain is if it is right even now. That will rest with whatever readers it may find.

J.McG.
August 1983

Preface to *Creatures of the Earth:*
New and Selected Stories

These stories grew in the mind and in the many workings of the material, but often began from as little as the sound of a chainsaw working in the evening, an overheard conversation about the price of cattle, thistledown floating by the open doors of bars on Grafton Street on a warm autumn day, an old gold watch spilling out of a sheet where it had been hidden and forgotten about for years. Others began as different stories, only to be replaced by something completely unforeseen at the beginning of the work. The most difficult were drawn directly from life. Unless they were reinvented, re-imagined and somehow dislocated from their origins, they never seemed to work. The imagination demands that life be told slant because of its need of distance.

Over the years there were two particular stories I rewrote several times, but I was never satisfied with them, and yet I would not let them go. I was too attached to the material. I stubbornly refused to obey the primary rule that if the writer finds himself too fond of a rhythm or an image or phrase, or even a long passage, he should get rid of it. When I came to write *Memoir*, I saw immediately that the central parts of both these stories were essential to the description of the life we lived with my father in the barracks, from which they should never have been lifted. No matter what violences or dislocations were attempted, they continued to remain firmly grounded, obdurately what they were.

Among its many other obligations, fiction always has to be believable. Life does not have to suffer such constraint, and much of what takes

place is believable only because it happens. The god of life is accident.*
Fiction has to be true to a central idea or vision of life.

[...]

John McGahern
March 2006

---

* In an unpublished essay, McGahern had written: 'It has been said that the god
of life is Accident, and we are both its priest and victim, and occasional
beneficiary.' (Untitled typescript, NUIG P71/1328.)

Introduction to
The Power of Darkness [1991]

Many years ago I was commissioned by the BBC to adapt Tolstoy's melodrama into Irish speech for radio. Most of Tolstoy's fiction was by then part of my mind, but I was unaware that he had written for the theatre. In fact, I had somehow assumed that he looked on the theatre as frivolous. The people who offered me the commission felt that the play could translate naturally into Irish country speech because of the strong religious presence there and the absence of a class system; in a similar British idiom they felt it could sound merely quaint or antiquated and even ridiculous.

The play was produced and it was well received. One of the good things about a publication or a production is that it generally kills off any emotion that still clings to the work, and frees the writer. That did not happen with *The Power of Darkness*. Over the years I kept returning to the play. I began an original play, but elements from the Tolstoy kept straying into the work, until it was abandoned. Even after that, between works of my own, I found myself returning again and again to *The Power of Darkness*.

I had come to realize that the language I used for the adaptation had been too colourful and idiomatic and that it skimmed over what was at the heart of the play. *The Power of Darkness* is a perfect description of that heart and is uncannily close to the moral climate in which I grew up. The old fear of famine was confused with terror of damnation. The confusion and guilt and plain ignorance that surrounded sex turned men and women into exploiters and adversaries.

Amid all this, the sad lusting after respectability, sugar-coated with

281

sanctimoniousness and held together by a thin binding of religious doctrine and ceremony, combined to form a very dark and explosive force that, generally, went inwards and hid. For anybody who might imagine this to be a description of a remote and dark age, I refer them to the findings of the Kerry Babies Tribunal in 1985. It is in the nature of things that such a climate also creates the dramatic hope, or even necessity, of redemption.

Several years afterwards, the play having gone through many versions, I showed it to others. What was pointed out to me, together with the many dramatic crudities, was that the play had moved so far from the original in the various reworkings that it was better to abandon the Tolstoy frame altogether and approach it as new work. After I finished the novel *Amongst Women* I returned to it for what I hoped would be the last time, as if it was new work, which it was, and was not.

I want to thank the playwright Thomas Kilroy for selfless and painstaking advice on the original version. [. . .]

John McGahern, Co. Leitrim, August 1991

Introduction to
The Power of Darkness [2005]

In the 1970s I was commissioned by the BBC to adapt Tolstoy's melo-drama *The Power of Darkness* into Irish country speech. It was thought that the play would translate naturally into Irish speech because of a reli-gious presence in the language and the relative lack of a class system.

I would have been glad of any work in those years, and was delighted with the Tolstoy commission. I admired the great novels, his autobiogra-phies and stories like 'Family Happiness' and 'The Death of Ivan Ilych', but didn't know then that Tolstoy had written a play. The play was produced with a very strong cast and it was well received.

Generally when a play is produced or a novel published it frees the writer from the material. This did not happen with *The Power of Darkness*. Over the years I kept returning to Tolstoy's melodrama. This was without any thought of production or publication. I had come to feel that the language I used was too idiomatic and colourful, and had skimmed over what was at the heart of the play. The title is a perfect description of that heart, and it was a moral climate I knew well from my own upbringing. Religious doctrine was used to enforce an abject conformity, and once self-interest came into play evil was easily dressed up as good.

When *Amongst Women* was published, I adapted sections of the novel for the BBC. They were read by the late Tony Doyle and produced by Pam Brighton. Brighton, who had worked as a theatre producer, asked if I had ever written a play. I showed her *The Power of Darkness*. By that time the play had gone through many reworkings and she felt that it had moved so far from the original that it was practically a new play. She sent it to the Abbey Theatre. Gary Hynes was the Artistic Director, and she decided to direct the play herself as the Abbey's contribution to the Dublin Theatre Festival.

During the previews the play went well, but it was met with such hostility by the first night audience that the actors found it difficult to act. The Dublin reviews reflected the same hostility.

I didn't come into the Abbey until late the next evening, and was met by Mick Lally at the door.

'God, John, we thought you weren't turning up. Have you seen the reviews?'

'No,' I said. 'I suppose they were bad.'

'Oh, they were much worse than that,' Mick said.

'What are you worried about, so?'

'No matter what they say, that play is alive,' Mick said. 'Andy O'Mahony liked it at one of the previews and has a show going out at 7.30. A car is coming for you in half an hour. *That*'s why I was worried. Get in that car and go out to RTÉ and talk about sex and sin and death – and especially Resurrection – to see if we can keep these swing doors open.' The car came and I went out to RTÉ.

I was leaving for America the next day and had visions of the actors playing to empty houses. It is not a pleasant feeling and one I was unused to. When a book is published there is not anything like the same sense of responsibility and public vulnerability. Luckily, this did not happen. The play and the production received good notices from outside critics covering the Theatre Festival. A controversy started and by the time the run ended the actors were playing to full houses.

I have rewritten the play for this production, and though it has moved far from its roots, I hope the truth first glimpsed through Tolstoy's genius is still dramatically present.

August 2005

VI

REVIEWS

Fact and Factotum

O'Neill: Son and Playwright, by Louis Sheaffer

Mr Sheaffer makes this claim for his biography of America's greatest playwright:

... it adds new pages, if not chapters, to O'Neill's history; it gives a portrait of the man different in some respects from the customary image, chiefly concerning his feelings towards his parents; and it offers both new information and some fresh thoughts on his plays, particularly in regard to their autobiographical content. Such a critical approach to his writings is, I realize, more or less unfashionable today as a result of the ascendancy of the New Critics, with their insistence that a text should be examined in a vacuum as it were, without any account taken of its author. Undoubtedly their credo has merit, for in the final analysis a work must stand on its own, yet O'Neill was one of the most autobiographical playwrights who ever lived, and knowledge of his life cannot but contribute to our understanding of his plays. Moreover, we can gain some insight into the workings of the creative mind, into the nature of creativity itself, by studying O'Neill's usage of his subjective raw materials, the liberties he took with the clutter of reality in his endeavour to reveal some of its inner truths.

He also relays something of his grindingly industrious method:

A glance at the section 'Acknowledgements' will indicate the wide range of my research; it was as thorough as a consuming interest could make it. In covering his one year at Princeton (1906–1907), for example, I wrote to all one hundred and eighty surviving members of O'Neill's class, and heard from slightly over a hundred. With those who had any recollection, however minor, I established a correspondence until I had learned apparently everything they could remember. A second round of letters to all who had disregarded my first query brought replies from about half. In addition to all this correspondence, I interviewed the half-dozen or so of his fellow students who had the most to tell.

The acknowledgements run to ten pages and several hundred names and sources.

The volume begins with his birth in 1888 at the Barrett House, a family hotel in what is now called Times Square, and ends with the appearance of *Beyond the Horizon* on Broadway in 1920.

Throughout there is a ponderous and simple-minded attempt to relate almost every event in his life to his work. There is much popular psychology: 'Seized by uncontrollable fury, like the time he had gone berserk at Princeton, he began hacking at things in the apartment, chiefly venting his rage on the legs of the furniture – possibly from the impulse toward castration'; there is some casual comedy, as when O'Neill, escaping to the sea and South America from his first marriage, is headlined in the New York *World* after his wife's family reported the birth of his first child: 'The Birth of a Boy / Reveals Marriage / of "Gene" O'Neill / / Young Man, In Honduras, / Doesn't Know He Is Dad / / May Not Hear News For Weeks / Working At Mine To Win / Fortune For Family'. The resounding cliché is never far away: 'At Betts he was struggling not only to grow up but, since nature abhors a vacuum, to fill the void left by his apostasy.' It has plenty of plain spice:

Over a round of drinks the foursome fell to talking of books, and O'Neill seemed surprised that Betty had never read *Thus Spake Zarathustra*. 'Thou goest to women?' he quoted at one point. 'Do not forget thy whip!'

'He wasn't joking,' Miss Collins recalls, 'at least he had a serious expression when he said it. I could have gone for him – my God, what eyes he had! – but he was in love with Louise Bryant, everybody knew it. I saw Gene a few times after that and he wanted me to go to bed with him. I wouldn't, though, I knew I would just be a convenience for him. Some time later I ran into him again and he said, 'Well, Betty, I'm no longer in love, what about it?' 'But now I am, Gene,' I told him, so I never did sleep with him. Wonder what it would have been like . . . I'm a little sorry now [said with a shrug and a smile] I didn't.'

There is even a central plot. O'Neill, the artist-hero, is constantly seeing a struggle between his Eyes and Mouth. While the Eyes pierce the Dantesque depths, the Mouth is weak and sensual and cruel. This is further externalized by the conflict between his Drinking and his Work. A supporting cast, the friends that come and go, as well as his own conflicting impulses, drag him toward one or the other. All is comfortably explained by the result: his destructive impulses provide the inspiration and material for his work; and all arrive happily festooned together on Broadway. In this sub-fiction the need to create character and atmosphere is replaced by the respectability of painful and laborious years of research and succeeded by certified fact.

In fairness, it should be said that any biography of O'Neill is close to the impossible. In his masterpiece *Long Day's Journey into Night* he drew so directly and powerfully on his life that any account will seem very much a newspaper report of what that great play causes us to imagine we had witnessed at first hand. This biography, too, is likely to give pleasure to the increasing numbers who prefer their novelettish reading researched and certified as having happened; and it will have served some honourable function if it leads even one or two people to the enjoyment of O'Neill's work.

Everybodies

Being Geniuses Together,
by Robert McAlmon and Kay Boyle

Robert McAlmon's name belongs honourably to the history of the little magazines of the 1920s. When he became with William Carlos Williams the publisher of *Contact* magazine, he became for Kay Boyle 'an element in my own rebellion against status, fuel to my own fury for independence, and I revered him as a man who, like Sherwood Anderson, exemplified the mounting protest … against the English literary tradition.' Not surprisingly, he had little use for Eliot:

Eliot appeals to the adolescent emotions of despair and defeat. His cerebral tearfulness, his liverish and stomach-achey wail, dominated his poetry during his college days, long before the war, at the time he was writing 'Prufrock', and with artifice having people come and go talking of Michelangelo, while the long-haired Pole plays Chopin. He became then quite a butler to the arts, the 'classes', and later to the Church.

Or the shrewd Mencken:

It simply was not in the minds of our generation (the younger generation then) to look on Mencken as a person with a feeling for literature. Axe-grinding articles, pieces with purported sociologic or documentary contents, and attitudes showing up the boobs for other boobs to chuckle at, this he could and did do, but his mediocre mind was dated pre-war and never sensitive.

Or the courteous and gentle Fitzgerald whom we meet here on the Channel ship.

But he did use the money he acquired through his marriage to the distinguished historical novelist Bryher to help and publish through

Contact magazine and the book publishing house Contact Editions the writers he believed in, and many of these were among the most important of his generation. He was the first to publish Hemingway but this relationship later gave way, after bull-fighting and trout fishing in Spain, to the brawl outside the Montparnasse bar and, as in other relationships, rancour on McAlmon's part: 'Some declare it is a great story, "Great Two-Hearted River". I find it is a stunt and very artificial, and I do not believe his mind works that way at all. I think he's a very good business-man, a publicity-seeker . . .'

McAlmon drank, he wrote, he published, he travelled, he danced, he sang, he met everybody he wanted to; but it grows clear that his realization that he was no genius, which seems closely linked to his alcoholism, came to dominate and canker his whole life:

Williams has often said that I have 'a genius for life', while in the same breath he bemoans his own New England soul and the fact that he has not ventured far or long from the town of his birth, where he practises medicine. He may be right about me. If absolute despair, a capacity for reckless abandon and drink, long and heavy spells of ennui which require bottles of strong drink to cure, and a gregarious but not altogether loving nature is 'a genius for life', then I have it . . .

he says, and Kay Boyle describes the outburst of self-vituperation when she said that perhaps the Black Sun Press would do a collection of his poetry:

The God-damned, fucking, quivering pieces of me! Good enough to be flushed like you know what down the drain! Stinking enough to be tacked on the barn door in warning to the young! . . . Fouled up enough for – what? You finish it! I'm fed up with whatever it is I'm carrying around inside this skin, rattling around inside these bones! . . . For Christ's sake, don't care about me! Stop it, will you? Let the God-damned pieces fall apart!

McAlmon wrote the original of *Being Geniuses Together* in 1934, on his life in the 1920s. It was published in 1938. For its resurrection Kay Boyle has revised and shortened it and added alternating chapters of her own. She draws certain parallels: they were both Americans who had married into European families where 'The moments of our daily lives had been placed suddenly in the hands of families-in-law of other nationalities, into the keeping of women and men we knew almost nothing about; and they, held static within the fixed boundaries, the fixed postures, of their own nights and days, became the custodians of our existences.' As well as revolting against literary traditions they were in revolt against their families-in-law. They both admired, with certain reservations on McAlmon's part, each other's work. They were connected with much the same people and small magazines, which were seen in Jolas's words as one continuous 'proving ground for the new literature, a laboratory for poetic experiment'. Boyle had worked on *Broom* in New York. She first met McAlmon through its editor Harold Loeb. In her relationship with Ernest Walshe she helped on *This Quarter*. *transition* published them both.

Neither of them writes well, even if McAlmon's garrulous clumsiness is preferable to Boyle's effusions: 'But if her flesh hurt the knuckles when one knocked for entry to her heart, there was within her a core of uncertainty as soft as the petals of a rose.' Often in the rounds of drinks and people and places and gossip and intrigue it is necessary to look to the top of the page to discover which of them is actually writing. Neither Boyle's French family-in-law or the interesting Ellermans or the various portraits of the famous ever rise above the level of caricature except in stray bits of dialogue: 'Fritz, you ged de taxi vor Meester Firbank. He is a goot man und a goot gustomer, put he is trunk.' Both of them are more concerned with measuring and exhibiting their own uncertain egos in every situation than with any wish to see. The liveliest and most sympathetically human of all the portraits is that of the wily Mr Joyce and his wife Nora; but more typical of the tone is this description of an encounter with Yeats:

He was staying in the same hotel as I, and as he was a friend of Ezra's, and I had been told he knew my work, I telephoned his room. It was morning, and he was leaving the next day and would be very busy. But 'Come up at once, and have coffee,' he suggested . . . Yes, he did look 'aesthetic' and somewhat deliberately vague, with his head in the clouds. Of course, some of his poetry is 'beautiful', but I found it too Irish twilighty and sweetly mystic. It is impossible to recall much of the conversation beyond courteous and hospitable greetings. He mentioned truth and beauty and art, and I gathered that he was going to enlarge upon the point that 'beauty or art is the eternal search' . . . I pleaded another engagement and bolted. Mr Yeats was entirely likeable, amiable and sympathetic. If he had been nearer my own age I would have stopped his sermon on beauty. As it was, I knew it was hopeless.

The pity is that with his energy, his candour, his charm, his good looks and apparent generosity, McAlmon was possibly good company. None of these qualities inhabit his language, and the often-mentioned icy stare that made people look closely at themselves and their pretences becomes no more than another posture. What the language does betray is a dreary and vicious commonplaceness.

Authors' Domains

Between Life and Death, by Nathalie Sarraute

Nearer to me, but not too near . . . a little to one side nevertheless . . . but rather far from all the others . . . at just the right distance . . . you my double, my witness . . . there, lean over with me . . . let's look together . . . does it emit, deposit . . . as on the mirror we hold before the mouth of the dying . . . a fine mist?

This is, one supposes, the description of the final bringing together of 'the world of literature and the world of life' spoken of in the blurb to Nathalie Sarraute's novel, her attempt 'to show some phases of the uncertain struggle between the complementary domains of life and death, merging into each other, that field where literary work develops impetus and grows or dies'.

The domains unfortunately never do merge. They remain embodied in two separate essays. The longer, an investigation into the creative process, is leaden with pretension, the kind of pretension Proust describes as next-door neighbour to stupidity; and it almost swamps the fine satirical talent the author displays in the remainder of the book, where she describes the comedy of the Word made Public, and now moving in the social fumes of position and vanity and fashion, with the consequent insecurity and insatiable need for reassurance of its creators:

He stretches out his arm, bends it again . . . 'I tear out the page.' He clenches his fist, then his arm drops, his hand relaxes . . . 'I throw it away. I take another sheet. I write. On the typewriter. Always. I never write by hand. I reread . . .'

All this huffing and puffing to describe the probably indescribable act of writing comes comically to resemble a laborious and meticulous count of the number of pubic hairs involved in the struggle in the hope of illuminating the sexual act. Then suddenly – 'We'll take it. That is, I think so. You feel in it, that's certain' – with the apparent announcement of the acceptance for publication of the work in question, the prose comes to life. The act has at long last become social, and in the social world of letters Madame Sarraute moves wonderfully at ease. Little in the glasshouse escapes her ironic eye: the egotism of authorship, the jostling for the little territories of recognition, the attendant crowds greedy to pedestal their false gods and at the same time tear them down. There is in particular one brilliantly malicious chapter on the author giving tea.

But even here affectation is not far away. It is as if Madame Sarraute realizes that nothing finally will justify the pretensions of her ambition but poetry. The metaphor, to take but one of her thematic repetitions, of the father seeing his darling daughter a wallflower, echoed later by the father taking his son to the city, and finally echoed at the very end by the mother taking the new-born child from the nurses, while courageously attempting to create a resonance of rhyme or music in the prose, never passes beyond that of another intricately-worked poetic cliché. One sorrows for all the wasted artifice and care that must have gone into the making, especially since one of the flattering illusions the demands of the book bestow on the reader is that while reading he, somewhere, somehow, is taking part in the writing of a book. But no matter how clever and intricate poeticism can be, it is no substitute for poetry. Of all the writers unfairly labelled together as the post-war French experimentalists, I have often wondered if the reason why Claude Simon is so little known in this country is simply that he is a true poet.

An Island Race

Achill, by Kenneth McNally

It is old thou art, o bird of Eacaill
Tell me the cause of your adventures;
I possess, without denial,
The gift of speaking in the bird language.

The whitetailed sea eagle and the golden eagle have disappeared from Achill, as have many of the island ways described in this book, and described beautifully in its extracts from Paul Henry's letters. Recently a priest was presented, on his transfer from the island, with a colour TV set, and this spirit can be set down beside the spirit of the naked iron cross that dominates the little harbour of Purteen even when it is awash with the bloated sharks that stink to heaven in hot weather. And on a Sunday evening in April if the big ghost of the redoubtable Mr Nagle passed through Keel and saw the football pitch against the long and beautiful Keel Strand, running from the white-washed blobs of the cottages to the beetling Menawn Cliffs, enclosed by a rectangle of cars hooting their applause for every score and tooting their annoyance at fouls and unfavourable decisions, he might reasonably have recourse to his Maker, He who is Alpha and He who is Omega. The same incongruity of the tooting cars against the sea and cliffs extends to local TV sets where to the words of *Bail ó Dhia oraibh go léir a chairde Gael ó Pháirc an Chrócaigh* a bull can sometimes charge around the arena. Along the same road by Keel and across the waters of the Sound, now spanned ironically by the Michael Davitt Bridge, Captain Boycott made his last journey from the Island on his way to Lough Mask and into the English language.

This admirable and carefully researched book records all this, as it does the soils, the plants, the weather, the fishing, the changing social life of the people, how they survived mostly through emigration, even then emigrating in groups, taking their island with them to Cleveland and to Glasgow.

For me two things in the book were particularly interesting: the account of Archbishop McHale's efforts to destroy the work of the proselytizing Missionary Settlement at Dugort, which adds yet another sordid note to the history of the Church in Irish education, greedy for power and careless or fearful of knowledge; and Mr McNally's dwelling on the natural courtesy of the Achill people towards strangers, which is unusual in many inland places, where the stranger is often looked upon with hatred and suspicion. Mr McNally states that this is probably because the Achill people, having at all times to emigrate in order to survive, found themselves as often as not in the position of stranger, so that when the stranger comes among themselves they treat him with an even more meticulous courtesy than they reserve for one another. This is probably true and I would like to think it rests as well upon an older truth, the knowledge that all men are strangers to one another, and that the tension of fear and attraction that this creates is ritualized into a generous courtesy. An Englishman told me that one Sunday forty years ago or more he watched de Valera drumming up votes round the island in a battered Ford by ranting against Britain and the British and that later some Achill men came up to him in the pub and said, 'Don't take it to heart what he said. He doesn't mean that. He has to say that. It's his job', which is a very charitable description of a politician.

Such labour has gone into the making of this book that I uneasily state my disappointment: that any spirit of the place, with the exception of the quotations from Paul Henry's letters, eludes the book completely. I thought longingly of *Sea and Sardinia*, and, more recently, of George Mackay Brown's wonderful tapestry of the Orkneys, and of a slender book of poems, *Malcolm Mooney's Land*, by W. S. Graham, which beautifully reveals the most elusive island of all, the First Person Singular.

Mr McNally may fairly protest that he did not intend to write such a book. He set out to write a different book. And that different book he has assembled scrupulously and well.

Memories of Newcastle

Kiddar's Luck and *The Ampersand*, by Jack Common

Jack Common was born in the working-class suburb of Heaton, Newcastle upon Tyne, in 1903, the son of a railwayman; and he died in 1968. These two autobiographical novels, on which his claim to permanence in the language rests, were written between 1949 and 1953 and they were first published by the Turnstile Press in 1951 and 1954. They are now both reissued in this single volume. Though admired by E. M. Forster and Orwell and Kingsley Martin, they went largely unnoticed when first published. His reputation was kept alive by a small minority who admired his work.

Kiddar's Luck, the title taken from Jimmy Learmouth at the Newcastle Hippodrome ('Hallo, kidders! How's your luck?'), recreates the world in which Jack Common grew up on Tyneside in the early years of the century, ending during the First World War when Kiddar reaches fourteen and has to think about finding work. He addresses a savage letter to an imaginary employer, invoking the god of luck, the only worker of true miracles among the poor.

The novel opens with the first meeting of his future parents, outside a pub; their courtship, families, marriage, the ominous death of their first child. Kiddar is conceived – 'I came upon the frost-rimmed roofs of a working-class suburb in Newcastle upon Tyne, and in the back-bedroom of an upstairs flat in a street parallel with the railway line, on which a halted engine whistled to be let through the junction, I chose my future parents' – and almost at once his life begins to go wrong. The mother breaks her leg. A young medico botches the setting, leaving ligaments between the bones. Forever after she is a partial cripple, takes to

298

drink and the pawnshop; while the handsome father grows ashamed, and starts to philander secretly. It is, in some ways, the situation of *Long Day's Journey into Night*, but Common's world can't afford tragedy. His defence is laughter. Even the horrible humiliation of the crippled mother's arrest in charge of a pram becomes just another little comic Calvary:

At that moment, her lame foot caught on the sweeping hem of her skirt, the pram-handle went down under her weight, the baby yelled from fright. Over comes the copper to help. Yes, but he did think she was drunk. He wanted to run her in; worse, he did run her in; kids, pram as well, all the way to Headlam Street Police Station.

God, I could see it so vividly, that shame-making procession, the flushed, protesting, limping woman still hanging on to one whimpering child; the smart young copper holding her free arm and trying to steer a pram-full of yelling babe past curious and unsympathetic bystanders.

The rare, intermittent consciousness of values other than the society's is Common's own.

There are wonderful small portraits, of the houses and streets and people: Mrs McGrewin, for instance, queen of the hockers:

She had reduced her household to a bareness which even Thoreau himself had never contemplated. 'Simplify!' said the New England philosopher. Well, she had simplified every room pretty near down to the original bare buff. Venetian blinds, being part of the fixtures, hung down in the front with no curtains behind them. There was one double-bed remaining doubtless in deference to her husband's humble need, for the rest, the children slept on the floor in rooms clock-less, vase-less, picture-less and dish-less – they drank out of jam-jars. In this near-nirvana of the necessities peace reigned.

The streets, the criers, the cluttered Victorian rooms, snow on hawthorn, the feeble gas lamps with their trembling arcs of shadow are all brought to such vivid life that they seem to cry out for quotation; the markets full of the smells of poultry and stale biscuit, the damp sawdust on the floor; the whiskey with sugar and a slice of lemon, the tub that was a port-wine barrel cut in two. The prose is shrewd, hurtful, ironic, humorous, seedily elegant. The voice is as slow and sure as the Tyne itself, a collective as much as an individual voice: yet nowhere is there anything like the quick individual rhythm that is unmistakably Lawrence, whether it be Nottingham or Sardinia. Though Common may complain about the innate injustice of the society, its reality and values are never in doubt. Poor as it is, it is totally conservative. Looking across a lawn through open French windows – in *The Ampersand* – on a rich family ending dinner, his mind journeys past envy to finally sicken of 'unreality', and he crosses the road and gets the first tram back to Heaton. The sense of injustice becomes another part of his Newcastle, as real and solid as the lower half of the port-wine barrel; and Common's own voice seems to merge and lose itself in the folk voice of Newcastle.

Common thought *The Ampersand* his masterpiece, but it is here his limitations show. The Kiddars of *Kiddar's Luck* become Clarts, but nothing else changes. The story follows closely Common's own life until he left Newcastle for London.

The sprawling world of childhood is sufficient to itself, but poverty is only an extension of a childhood deprived of its sense of growth and wonder. To develop, a writer of talent – and Common had rare talent – has need of a central idea or vision; and this Common does not seem to hold, or even want to hold, and he is too honest to avoid it:

He was drawn to this huge, mute community that lay shut up in half-houses, family by family, under the uniform-tile, each of them maintaining a warm hearth against all hazards by the slender defence of a weekly wage . . . What he knew was that he wanted both to be good with his kind and at the same time fulfil the separate needs of his nature.

These will be forever irreconcilables. The writer, naturally egotistic, if he cannot choose silence and is forced to go on, must hold life in his vision, and reflect it in the light of the idea, not in its own light. Deprived of this tension, much of *The Ampersand* dwindles to something all too like life, but since Common was undoubtedly a poet there are many wonderful individual things:

Though but an image, replica at most, this second appearance of the same scene had a concentration which gave it an extra-reality. Perhaps the twice-known is somehow more perfect. In being recorded, even briefly, the temporal event reveals that its inner structure is eternal. Truth is always twice-told; beauty that which has been most often witnessed.

The sights of Newcastle and the Tyne are always and often witnessed and twice told:

The old coaly Tyne himself threw up oily twinkles and saucer eddies as he swam out of the deep-green shadows of the bridges, breasted the open day, slapped and sucked at the grey or rust-brown hulls of the cargo ships moored at the quayside. Their salted upper-structures caught at the crystal air. A monogram or colour-band on the tilted smoke-stack was amazingly vivid in it. Lower than their decks, cream-yellow crates in towers held the quays. A tug in swift, swan-like motion forced a weal across the water, and voices on it made tiny delayed sounds. Smoke and steam puffed up from sundry places to expand and die from the over-brightness of the great afternoon.

I like to imagine the sad, limping mother leafing through these pages, and replying as W. C. Fields's mother is supposed to have replied on being asked 'Don't you think your son, Mrs Fields, has a fantastic imagination?' 'No,' Mrs Fields answered sadly: 'What I never realized was that he had such a good memory.'

A Bank of Non-Sequiturs

Tom Corkery's Dublin, by Tom Corkery

This is a lovely book. I might be tempted to refer to it as a bewk, so contagious is its idiom, were it not for the certainty of being blowed out of it by the citizens, with their inexhaustible arsenal of non-sequiturs, that come to such vivid life in its pages. Here is Mr Corkery's own critic:

'His nibs hyar,' explained Methusaleh to the Venerable One, 'is a rare dab hand with the pen.'

The Venerable One had the cold eye and the tight lip of the congenital icono-clast. He looked at me with obvious distaste. 'An amatewer writer, is it?' he sneered.

It was squelch or be squelched. 'Ectually,' I spoke in superior tones, 'ectually I get paid for it.'

It was the wrong answer. The Venerable One turned his head to the bar and bayed. 'Ye git paid for it, hah! An' will ye tell me wan thing. Will ye tell me isn't it a tarrible thing for men to be coming inta a boozer for a jar an' them men talkin' words, and another man to be writing down them words an' gettin' paid for it?' . . .

'It's a damn sight easier for you to talk them than for me to write them' . . .

He allowed me a few minutes' swagger. Then he came at me. 'I suppose that yew,' he queried, 'being as ye are an amateur writer an' all that, would have a great knowledge of Dublin?'

I saw my danger and, downing my pint, I rose for what was intended to be a swift tactical retreat. But even as I did so my old friend Methusaleh, in his enthusiasm, unwittingly stabbed me in the back.

'Sairtindly he has,' declared Methusaleh, 'why the man is a walking bewk of this town.'

The Venerable One struck. 'Fair enough, me walkin' 'bewk,' he roared. 'Can ye stand yer ground and answer a few queskins of Dublin history?'

'Sairtindly he can,' enthused my admirer and patron. 'Ask him any queskins ye can think of.'

The Venerable One winked at his friends in the bar. 'What,' he demanded, 'was channel twist?'

And that was only the beginning of the end.

The pieces were first written as a series of articles in the *Irish Times* in the 1950s. They gave much pleasure then and are here collected for the first time. They stand both the test of collection and time with remarkable freshness. They are quiet, shrewd, sly, affectionate, traditional, unobtrusively skilful and, above all, humorous. They celebrate place and character and custom, are as thronged and full of good things as their beloved Moore and Henry Streets on a busy Saturday. Change is resisted; but, when it comes, what has passed is properly mourned: the old west terrace of Croke Park, the four-legged fellas, the Gaiety gods:

The seat of the intellect is in the dress circle, but the promenade of the emotions needs a spacious gallery in which to express itself. But a circle of cushioners puts a careful limit on rapture. How do you roar or boo or whistle or scream in a circle, and to stamp your feet on a carpet is just about as rewarding as to try and slam a swing door.

What, then, of the author of all this? I think it can be legitimately asked, since this Dublin has the charm and flavour of a singular personality. Sometimes he is a cinema manager, always curious. Here he is dealing with a new employee:

I sent him off to clean a plate-glass window from the top of a ladder, and then, overcome by curiosity as to the Beau Brummel waistcoat, I went out to discover the origin of the species.

'What do you call that?' I indicated the garment.

He looked down at the waistcoat with pride. 'That, baaws, that's a Mississippi Waistcoat.'

'Does it come,' I asked in all innocence, 'from Mississippi?'

'Naw, baaws,' he said patronisingly. 'It's called a Mississippi Waistcoat because Rock Hudson wore it in his picture *The Mississippi Gambler*. All the chaps is goin' in for it now, baaws . . .'

More times he is a student, a watcher, a bystander, and that single disastrous time with the Venerable One, a writer. Always he is a lover. Abroad for him is the view from the lower deck of a bus for a man who usually travels on the top deck. When he goes with the citizen to Smithfield in pursuit of a secondhand piano he is dismayed when he runs into a half-countryside, bales of hay, cartwheels, straw sticking out of the piano, and finds himself offered a clatter of ducks by the man in the pub. He is dismayed because he thought he *knew* this neighbourhood. On the rare occasion when he cannot extend a personal liking to his places and characters, he never fails to honour them: 'Some folk refer to him loosely as a chancer; others pithily as a bum; most just call him a scrounger. But in those quarters where people are reared to have an exact word for everything he is known simply as the "ball-man".'

Because he is a lover, he is also a moralist, always anxious for his city; and he knows that the only happy resolution to this dilemma is humour:

. . . Lissen John: wait'll I tell ye thar he was the bleedin' oul' bowler seven lengths a the field the sun mewen an' stars between him an' the rest a the bleedin' bowlers lissen what does he do the bleedin' bowler down he flops over the last huggle twenty-five brick down the swannee over the last huggle the bleedin' oul' bowler an' me going to Galway wid the missus a Monday. Lissen John; could ye – I mean what way are ye fixed at all – I mean ye know me that's wan thing about me I never ask only . . .

And his Pro-Cathedral and Law Courts and House of Parliament is the Dublin pinthouse, where your empty tumbler should be as ringed as a zebra.

There are forty-five photographs in the book. They are all interesting. Many of them are beautiful. Yet, at best, they seem to me irrelevant, at worst to tend to make their own cliché of the accompanying text. There is an Epilogue, an attempt to sum up this Dublin world, and here Mr Corkery's sure taste temporarily deserts him; but these are cavils. The book is an occasion for celebration.

Local Hero

Speech for the launch of *Deported: The Story of Jimmy Gralton, Effernagh, Gowel, Co. Leitrim 1886–1945,* by Des Guckian

I have to confess I had not heard of Jimmy Gralton until Packie Gralton and Des Guckian came to see me a short time ago. I grew up and went to school all round here, and, like Des Guckian and many others from this area, spent five years with the Presentation Brothers in Carrick-on-Shannon; and that I never heard of Jimmy Gralton in all these years can, I think, demonstrate only one thing: the effectiveness of the conspiracy of silence and suppression around his name and life.*

Jimmy Gralton had been deported. In the ugly phrase, he had become a non-person. Tonight, in the centenary year of his birth, with the publication of Mr Guckian's work, we are seeing the deep wrong done to Gralton being, to some extent, put right.

---

* Jimmy Gralton's name is as unknown now as when McGahern wrote this essay. Gralton was born in Gowel, County Leitrim, in 1886. Like many young men of his generation he emigrated, first to Britain and eventually to the United States, where he obtained citizenship in 1909 and became a committed socialist, eventually joining the American Communist Party. Gralton returned to Leitrim after the end of the War of Independence and became involved in organizing the small farmers in a struggle for more rights and better conditions. Gralton was denounced from the Catholic pulpit as a 'Communist agent' and eventually a deportation order was issued by de Valera's Fianna Fáil party. After a manhunt around Effernagh, which Des Guckian's book follows closely, Gralton was deported as an 'undesirable alien', the only Irishman ever to have been deported from the independent Ireland. The story would have appealed to McGahern, who believed that the radical social ideas of the 1916 Proclamation had been wilfully ignored by a succession of post-Independence governments (see his essay 'From a Glorious Dream to Wink and Nod' elsewhere in this collection).

I wish to make a few short general remarks. The true history of the 1930s, 1940s and 1950s in this country has yet to be written. When it does, I believe it will be shown to have been a very dark time indeed, in which an insular Church colluded with an insecure State to bring about a society that was often bigoted, intolerant, cowardly, philistine and spiritually crippled. 'Whatever you say, say nothing' were its watchwords.

Such a society and a man like Gralton could hardly avoid coming into violent collision. Mr Guckian shows this clearly and shows too how feeling and opinion against Gralton were unscrupulously manipulated.

The role of Gralton's neighbours is happier. I have a sense that there is a very old knowledge and tradition in the localities of Leitrim, a knowledge and tradition so hidden as to form a kind of secret society. The mind of this society is deeply suspicious of both Church and State, of all sects and isms and classes. Its only allegiance, and it is a fiercely held allegiance, is to what I would describe as the decently human. Gralton's neighbours had watched him with his father and mother, had worked with him and played with him. They knew their man and they knew him on their ground. No one, no Church nor State, was going to convince them that Gralton was other than the man they knew. Even more than Gralton's name, we are honouring the sense of justice and fair play those neighbours held against all odds. Without them we would not be here tonight.

Mr Guckian's account of Gralton is simple and factual and moving. I found its plain style a delight: 'He and his sisters were home for bonfire night. They were home for the bonfire dance in Effernagh.' Though I suspect that Gralton's importance may yet turn out to be more than local, I think it wonderful that these local histories are now being written. I admired very much Father Liam Kelly's book on Kiltubrid.

All things begin in one person and one place, no matter what they grow to or where they end. These local histories speak to us more intimately than the great histories of state, and are more fruitful subjects for our reflection simply because they are closer to our own lives.

In his foreword, Packie Gralton writes: 'When I asked Des Guckian to write this book I said to him that there was no blame to be attached to those local people who felt they were doing right by opposing Gralton.' It is pleasant to end with such generous words. We should now be mature enough and big enough as a people to reciprocate that generosity. No person or party or church or nation is in possession of the whole truth. Anybody who asserts otherwise lies against the very nature of our human situation. If we are lucky and true we may reflect human bits of it. Certainly, no blame is attached to those people who supported Gralton. Tonight we are in their debt. They and he served human liberty.

New Victory for Gilchrist

Victory over Japan, by Ellen Gilchrist

Ellen Gilchrist's first book, *The Land of Dreamy Dreams*, was a wonderful collection of stories. This was followed by a long novel, *The Annunciation*, the chief interest of which was how anyone as talented as Gilchrist had shown herself to write so badly.

With *Victory over Japan* she has reclaimed her own territory. She depicts women of the American South, wilfully and eternally young, refusing equally to grow up or to grow old. Wish and desire, dream and fulfilment, law and lawlessness are all mixed up as they weave in and out of the lanes of traffic.

There is a great naiveté and a great shrewdness. They rule by the American Dream and are ruled by it. Violence is everywhere, dreams of violence and actual violence, and linked to it is the fierce pursuit of money and pleasure. If everything seems possible, how are we to know what we want or feel, and the resulting confusion becomes the breeding ground of violence; and increasing violence is required to make anything seem real. Nathanael West wrote about this stasis with a cool savagery that would be alien to Gilchrist. She seems at least half in love with her material, but her brilliant, watchful prose reveals the same emptiness, and never more effectively than when she allows her characters to speak for themselves.

The collection is split into four sections. The last, 'Crystal', is told by Miss Crystal's black maid, Tracaleen. The world is unmistakably Gilchrist's, but she is no ventriloquist. The adopted voice is only really effective when dealing with pure farce: 'I was trying to get to the part where Miss Crystal sent notices to all her friends and told them she wasn't going to any more funerals so if any of them was getting the idea of shooting themselves, to count her out.'

In 'Defender of the Little Falaya', Gilchrist writes about the same family in her own voice. Crystal's son and his girlfriend descend on the bachelor brother of Crystal's Jewish second husband. There is a typically sharp portrait of one of her young heroines, Roxanne. 'She smiled deep in his face. She was very good at this. She had survived three stepmothers.'

Instead of kicking them out, the brother stays to share their meal, gets high on mushrooms in the paella, and, having visions of golden lions and deaf people, almost drowns off his private beach, bringing out all of Roxanne's moral refinements. 'There wasn't enough mushrooms in that stuff to get a robin off. And now we're going to jail for murder.'

The young heroine of the third section, Nora Jane, is taken straight from Gilchrist's first book. Dressed as a Dominican nun, she robs a bar in New Orleans so that she can join her love in California. Gilchrist's intelligence and eye and ear are light and true and very funny as she follows the delicious Nora Jane around California. In Faulkner's sour phrase, it is the world thronged with the bodies of gods and the mind of the pea. There are even twinges of morality, but when they come her characters find it more reassuring to contemplate the life of the whale.

All things are possible, or almost so:

'You can drive my car,' he said. 'You can drive it all day long. You can drive it anyplace you want to drive it to.'

'Except over bridges,' she said. 'I don't drive over bridges.'

'Why not?'

'I don't know. It always seems like there's nothing underneath them. Like there's nothing there.'

It is an exact metaphor.

And it is stranded on a bridge in the middle of an earthquake that we leave Nora Jane singing to a band of children who are stranded in traffic too. All Nora Jane had ever used her voice for was to memorize phonograph albums in case there was a war and all the stereos were blown up. 'Now, in honour of the emergency, she took out her marvellous voice and wonderful memory and began singing long-playing albums to the children.'

All this is wonderfully done, but it is the first section, the Rhoda stories that seem the solid achievements of the volume. They are closest in tone and material to *The Land of Dreamy Dreams* and all deal with forms of violence. In the title story hints of domestic violence ripple out to the violence of war and back home again. In 'Music', the violence of adolescence, 'a holy and terrible age,' is matched beautifully against the restless sexual energy of the millionaire father, king of Blue Gem coal, whose violent simplicities are the expression of emotional and intellectual vacuity.

The final story gathers in all of Ms Gilchrist's striking virtues. Her archetypal heroine, part bitch, part goddess, part child, now thirty-two and on the point of divorce, wakes in a dream of violence. The light of day circling the plants she waters in her luxurious room tells her that the divorce will mean a painful drop in her income, but 'Dolphins don't have anything, she told herself. A hawk possesses nothing. Albert Einstein wore tennis shoes.'

A Solid Gold Novel

The Golden Gate, by Vikram Seth

In those old, useless arguments about the upperosity of verse contra prose even the more obtuse disputants were able to agree that poetry was found more often in verse than in prose but that in the vast general practice of both it was recognizable only by its absence.

They are separate disciplines. I find the prose of the American novelist John Hawkes – *The Lime Twig*, *Blood Oranges* and others – eventually deadening in spite of the stunning poetic brilliance of the images because his rhythm belongs essentially to verse, what George Saintsbury (1845–1933) called blank prose. I bring this up since *The Golden Gate* is a novel of conventional length, written not only in verse but in the sonnet form throughout. Patrick Kavanagh once described the sonnet as the 'envelope of love'.

The preoccupation of *The Golden Gate* is with human love and, conversely, with the enemies of love. It is beautifully free of all the confusions verse v prose seems to generate. Prose is not allowed entrance. A tone that never falters is set at once in the table of contents:

1. The world's discussed while friends are eating.
2. A cache of billets-doux arrive.
3. A concert generates a meeting.
4. A house is warmed. Sheep come alive.
5. Olives are plucked in prime condition.
6. A cat reacts to competition.
7. Arrests occur. A speech is made.
8. Coffee is drunk, and Scrabble played.

9. A quarrel is initiated.
10. Vines rest in early winter light.
11. The Winking Owl fills up by night.
12. An old affair is renovated.
13. Friends meditate on friends who've gone.

The months go by; the world goes on.

The friends are a group of people, mostly young, and their pets –
several cats, an iguana – who live within driving distance of the Golden
Gate Bridge in California in the 1980s. There is John, a handsome,
successful young executive who suffers from egoism and loneliness; his
devoted ex-girlfriend Janet, who is a sculptor by day and a drummer
with the Liquid Sheep band by night; Phil, a divorcee and drop-out of
Silicon Valley, who looks after his young son and garden and works for
the peace movement.

Through a lonely hearts ad the Dorati family become intertwined
with them: Liz Dorati, a young lawyer, her sister Sue, a cellist, their
brother Ed, owner of the iguana, torn between his homosexuality and
church teaching; the family vineyard in the Sonoma Valley, the father
Mike Dorati, who's been farming his benchland loam for forty years,
and the ailing mother who longs for grandchildren.

Nothing much – or everything – happens, as the table of contents
suggests, depending on your point of view. People work, converse, fall in
love, fall out of love. They marry, have children, enjoy or suffer their cats,
listen to music, drink coffee, read books, play Scrabble, try to pick one
another up in the Winking Owl, walk on the seashore. Young people are
killed in a car crash. An older woman dies. The rest live on. Its message
is unambiguous: Earth is the only place for love. We must ensure that it
is passed on. It is no place for enduring grudges. We must give and try
to receive all the sweetness that we can. We must love one another or die.

Then there is the overlord of this creation, the omnipresent narrator,
wielder of the sonnets, eavesdropper, buttonholer, nudger, prompter,
philosopher, scholar, poet, half mortal and half god. He is his own best
creation, a true fiction. Though Mr Seth was born in Calcutta and took
his undergraduate degree at Corpus Christi College, Oxford, his narrator is in that pure American line that runs from *Huckleberry Finn*

through *Catcher in the Rye* with the exception that he at all times stays out of the action.

The verse is able to do certain things with an élan that would be impossible for prose. Because of its distancing effect, it restores many clichés, even platitudes – love is blind, the eternal triangle, she's dynamite in bed – to the happiness which must have given them their first currency. Above all, he can write well about blessed banality without abandoning wit or irony or compassion:

> Liz, now addressed by John as 'honey,'
> Responds to him with 'funny bunny.'
> Their diction has, alas, become
> Incomprehensible and numb.
> Their brains appear to be dissolving
> To sugary sludge as they caress . .

> Judged by these artless serfs of Cupid,
> Love is not blind but, rather, dumb.
> Their babblings daily grow more stupid.
> I am embarrassed for them. Come,
> Let's leave them here, the blesséd yuppies,
> As happy as a pair of puppies . . .

> Let's leave them to their fragile fictions –
> Arcadia, Shangri-La, Cockaigne –
> A land beyond the reach of pain –
> Except for two slight contradictions,
> To wit . . . but what transpires next
> Is furnished later in this text.

The book comes with much deserved praise. Gore Vidal describes it as the great Californian novel, which is perhaps more relevant than the great Carlow novel, but he is nearer truth when he describes it as a joy. It is a traditional novel, at ease with its world and its value, compulsively readable, written in verse that is a pure delight.

Who's a Clever Chap?

End Papers, by Breyten Breytenbach

The good things in this book are all straight reporting. There is a very moving tribute to Desmond Mpilo Tutu, a view of the blind Borges receiving the Legion of Honour in Paris, a vivid report of America as the writer goes coast-to-coast on a promotional trip: 'I took part in a live television show: with the two brown-pasted platinum-smiled spokes-people. I sat on a stage that rotated slowly before audience and camera and offstage a man stood holding up placards to tell people to clap or to OHHHHHHHH . . .'

But these interludes are few amid the essays, letters, addresses to cultural gatherings, what he calls Articles of Faith, workbook notes, struggles with his alter-ego and the interspersed poems that make up the book. There is much about South Africa, but it is so often used as a sounding board for ideas and theories and intellectual posturing that even it grows unreal, disappears in the rhetorical smoke.

There is even more about culture, which seems to be confused with politics. 'Politics is a matter of magic,' he writes, 'and therefore ritual, and not of rationality.' If one were to substitute *poetry* for *politics* it could be a true and interesting definition of a certain kind of poetry, as would its opposite be true of the work of Alexander Pope, the removal of all magic from poetry; but as it stands it is nonsense.

Elsewhere he says that art-cultural writing is as necessary as breathing, when they are never more than serious luxuries and a great deal less than that beside some of the terrible things his book dances in and out of. The confusion is so pervasive that one wonders is it endemic or plain wilful or something worse. Certainly, he wants all things at all times in all ways.

Typical of his method is the opening of 'Berlin', where he confronts a classical problem:

The two poles remain freedom and restriction. And, like other pairs of opposites, the one exists only in terms of the other. Even quite recently Claude Levi Strauss asserted that we cannot express ourselves unless there are limitations. It was a reference to Gide's well-known: 'Art lives on restrictions (or obstacles) and dies from freedom.'

That is fairly stated. It is a truth that has always been with us and will not go away. What he proceeds to do is to stand the question on its head: 'I should like to express the same in trying a somewhat different tack. Namely that freedom can be uttered only through structure. Even: that structure is the embodiment of freedom.' This gradually frees him from any responsibility. He can then race away in a series of personal handstands and press-ups that end as a rhetoric that has completely shed the original question:

But what is a working truth, an organic or even an organizational law. Metamorphosis, after all, 'manifests' or accomplishes itself from form to and into form. It has no truck at all with repression. (The structures I have now in mind concern rhythm and pattern and repetition and reason and space, edges of the silence, rims around silences, signs of and towards meaning, the play between matrix and fuck-all, which is what text is all about, and jutting from those all the relationships . . .)

One feels it could continue forever. As he says in a different context: 'But if you have nothing to say it is still no reason for shutting your mouth. If I may quote God.'

Elsewhere, friends are embraced, and there are some sideswipes, notably at Coetzee's formidable intelligence. Even expressions of self-disgust find their way into the melting pot. Breytenbach spent several years in prison in South Africa for his beliefs, but the printed word is pitiless in these matters.

I found the book pretentious and confusing, unrelenting in its self-regard, full of the big words. Just causes can have some sorry messengers, and there are forms of cleverness even worse than ordinary dimness.

Sicily – A Land of Extremes

The Wine-Dark Sea and *Sicilian Uncles*,
by Leonardo Sciascia

She thinks the Italian gentlemen were right to haul Ettore Albini, the critic of the *Secolo*, from the stalls because he did not stand up when the band played the Royal March. She heard that at supper. Ay. They love their country when they are quite sure which country it is.

Joyce's lines, written in Trieste, could describe much of Sciascia's satiric vision of Sicily. This world is as opportunistic as it is deeply political. It is without mystery as it is, despite the ubiquitous presence of the Church, without religion. The Church is seen, with the family and the Mafia and the different political parties, as just another corrupt system among competing systems.

In this brutal, cynical, colourful, farcical interplay the individual is hardly ever allowed a moment of his own light. Even at his most free he is chained to others as closely as the prisoners are chained together on the steamship deck. Consequently, the few individual gestures acquire an extraordinary poignancy.

Pepé, for instance, in *Sicilian Uncles*, works like a dog for the Baron all the hours God sends, but the Baron is having an affair with Pepé's young wife Rosalie and wants him out of the way. He is arrested. In a great display of hypocrisy, Rosalie rushes to the Baron, the Baron to the authorities, and discovers that, alas, the arrest isn't the mistake they had first thought it to be. Though he had done nothing except work, Pepé finds himself chained with the chemist and doctor, both anti-royalists, and the thirty or so other prisoners. The women come to the quay, bringing bundles of linen and things to eat for the prisoners. Rosalie, too, arrives with her bundle. The soldiers pass each bundle from hand to hand, shouting out the name of the prisoner, and as soon as each receives his bundle he waves his chained hands so that his relatives can see he has got it. Rosalie calls out to Pepé from the quay:

'There's something to change into, I've brought you all new things, and there some cigars the Baron's sent you, and some of the fine wheatbread you like.' But Pepé lifted the bundle up, opened his hands and let it drop into the sea. Everybody shouted out in amazement, then there was silence. Pepé shouted, 'You should've brought poison, because if I live I'll tear your heart out, and the heart of that . . .' A soldier gave him a blow in the ribs with his rifle-butt and he was silent. He remained leaning against the ship's rail, lost, his eyes running with tears.

The Baron continues his affair with Rosalie amid much farce and some bliss. They produce a son. The doctor and chemist return to take their place in the corrupt castle at the next political upheaval, but Pepé disappears from the text as completely as the Fool in *King Lear*.

There are thirteen stories in *The Wine-Dark Sea*. Twelve of them are short, more like parables or elongated jokes and ironies than stories. In 'The Long Crossing' peasants pay a travelling salesman part of the passage money to America. They are taken aboard the ship at night, spend a terrible week at sea, and after parting with the final payment are put ashore again at night. In the morning they discover themselves not in America but in a different part of Sicily. In 'Guifa' a mythological simpleton, a mixture of cunning and stupidity, is encouraged to shoot a red-crested bird. There are many birds, but Guifa has only eyes for the first living thing that comes along with a red head, and from behind a hedge shoots the cardinal out on his morning stroll. He also gets away with it.

Sciascia has been likened to Pirandello, but he does not have either his dramatic intensity or individual focus. None of these tales can even mildly compare with Pirandello's 'A Soft Touch of Grass' or 'The Rivers of Lapland'. Only in the long title story has his true talent room to flower, when a couple with two spectacularly awful children, a girl entrusted to their care, and an engineer travelling to take up work in Sicily are all thrown together in a railway compartment on the two-day journey from Rome. Somehow he makes the journey a complete representation of existence in a particular society, in its prejudices and fears and hopes and longings, not least the longings for sleep after it all.

This ease and mastery are to be found abundantly in the four novellas that make up *Sicilian Uncles*. Each is set in a historical phase. The weakest, 'The Death of Stalin', is the one closest in time. Here a cobbler, a political activist, communist and anti-clericalist, hero-worshipper of Stalin for most of a lifetime, is forced to face the discovery that the life of his hero has been far from untainted and to comically resolve his dilemma in human and local terms.

Without condescension and without rancour the worlds of the weak and ignorant and exploited are given a voice amid the barbarous pageantry of their masters. The effect is that of a very strange, intensely moving poetry.

A Plain Tale from a Desert Island

Foe, by J. M. Coetzee

J. M. Coetzee's *Life and Times of Michael K* was a remarkable novel that deservedly won the Booker Prize in 1983. His essays and articles have been distinguished by a rigorous intelligence.

Foe seems to be both an act of homage to Daniel Defoe and an engagement with the great master of plain style. In it a new version of *Robinson Crusoe* is superimposed on the original. It is both fable and allegory, an enquiry into the nature of art or story, of fact and fiction, of illusion and reality.

Susan Barton is cast up on Defoe's island and is found by Friday. She suffers the boredom of the island as she watches Cruso pass the time by building. She does not offer to join Cruso in this work, for she holds it to be a stupid labour. Her days are spent walking the cliffs or along the shore, or sleeping. She confesses that if she ever gave up hope of being rescued that she would try to have a child by Cruso in order to break up the morose silence in which they lived.

There is no law on the island except the one commandment that you must work for your daily bread. There is no need of law since there are no desires. The desire to escape is outside the life of the island and is irrelevant.

To Susan's joy, a ship arrives. Cruso is too ill to protest as the sailors carry him to the ship, and Friday is captured and taken aboard. On the voyage Cruso dies and is buried at sea. Susan arrives in London with the mute Friday as evidence of her life on the island. She becomes a character in search of an author, hoping Daniel Foe will write the story of the island and make their fortune. Foe, however, is more interested in the story of Susan than in the history of the island. The battle lines are drawn between writer and subject, and the enquiry which is the novel's true theme begins.

It is an intriguing theme. Coetzee scrupulously echoes the world of Defoe's London, as he does his style, and yet the novel never really comes to life, it hardly ever rises above a kind of tasteful literary cartoon. Why this is so is not easy to ascertain. Even the formal beauty of much of Coetzee's writing seems only to heighten the sense of unreality. Perhaps, in spite of all its elegant plainness, it is essentially too literary, not a palimpsest but a shadow cast upon a shadow; and yet Virgil led at least one great poet to the very gates of Paradise.

Simenon – Far from Maigret

The Outlaw, by Georges Simenon

The Outlaw was published in France in 1943 and wears only the flimsiest trappings of the detective novel. This is almost certainly why it has waited so long for translation into English. In fact, it reads like a brilliant short story that has been teased out and weakened to the novel's length and weakened still further by the conventions it sometimes follows. There are also many moments in which it bears an uncanny resemblance to Camus.

The opening is perfection in its simple starkness. A man and a woman are walking the night streets of Paris. They have no money and nowhere to sleep. She is anxious. He is irritable. They have walked all the way from an unfinished street at the far end of Grenelle, which is not even on the maps of Paris, to see if Lartike will give them a room for the night. They knock on his door and call out. They can see a reddish halo from a lighted stove, a shadowy fixture on the bed, but they receive no answer, and turn once again into the streets. The St Paul cinema is spilling out its crowd.

Nushi asks Stan the time. The question is a serious mistake: he has no watch, nothing of the slightest value, and becomes enraged. They try to slip into a cheap hotel, not any cheap hotel, a hotel off the Rue de Birague, off the Place des Vosges, a hotel where some guests sleep four or five to a room. They are faced by the manager. Again they find themselves on the streets, the delivery area of Les Halles, in front of a ten-ton lorry with a name on its side, the word NANTES and a telephone number. Men are unloading cabbages:

One after the other, the cabbages came down from the back of the lorry, thrown by a man who took them from under the tarpaulin. In the street, another man caught them, a sort of tramp in unidentifiable clothes which he had packed with old newspapers for warmth.

Each cabbage arrived with a tangible impact, strong enough to knock the old man over. He would wait a moment, then throw the cabbage to his right, where a tall young man would catch it and throw it in his turn to the market worker who was stacking the vegetables in a neat pile on the pavement.

None of them paid any attention to the others. The cabbages were pale, and dotted with diamonds of ice which were abrasive to the touch.

Stan takes his place in the line. When the four thousand cabbages are unloaded, he receives ten francs. With the money, they buy two hard-boiled eggs and two coffees. Without identity papers or qualifications, he has hardly any choice but to turn to petty crime. He attempts to rob a taxi driver and fails. Then he meets Frida, a promiscuous beauty he knew in his youth in Poland, but he is frightened by the gang of toughs she has built around her.

He is frightened still further by their violent plans for robbing a farm he once worked on, but thinks he can get his hands on the money he craves and at the same time free himself from their clutches by betraying them to the police. In the meantime, Nushi gets a job in Dr Storm's house and Stan goes into hiding in her room.

Simenon is a moralist, he is concerned with what constitutes fairness and its opposite, happiness and unhappiness, and he is fascinated by the criminal mind. This is so brilliantly portrayed during Stan's long incarceration in Nushi's room that the conventional denouement, when it comes, is practically unnecessary. All through the novel, the streets, the seedy rooms, the bars and restaurants, the conversations are so completely realized that it is as if one has already lived them. The translation by Howard Curtis is as sure-footed as it is unobtrusive.

From 'Critic's Choice'

The Greeks and the Irrational, by E. R. Dodds

I find re-reading becoming increasingly more a part of my reading. Of the books I re-read this year none gave me more pleasure than *The Greeks and the Irrational,* by E. R. Dodds.

Dodds was an Ulsterman. He gave Louis MacNeice his first job in Birmingham and lived to become his literary executor. In the book he deals with one aspect in the history of the mental life of Greece, and throws light on much else. For someone taught to confuse religion and morality, as I was, to come on the following is like finding a clear spring:

I need hardly say that religion and morals were not initially interdependent in Greece or elsewhere; they had their separate roots. I suppose that, broadly speaking, religion grows out of man's relationship to his total environment, morals out of his relation to his fellow-men.

[...]

The Hero We Didn't Know

The Real Life of Alejandro Mayta,
by Mario Vargas Llosa

This can be described as a search for the unknown intellectual revolutionary.

As a child at the Salesian School in Lima, Mayta was always talking about the poor, the blind, the lame, the orphaned and the mad people wandering the streets. His classmates thought he'd become a priest. After his mother died he was brought up by an aunt, and instead of the priesthood he joined the fragmented revolutionary movement on the far left. There he attended endless meetings, translated, wrote articles, sold copies of the *Worker's Voice*, always in argument, always dissenting, a member of smaller and smaller groups.

His life might have continued in this manner into old age except for a chance meeting with a young lieutenant named Vallejos, handsome, privileged, decisive, the opposite of Mayta. Through a shared streak of idealism they come together, and Mayta's life is pushed from the world of ideology to violent action.

Twenty years later, and Peru now full of terrorist activity, Vargas Llosa sets out to trace Mayta's life's course. He seeks out the people one by one who knew Mayta. Most of them have remained obscure, some have attained positions of power and consequently stand to lose by association. We see these people through the novelist's eyes and Mayta through their eyes.

The time in which Mayta lived is also set against the more violent and complicated present time – Peru as it was and Peru as it is today. Interwoven with the investigative interviews and descriptions is the novelist's own dramatized fantasy of events; in short, the actual novel he is researching. 'My job is to listen, observe, compare stories, mix it all together, and weave a fantasy.' It is a method that allows him almost absolute freedom.

He can move from his own privileged position into the appalling slums, reflecting on Mayta and the shameful economic divisions of Peru. Talking with a successful politician who once knew Mayta, he enters the halls of power and corruption in present-day Peru. As the novelist, he can enter Mayta's mind and dramatize important moments in his life.

The entire first half of the novel collapses beneath the limitless scope it allows itself, suffocating particularly beneath the weight of the ideological cant it attempts to render. To do this would require a darker and more savage talent.

But, against all odds, he saves the novel when the scene shifts from the city to the mountains. The pathetic insurrection, when everything that could go wrong does go wrong, is beautifully caught. Vallejos is sure-footedly represented in action to his inevitable death in battle. Mayta is captured and enters the underworld of Peruvian prisons. The novel grows steadily in dignity as it traces Mayta through the savage teeming underworld. The world of the present and Mayta's world begin to echo one another perfectly.

When we come face to face with the living Mayta, working in an ice-cream parlour, a wife and children in a shack in one of the shanty towns, many of the novel's assumptions about him, imaginative and otherwise, fall away; and in the end, with a gentle diffidence, Mario Vargas Llosa's novel manages to state eloquently a simple enduring decency amid all the facts of the surrounding darkness, and to do so in spite of the novel's own unpromising beginnings.

A Family at War?

Monkeys, by Susan Minot

This meticulous short novel sketches the life of the large prosperous Vincent family at different intervals as they grow up between 1966 and 1979 in Massachusetts. Their Catholic mother, Rose Vincent, vivacious and capable, is the dominant figure, and the 'monkeys' of the title is her term of endearment for her seven healthy children. At the beginning, their father, Gus Vincent, has already withdrawn into heavy drinking, reading and gardening.

In the opening chapter, 'Hiding', the mother and children attend Mass without the father. Then they all go skating to Ice House Pond:

Dad played hockey in college and was so good his name is on a plaque that's right as you walk into the Harvard rink . . . He goes zipping by and we watch him: his hands behind him in a tight clasp, his face as calm as if he were just walking along, only slightly forward. When he sweeps a corner, he tips in, then rolls into a hunch, and starts the long side-pushing again . . . Mum practices her 3s from when she used to figure skate. She pushes forward on one skate, turning in the middle like a petal flipped suddenly in the wind.

The parents are pictures of perfection, and the monkeys fall about on the ice as they try to copy them. At home, Gus reads as he sips gin and beer, and then mysteriously drives down town alone. While he's away, the monkeys and their mother hide in the linen cupboard upstairs so that he returns to an empty house. 'Anybody home?' he bellows, finding the house empty; and then shouts, 'Hello?' But that is the extent of the pursuit. He wanders into the television room, turns on the set, and sits to watch football. They all have to scramble out of their hiding place with a feeling of anti-climax:

Then we hear the deep boom of Dad clearing his throat and look up at Mum. Though she is turned away, we still can see the wince on her face like when you are waiting to be hit or right after you have been . . . We're stalling, waiting for Mum to finish folding, waiting to see what she's going to do next because we don't want to go downstairs yet, where Dad is, without her.

Thirteen years later we find the father and children engaged together in the ceremony of scattering their mother's ashes into the ocean. In between, we see them at their grandparents for Thanksgiving Day, with uncles and aunts and cousins, their mother and father trying to paper over the many cracks of hostility and general unease. Another year they go on holiday to the Bahamas. In 'Wildflowers', a complete short story in itself, they are at their summer house on the ocean among even richer neighbours than themselves. Though by this time Rose Vincent has stopped listening to the Pope, she has her last child in order to assert herself against a sense of being excluded from her neighbours' footloose, jetsetting ways.

As they grow, the monkeys begin to hold wild parties in their parents' absence. The father gets drunk at an important dinner party, but he is delinquent in the face of family pressure to quit drinking. His son crashes the car. Rose Vincent is killed by a train. Their father remarries. Together they scatter her ashes in the ocean and return to land, '. . . following at one another's heels, no one with the slightest idea, when they raised their heads and looked around, of where to go next.'

There are many exquisitely accurate vignettes scattered throughout the novel, single sentences that seem like painting: 'The wind dies down at that time of day and the bay past Clam Cove, its mud flat shiny, was pearly and still, a silk tablecloth with sailboats sitting on top, motionless.' Yet I found the whole ultimately dissatisfying, in spite of its virtues. In much the same way as the Vincents are imprisoned in an unexamined idea of the family, the novel seems to be trapped within its own neatness. The form of the short story at work within the novel abets the sense of constraint. Ms Minot has clear and sure talents, but in the end the novel becomes as much its own situation as the Vincent family it describes.

When the Magic Fails

Drunk with Love, by Ellen Gilchrist

Ellen Gilchrist is a magical writer. She is poetic, lyrical, sensuous, passionate. These adjectives can be pejorative descriptions of much prose, and yet she can make them true. When she does, the work is also intelligent, witty, ironic, sure-footed and sometimes funny. At its heart is a craving for some ultimate violence that will steady both the mind and senses, and when that violence draws too close there is an ambiguous reaching back for the despised everyday.

In Gilchrist's world the everyday is mostly alimony, air-conditioning, alcohol, hot showers, hotels, good food and wine, sometimes marriage and nearly always youth and beauty. It is writing that requires nothing less than perfect pitch. When it is less than perfect, it degenerates fast into whimsy, farce and things worse.

She found that perfect pitch and sustained it for almost the entire length of her first collection of stories, *The Land of Dreamy Dreams*. After a forgettable long novel, *The Annunciation*, she reclaimed much of her talent in *Victory over Japan*. With the second book of stories, it seemed that the novel was, perhaps, a wrong turning, unsuited to a natural writer of short fictions.

Drunk with Love is a new collection of stories. While it is not as disappointing as *The Annunciation*, the worst of it resembles the novel. Some of the stories read like a tired reworking of the abandoned scraps of material from the previous collections. Gilchrist has returned time and again to the same characters and scenes, mostly successfully in *Victory over Japan*. It is more daring and honourable than superficial authorial camouflage but it has obvious dangers, above all the substitution of the imagination for knowledge, since it has all been possessed imaginatively before. In simple terms, it becomes too easy. The short work loses tension without having to take on the novel's responsibility of creating its own larger credible world.

This is nowhere more obvious than in the title story. We meet the delicious Nora Jane Whittington again, back with her first lover Sandy, pregnant with twins, and awaiting tests to discover who has fathered them. Going through tired motions, in lieu of a resolution the story delivers this piece of whimsy. Nora Jane's twins are talking to one another inside her womb, a poor parody of some of Gilchrist's best work:

'Nice night tonight.'
  'I wish it could always be the same. She's always changing. Up and down. Up and down.'
  'Get used to it. We'll be there soon.'
  'Let's don't think about it.'
  'You're right. Let's be quiet.'
  'Okay.'

The two good stories come late in the long collection. 'The Blue-Eyed Buddhist' and 'Belize'. Again, the characters and places and dilemmas are familiar. What is new is the underwater world they force themselves to move in, which both fascinates and threatens. In both stories the prose sheds its tiredness and comes gloriously to life. The imagination quickens. The wonderful eye and ear steadies. The quality of the material ceases to matter.

It does not last for long. In the final story we meet up again with Anna, the writer. She is now a world-famous author, living in New York, having an affair with a married doctor and unable to write. Instead of running away to the mountains again, in the end she decides to open a brand new box of twenty-five per cent cotton bond and sets it on a table beside her typewriter. Then 'She pushes her hair out of her face and begins to write.' The whole story is as thin as life, as uninteresting as all mere self-expression.

Journey along the Canal Bank

Patrick Kavanagh: Man and Poet,
edited by Peter Kavanagh

There was a definite sense of excitement about Kavanagh's presence in this city when I was young. Part of it was his extraordinary physical presence, his violent energy. There are impressions of this quality in the book, but no one captures it better than John Arden:

My personal knowledge of Patrick Kavanagh is confined to an alarming vision one evening in a Baggot Street bar, nearly thirty years ago, of a fierce, ageing face, dark with anger, suddenly towering up under a shapeless hat from among a group of men crowded round a table – it was raining outside and everyone's clothes were sodden and steaming in the warmth – furious quarrelling words, an arm all but sweeping the pint-glasses off the formica, bleats and cries of 'Ah, now Paddy, ah now – no, no, no, hold on there' – and then a slow, pacified subsidence and the conversation once again general and harmless. I was told who he was and I looked at him with awe: but I did not feel at all that I wanted to make his acquaintance.

In better humour in the morning, Kavanagh would make his walk to Parson's Bookshop into an important public event, and a few hours later claim, with equal authority, that he was the most private man in the world.

Beyond all this he had already, singlehandedly, in *The Great Hunger* and the poems around that work, brought a world of his own vividly to life. The dumb world of de Valera's dream had been given a true voice.

He had an individual vision, a vigorous gift for catching the rhythms of ordinary speech, and he was able to bring the images that move us into the light without patronage and on an equal footing with any great work.

More than a decade later, after a bout with lung cancer in a Dublin hospital, he recovered a new world in *Come Dance with Kitty Stobling* along the banks of the Grand Canal and other city places. The vision was lightened and deepened. 'The axle-roll of a rut-locked cart' became 'the inexhaustible adventure of a gravelled yard.' No longer having to climb away from that original child's country to struggle with the Great Immensities, these later poems are steeped in space and time while still happening in one dear, specific place. What they have in common with the early poems is the genius that restores the dramatic to the ordinary and the banal.

I remember well the excitement of reading poems like 'Prelude' or 'Auditors In', or 'Kerr's Ass' or 'The Chest Hospital' for the first time in manuscript. The occasional prose he wrote for the *Irish Farmers' Journal* and other newspapers was always lively, and there was a chance of happening on a fresh insight. There were times, too, when his utterances were unfair and, in Heaney's phrase, 'inelegantly opportunistic'; but had they been more elegant it is unlikely that their moral quality would have been any the more fragrant. It did not matter. To some extent, we were all partisans. We felt an exhilaration at the possibility that literature could belong again to the streets rather than to the Church and university and the worn establishment.

There are good and interesting things in *Patrick Kavanagh: Man and Poet*, but the volume as a whole is curiously depressing, not a quality much associated with Kavanagh. Part of the trouble is a confusion for which Kavanagh himself was largely responsible. Not only was Kavanagh a man of talent but he was a man with a message: 'There are people in the street who steer by my star!' What this message was he never manages to make clear. The message appears in many different guises. Art as a kind of fun, something dangerous and mystical, an entertainment, a profound and holy statement of the failure of man's mission. Sometimes it was confused with life and sometimes with religion. In a not unusual Irish strategy, it defined itself more by what it was against – dullness, insincerity, solemnity – than by what it was; and, in time, became a general flailing about. In one of the lectures printed here,

Thomas Hardy and Michael McLaverty together go out the window in one heave-ho, and there is a sonnet on Yeats I hadn't read before which could safely qualify for inclusion in any volume of Verse and Worse.

What the message was is unimportant, but it was something Kavanagh passionately believed in and that we have to take on trust, and it provided a platform that lifted the important poems. In the weaker poems it often appears as posturing; without the talent it becomes ridiculous. In embracing the whole dogma, Peter Kavanagh places a burdensome emphasis on the work while excluding much of the best writing done on Kavanagh.

Kavanagh had much to endure, both as man and poet, and the pilgrimage from Mucker to the banks of the Grand Canal must have been one of the longest journeys ever taken in Ireland, and in a bad time. A philistine Church was combining with an insecure State to create a society as pedantic as it was inward-looking. Dabs of local colour and cowboy novels in Irish would do with a few bows towards Letters by way of Thomas Aquinas. This is an exaggeration, but the country itself was not far from being a caricature, where people could debate solemnly whether Einstein or de Valera was the greater mathematician. Given the place and time and Kavanagh's temperament, the surprise is that the journey did not turn out worse. And I doubt if any earthly city, let alone Dublin, could have satisfied the weight of Kavanagh's expectation. It was out of the failure that the best work was won: the millstone became the star.

William Blake is mentioned many times throughout the book. D. H. Lawrence, another visionary with a message, is never mentioned. Though of very different temperament, he and Kavanagh emerged from similar backgrounds into societies in which they felt, or were made to feel, outsiders. There are other similarities: their passionate care for genuineness of feeling, their violent reaction to bourgeois art and society, their hatred of the smug response, their quickness to spot any phoniness of emotion (Kavanagh, for instance, identified the emotional vacuity of Column's verses which were then one of the staples of schoolbooks). It is fair to add that Kavanagh's messianic zeal never led him into the areas of extreme silliness into which Lawrence plunged, and Kavanagh's work as a whole is pervaded by a strong saving sense of the comic, which was a closed world to Lawrence.

The most remarkable similarity is the use of satiric doggerel. Kavanagh's use of doggerel can be roughly paraphrased by 'Roll out the dice, boys. Anything goes. *Frog* rhymes perfectly with *bog, catharsis* with *arses.*' The main difference between the two is that Lawrence's fire was the better directed, perhaps because he was the more completely cut off. The Kavanagh of 'The Paddiad' and 'Sensational Disclosures!' is a blunt instrument compared to Lawrence's later satires, but Auden could be describing them both in his brilliant definition of this kind of doggerel as 'the weapon of the outsider, the anarchist rebel, who refuses to accept conventional laws and pieties as binding or worthy of respect. Hence its childish technique, for the child represents the naive and personal, as yet uncorrupted by education and convention.'

Child, lover, braggart, fool, knave, are only a few of the epithets that come to mind when I think of Kavanagh. His extraordinary physical presence, whether seated in a chair or walking up a street with his hands clasped behind his back, always managed to convey more the sense of a warring crowd than of a solitary person. He was also a true poet, and I believe his violent energy, like his belief that people in the street steered by his star, raised the important poems to permanence. They have now moved from Mucker by way of the Grand Canal and the Chest Hospital to their own place on Parnassus.

From 'Higgins Goes to the Brinks'

Outlaws, by George V. Higgins

This interesting crime novel sets the first of its many leisurely themes at once:

At about 9.50 in the morning the Brinks armoured truck carrying its driver and two guards, all in uniform and armed with Smith and Wesson .38 caliber revolvers, arrived at the Danvers Mall branch office of the Essex Bank and Trust Co. The cargo consisted of forty thousand dollars in small bills and coins. A light mist was falling.

Between passages of such straight reportage it continually – and often dramatically – moves its point of view as the plot slowly unfolds: to a dinner party, a musical gathering, bars, restaurants, hotel rooms, airports, police stations, jails and, most often and most successfully, to the courtroom itself. Here Higgins's touch is masterfully sure. The long speeches never grow tedious. In fact, the slower the movement the more riveting the drama becomes. There is a fascinating use of courtroom ritual, underpinning the story like rhyme.

   [. . .]

In the courtroom drama, when it is at its slowest and most reflective and in the scenes around Boston, the novel is at its most compelling. It is less so when it flits Bond-like round the world: but it is still entertaining and interesting.

It's All in the Mind

Blackbird, by Tony Cartano

Tony Cartano is a leading French novelist of his generation and has recently been runner-up for the Goncourt. This strangely literary labyrinthine novel is his first work to appear in English.

'A cage in search of a bird', the prefatory quote from Kafka, describes the novel well, and there are direct and indirect references throughout to the author of *Metamorphosis* and *Letter to my Father*. It is at once a game and a serious search, and it is set insecurely in the literature of identity and detection. Is the self real or imaginary, fixed or subject to metamorphosis? Who is sane and who is mad? And who, particularly, is Blackbird?

We first meet Blackbird through the brilliant notebooks he himself is keeping in Bellevue Hospital in New York, where he's been a mental patient for thirty years. He claims to be the Czech writer – Kafka? – who supposedly died of tuberculosis. Maximilien had been his mentor, Milena the love of his life. These and other parallels are clear but rough and questionable. News of Milena's death reached him, the notebooks tell us, while he was giving piano lessons in New York, having left her long before; and it was the effect of this news that caused people to say that he was mad and to have him put away.

Through the notebooks he is cancelling his own stricture of silence to Maximilien and 'christening my death pangs with a second life'. In the notebooks he is another man, Anton Huka, who moved from Prague to Vienna with his Jewish father and mother when he was sixteen or seventeen. There his father's fortune grew from the first butcher's shop to the enormous meat empire Huka and Son, with the blackbird as its emblem.

335

The father wanted the son to succeed him in the family business, but the son was equally determined to separate himself from the father and to establish himself as a writer. It is this struggle that leads him to Maximilien, Milena, Berlin, Paris, Spain and finally New York.

Side by side with Blackbird's notebooks, Clockwork's notes are set down. Clockwork is the doctor in charge of Bellevue who has become obsessed with his patient and intent on finding out who he really is. This pursuit takes him to Paris and Vienna. In Paris he is convinced that he has run him to earth as the famous pianist and surreal composer Antoine Choucas, who, in 1935, murdered his father, the wealthy industrialist Louis Choucas, and disappeared. Clockwork is triumphant, but Blackbird greets the discovery with derision. Battle is joined. The notebooks reveal that Huka and Choucas met during the Spanish Civil War and that after the war Huka emerged as one Blackbird in New York. A trip to Vienna in search of Huka only deepens Clockwork's confusion as the novel moves towards its resolution.

The labyrinth of the notebooks and Clockwork's notes are echoed throughout the book in a simple bestiary of the blackbird, where the language is as poetic and virginal as the notebook is prosaic and complicated.

Primary experience is eschewed throughout. The climate of the novel is the cultural and political movements in the great European cities between the wars. Its place is the modern mind. Kafka's Prague is Freud's Vienna. Clockwork lurches toward Blackbird. Reality can be the madman's ball. So complicated and intricate is the play that one can never be quite certain whether the book itself is merely an elaborate game or a tragic statement on the nature of man's own identity.

The power struggle in American poetry in the 1950s and 1960s between the Beats and the Traditionalists was once defined as the 'Cooked' versus the 'Raw'. *Blackbird* is definitely cooked, and it is exceedingly well done.

Poor Account of Chilean Life

Of Love and Shadows, by Isabel Allende

Chekhov once stated that there are two sentimentalities – the obvious one of tears, the other of violence, and that they are essentially the same condition, for all their spectacular differences.

The sentimentality of *Of Love and Shadows* is that of violence as it attempts to paint large present-day Chile under the rule of the Junta. Side by side straight reporting of state kidnappings, torture and murder have to live with bravura descriptions of private passions and premonitions. The straight reporting is the more effective, but such is the unrelenting foolishness of the writing that it becomes increasingly difficult to take either seriously:

. . . Then, when he felt her body vibrate like a delicate instrument, and a deep sigh issued from her lips to give breath to his own, a formidable dam burst in his groin, and the force of that shuddering torrent swept over Irene, washing her into gentle seas.

They awaken at the first morning light and chattering of sparrows, giddy from the meeting of their bodies and the complicity of their souls. Then they remembered the corpse in the mine and were catapulted into reality. With the arrogance of mutual love, but still trembling and awestruck, they dressed, climbed on the motorcycle, and set off for the Ranquilio home.

Everywhere is the violent drama of extremes. In a tone of unrelieved mockery, the novel opens in a geriatric home for the well-heeled, with all its inmates locked into the pathetic worlds of their delusions, plainly a parable of the country and its rulers and their camp followers. The home is owned by Beatriz Alcántara de Beltrán, spoiled and pampered

337

with the luxuries the Junta provides for those it favours – delicacies of food and drink, beauty salons, ski slopes, luxurious hotels, private beaches. These luxuries, which she grows dependent on, isolate her from any political reality, much as their delusions isolate the old rich people that she keeps in her home.

Beatriz's daughter Irene, a journalist on a fashionable magazine, engaged to an army officer, breaks free of this unreal world. In trying to trace a young girl abducted by the military, she stumbles on a cave filled with mutilated corpses, people like the girl who had disappeared overnight: and she falls in love with Francisco Leal, a photographer on her magazine, son of an émigré Spanish intellectual. After recovering from an assassination attempt, Irene goes into hiding with Francisco, and later they go together into exile.

The people, no less than the situations and emotions, are all equally overblown and unreal. Irene's military fiancé, another inflated personage, dies in a failed coup, attempting to recover honour to the military. As the unhappy couple go into exile, amid panoramic views of mountain and forest, all that's missing is the sound of Wagner.

From what can be glimpsed through the whole palpitating charade, Ms Allende's own political position appears decent and humane, but nothing comes well out of writing of this quality. Fortunately or unfortunately bad writing is always its own situation, and long before the end I wanted Joyce's woman with her saucepan to enter and declare, 'I cooked good Irish stew.'

Yours Sincerely, D.H.L.

The Letters of D. H. Lawrence, Volume IV, edited by Warren
Roberts, James T. Boulton and Elizabeth Mansfield

That Lawrence is so patronized in England must have roots deep in that
country's class-ridden consciousness. Recently I saw his own burlesque
of himself in London – 'Poor D.H.L.' – taken at face value.

Anybody who wrote the early scenes of *Sons and Lovers*, much of *The
Rainbow*, at least a dozen permanent stories, some brilliant travel
sketches and original criticism, certain poems that are part of the
language, can never be poor; and he turned out to be, as well, a master
of satirical doggerel. It is also true that much of what he wrote is posturing nonsense. He was never middling, and for that instantaneous spontaneity Lawrence passionately believed in, the good and the plain awful
were almost certainly interdependent. For him there never could be that
'calm that is an ordered passion',* and he was puritanically consistent:

Alice Corbin came here along with us. I like her very much. But her mouth talks
of freedom and her eyes ask only to have freedom taken away; *such* freedom.
The Land of the Free. Thank God I am not free, any more than a rooted tree is
free.

He wrote this about India:

But all this 'nationalism' and 'self-government' and 'liberty' are all tripe. They've
no more notion of liberty than a jackal has. It's an absolute farce. The whole
thing is, like Bolshevism, anarchistic in its inspiration – only anarchistic: just a

---

* The phrase was attributed by W. B. Yeats to his father, the painter John Butler
  Yeats, and McGahern quoted it on several occasions. See W. B. Yeats,
  Autobiographies (London: Macmillan, 1955), p. 66.

downthrow of rule, and a chaos. And anyhow, the dark races *don't have* any sense of liberty, in our meaning of the word. They live and move and have their being according to the inspiration of *power* – always *power*, whether private or public, just or unjust. They can't understand the stuff we mean by love or liberty. We can't understand it ourselves anymore, it seems to me.

And in the following he may have described himself more fully than he intended:

I don't believe either in liberty or democracy. I believe in actual, sacred, inspired authority: divine right of natural kings: I believe in the divine right of natural aristocracy, the right, the sacred duty to wield undisputed authority. Naturally I find myself in diametric opposition to every American – and everybody else, besides Americans – whom I come across.

Increasingly the tone becomes one of hatred, a ranting, a lashing about. One cannot but applaud his old father who half-soled his shoes with tin instead of the requested leather when Lawrence was a fledgling author, 'So that thou can hear theyself coming.' Increasingly, too, all the moving about, the restlessness, seems to be a kind of death-longing, in spite of all the protestations that he is travelling towards the sun. The reactions to places and people follow a predictable, almost geometric, pattern: an initial excitement, a brief settling down during which he is happy for a while, and then the inevitable turning away in hatred.

As in the best work, it is when he takes leave of people and ideas and loses himself in a scene that the writing becomes vital and true:

The weather has been beautiful again. Our *podere* is being ploughed. Comes a black, Saracen man, a little young woman in a yellow kerchief, a barefoot boy, two cows, a young silver bull with black eyebrows, a fine merino sheep, a black-and-brown goat, and a yellow dog: and an ass, oh dear Lord, that sings for twenty. The man with the two cows ploughs, the woman cuts the long grasses, and runs after the boy with high-upraised stick, wants to hit him: the bull goes lonesomely about, and flirts with us, the merino sheep keeps near to man and dog. They all sit together and eat under the sorb-apple tree, and the cows get hay, the dog gets bread, the people eat bread and onion, drink wine with water.

It is as if some ever-present threat has been momentarily lifted, and the writing becomes pure seeing.

Such a writer as Lawrence is always better served by a Selected Letters, such as Aldous Huxley's Penguin volume, than by a full collection. These letters were written from June 1921 to March 1924. They have been edited with painstaking scholarship. The introduction by Warren Roberts is useful, but his claim for Lawrence's greatness as a letter writer is not justified by the text. There are occasional gleams of greatness. There are attractive qualities, his attitude to money, for one thing; his hatred of the phoney.

But there is much more that is just unattractive. The minor prophets demand a tolerance they seldom give. Auden's brilliant essay on Lawrence's verse seems to be not only true but also imaginatively generous, extending to his whole personality. No one needs to feel sorry for him though. He was, among other things, a man of genius who wrote well: 'Now we are off to America there is a strong North wind, the sea smoking its spray, and dark grey waves, and this big ship rolling!'

Getting Flaubert's Facts Straight

Flaubert, by Herbert Lottman

It must be very difficult to write a life of Flaubert. The true biography is in the brilliant letters, translated and superbly edited by Francis Steegmuller in the two Faber volumes. Any other life must be largely a reordering of these letters, the Goncourt Journals and such, in the light of fresh scraps of relevance as they become available to scholars – that, or personal interpretation.

In his preface, Herbert Lottman states firmly what his own position is: 'The present writer believes that biography is nothing if not history; that is to say, the best arrangement of verifiable fact must precede any attempt to interpret fact.' For the most part, he sticks scrupulously to this method throughout the book: he is hard on previous interpreters and he does not inspire much faith himself whenever he strays from his own method. What he has done is to organize an enormous amount of material into relatively few pages; and the book leaves no aftertaste of one's having been taken through a thousand newspapers. Yet the final effect is that of a certain dullness and claustrophobia. Given the nature of Flaubert's life and Lottman's view of biography, probably this was inescapable.

Flaubert's background was professional: his father was a doctor; his mother's father was a doctor; his brother, Achille, became a doctor. When his father required him to choose a profession he pretended to pick law. He escaped without qualifying by producing the symptoms of serious illness. Never again was he to try for a place in society and all his life he appeared to see it as a necessary mixture of fools and sharks. He feared the working class as much as he despised his own. The only result of democracy would be to raise the workers to the same level of stupidity as the middle class. 'If ever I take an active part in the world it will be as a thinker and demoraliser. I shall only tell the truth but it will be horrible, cruel, naked.' The position of an established writer seemed to him as shabby as all the rest.

For almost all of his fifty-nine years he lived within his family. For thirty-five years he lived in the family house at Croisset, and most of that time with his mother. 'Are you then guarded like a young girl?' his exasperated mistress, Louise Colet, was driven to demand. There were two trips abroad: an eighteen-month tour of Egypt and the Near East in 1849–51 with his friend Maxime Du Camp and a brief trip to Tunisia in 1858 in preparation for *Salammbô*. And there were regular trips to Paris for sexual and literary diversion. All this was possible because of the great wealth his surgeon-father had accumulated. After his mother's death in 1872 he continued to live at Croisset and he lost all the family wealth, not in extravagance or dissipation but in rescuing his niece Caroline's husband from his disastrous commercial ventures. He died at Croisset in 1880.

Flaubert wrote at the height of the nineteenth century. For him and his circle, art was the only true religion. Style was everything. Life itself was seen as having little value except as material for art. The logic of this is unpleasant. The artist becomes the only true human being. The rest, rich and poor alike, are dirt. Such an extreme position has, naturally, excited passionate opposition ever since, most of it political, and it has often led to another confusion – that of identifying art with life. There is some justice in Erich Auerbach's objection: 'What finally emerges, despite all their intellectual and artistic incorruptibility, is a strangely petty impression; that of an upper-bourgeois egocentrically concerned over his aesthetic comfort, plagued by a thousand small vexations, nervous, obsessed by a mania – only in this case the mania is called "Literature".' But it is more applicable to the Goncourts than to Flaubert. Flaubert was finally too big. Henry James is mentioned only twice in the biography, once unnecessarily, both times caustically. Lottman could have done with James's dissenting intelligence in the Paris sections.

Ideally, Flaubert would have wished to have written about nothing: 'a book without exterior attachments, which would hold together by the internal strength of its style'.* He admired Molière's style but he was a bourgeois compared to Shakespeare. 'Molière is always for the majorities while the great William is for nobody.' We are close to the famous statement that the artist is like God in nature – everywhere present, nowhere visible. 'As for revealing my private opinion of the people I bring on stage, no, no! a thousand times no! I do not recognize my *right* to do so. If the reader doesn't draw from a book the moral it implies, either the reader is an imbecile or the book is false because it lacks exactitude. For the moment a thing is True, it is good.'

Through the correspondence we get glimpses that in his circle of friends conversation too must have been near to the level of art, something we can only imagine now. George Sand appears as an amazingly attractive person, but Flaubert will have none of her recipes for literary success: 'To try to please readers seems to me absolutely chimerical . . . Success is a result; it must not be a goal. I have never sought it (though I desire it), and I seek it less and less.' The gentle Turgenev is the most attractive of all, sometimes falling silent before Flaubert's impossible energy.

In matters other than literature Flaubert can, as often as not, be a lord of self-contradiction, but on literature he is always surefooted. He abhorred the stupid label *realism*, which was often attached to his work:

I think that rounding out a sentence is nothing. But that *to write well* is everything. Because: 'Good writing implies strong feeling, accurate thinking, and effective expression.' (Buffon.)

The last term is thus dependent on the two others, since it is necessary to feel strongly in order to think, and to think in order to express.

He saw Form and Matter as two abstractions. One never existed without the other. Likewise the word and the idea. His good influence is everywhere. The great Portuguese novel *Cousin Basilio* is steeped in *Bovary*. Flaubert is one of the great clerks in the sense that Joyce said Thomas Hardy was in his attitude of poet in relation to his public:

* McGahern substantially misquotes this famous line from Flaubert's letters, possibly citing it from memory. See *The Letters of Gustave Flaubert 1830–1857*, translated and edited by Francis Steegmuller (London: Faber and Faber, 1981), p. 154.

... an honourable example of integrity and self-esteem of which we other clerks are always a little in need, especially in a period when the reader seems to content himself with less and less of the poor written word and when, in consequence, the writer tends to concern himself more and more with the great questions which, for all that, adjust themselves very well without his aid.

The fresh information in the book changes little or nothing; for instance, the long affair with his niece's English governess, Juliet Herbert, is described carefully and well, but it appears to be no different from the other affairs except in its discretion. Flaubert wanted pleasure but not the burden of a relationship: 'taking the rust off my sword' and 'fucking like a donkey' are two of the typical phrases he uses to describe the secret trysts. I can't imagine any new information adding anything essential to our knowledge of Flaubert. He seemed hardly to change at all in what, for that time, was a fairly long life. He came on his central ideas very early and they served him 'till his death.

I have much sympathy with Herbert Lottman's approach to biography. The facts are painstakingly assembled, and it is useful and interesting to see them in this formalized way, but I think the real difficulty for any biographer of Flaubert is that the life has already been written in the great letters.

Sagas from the North

The Masked Fisherman, by George Mackay Brown

An almost lost beauty and poetry live in George Mackay Brown's work as naturally as the sea air his people breathe and the harsh northern landscape they inhabit. In the best of these stories there is a strange sense of timelessness, as if the people, as well as the setting and action, existed outside of time. Though they often stretch across centuries, from the first century to the early part of the twentieth, the unit of time throughout is that of the day, the endlessly repeated single day that breaks out afresh on the action, reflecting the lives of the men and women as they continually set out and return.

These stories reach out past Grimm and Andersen to the northern myths and the *Orkneyinga Sagas*. For all the poetry, they are true storytelling. The prose is clear and vigorous, and it hardly ever degenerates into poeticism; the ballad rhythms are too cunningly varied to ever fall into the monotony of blank prose. Often a movement long enough to claim a whole chapter from a different writer is accomplished in a few simple sentences: 'The girl brought them shell fish. They left the empty shells on a stone. They rowed North.'

The two weakest stories in the collection attempt to echo and mix this timeless world with the present day. Curiously, they are both 'literary' as well. 'The Eve of St Thomas' stretches across several generations. We see the fisherman Aaron Rolfson hungover after the night of the first tasting of the winter whiskey at the smithy's. Painfully, he is trying to bait his lobster creels when he is visited by his wife-to-be, Norda. She stops the work, reminding him that it is already the morning of Thomasmas Day and that to continue working on that day would certainly bring them bad luck. She persuades him to go back to bed. She sings to him and he is soothed.

In the long second part a direct descendant of the people, a successful writer suffering from writer's block, returns with his wife to the island, seeking to renew his talent at its source. The result is to change the world Mackay Brown so often brings to true life into the poor gaudy beads of local colour: 'The sun plucked this morning a brighter string on the great harp of light.'

Much the same happens to 'The Corn and the Tares', which centres on the fact that two of the most famous poets of the North, Kolba Hrunga and Edwin Muir, though separated by seven-and-a-half centuries, were both brought up on the same farm on the island of Wyre. It did return me, though, to the magical early pages of Muir's *Autobiography*.

These two stories stand out because the others are so pure and sure-footed. The title story is a brilliant reclaiming of an incident in the Viking period on Orkney. 'The White Horse Inn' is a delight. Here, several stories – that of 'The Fisherman', 'Harvester', 'Spinster', 'Master of Choristers', 'Lamplighter', 'Schoolmaster' – flow in sure mastery of form to 'The White Horse Inn'. After the drinkers have gone from the inn and the glasses are washed and wiped the story closes with an account of 'The Innkeeper'. The whole is perfection. 'The Tree and the Harp' is no less so, and there are many other delights.

In his brief introduction the author states: 'From the wheel of the year came, wavering and lovely, the dances of Johnsmas in summer and the boisterous Yuletide reels. A northern story-teller must try to order his words into the same kind of celebration.' In these beautiful stories he does just that.

The Man Who Fell in Love with His Dog

Ackerley: A Life of J. R. Ackerley, by Peter Parker

J. R. Ackerley's reputation rests on four short books and his letters. Only three of the books were published in his lifetime. The bleak and funny *My Father and Myself*, which Ivy Compton-Burnett said would be more accurately entitled *Myself and My Father*, was published after his death, which took place in 1967 when he was seventy-one.

The first and most popular of his books, *Hindoo Holiday*, is a thinly disguised account of the six months Ackerley spent in India as secretary to the Maharajah of Chatarpur, a minor Native State. The visit was more or less arranged by Ackerley's lifelong friend E. M. Forster, and it began as letters to the novelist, describing the court. His Highness was more interested in Western literature and philosophy than affairs of state and his reign was characterized by 'financial mismanagement and sexual misdemeanour, these two elements combining in immensely expensive productions of Hindu plays written by himself and performed for his pleasure by an unruly company of boy actors'. Forster was to claim that these letters revitalized *A Passage to India*, which he was writing at the time.

Years of craftsmanship were to go into Ackerley's book before it was published in 1932. It was the first and last of his books to meet with instant success and it is rare among books about India in that it contains not even a taint of patronage.

His next book, *My Dog Tulip*, a celebration of the Alsatian bitch Queenie who dominated his life for years, did not appear until 1956. The 1960 novel *We Think the World of You* recreates Ackerley's love affair with Freddie Doyle, a petty criminal, and it tells how that love was transferred to Queenie when Ackerley took care of her after Freddie had been sent to jail. What all the books have in common is Ackerley's superb prose.

Ackerley was literary editor of the *Listener* from 1935 to 1959 and one of the great editors of his time. (With characteristic modesty he played this down: 'I have been lucky with my team.') Leonard and Virginia Woolf, Forster, Isherwood, Kenneth Clark and Wyndham Lewis were among the writers he persuaded to review for him regularly. Against formidable opposition he contrived to keep open a forum for young writers and dissenting ideas. Auden is the most distinguished of those who have recorded their indebtedness to him for giving them work and space when they were young. Philip Larkin was one of many of the unknown poets that he published for the first time outside college magazines.

As a literary editor he remained remarkably unpartisan, and he was prepared to allow attacks if they were fairly argued on books that he himself admired; but 'There is a step from not being kind to being actually cruel that I am not prepared to take,' he wrote when rejecting one particularly brutal review.

His father, Roger Ackerley, came from humble origins and through luck and charm and business astuteness he made a fortune in fruit importing. His mother had been an actress before her marriage, and a beauty. Ackerley had an older brother who was killed in the Great War and a sister whom the father particularly indulged, with disastrous consequences. Ackerley was himself wounded in the war and taken prisoner. After the war he went to Cambridge. A poem entitled 'Ghosts' stirred Forster to write to him and their long friendship began.

The family's lavish way of life disappeared with the father's death. Roger spent everything as it was earned. A second household that he had maintained in secret was revealed. This has been also written about by their half-sister Diana Petre in *The Secret Orchard of Roger Ackerley*. The death changed Ackerley's circumstances as much as his perception of his father. Not only did he have to earn his own living but he had to support and look after the rest of the family. This was to prove particularly difficult in the case of his sister Nancy and Ackerley had not the necessary firmness to keep her at bay.

All through his complicated life Ackerley pursued obsessively among the working class an idealized love – 'the Ideal Friend' – until it found, at last, its strange quietus in Queenie. While he might acknowledge with Wilde that truth is rarely pure and never simple, he could hardly do so with his heart. This obsessiveness alarmed and saddened his friends. When you go down a mineshaft, Forster counselled, enjoy the lumps of coal, don't look for gold. Late in life Ackerley took up Rights of Animals with the same obsessiveness.

Ackerley had great luck in his biographer. Parker's handling of the difficult material is perfect and he is alert throughout to the rich, black humour that Ackerley himself exploited so well. One feels engaged with a true intelligence from the beginning of the book to the end. All the minor characters are brought to life. Forster in particular is vividly alive, a wise, intelligent kind of nanny, addicted to giving his friends, and even lovers, lectures about money and full of enlightened common sense.

Mr Parker does not flinch from unflattering facts. His analysis that Ackerley never faced his own homosexuality is convincing. 'Frank as he is, Mr Ackerley is never quite explicit about what he *really* preferred to do in bed,' Auden complained when reviewing *My Father and Myself*. 'My own guess is that at the back of Ackerley's mind lay a daydream of an innocent Eden where children play "Doctor."'

This seems to be near the truth, and would not matter if the same romanticism or evasiveness did not extend to the work. It is most obvious at the end of *We Think the World of You*. The beautiful prose, with its Biblical echoes, is not quite able to disguise that the very real implications of the novel are being shuffled to one side as the narrator retreats into the 'darkness of my mind'. In not shirking any of these implications Mr Parker properly honours his material. Joe Ackerley was a man of enormous charm, and he wrote well.

The Life, the Work and the Hurt

Novelists in Their Youth, by John Halperin

The central argument of *Novelists in Their Youth* is that much, if not all, of a writer's work can be revealed through an examination of the life, particularly of the early formative years. John Halperin is a distinguished academic. Among his previous works are *The Life of Jane Austen*, *Gissing: A Life in Books*, and *C. P. Snow: An Oral Biography*.

In this new book the early years of Henry James, Hardy, Gissing, Conrad, Maugham and Edith Wharton are examined. These authors all shared a community of interests (whatever that means), and all were published between the 1860s and the 1920s. But they were chosen more for the fact that Halperin found in each subject something that made them feel 'marginal or isolated'. He describes this as a psychic wound that never heals and links it to creative power, arguing that this impossible wound shaped the writer and, consequently, gave form to everything he or she produced.

In James's case the rootlessness of his upbringing instilled all kinds of uncertainties and dualities in the growing boy, culminating in his inability to answer the call-up to the Civil War, which resulted in a feeling that he could never take an active, approved part in life. Instead, he would live through the lives of others as observer and recorder.

Professor Halperin places James's own description, 'an obscure hurt', firmly in the psychic. Apparently, cruder critics have explained the origin of the phrase with an incident that involved a fire engine and a fence, and such is the nature of James's elliptical genius that the argument itself seems to become another small comic Jamesian refraction.

With Hardy the hurt lies in humble origins, his early obscurity and failures and exaggerated class consciousness. This led him to dramatize, aggrandize and hide. His pessimism is attributed to basic insecurity. There are times in this chapter when Halperin turns away from the more pliable prose to glance uneasily at the great poetry which will not fit into any thesis.

On Maugham and Gissing he is the most persuasive. These are the two writers whose work I know least well. With Gissing it is class again, plus a neurotic identification with his dead father. Maugham's wound is his mother's death in Paris, to be followed shortly by his father's death and his own expulsion from Eden into the care of a self-absorbed vicar-uncle in Whitstable. The chapter on Gissing is the most eloquent in the book and tempts this reader to try the novels again.

The intense solitude of the early years Conrad shared with his father, a political exile, is the shaping influence on his life and work. Edith Wharton's feelings of imprisonment in the rich but philistine society of old New York hurt her into speech.

Prefacing each chapter are three formal quotations – 'skyhooks' the Americans call them – with at least one quotation from Proust's great novel in all of them. Four of the five quotations that preface Professor Halperin's own introduction come from the same source. Consequently, it is worth looking carefully at what is said about Proust – again, there is another quotation, this time within the introduction: 'Everything we think of as great has come to us from neurotics. It is they and they alone who found religions and create great works of art . . . Without nervous disorder there can be no great artist.'

'Proust means, of course, that we must study the artist in order to know the work,' Halperin concludes, and goes on to show how '[Proust's] own biographer, George D. Painter, acknowledges this readily enough.' Painter might acknowledge this, but Proust himself would disagree. In the great critical fragments that make up *Contre Sainte-Beuve* Proust states clearly that he sees the biographical method as essentially idle, since the recognizable, everyday personality of the artist bears, at best, an uncertain relationship to the inner spirit that creates, what he calls *le moi profond*, which operates according to its own mysterious laws, a variant of Flaubert's 'God in Nature': and he asserts that to argue from the former to the latter is foolish. In fact, in the short brilliant essay

On Reading, Proust goes further and dismisses the biographical method as one of the many pleasant forms of moral idleness.

The modern fashion for biography has overtaken Proust's position but it hardly invalidates it. Professor Halperin writes that 'This book has been written with the common reader in mind – the reader who is interested in fiction, in history, in biography.' This may account for the quality of some of the prose: 'A man or a woman who creates a great work is nonetheless a man or a woman.'

The many prefatory quotations, the uncertain tone of the introduction, in which true aesthetic theories are often raised only to be lost or confused in what follows, make one suspicious that this is just another exercise in bookmaking. It may be that a learned man is attempting a difficult simplification. There are a few hits at the deconstructionists. While his own method is certainly more entertaining (there is a detail of Hardy throwing a knife at an insect on the wall during a luncheon at Max Gate), it appears to me equally futile.

Thinking of the enormous publishing and academic industries that now surround true original work – the Collected Letters in several volumes, the Biographies, the Studies – I wonder if the overall result is not to turn those works back into the confusion and trivia and brittleness out of which they somehow contrived, magically, to emerge. We do not need knowledge of Shakespeare's 'obscure hurt' to enjoy or suffer with Falstaff or Ophelia or Hamlet or Lear.

An Immaculate Mistake

An Immaculate Mistake, by Paul Bailey

I first came on an extract from this book in the Bloomsbury miscellany *Soho Square*. The prose had a remarkable warmth and tenderness, evoked an exact time and place with great clarity, and the piece was exasperatingly brief. Almost the same can be said of *An Immaculate Mistake*.

Paul Bailey grew up in Battersea, South London, in the 1940s and 1950s, the son of a road sweeper and a domestic servant. His arrival was late and unexpected: 'You were our mistake,' the mother who dominates the book told him when she was old and letting go of her secrets. 'We didn't plan to have you, is what I'm saying. People like us had to be very careful when it came to having children. You took me by surprise and your poor father, too. That was typical of you – determined to be different.'

Paul Bailey continued to be different – if not quite with a vengeance; it was more than exasperating. He was clever, winning a scholarship to the local grammar school. There, he played Sarah, Duchess of Marlborough, in the school play. It was the lead part, but to his mother it all sounded 'funny'. And he wasn't 'natural'. He bought his mother a bunch of red roses from a florist in Chelsea, but as soon as he turned into their street the jeering and whistling began. 'Why were they calling me names?' he asked his mother. 'Because it's not natural,' she replied. 'You should have got the woman in the shop to cover them up for you.' There was the danger of becoming known as the Oscar Wilde type in that poor South London street: 'Be careful when you bend over,' the street joke went, 'or you might find that Oscar Wilde behind you, sticking his green carnation in where he shouldn't.'

From grammar school, by way of the provincial theatre, he passed to drama school. Though he was to play the lead role in Ann Jellicoe's *The Sport of My Mad Mother* at the Royal Court, his dream of playing Hamlet or Richard II finally came to no more than walk-on parts at Stratford. Instead, he went on to be the distinguished writer and critic that he is. To his mother this meant that he never managed to learn to know his place: 'It's high time you knew your place in the world. I knew mine when I was younger than you are, with no books to help me . . . If God had meant you to be a duke or a lord He would have given you a duchess for a mother, not a servant like me.' 'I've no wish to be a duke. I only want to be an actor.' 'There's wanting and then there's wanting,' she observed, mysteriously.

His gentle, diffident father stood no chance against this woman. He died in 1948, able to give vent to all the suppressed violence of his feelings only during his last ravings. The mother's world is riddled with class; she craved respectability: 'If people ask you what your father does for a living, say he works for the council.' Her obsession with personal cleanliness and neatness of dress gives rise to the title word, 'immaculate'.

People who complain of class consciousness in Ireland can never have experienced its full ferocity as it exists in the South of England, especially in the lower rungs in the system. I once worked in a primary school in Essex where there were at least eight different class categories among the twenty or so teachers who worked in the school who would all be described as lower middle class. For an outsider it was often comic, sometimes sad, and only vaguely comprehensible; but not for those within. Were it not for the fact that it pervaded their every fibre, I often thought that with a bit more effort they could all have squared the circle and reached old Crusoe's island. For someone like Mr Bailey to have come through such a system must be close to miraculous.

The book dispenses with a conventional narrative and is made up of fragments or short scenes, sometimes interconnected, more often not. Many are moving, some are very funny:

. . . a congenial young woman with whom I was endeavouring to make love on a friend's divan suddenly began to giggle. I persevered. 'What's the matter?' I asked, when her giggling became uncontrollable. 'You are,' she answered, pushing me off. 'You're the matter. You're soft where you shouldn't be. You want a man, don't you?' 'Yes,' I astonished myself by admitting. 'So do I,' she said, without malice. 'Let's go and get drunk.'

The homosexual scenes are less sure. There is an innocent affair with a Plato-reading bus conductor that reminded me of the flawed passages in Forrest Reid's *Apostate*, that sometimes brilliant evocation of Victorian middle-class Belfast. As in *Apostate*, philosophy or self-improvement and plain sex seem to make poor literary bedfellows, and like *Apostate* this book is so well written that it seems churlish to say that there should be more, that something has been omitted or put to one side or written around; but the feeling stays. What we have is a portrait that is without rancour, is full of affection and humour, even wistfulness, for his powerful and caring parent.

Travails with the Not So Merry Pranksters

Off the Road, by Carolyn Cassady

Carolyn Cassady married Neal Cassady and they had three children. Neal Cassady was a lover of Allen Ginsberg and *Howl* is dedicated to 'N.C., secret hero of these poems'. He was also Jack Kerouac's best friend. They travelled across America together and the journey became the basis of Kerouac's *On the Road*, Cassady as Dean Moriarty to Kerouac's Sal Paradise; and he is dramatized as a kind of neo-Nietzschean hero in several of Kerouac's other novels.

Cassady signed his letters to Ginsberg 'Your other half', and to Kerouac 'Your brother'. Carolyn Cassady was to find her husband and Ginsberg together on one of Ginsberg's visits to the house years after their marriage. The prose is a fair example of the melodramatic foolishness of much of the writing:

Allen must have been with us about six weeks when one afternoon our idyllic life came to a shattering end. Neal and Allen had been in the latter's room for some time. I had a question to ask Neal, so I tapped on the door as a matter of courtesy and, not waiting for an answer, opened it and walked in. The question stuck in my throat at what I saw before me. The force of the shock nearly knocked my head off, or so it felt. I backed out and shut the door, my insides turning sickening cartwheels. In that brief instant the picture registered *in toto*. Allen had lifted his head toward me quizzically, but I was gone – to tremble, pace, cry to heaven, wring my hands and fight down the revulsion that threatened to turn me inside out.

By the time they'd put on their pants and come out, I was sitting miserably on the edge of the couch, staring at the floor and trying to figure myself out.

Out of anger and frustration and loneliness Carolyn started an affair with Kerouac, her husband giving them his ambiguous blessing: 'You know what they say, "my best pal with my best gal."' So it can be said, in most senses, that she married into the heart and head and pants of what was later to become known as the Beat movement.

Cassady was vague and shifty about his background. It appears to have been poor, alcoholic, broken. While he grew addicted to drugs, unlike Kerouac he was never much drawn to alcohol, and some of his own childhood may have been spent in Boys' Town. Carolyn Cassady is equally vague about her own origins other than that they were academic, middle-class, conventional and puritan.

The moment Cassady first looked at her she felt a 'physical stab' and his eyes were like 'lasers', but he was married. Later the same night she found him outside her hotel bedroom, saying his under-age wife had thrown him out, and pleading for a bed for the night. He got into her bed at once and fell asleep. She remained awake all night.

This relationship continued chastely for several weeks. She was flattered by his intellectual interest in her – the men she had met up till then had been interested in her body only. The chasteness ended when Ginsberg came to stay with them in their small room. With his friend and lover lying a few feet away in the darkness Cassady had sex with her for the first time. She cried out with pain and Ginsberg mistook the cries of hurt and shame for ecstasy.

All through the marriage she complains of the unsatisfactory nature of their physical relationship. Cassady seems to have made love with all the delicacy of a jackhammer. In spite of obvious lies and infidelities she grew determined that her love would triumph. What emerges is a picture of a not uncommon type of young American woman whose earnestness is matched by almost total naiveté. Not only is this book a loud confessional outpouring but a covert attempt as well to deify Cassady and her love for him.

Cassady had a rugged, movie star's good looks, great energy and charm, and he wanted to be a writer. He seemed unable to be alone for any serious length of time, and he was never happier than when hitting the road 'any time and place' with a car, a new girl and buddies; and there was always the dream of a commune, buying a ranch and living there with his pals and gals in an earthly Eden.

He was fond of reading aloud. I wonder which passages of Proust he and Kerouac used to read to one another. (Unlikely that it was the Euclidean, 'Fashion which is begotten from the desire for change is quick to change itself.') There was also the search, which both the Cassadys shared, for the Philosopher or Guru who would explain the world.

The book traces the course of their disastrous marriage, the birth of their three children, their estrangement and reconciliations and eventual separation. During much of this time he worked as a brakesman on the Southern Pacific Railway. This suited his temperament and he had no difficulty in charming his fellow workers. After his jail term for drug offences he found work in a tyre recapping shop. There were more prison terms as his drug addiction grew.

Towards the end he was the bus driver of Ken Kesey's group The Merry Pranksters. They went up and down the coast giving shows called 'Acid Tests': Kool-Aid spiked with LSD or other drugs, hard rock music, Day-Glo paint and flashing lights. The destination of the bus read 'Further'. There's a cast of hundreds including Kesey – in his Superman suit, white tights, red boots, red and white satin cape, a red, white and blue sash across his bare chest – Gregory Corso and Grandma Go-Go. At forty-three Neal Cassady was dead of despair and drugs. He was found beside a railway track.

Threaded in and out of *Off the Road* is Kerouac's story, the struggling author who often stayed with the Cassadys, and at that time he seems an attractive figure: the huge success of *On the Road*, Kerouac appearing drunk on TV talk shows while Cassady was in San Quentin prison, his marriages, his increasing paranoia and alcoholism. Less than a year after Cassady's death Kerouac was dead at forty-seven. Ginsberg, who survived, appears more detached, literary and calculating.

The book is dedicated to Helen and Al Hinkle. Whenever Helen Hinkle appears the writing acquires a much-needed lightness. Helen and her husband set off on their honeymoon with Cassady. As usual Cassady was driving. His charm did not work on Helen and they hated one another. After a while she wanted out. On Christmas Eve she took the train to New Orleans and booked into a hotel to wait for her husband and Cassady. They had continued on by car. When they didn't turn up and her money started to run out, she moved from the hotel to a whorehouse, and finally to William Burroughs's house. Her account of this crazy household is the best thing in the book:

Bill had this cat thing. He had six or seven cats, and each evening he tied them with *string* . . . tying up their feet . . . and *bathed* them. You'd hear these terrible shrieks and it was all so *insane*, but they acted as though it was perfectly natural.

Then there was the lizard tree, this grotesque, ugly tree outside which was – ugh – literally *covered* with lizards. It was one of Joan's duties to rake the lizards off the tree every night. I don't know why she didn't try poison. I'd step out on the veranda after dark, and she'd be raking lizards off the tree in the moonlight.

Burroughs later shot Joan through the forehead while shooting beer cans off her head.

After Cassady's cremation Carolyn Cassady acquired his ashes. One of his other women was so persistent in her demands for the ashes that she was eventually forced to post a few spoonfuls in a little box. The woman's plan was to buy a tree in Washington Square and bury the ashes beneath the tree, accompanied by an old-fashioned quarter:

You know – those old quarters that had an eagle on the back? Well, when you look at it one way it looks like an eagle, but going the other way it looks like a cowboy with a hard-on. Don't you think that's terribly appropriate for Neal?

This is a disturbing and troubling book.

On the Edge of the Dream

Wildlife, by Richard Ford

Richard Ford's third novel, *The Sportswriter*, was a remarkable evocation of an America that seldom finds a voice, small people in trailers and diners and stolen cars and motel rooms who are trapped on the edge of the Dream. Their insecurity is palpable as they attempt to make the necessary accommodations that will enable them to stay happy and get by; and yet Ford, in the miraculous contradiction of art, makes that very uncertainty sing.

The profession of the sportswriter, Frank Bascombe, allows Ford to move anywhere in America, involved and yet separate. There is at once a sense of vastness and a sense of particular lives in exact places, and the tension between this specificity and the blurring vastness with which it is surrounded gives a poignancy that Ford has made his own. Nothing in the novel is more memorable than the wasteland of Detroit, city of lost industrial dreams, where Frank Bascombe goes with his failed marriage and new girlfriend to write an article on a football star, now confined to a wheelchair with a spinal injury, and half-crazed. It is both an acute examination and a celebration:

I have read that with enough time American civilization will make the Midwest of any place, New York included. And from here that seems not at all bad. Here is a great place to be in love; to get a land-grant education; to own a mortgage; to see a game under the lights as the old dusky daylight falls to blue-black, a backdrop of stars and stony buildings, while friendly Negroes and Polacks roll their pants legs up, sit side by side, feeling the cool Canadian breeze off the lake. So much that is explicable in American life is made in Detroit.

The Sportswriter was followed by an even better book, the short story collection *Rock Springs*. The prose is hardbitten, exact, humorous, and it has an unspoken tenderness as it celebrates moments of happiness that would not be so intense were they not so threatened. The dialogue is witty and true and has the courage to embrace a great ordinariness:

'I'll come join you in a little while,' Sims said. 'I'm not sleepy yet. I'll have another one of these, though.' He drank the last of his gin from his plastic cup and jiggled the ice cubes.

'Who's counting?' Marge smiled. She had a pill in her hand, but she took a leather-bound glass flask out of her purse and poured Sims some gin while he jiggled the ice.

'Perfect. It'll make me sleepy,' Sims said.

Marge put her pill in her mouth. 'Snoozeroosky,' she said, and washed it down with the rest of her drink. 'Don't be Mr Night Owl.' She reached and kissed Sims on the cheek. 'There's a pretty girl in the sleeping car who loves you. She's waiting for you.'

'I'll keep that in mind,' Sims said and smiled. He reached across and kissed Marge and patted her shoulder.

'Tomorrow'll be fine. Don't brood,' Marge said.

'I wasn't even thinking about it.'

'Nothing's normal, right? That's just a concept.'

'Nothing I've seen yet,' Sims said.

'Just a figure of the mind, right?' Marge smiled, then went off down the aisle toward the sleeper.

The very constraint of the short form inhibits the over-descriptiveness and homespun philosophizing that flaws sections of *The Sportswriter*, and the whole book has the unmistakeable feel of permanent work. The novel that preceded *The Sportswriter* was an uneasy thriller, *The Ultimate Good Luck*, set among drug-runners in Mexico City. The novel contains some good passages, but for the most part it flounders around in a welter of flashbacks and unreality.

In *Wildlife*, Ford seems to be going over the same ground he covered memorably in *Rock Springs*. In fact, the very title appears to have come from a passage in 'Optimists': 'And all these duck got up, all except for one that stayed on the ice, where its feet were frozen, I guess. It didn't even try to fly. It just sat. And Judy said to me, "It's just a coincidence, Dottie. It's wildlife. Some always get left back."'

At the start of the novel Joe Brinson has moved with his parents, Jerry and Jeanette, to Great Falls, Montana, because Jerry, a golf pro, sees money being made in the oil boom and hopes some of it will come his way. Once there, he is soon fired from his coaching job and grows too demoralized to look for other work. Jeanette becomes a swimming instructor ('Don't be afraid of it. It's all fun. Think about all you've missed'), and meets an older wealthy man, Warren Miller. When Jerry does force himself to work and goes off to fight a forest fire, Jeanette is left alone. The metaphor of the fire is used with surprising clumsiness.

On her own, Jeanette starts to try out her own uncertain frustrated sexuality. She invites Warren Miller to her house, and then takes Joe to dinner to his. There she gets drunk and does a dance of frustration and seduction, to the intense discomfort of her son, who pretends he isn't present. 'I guess I'm very inappropriate,' she says at the end.

Ford brings this woman of thirty-seven to vivid life as she attempts to deal with a marriage that has died. Her husband too is vividly captured: it is easy to imagine both of them all the years before when she was the beauty queen and he the golf star of a small college. Now, when he is about to be forced from the golf club, apparently for stealing, all he says is, 'He'll fire me. These things have a feel. I've been fired before. He doesn't have to have a reason,' and it is closer to nihilism than despair. Nothing as good can be said of the other characters.

Their son of sixteen seems to have no friends and no life outside his parents and is crushed beneath the weight of authorial consciousness that he is forced to carry, serving both author and character equally badly. Warren Miller too never manages to emerge out of the generous labels and tags of his wealth. Setting fire to Miller's porch becomes a thin echo of the fatal blow in 'Optimists'. The feeling grows that a short, short story is being strained to novel length. The prose loses its fine edge and turns both sugary and ungainly:

I wondered . . . if I would ever see the world as *I* had seen it before then, when I did not even know I saw it. Or if you just got used to parting with things, and because you were young you parted with them faster; or if in fact none of that thinking was important at all, and things stayed mostly the same in spite of small changes, so that when you faced the worst and went past it what you found there was nothing. Nothing has its own badness, but it does not last forever. And what there is to learn from almost any human experience is that your own interests do not usually come first where other people are concerned – even the people who love you – and that is all right. It can be lived with.

This disappointing novel adds nothing to *Rock Springs* or *The Sportswriter*, but neither can it take anything away from what is already a permanent achievement.

Patriot Games

Michael Collins: A Biography, by Tim Pat Coogan

In the town of Granard in the low Cavan/Longford mountains, a surprisingly attractive Victorian canopy of iron and glass covers the entrance to the Greville Arms. Inside, a large blown-up photograph of Michael Collins in full uniform hangs above the handsome fireplace, his hand hovering over his holstered revolver. All through the decades of Eamon de Valera's presidency it hung there arrogantly, as it still does today in Charlie Haughey's Ireland. For this was the home territory of Seán MacEoin, a blacksmith turned guerrilla leader and later a general in the Free State Army, Collins's close friend; and the Greville Arms was owned by the Kiernans, Kitty Kiernan being one of the four glamorous sisters of the hotel, and the woman who was about to be married to Michael Collins when he was shot dead in August 1922 during the Civil War. It is this allegiance to the local and personal above the narrow rule of Church and State that has kept most of the people of Ireland as relatively sane as they are.

Tim Pat Coogan's father was, like Collins and MacEoin, one of the young men who helped found the Free State. From 1967 to 1987, Coogan was editor of the *Irish Press*. By then the *Press* was as much an institution of the Fianna Fáil party as a newspaper, originally founded by contributions from patriotic Irish-Americans, but effectively appropriated by de Valera for his family and used as a party instrument. As editor, one of his most ill-judged decisions was to publish on the front page Charles Haughey's political obituary during a power struggle within Fianna Fáil in 1983. How premature it was can be seen by the fact that Mr Haughey is now Taoiseach and Mr Coogan is a freelance writer.

However, his background and career have given Coogan access to a wide diversity of sources. This is crucial in a country where there is often a great difference between what is said and what is thought or known. One of Coogan's sources, David Nelligan, a double agent who worked for Collins, was 'one of the most remarkable figures of the period. He was drawing five pensions when I first met him in the 1960s – an old IRA pension, one from the RIC, the Irish police force, the Irish civil service – and the British secret service.' The extract from Kathleen MacKenna Napoli's unpublished memoirs is so vivid that they seem to demand publication in their own right. Coogan uses all such sources well.

He does not dwell much on Michael Collins's background or upbringing. Collins's father was in his sixtieth year when he married a local girl of twenty-three – the age difference was not unusual in the agrarian economic conditions of the time – and they went on to have the usual large family. Their ninety-acre Cork farm would have been seen as relatively prosperous. Michael, being a younger son and good at school, passed the Post Office examinations and was given a job in the Post Office Savings Bank in West Kensington. He was tall, athletic, handsome, and was soon prominent in the sporting, dancing and political societies of the London Irish. All the time he read widely and was very fond of the theatre, especially of Shaw and Barrie. Through night school, he moved from the Post Office to a firm of City stockbrokers, where he was put in charge of the messengers, then passed the civil service examinations that allowed him to join the Board of Works as a clerk. The single most important act of his life in London was his induction into the IRB, a secret organization descended from the Fenians. This was to lead him directly into the 1916 uprising in the General Post Office in Dublin, and his now-mythical place in Irish history.

Coogan's prose is best when it stays workmanlike and factual. There are occasional ill-judged forays into the poetical, but overall these are mercifully few. Sometimes he wanders off into woolliness and generalization, but, more often than not, these moments are rescued by the astute use he makes of his sources and the tact of his anecdotes. The following, for instance, perfectly illustrates the private and public attitudes to violence of sections of the clergy:

Not only was the Squad absolutely convinced of the rightness of their actions, they were soldiers fighting a far stronger enemy by the only means at their disposal; others, sometimes in highly significant places, shared this view. Byrne, for example, remembered going to confession to 'a great priest, Father Moriarty of South William Street. I told him: "I shot a man, Father." "Did you think you were doing right? Had you no qualms about it?" he asked me. I told him I didn't have any qualms, I thought I was doing right, and he said, "Carry on with the good work," and gave me absolution.'

Collins owed his amazing success, in smashing the entire British intelligence network in Dublin, to the small fiercely disciplined group he gathered round him, to his own effective counter-intelligence, a wide network of safe houses, personal courage, ruthlessness, great charm, calculation and luck. Coogan's account of how the most wanted man in Britain and Ireland was able to move openly in a business suit about Dublin on a bicycle is as convincing as it is masterly.

The two most fascinating aspects of the book are its subject's relationship to de Valera and the whole alarming chapter on the setting up of the six counties. There can be little doubt that de Valera manipulated history to show himself as he wished to appear, and there is even less doubt that this biography of Collins must be extremely damaging to that image.

As Coogan sees it, de Valera manipulated Collins into an impossible position throughout the Treaty negotiations, having earlier ascertained for himself the limits of what could be obtained from the British and knowing this to be unacceptable to the extremists. Coogan sees the Civil War, which was in every way a tragedy for Collins and which he tried to avoid in every possible way short of capitulation, as being largely brought about by de Valera's egotism. 'The majority has no right to be wrong,' de Valera declared and appealed to the extremists.

De Valera's genius, Coogan argues, was for obtaining power without any burden of thought or policy, other than holding on to power, and this was to extend beyond de Valera's time into the Fianna Fáil party as it exists today. 'Pragmatism' is the public catchword, but at the grass roots it becomes 'We'll look after you if you are one of us and will get you if you are agin us.' A whole powerful system of clientelism has sprung up where loyalty to party appears to be valued even above the law.

If Coogan's view is unflattering to the roots and development of Fianna Fáil, it is hardly less so to the Fine Gael image of Collins as the lost leader of honour and integrity, a view this party has long held of itself. In the most engaged chapter in the book, 'Setting up the Six', it is clear that what Dr Fitzgerald thought and got from Mrs Thatcher – the Anglo-Irish Agreement – is exactly what Collins tried to get from Lloyd George, and failed. Moreover, he seemed to have had no intention of honouring such an agreement, but simply to use it as a stepping-stone to destabilize the six counties and force them into a united Ireland. He had already started down that dangerous road when the Civil War took all his attention, and then his life.

In his conclusion Coogan speculates that, because of the width of Collins's interests and his practical abilities, Ireland would have become a better and more open country had he lived. Who knows? Many of the best men found that they had no place in the Ireland they had helped to bring about. Under de Valera the country became more sectarian: de Valera himself developed into a kind of lay cardinal, who said he had only to look into his own heart to know what the people of Ireland thought. Yet, when asked why people were streaming in droves to the cattle boats, he had to confess that he didn't know. Coogan has written a timely and, I believe, a courageous book.

The Beautiful and the Damned

The Short Stories of F. Scott Fitzgerald:
A New Collection, edited by Matthew J. Bruccoli

Extraordinary work in the short story has come continuously out of North America in a comparatively short length of time. I think of Melville's 'Bartleby', Ambrose Bierce's *In the Midst of Life*, Sarah Orne Jewett's *The Country of the Pointed Firs and Other Stories*; also, Flannery O'Connor, Hemingway, the Faulkner of *Go Down, Moses*, Eudora Welty, J. F. Powers. Among recent books are several collections by the superb Canadian Alice Munro, and Richard Ford's *Rock Springs*.

As soon as I set these names down, many more come to mind which jostle rightly for their place, and there are, no doubt, many more still whom I have neither heard of nor read. What there is is an extraordinary richness which looks like confronting time and change more serenely than that patriot whale, The Great American Novel. Scott Fitzgerald's brilliant description of the technique of the short story as 'a short sharp cough' is worth a truckload of manuals, and yet, on the evidence of this massive volume, he was, for the most part, a poor or indifferent writer himself in the same form.

Charles Scribner III furnishes the foreword. His great-grandfather accepted *This Side of Paradise* for publication in 1919. His grandfather was Fitzgerald's friend and publisher in the latter part of his career. 'At the time of his death his books were not, as was later supposed, out of print with his publisher. The truth is sadder: they were all in stock at our warehouse and listed in the catalogue, but there were no orders.' His father presided over the posthumous success, and Charles Scribner III became the first of the Scribners to be introduced to Fitzgerald's work *in the classroom*. Through his father he was to 'meet and work with the author's talented and generous daughter, Scottie, and her collaborator and advisor, Matthew J. Bruccoli'. 'The ultimate effect [of Fitzgerald's stories], once the initial reverberations of imagery and language has [sic] subsided,' he concludes, 'transcends the bounds of fiction.'

In his preface, Bruccoli complains that Fitzgerald's short stories remain a misunderstood and underrated aspect of his career, and he takes issue with those critics who dismiss them as hackwork. Then he tells us how the stories should be read: 'Fitzgerald's stories now require two approaches. One should try to read them as though for the first time as they originally appeared – for the pleasure of their style, wit, warmth and versatility. They should also be read in terms of their role in the canon of a great writer.'

We are also informed that it is 'necessary to understand Fitzgerald's finances in order to evaluate the influence of his short stories on his career'. If this is true, then an understanding of Professor Bruccoli's finances should be equally necessary in order to evaluate the influence of Fitzgerald on his career, should anybody want to pursue such foolishness. The professor then proceeds to put all on show (160 stories were published in the short lifetime), and the general effect is fairly numbing.

What does emerge, beside the fact that Fitzgerald's talent appears ill-suited to the constrictions of the short form, is how fragile that true and beautiful talent was. A whole delicate confluence of theme, character, material, even atmosphere, had to happen before he was able to place his own indefinable genius on the work, and if one of the factors was missing, the collapse into the commonplace and banal was immediate and inevitable. Those true moments are rare in this book, and when they happen it is almost always in the longer pieces like 'May Day' and 'The Rich Boy', which are more like short novels than short stories; and I think only 'The Rich Boy' can stand with any ease beside *The Great Gatsby* or *The Last Tycoon*. It includes the sentence 'They [the rich] are different from you and me,' which gave rise to many misquotes or variations, beginning with the Hemingway dialogue.

Ring Lardner thought that 'The Rich Boy' should have been enlarged into a novel. This troubled Fitzgerald who protested that it couldn't be stretched into anything bigger than a novelette. Whatever the rights, 'The Rich Boy' is remarkable work and pure Fitzgerald. It is the story of

Anson Hunter, a rich New Yorker, and different from you and me. The perfect tone is caught at once:

Anson accepted without reservation the world of high finance and high extravagance, of divorce and dissipation, of snobbery and of privilege. Most of our lives end as a compromise – it was as a compromise that his life began.

and is held to the final sentences:

I don't think he was ever happy unless some one was in love with him, responding to him like filings to a magnet, helping him to explain himself, promising him something. What it was I do not know. Perhaps they promised that there would always be women in the world who would spend their brightest, freshest, rarest hours to nurse and protect that superiority he cherished in his heart.

In between, there are wonderful portraits, especially of women and rooms and great houses all playing like lights on the dark central object of Anson Hunter. The effect is that of a whole world revealed and perfectly understood.

The pity is that 'The Rich Boy' and the small quantity of true work is buried in such a mausoleum of tired, indifferent prose. Literature in our time is far more endangered by a surfeit of material and commentary than by neglect. With advocates like Bruccoli it needs no enemies. I wonder what the historian J. A. Froude would say today. More than one hundred years ago, in an essay on Homer, he wrote:

But the person of the poet has been found more difficult of elimination than a mere fact of history. Facts, it was once said, are stubborn things; but in our days we have changed all that; a fact, under the knife of the critic, splits in pieces, and is dissected out of belief with incredible readiness. The helpless thing lies under his hand like a foolish witness in a law court, when browbeaten by an unscrupulous advocate, and is turned about and twisted this way and that way, till in its distraction it contradicts itself; and to escape from torture, at last flies utterly away, itself half doubting its own existence.

Cool World

Cooler by the Lake, by Larry Heinemann

'Maximilian Nutmeg was a mildly incompetent, mostly harmless petty crook, always hustling for money. He would wake up in the middle of the morning, listening to the traffic coasting through the stop signs at the corner, and run easy-dough "Max makes a million" schemes through his head.' Thus the opening of Larry Heinemann's superb *Cooler by the Lake*.

Max lives in the house where he was born in Chicago, with his adoring wife Muriel and their son Robert:

Robert had been conceived the night of September 22, 1959, when Bill Voeck's White Sox beat the Cleveland Indians four to two to clinch the American League Pennant, and Max and Muriel went for one more roll in the hay, and bingo! Max hit the bull's eye and Muriel got pregnant, about which Max said, 'That's just great. The White Sox win the fucking pennant and we get fucking pregnant!'

Also living in the house is Max's sister Belle-Noche, and the four children she has brought into the world – each more blindingly ugly than the last – without bothering to marry their fathers. Max and Belle-Noche's ninety-four-year-old mother sleeps past noon and Easy Ed, another petty crook, who sleeps with daughter Amaryllis, has also moved in with the Nutmegs to save on the rent. The house crawls with cats and kittens, and its happily chaotic domesticity is presided over by two ferrets in a cage. They could have all walked straight out of a cartoon.

Max had been cruising the city's alleys at night with Easy Ed, stealing batteries, truck tools and spare tyres, when his next easy-dough brain-wave struck: to dress up and haul an old, empty gas can downtown to peddle a hard-luck story about how he ran out of gas on his way to an important wedding/luncheon/conference. Sometimes he found himself addressing a single person; other times, especially at intersections, he gathered a crowd. No story was too far-fetched or fantastical or just plain crazy, and it always brought in plenty of dough. People are practically queueing up to swallow his stories, and then he comes upon Loretta Spokeshave's grey leather wallet, and feels compelled, against all morals and every known reason, to return it. He can't eat, sleep, drink, fuck or beg until he manages to get the wallet with its eight one-hundred-dollar bills, credit cards and love letter back into Loretta Spokeshave's rich hands. The apple has entered the easy-dough Eden.

Both nature and reality are excluded ruthlessly from *Cooler by the Lake*. In this completely man-made, machine-driven universe, everything has an obvious explanation, a brand name and price tag, bought or stolen, used or thrown away. Baseball and horse racing, the Chicago Bears and Bulls, are perfect metaphors, as is TV. Death is gossip overheard in the transit system. Love or sex is a home run belted high into the bleachers of Wrigley Field. When Max spies the wallet on the pavement, his first fear is that it was put there in order to set him up for a live TV show. When lovers meet in the parking lot in front of the Nutmeg house they are watched and discussed as if they were part of a breakfast soap.

Larry Heinemann's achievement is to create a heightened, artificial, real/unreal language in which these cartoon people live out their real/unreal lives in a throwaway world. Only towards the end, when all the good things are being probably too neatly gathered into Deadwood Dave's Saloon Bar heaven, does the exuberance sometimes wander and blur, but this is no more than a minor hiccup in what can only be called a triumph. The publishers describe the novel as a reckless comedy. It is, in fact, a classical farce, a sharp allegory of the present-day US by a writer of enormous talent and originality.

The Adult Mysteries

Across the Bridge: Stories, by Mavis Gallant

Mavis Gallant has written much short fiction. More than a hundred stories have appeared in the *New Yorker* alone, and all but two of the eleven in her new collection, *Across the Bridge*, appeared in that magazine.

Mrs Gallant's world is urban and deeply conservative. (Most of the stories are set in Montreal or Paris.) French is the natural language of many of her characters, and it is a palpable presence in her lucid, elegant sentences. Here, accent is as much a means of defining social position as clothes or jewellery, furniture or address. The general climate of the bourgeois or petit-bourgeois world she describes is philistine, never more so than when airbrushed with culture: Proust or Chateaubriand are interchangeable with Gucci or Armani. Her prose can move seamlessly from the present to the past and back again, as if they were one time and the same country, and from a bright, slangy vulgarity to passages of formal beauty. The vantage points she uses to view what she describes as 'the adult mysteries' – change, death, absence – are often those of a child or someone grown old or, as in the case of the superb story called 'Forain', a neutered intellectual: 'He was thirty-eight, divorced, had a daughter of twelve who lived in Nice with her mother and the mother's lover. Only one or two of Forain's friends had ever met the girl. Most people, when told, found it hard to believe he had ever been married.'

Some of Mrs Gallant's characters remain childlike all their lives. 'She was barely forty-five,' the author says of Mme Carette in 'The Chosen Husband', 'but a long widowhood strictly observed had kept her childish, not youthful.' Mrs Gallant is a scalpel-sharp anatomizer of various forms of stupidity, and while this skilfulness can often seem just and very funny, sometimes it leaves behind an unpleasant aftertaste, as if the witty, controlled prose is functioning at the expense of her characters.

For all its urbanity, her world is curiously old-fashioned. The young are unaware of sexual revolution. In two of the most accomplished stories, a daughter lives at home waiting for a suitor to turn up. In 'The Chosen Husband', she waits with her child-mother and older sister in genteel Montreal. Marie's suitor has been provided by Uncle Gildas, 'an elderly priest with limited social opportunities, though his niece believed him to have wide and worldly connections'. This is a small, savage portrait:

Nowadays, shrunken and always hungry, he lived in retirement, had waxed linoleum on his floor, no carpet, ate tapioca soup two or three times a week. He would have stayed in bed all day, but the nuns who ran the place looked upon illness as fatigue, fatigue as shirking. He was not tired or lazy; he had nothing to get up for.

The suitor's awfulness is all but outweighed by what *he* has to face:

Of course he was at a loss, astray in an armchair, with the Carettes watching like friendly judges. When he reached for another chocolate, they looked to see if his nails were clean. When he crossed his legs, they examined his socks. They were fixing their first impression of the stranger who might take Marie away, give her a modern kitchen, children to bring up, a muskrat coat, a charge account at Dupuis Frères department store, a holiday in Maine.

In the title story, similar material and an identical plot are transposed to Paris. The ingénue sketches the beehives in the Luxembourg Gardens, is the only child of a prosperous ear specialist and lives at home with her father and mother. Though set during the early 1950s, 'Across the Bridge' is as timeless as a fairy tale. 'I cannot say what was taking place in the world that spring,' the narrator tells us; 'my father did not like to see young women reading newspapers.' Everything about the story is pure stock, except the writing. The material is, in fact, a staple of much popular romantic fiction, which Mrs Gallant subverts with exactitude, intelligence and dry wit.

There are places in the collection where the strain of the magazine short story form shows, particularly in the endings. '1933' is a delicate memoir of Montreal – like a yellowed photograph – in which the Carette family is first introduced. Nothing in the story justifies the violence of its ending, which gives it a dramatic weight it is too frail to carry. 'Dédé' contains much that is brilliant, especially a cruelly observed Sunday luncheon in a magistrate's house in Paris. It also shows Mrs Gallant's remarkable gift for introducing whole lives and future histories in a few swift, brief strokes:

The Brouets are tolerant parents, ready for anything. They met for the first time in May of 1968, a few yards away from a barricade of burning cars. She had a stone in her hand; when she saw him looking at her, she put it down. They walked up the Boulevard Saint-Michel together, and he told her his plan for reforming the judiciary.

But for all its qualities, the story does not grow, and when the ending comes it seems contrived.

In stories like 'From Cloud to Cloud' and 'Florida', which move to the United States, where the Carette grandson from Montreal enlists in the Marines after his father's funeral and later starts married life as a motel manager, the results are even more uncertain. The clear, confident prose of Mrs Gallant's best work begins to lose focus.

Nothing could be more different from 'Florida' than 'Forain', a story that is as close to perfection as possible. Forain is a French publisher of Eastern European writers in translation. We meet him first at the funeral service of his star author, Adam Tremski, who 'for some forty years had occupied the same walkup flat on the fringe of Montparnasse' and to whom fame had come too late to make material difference. Mrs Gallant has always written well about the Parisian émigré world, but never better than here: 'The mourners climbed the church steps slowly. Some were helped by younger relatives, who had taken time off from work. A few had migrated to high-rise apartments in the outer suburbs, to deeper loneliness but cheaper rents.'

Forain is the person through whom she views this small, idealistic, impractical world. He is a perfect filter: 'Here, Forain had noticed, tears came easily, not only for the lost friend but for all the broken ties and old, unwilling journeys. The tears of strangers around him, that is; grief, when it reached him, was pale and dry.'

'Forain' also allows the mordant prose to range out from Tremski's immediate family and concerns to the overlords of these clerks of literature:

Well, of course, his thimble-size firm had not been able to attract the leviathan prophets, the booming novelists, the great mentors and tireless definers. Tremski had been at the very limit of Forain's financial reach – good Tremski, who had stuck to Forain even after he could have moved on. Common sense had kept Forain from approaching the next-best, second-level oracles, articulate and attractive, subsidized to the ears, chain-smoking and explaining, still wandering the universities and congresses of the West . . .

Forain's own little flock, by contrast, seemed to have entered the world with no expectations.

The author's sharp eye misses nothing; each detail is exact and telling:

Mourners accustomed to the ceremonial turned to a neighbour to exchange the kiss of peace. Those who were not shrank slightly, as if the touch without warmth were a new form of aggression. Forain found unfocused, symbolized love positively terrifying. He refused the universal coming-together, rammed his hands in his pockets – like a rebellious child – and joined the untidy lines shuffling out into the rain.

In 'Forain', Mavis Gallant has written an elegy that is also a true celebration: it is a small marvel of wit and feeling and rare tact.

The Forging of the State

Pleasant the Scholar's Life: Irish Intellectuals and the Construction of the Nation State, by Maurice Goldring

Maurice Goldring has been described as France's leading historian of Irish culture and is Professor of Irish Studies at the University of Paris. His book has been written and revised and added to over very many years. The early chapters are heavily revised versions of *Faith of Our Fathers*, first published in French in 1976 and published in Dublin in 1982.

Goldring was then a Marxist and a member of the French Communist Party. He is no longer a communist, has abandoned large chunks of what was once part and parcel of his Marxism, but some of it he retains as useful for the examination of class conflict.

Indeed, in the collapse of the various forms of the communist organizations inherited from Leninism he perceives many similarities with the self-definition of the early Dublin intellectuals as well as with the violence of the paramilitaries. They all shared the idea of themselves as a self-selecting elite which knows what is best for the people: 'Thunderous excommunications, whether in republican ranks or cultural circles, share the same logic as Communist parties, with the resulting danger of a totalitarian state. Democracy, on the other hand, must first learn to recognise that different ideas must be understood, tolerated and maybe even considered as not necessarily wrong.'

Goldring's principal focus is on the interplay between intellectuals and mass movements and how, towards the turn of the century, they combined to forge an Irish national identity. In fact, he defines the difference between a revolt and revolution in exactly those terms: revolt never turns into a revolution until it succeeds in attracting to itself a sufficient number of intellectuals able to give it theoretical cohesion; that is, 'to understand the complexities of the present or to dream about the future'.

To illustrate his argument he points to Iran, South Africa and the black uprisings in American cities; and he separates the present Troubles in the North from the revolution that led to the founding of the Free State: 'In contemporary Ireland, especially the North, the major political movements, both nationalist and loyalist, do not have intellectuals, as I have used the term, in their ranks. There is a great deal of propaganda but no intellectual creation that is rooted in the political struggle.'

With remarkable clarity and compression, he traces the forging of this cultural nationalism in the nineteenth century through the unearthing of the lost Gaelic past, the rediscovered legends and folklore, the myths of the wandering poet deprived of his patrons, the dispossessed aristocrats fallen on hard times. In Yeats, these impoverished gentry become Knights of the Sheep, and Goldring observes the same process continuing into our own time among some celtophiles as they attempt to discover traces of feminism and primitive socialism in ancient Irish societies.

Countless hands struggled to set their own imprint on the nineteenth-century myth, the thousands of *Nation* poets as well as powerful figures such as Yeats, AE, Pearse; and long before it reached sanctification during the de Valera era in Corkery's *The Hidden Ireland* it had acquired the necessary vagueness that allowed it to work. People as different in personality and opinions as D. P. Moran, George Russell, Michael Collins, even Yeats and de Valera, were able to stand on the common ground it provided. The nature of the myth was vague and rich enough to contain contradictory interpretation.

Goldring details how essentially middle-class the whole movement was, like this Sinn Féin Directive: 'It is your right to compel your tailor, if he is unwilling, to make your coat of Irish cloth, to compel your grocer to sell you Irish eggs, to compel your public servants to acquire some knowledge of the Irish language and help Irish industries' – when the masses had neither a suit nor the makings of a suit. Faced with the appalling poverty of the time, the collective misery, all Sinn Féin could resort to were platitudes couched in terms of morality and individual conduct.

It was likewise with the Gaelic League, founded to revive the language, which was to have such a profound influence on the future state. All civil servants would have to learn Irish, though it could have no practical use in courthouse or post office. All top servants would have to speak and write Irish perfectly, know its literature and understand its art. The sole function of this was ideological: it was a mark of patriotism and loyalty, and a passport to the highest positions in the State. (On a more elementary level, they failed to understand that a starving child cannot be taught Irish.)

In his analysis of the best-selling *Speeches from the Dock*, which served as a kind of popular history and was regularly updated, Goldring observes that in order to be included one had not only to be eloquent but wealthy as well. It was a people's history of nationalist and Catholic Ireland from which the people were excluded. All that Goldring deduces rhymes perfectly with the wonderful, patronizing phrase, *caint na ndaoine*.*

The slow evolution of cultural nationalism through the great political movements, its place in the essentially pragmatic and constitutional movements of O'Connell and Parnell, is traced to 1916 by way of the romanticism of Davis and the Fenians. 'The form of combat and the beauty of gesture took over from the search for precise objectives. The Fenian leaders theorized about their successive defeats and transformed them into victories.'

Goldring contrasts this attitude tellingly with that of the French socialists to the Paris Commune and 1871 massacre, and continues: 'When there are no real battles going on, only sham ones, when a long and monotonous war is replaced by a series of warlike declarations and desperate deeds, then the poet has every chance of succeeding.' After the fall of Parnell, this romantic nationalism had a free field and took over: the use of arms in poetry and poetry in arms.

The Catholic Church is seen as ambiguous, if not hostile, to this new nationalism, especially its romantic branch which had its own canon of martyrs. This ambiguity sprang from tensions within the Church itself – young priests attracted to nationalism, aged bishops taking direction from Rome – and this was to some extent resolved in the use of the

---

* See p. 126.

Christian Brothers to counter the Whig ministry of Earl Grey's plan to establish a non-religious system of education.

The Catholic bishops were totally opposed to this scheme. They wanted what they want today, Catholic schools for Catholic children. Steeped in rebellion against the godless English, the Christian Brothers schools were seen as national as well as Catholic, and their textbooks were more nationalistic than other schools. There was a class dimension too: they catered to the urban poor, and many of the future IRA leaders were to get their education from the Christian Brothers. The Jesuits and Dominicans, in contrast, were seen as providers of schools for West Britons. Gradually, rather than oppose the rising tide, the Church sought to colour nationalism with its own brand, so that it became the only 'true' one.

This Irish brand of cultural nationalism is seen by Goldring as essentially foreign, deriving from German romantic nationalism of the early nineteenth century, which began with the conquest and domination of that country by France and the French Revolution, but it did not enter France itself until about 1870, when it was state-instituted. Goldring details with wonderful clarity the different forms it took, its essential nature and characteristics. Pearse's ideals of blazing patriotism and blood sacrifice can be found in Fichte, and the idea of a pure race is never far away in either.

The construction of the tradition of violence in Irish cultural nationalism at once made its use easier in future conflicts such as that in the North. Where there is no tradition to support it, violence becomes more difficult to institutionalize. Once this happens, though, Goldring sees little point in its criminalization, and he believes the violence will not disappear until it is absorbed and is able to express itself through normal politics, as in the other European democracies. As he differentiates between the violence in the North and the revolution that led up to 1922, he also separates that violence, loyalist as well as nationalist, from purely social upheavals.

Probably the finest single chapter in the book is 'Intellectuals and Labour', which concentrates on the conflicts surrounding the 1913 Dublin lockout and strike. Everybody had to come off the fence. Archbishop Walsh claimed that indiscriminate charity could become a source of demoralization, which has uncanny echoes of later conflicts. In the face of the outcry against sending starving children into unholy England to be fed, Shaw quipped: 'There were some dwellings in Dublin that if they took the children out of them, the adults would misbehave themselves.' The old and ever-present cry went up, that those stating the facts were writing for the English. It is a sorry episode, beautifully detailed and analysed.

By 1913, emigration had acquired a cultural stamp: the crossing to the United States, the land of the free, was seen as noble; the crossing to Britain as servile, though the early Irish communities there had contributed much to both the Labour and Chartist movements. It was to the United States that nationalist leaders naturally turned, and the various cultural organizations played an important part in attracting Irish exiles to the nationalist cause. Goldring states this with some acerbity: 'Exiles, of course, had long been separated from Irish reality – though one sometimes wonders if those who had stayed behind were more familiar with "reality". The exiles remembered a mythical country and were delighted to encounter people and organizations who told them that their recollections could come true.' The one exception to the dominance of this traffic was in 1913 when labour issues took precedence over the nationalist question and the strikers turned to England for help.

Professor Goldring has obviously a long acquaintance with this country and is not afraid to use his direct experience, as in this vignette of the MacEntee-Cruise O'Brien households, to illustrate an aspect of class displacement:

In the late 1960s, I had the privilege of attending a conversation between the late Sean McEntee [sic], then the last survivor of the 1916 Rising, and Conor Cruise O'Brien. Conor Cruise O'Brien, as is his wont, provoked McEntee with a sweeping statement: '1916 was a mistake,' he declared. Sean McEntee replied, 'Maybe it was, but I'm glad I was part of it.' McEntee's daughter Maureen added, with superb clear-sightedness, 'Conor, your grandfather was a member of the Irish Parliamentary Party. You were part of the elite. My father was the son of a publican. He would never have become minister without 1916. We would not have a fine house, his children would never have been to the best schools.' Ruefully, Conor Cruise O'Brien answered, 'Exactly, your people pushed mine aside.'

Less persuasive is the use of scenes from certain literary works, such as *The Valley of the Squinting Windows*, to illustrate sociological argument. There is a serious misreading of the power of the poet Dunleavy in *The Islandman* that not even the *Fíor Ghaeilgeoirí* – not to speak of the Dublin poets Goldring has in mind – would swallow. Such poets as Dunleavy were as widespread as bonesetters throughout Ireland. His use of Ernie O'Malley is tentative (this unease seems to be shared with many historians), though *On Another Man's Wound* is the only work I know of a very high literary quality to have emerged directly from the violence.

There are a few rhetorical passages towards the end of the book which tend to confuse thought with action and stand out because they are at odds with the rest of this carefully wrought, subtle and intelligent work. The book's focus is narrow, but is all the more powerful for that: there is no doubt that it is provocative, probably intentionally so:

I hope I have been able to show in this book that cultural nationalism was an essential process in forging the identity of the Irish people in the sense that it helped to delineate culturally who was an Irish citizen and who was not. The Irish citizen was a Catholic, a Gaelic-speaker and a man. Women and Protestants were definitely not citizens, culturally speaking. The cultural nationalist phenomenon was so strong that no law was required to exclude 'aliens' from the avenues of political and cultural power.

Elsewhere he asserts:

. . . the tasks of changing and interpreting the world are not the same, and no book of political science has ever changed reality; this means, for example, that my own opinions about modern Irish politics have no special weight simply because I have written books about Irish history. It is quite sufficient if the academic or writer provides food for thought.

This he has done handsomely.

Shadows of a Summer Night

Sunday's Children, by Ingmar Bergman

The Swedish director Ingmar Bergman's second autobiographical novel, *Sunday's Children*, is at first set securely in the past, in the summer of 1926, at the ramshackle, eccentric house built by Pastor Dahlberg, high above Dufnas village. The author's mother has rented it as a summer house, within walking distance through the forest of her own mother's 'grand and tasteful' country mansion, Varoms. The novel's protagonist – like the protagonist of the film it inspired, directed by Mr Bergman's own son Daniel – is the eight-year-old Pu Bergman, a Sunday's child like his father. Children born on that day were said to have special gifts of clairvoyance, to be able to conjure up ghosts and spectres, to foretell the future.

Assembled with Pu and his mother are his older brother, Dag; their young sister, Lillan; Moster Emma, 'a leftover overweight dinosaur from Father's family'; Marta Johansson, an ailing retainer; and the dark beauty, Marianne, 'broad-hipped and high-bosomed', who is tutoring Dag in German and mathematics. In addition, there are two remarkable maidservants: old Lalla, who deserted the grandmother's establishment at Varoms to give her darling, the children's mother, all the help she needed; and the earthy Maj, who is in charge of little Lillan. The whole household is in place as the novel opens, ready for the father's arrival from Stockholm.

In one of the many beautifully realized set pieces through which the psychological drama is developed, the family waits at the tiny railway station at Dufnas, where 'the bright sunlight is blazing down'. Pu's mother 'is wearing a light summer dress with a wide belt around her narrow waist. Her hat is yellow and wide-brimmed. As usual, Mother is beautiful.' But all the essentials for a disaster are already in place.

As recalled by readers of Mr Bergman's previous novel, *The Best Intentions* (and viewers of the film of the same name), the wealthy Akerbloms strongly opposed the alliance of their well-guarded only daughter with the young theological student Erik Bergman. 'In himself, the future pastor might have been a mother-in-law's dream: ambitious, well brought up, tidy and relatively handsome,' the author writes in *Sunday's Children*. The formidable Anna Akerblom, however, had 'an eye for people. She saw something below the irreproachable surface: moodiness, oversensitivity, a violent temper and sudden emotional coldness. Mrs Anna also believed that she well understood her daughter, the family's bright and slightly spoiled central character. Karin was emotional, cheerful, clever, extremely sensible and, as already mentioned, rather spoiled.'

Severe hostilities broke out. Bitter words were traded. Erik felt rejected and badly treated: 'he never forgot a real or imagined injury.' Karin's will proved as formidable as her mother's. She had made up her mind to spend her life with Erik Bergman, and she would have her way. The young pastor was finally, reluctantly, accepted:

The tone became friendly and superior, courteously attentive, occasionally heartfelt, all the roles acted out. No one was to put familial unity at risk.

Hatred and bitterness remained, invisible and below. It was revealed in subordinate clauses and sudden silences, in imperceptible, absent or strained smiles. It was all extremely sophisticated and kept strictly within the narrow confines of Christian forbearance.

One of the difficulties that carried over from the conflict was the organization of the summer holidays. Karin had spent her childhood summers at her parents' house; to her it was 'obvious that her beloved should like Varoms, Dufnas, Dalarna in the same way she did'. Erik acquiesced, eager to please his young wife. When the children appeared, they also became fond of their grandmother's country house. 'Silence and courtesy, the silences and the subordinate clauses becoming more and more tangible as the idyll solidified.' Then, over a number of summers, Erik contrived on various pretexts to absent himself, and

Karin saw, too late, that something had to be done quickly if calamity was to be averted. Renting Pastor Dahlberg's house was both a compromise – within walking distance of Grandmother's, they could still have Sunday dinners there – and 'a silent prayer for forgiveness'. But when his father eventually arrives in the summer of his adoring son's eighth birthday, he is 'restless, absent-minded and melancholy'.

Very like a slow, formal movie, the magical summer, with its domestic dramas, unfolds in richly observed scenes: a dinner party; an archery contest; childish games and battles; a walk to a farmyard where two calves are being slaughtered; the unannounced visit of the grandmother at the house, accompanied by her black-sheep son, Uncle Carl (his is a masterly comic portrait). And then there is Pu's dramatic trip by bicycle and train and river ferry with his father on the Sunday that Pastor Bergman is to preach at Granas Church.

Despite its sombre shadows, there is a great sense of playfulness throughout the novel. A courtly yet ironic invitation is even extended to the reader: 'Do please enter the picture. You can stand there by the door out to the veranda or sit on the curvaceous sofa below the wall clock.' Like a painter who works the outer edges of the canvas as carefully as the centre, Mr Bergman, aided by his able translator, Joan Tate, brings casual events and people met by chance as vividly to life as the main characters in the story. There are delicious allusions and touches of humour, but they are never more than incidental to the rich fabric of observation, as when Pu, bored during his father's long sermon, keeps his interest alive by looking at the church's murals and stained-glass windows: 'Mary Magdalene, that must be the sinner . . . Close by, Death is sawing down the Tree of Life, a terrified jester sitting at the top, wringing his hands: "Are there no special rules for actors?" '

In the central scene, Pu is awakened by voices from his mother's room and crawls out onto the landing to witness the terror of his parents arguing, seeing his own small world suddenly without boundaries. The scene is devastating in its impact, probably because it is so formal and underplayed.

The flashback technique of general fiction is subverted in a few haunting sequences scattered throughout the book. Instead of bringing the past to life in order to illuminate the present, the author takes us from the magical summer of 1926 to the cold spring of 1968, in Stockholm, where the ageing Ingmar Bergman goes to see his eighty-two-year-old father, a recent widower. Thus the future is visited to illuminate the past, to preserve in even deeper dyes the indelible psychological hues that lie at the heart of the drama. This Sunday's child has exercised his birthright to try to redeem himself and his father – and the whole broken world of love.

Chekhov and Martin Luther are the only writers mentioned in the text, once each and in passing. But so careful is the work that I doubt if it is as casual as it appears. In this novel, as in the film *Wild Strawberries*, Chekhov's good influence is everywhere, though what Mr Bergman has made of it is uniquely his own. I know of no recent work to which Chekhov's famous definition could be more truly applied:

Writers who are considered immortal or just plain good and who intoxicate us have one very important trait in common: they are going somewhere and call you with them ... The best of them are realistic and paint life as it is, but because every line is saturated with juice, with the sense of life, you feel, in addition to life as it is, life as it ought to be.

A Legend after His Own Lifetime

The Love of the Last Tycoon: A Western,
by F. Scott Fitzgerald

In the half-century since his death, the life of F. Scott Fitzgerald has become more famous than his work. Scott and Zelda and Sheila Graham are more easily identifiable than Carraway or Daisy or Jordan Baker or Anson Hunter. Of all Fitzgerald's creations, Gatsby alone might have a chance of popular recognition.

By the time he died in Hollywood in December 1940, Fitzgerald was largely forgotten and unread except by his fellow writers. The judicious editing and promotion of his work by Edmund Wilson contributed much to his post-war resurrection. Since then, a stream of memoirs and biographies has turned him into the literary embodiment of the Jazz Age. His own assertion that 'There can never be a good biography of a good novelist . . . He's too many people, if he's any good', goes unheeded. Along with Hemingway and Faulkner, his reputation is now more or less unassailable within the universities and dwarfs that of other good writers of the time, such as Willa Cather or Nathanael West.

Among the forty books about American literature that Matthew J. Bruccoli has written or edited is a biography of Fitzgerald, *Some Sort of Epic Grandeur*. A few years ago he collected and edited the 160 stories Fitzgerald published in his lifetime into a single volume. In his preface to the stories was the bizarre statement that it was necessary to understand Fitzgerald's finances 'in order to evaluate the influence of the short story on his career', and what emerged was that everything Fitzgerald wrote was important to Professor Bruccoli because Fitzgerald wrote it and thus had its role in the canon of a great writer.

It was a dismaying volume to read from cover to cover, and I thought it was a disservice to Fitzgerald's work. Hidden among much that was indifferent was a small body of exquisite prose which cried out to be selected and set free. (A similar disservice was done to Philip Larkin soon after his death through the fattening of the *Collected Poems*, though not on anything like such a massive scale.) In our time too many pages, not too few, demand space on our shelves and in our minds.

The industrious Matthew J. Bruccoli has now edited *The Last Tycoon* in the Cambridge University Press's definitive printing of Fitzgerald's work and restored its original and quite dreadful title, *The Love of the Last Tycoon: A Western*. I opened the book with misgivings, but to my relief I did not find the text of the fragments that make up this unfinished novel much added to or much different from the 1965 Penguin, edited by Edmund Wilson.

What is new are several selected facsimiles of Fitzgerald's working notes. There is an editorial note by Bruccoli, taking issue with Edmund Wilson's 'cosmeticised text', followed by a lengthy introduction in which, among other things, we are instructed on how the unfinished work should be read. Wilson's original introduction is shorter than Bruccoli's Note, and is far more courteous and persuasive than either the Note or the new introduction. Though it's of no great consequence, I found Wilson's 'cosmeticised' text preferable to Bruccoli's.

What then of the text itself? I first read it when I was young and always remembered it with affection. Part of its charm was the very fact that it was unfinished and still held within it the fascination of the possibilities of any uncompleted life. Re-reading it, I am not so sure that the large claims made on its behalf are justified. The love-struck Cecilia Brady's narrative reaches a dead-end long before these fragments come to a stop and never illuminates anything much, least of all the object of her infatuation – the central figure of Monroe Stahr. The portrait of Stahr is further weakened by a romanticism intellectuals are often drawn to project onto powerful men of action. What survives are some superb descriptions, like the plane flight in bad weather and the love scene between Kathleen and Stahr, which just about skirt banality:

It was a fine blue night. The tide was at the turn and the little silver fish rocked off shore waiting for 10:16. A few seconds after the time they came swarming in with the tide and Stahr and Kathleen stepped over them barefoot as they flicked slip-slop in the sand. A Negro man came along the shore toward them collecting the grunion quickly like twigs into two pails. They came in twos and threes and platoons and companies, relentless and exalted and scornful around the great bare feet of the intruders, as they had come before Sir Francis Drake had nailed his plaque to the boulder on the shore.

Edmund Wilson suggests a reading of *The Great Gatsby* alongside *The Last Tycoon* 'because it shows the kind of thing that Fitzgerald was aiming to do'. From the evidence the fragments provide it is difficult to see now how he could have managed it. Almost any work compared to *Gatsby* would suffer: it must be one of the most perfect novels ever written. Technique and tact and moral sensibility are as finely tuned as in any of Turgenev's great novels, and yet it is as American as Hollywood.

After *Gatsby* I would reach for *The Crack-Up*, with its bleak good humour, the dry clarity, so reminiscent of Carraway, the dazzling powers of description. Beside it, I would place a good half-dozen of the stories, among them 'The Rich Boy', 'May Day', 'Babylon Revisited'. There are things in the other works, such as those mentioned in *The Last Tycoon*, that I might wish to read from time to time, but what is already there is a quality of achievement that should be enjoyed and honoured as long as fiction is read.

A Critic Who Was One of the Elect

Edmund Wilson: A Biography, by Jeffrey Meyers

All four grandparents of Edmund Wilson were born in New York State. The Wilsons had emigrated from Londonderry in the middle of the eighteenth century and were among the first settlers in central New York. His maternal ancestors, the Kimballs and the Bakers, sailed from England soon after the Mayflower. A direct ancestor was Cotton Mather, the celebrated seventeenth-century divine and zealous witch-hunter, many of whose characteristics Wilson shared – intellect, bookishness, linguistic ability, temperament, energy, productivity and multiple marriages. In *Patriotic Gore*, Wilson, a lifelong atheist, found the Calvinistic Mather an extremely neurotic and tormented man: 'When anything goes wrong with Mather,' he observed, 'from a toothache to the death of his wife, he is likely to fall into a panic lest he not be, after all, elected, and to be stricken by a paroxysm of guilt.' Wilson's daughter Rosalind remarked that her father, a notoriously difficult patient, in hospital and out, 'is very demanding. He screams constantly and no one knows whether he's dying or whether there's no pepper on his tray.'

Wilson descended from a line long established in the professional upper middle classes, preachers, lawyers, doctors, men of letters. From them he inherited a deep hostility to the commercial mentality of the capitalistic class: 'He felt that he and his forebears represented the idealistic spirit that studies and understands, and opposed the materialistic spirit that acquires and consumes.'

To some extent, this clash was present in his parents' marriage. His father, the son of a Presbyterian minister, was a brilliant trial lawyer who became Attorney General of New Jersey and just missed being appointed a judge of the Supreme Court under Woodrow Wilson; but in private he was neurotic, hypersensitive, hypochondriacal and domineering. Helen Kimball was the daughter of a wealthy physician, pleasure-loving, lively and shrewd, fond of dogs, gardening, bridge, antique collecting – and she could, like her son, be blunt.

Edmund Wilson was a spoiled and neglected only child. He was brought up in the fashionable suburb of Red Bank, New Jersey. The family spent its summers in the ancestral stone house his mother inherited, in Talcottville, north of Utica in upstate New York, and the house was to play an important part in Wilson's life. The family maintained its roots, Wilson wrote, and had never really departed very far from the 'old American life of the countryside and the provincial cities with its simple tastes and habits'.

At all his schools Wilson was drawn to outstanding teachers to whom he remained loyal throughout his life. At Princeton he found Kemp Smith, a Scot, who had written on Descartes, Hume and Kant and was a master of technical philosophy; but for Smith philosophy meant the study of everything men had thought about themselves and their world. Even more important to Wilson than Kemp Smith was Christian Gauss. Wilson took Gauss's classes in French and Italian, learned to study every word when reading a foreign language, and under Gauss's guidance developed an intense and lasting admiration for Dante and Flaubert. Gauss and Smith were to remain lifelong friends – as was Scott Fitzgerald, his fellow student:

To Fitzgerald, Wilson appeared smug and arrogant, a well-dressed and withdrawn grind, while to Wilson, Scott seemed ignorant, shallow and foolish. It was understood between them that Fitzgerald was the brash superficial upstart, destined to make a splash but perhaps also doomed to failure, while Wilson was the solid intellectual who would set him straight.

In *My Lost City*, however, in spite of the fact that there are supposed to be no second acts in American lives, Wilson became for Fitzgerald a romantic symbol of New York. There was even to be a third act, when Wilson edited and introduced Fitzgerald's posthumous works and rescued his reputation from near-oblivion. Unlike Fitzgerald and Hemingway, another talent he was first to promote, Wilson was to live into old age and recognition as the most distinguished American man of letters in the twentieth century.

To write this masterly and readable biography, Jeffrey Meyers had to cover enormous ground. Wilson published fifty books. As well as the great critical works and autobiographical memoirs on which his reputation rests, he wrote novels, stories, plays, poems, a vast amount of journalism, and the private diaries he kept were to run to volumes. For most of his life he was combatively engaged in political causes and literary disputes. He was a heavy drinker, had four marriages, several mistresses and was a compulsive chronicler of his sexual adventures. Nothing seems to have been real for him until it was written down. Raymond Chandler, retaliating to Wilson's attacks on the detective novel, remarked that he made fornication as dull as a railway timetable, but the accounts have a dogged, naive candour that is often touching. He learned several languages, travelled widely, knew many of the great names of twentieth-century literature, and a number of them, like Fitzgerald, were friends.

Wilson had a melancholic streak but believed all his life in human progress. Not only does Jeffrey Meyers admire Wilson but a real liking of the man and a fascination with his contentious, complicated character shine through the book. He takes issue with John Updike's judgement that 'after 1930 his biography becomes largely bibliography' and states what draws him to Wilson: 'I admire his curiosity, energy, intelligence and erudition, his clear thought, pure style and good taste, his personal courage, defense of the underdog and constant struggles against mindless authority, his loyalty to friends and generosity to many writers, his independence and integrity.'

When Wilson's first books appeared, what surprised Fitzgerald, among others, was the lack of any sense of shape, and Meyers admits that this remained largely true of all his work. What he had was an uncanny ability to find the vivid, human detail that would bring his subjects to life, more interested in the vigour of thought and images than any overall shape. Meyers himself seems to have adopted much the same method. There is no attempt to write an exhaustive account, but a rich and vivid life does emerge. He is helped by the clarity of Wilson's own writing, the forcefulness of his views and of not being afraid to be wrong. Among the writers he disliked were Kafka, Frost, Pound, Hart Crane and Wallace Stevens, 'the voice of a helpless pierrot imprisoned in a functioning businessman.'

Wilson's personality made a vivid impression on the people he met, and many of those close to him could write well. Louise Bogan, the lyric poet and critic, his friend and for a brief time his mistress and later his colleague at the *New Yorker*, gives this picture of him between marriages in the 1930s:

Bunny [Wilson's nickname] kept turning the ice-box off, every night, in some mistaken hope that it would stay cold by itself, and in the morning the food smelled like a charnel house, and there was never enough gin, because he ordered, out of a desire for work and sobriety, only one bottle at a time, and then he and I would polish that off, and it would only be ten o'clock in the evening, and we'd be in the middle of an argument, with no gin to help us carry it on, and Edmund would sit there and say: 'I'll get a case of it; that's the thing to do: get a case of it!'

Wilson travelled widely and turned his travels, like everything else in his life, into long articles and books. Anglophobia runs through his encounters with the English:

Their rigid hierarchies, class distinctions and studied reticence, their arrogance, rudeness and cutting remarks grated against his more democratic manner ... [and he] particularly disliked the intellectual dishonesty in what he called 'the Oxford brush-off: getting rid of importunate and troublesome questions by laughing gently about some aspect of the country or class or person which is totally irrelevant to the question in hand.'

Detail to vivid detail is added to point up a whole, intriguing picture. Eliot appears 'speaking English with a most careful English accent as if it were a foreign language which he has learned extremely well'. Roethke walks on for one dramatic scene at Princeton and disappears. A skirmish with Evelyn Waugh in London is presented like a scene from a play.

Very typical of Meyers's method is his account of Wilson's relationship with Auden. They both admired each other's work and got on well. In his review of *Upstate*, Auden identifies them both as belonging to the same class, 'called in England Upper Middle Class Professional ... Mr Wilson and I were both, thank God, brought up on the Protestant Work

Ethic but, though I generally think of myself as fairly industrious, he makes me feel a lazybones'; and in writing about Wilson's *Apologies to the Iroquois* he noted his individuality and independence, and remarked that he 'is a specimen of that always rare and now almost extinct creature, the Intellectual Dandy'.

Wilson writes to a friend:

I've been seeing quite a lot of Auden and having a very good time with him. I find him very easy to talk to now and great fun . . . He is really extremely tough, cares nothing about property or money, popularity or social prestige – does everything on his own and alone.

In his essay on Casanova in *The Wound and the Bow*, Wilson remarked that a mistress of the great lover had urged him to remember her by writing her name on their window with a diamond. Wilson imitated this practice by encouraging friends to write poems on his window panes with a diamond pencil. The poems on the windows of the bedrooms described sleep; and the lines of Auden's nocturne, 'written, like Dorothy Parker's poem, after quite a few drinks – looked wobbly as well as dreamy: "Make this night loveable . . ."' We do not meet Auden again until Wilson, when teaching at Harvard, goes to a reading Auden gave at Sanders Theatre.

Through all these dramas, the ordinary domesticities of most nights are never obscured: having a drink, opening a book, playing with the cat, going to sleep. This book is enough to restore some faith in the over-worked and tired genre of literary biography.

The Tragical Comedy of the Men of Ireland

Angela's Ashes, by Frank McCourt

This vivid, disturbing and funny 'memoir of a childhood' has more the sense of a novel or drama than strict memoir. The bravura note of the whole work is struck at the very opening passage, together with a laconic, deflationary matter-of-factness:

When I look back on my childhood I wonder how I survived at all. It was, of course, a miserable childhood: the happy childhood is hardly worth your while. Worse than the ordinary miserable childhood is the miserable Irish childhood, and worse yet is the miserable Irish Catholic childhood.

People everywhere brag and whimper about the woes of their early years, but nothing can compare with the Irish version: the poverty; the shiftless loquacious alcoholic father; the pious defeated mother moaning by the fire; pompous priests; bullying schoolmasters; the English and the terrible things they did to us for eight hundred long years.

Above all – we were wet.

Angela's Ashes is the story of the McCourts: the author's father and mother, Angela and Malachy McCourt, their seven children, the four who survived, the three who died, the children's grandparents, relatives and neighbours. Angela and Malachy met in Brooklyn during the Great Depression. She had been sent out to America by her mother 'where there's room for all sorts of uselessness'. Malachy had to be spirited out of Ireland because there was a price on his head for some act he had done in the old IRA. They were a disastrous couple: he couldn't resist drink or company; she couldn't resist him or the different forces that beat her down. When she is pregnant he considers fleeing to California, but is dragooned into marriage by Angela's cousins, the fierce MacNamara sisters, in a scene that could have come straight out of Mack Sennett or early melodrama. The author comes into the world four months after the marriage and his baptism furnishes another occasion for knockabout farce.

Not until Frank McCourt is three, and his brother Malachy is two, does the author enter the narrative in his own right. The tone does not change. This adds to the impression that what we are reading is a novel rather than a memoir and that the material has been re-imagined or reinvented. Soon afterwards twin boys are born and a sister who dies after seven weeks. There are brief good times when the father has work and there's food and warmth in the flat and he tells the boys stories of Ireland's mythical past. He is never able, though, to resist drink for more than a few weeks, rolls home singing rebel songs having squandered his wages in the bars to insist on lining up his troops – the small boys – and making them promise to die for Ireland when they grow up. He loses his job. The children go hungry and the mother is unable to cope. They beg round the bars. A greengrocer who sees the two older boys steal bananas to try to stop the hungry crying of the twins in the pram gives them a parcel of food. The neighbours help, but the family descends to such a state of squalor that Angela's cousins, the fierce MacNamara sisters, are sent for. They decide that the only remedy is for the whole family to return to Ireland, and they write to Angela's mother in Limerick, who sends the fare. They put them on the ship to Ireland.

Their first port of call is the small house of Malachy McCourt's parents in County Antrim in Northern Ireland. They are given food and cramped shelter but no encouragement to remain. Malachy is told that pensions are being handed out in the Free State to all who fought for Ireland, and the family are put on a bus to Dublin. There he leaves the mother and smaller children at the bus station and takes Frank with him in search of a pension. When they return empty-handed the children are crying with hunger and the mother distraught. A policeman takes the family to the Garda station where they are fed and allowed to sleep on the floor. The cells are crammed with drunks and prostitutes. The next day the policemen make up a collection for the train fare to get them to Limerick. Malachy McCourt is one of the walking wounded of, among

other things, all the romantic myths that were unearthed and popularized in the nineteenth century and used to create a glorious mythical
past from which the Irish were dispossessed. On the way to the train he
insists that the taxi stop at the GPO to show his son Cuchulain's statue:

The driver says, Now what in God's name is this all about? What's this fellow
doin' with the long hair and the bird on his shoulder? And will you kindly tell
me, mister, what this has to do with the men of 1916?

Dad says, Cuchulain fought to the end like the men of Easter Week. His
enemies were afraid to go near him till they were sure he was dead and when
the bird landed on him and drank his blood they knew.

Well, says the driver, 'tis a sad day for the men of Ireland when they need a
bird to tell them a man is dead. I think we better go now or we'll be missing that
train to Limerick.

The same setting also provides one of the funniest scenes in Samuel
Beckett's first novel.

Limerick had the reputation of being the most Catholic and puritan
city in Ireland, with its large sodalities and congregations. Heinrich Böll
highlighted the city in his romantic hymn to Catholic Ireland. The
poorest of the poor of Ireland lived in the lanes of Limerick, small
houses on either side of narrow lanes into which Angela McCourt had
been born and was now returning to penniless with her whole family.
The people of the lanes were practically invisible in their poverty and
resignation. One of the finest Irish novelists of this century, Kate
O'Brien, grew up in the Catholic merchant class of Limerick. Her
father's large house would have stood little more than a mile from the
McCourt lane and his people do not even enter her work by the back
door. The classes could not have been further apart had either been in
Morocco.

Angela's mother met the family of six at Limerick station, walked
them through the park to her small house, and next morning paid two
weeks' rent for a room in Windmill Street where the children's aunt lived
in a flat with her husband. She then gave Angela money for food, loaned
her household utensils, and told her she could do no more. The family
of six would have to rely on the dole and whatever could be scraped
from public assistance and the Vincent de Paul. In Windmill Street

Oliver is the first of the twins to go. After the death, they move to another room, which has the advantage of being close to Leamy's National School. Here the McCourts come up against racial violence from the other boys because of their American accents, and severe corporal punishment from the master within the school as a part of lessons.

Frank McCourt rails against the unfairness of such schools as Leamy's, as does the headmaster, Mr Halloran. Other schools send out the professionals who will manage the world. No matter how gifted the boys are in Mr Halloran's charge, Leamy's can send out only messenger boys, thieves, labourers.

Eugene sits looking out the window, waiting and calling to his dead brother, until he too dies and the family move again. As the Shannon floods the downstairs in winter, the family move with a picture of the Pope, brought all the way from Brooklyn, to the warmth of upstairs and call it Italy. In summer they would move downstairs again to Ireland.

Two more boys replace the twins, when the mother declares she has had children enough. Because of his Northern accent the father finds it almost impossible to get work in Limerick, but when he does the same pattern is repeated. After a few weeks at work, he comes roaring and singing down Roden Lane to get the boys out of bed in the middle of the night to promise to die for Ireland. He also fairly regularly drinks the weekly dole money, and when that inadequate defence is gone, they beg, they steal, they go hungry. Then he goes, like many of the other men from the lanes, to Coventry, where there is plenty of work in the munitions factories during the war, but fails to send money home. Eventually, he disappears out of their lives and into England for good. One of the many poignant moments in the book is the waiting all day for the telegram boy to arrive at the door with money from England. The mother falls sick and the children start to provide for the house, one of the brothers begging at the front door of rich houses while the other steals from the back, and eventually they start to break up the flimsy walls of Italy for firewood.

McCourt himself almost dies of diphtheria, but he grows up to discover love and sex, to become a telegram boy in the post office and later a clerk in Easons, the newsagents. He saves much of the fare which enables him to return to America by writing threatening letters for a moneylender to poor neighbours of the lanes.

Outside this world stood the Church, the cinema, the library. The doors of the Church were shut against such as the McCourts. The magical world of the cinema was open to them whenever they had the admission money. In the library young McCourt could move at ease and leisure through the world of the mind until he is caught with his nose in unedifying texts.

Given such a life, the expectations must be of a work of unbearable pathos, but nothing could be farther from the reality of *Angela's Ashes*. The explanation is, as usual, in the language, in the style. McCourt has crafted a highly artificial language culled from many sources: prayers, blasphemy, poetry, song, slang, Church doctrine, the cinema and much else. It is a language of exaggeration and distortion, and is an echo of the language people use to obscure or revenge themselves on their circumstances or to raise it to importance. Primarily, it is the language of farce. Despite the differences in setting and form, the Irish work it most reminds me of is that classic farce, Synge's *The Playboy of the Western World*. The characters, for all their vividness, represent types rather than individuals. Were the work to be viewed as other than farce the concluding chapters would be a serious lapse of taste. But it is not simple farce. The streets, the lanes, the bars, the rooms, the shops, the landscapes are evoked with scrupulous accuracy.

The dominant style is varied with a laconic matter-of-factness: 'Grandma caught a chill the night we had the trouble in Roden Lane and the chill turned to pneumonia. They shifted her to the City Hospital and now she's dead.' The farce is never allowed quite to filter the very painful underlying reality.

There are questionable moments in the work. At times its American focus shows. The word 'souper' (a person who exchanges Catholicism for a bowl of soup) would not have required a longwinded explanation in the Limerick of the time. A work as good as *Angela's Ashes* does not need to export local colour, even of a historical nature. Old literary jokes, like the excellence of Shakespeare making him Irish, are made to stand uneasily in the material. The reference to the great *A Modest Proposal*, when it appears, seems even more forced. A certain cinematic predictability invades some of the comic set pieces. But these are small cavils compared to the overall quality and spirit of the work.

Tragedy has been described as a great kick at passive suffering.* The world of *Angela's Ashes* is not a tragedy but it is a great kick at the resignation, the humiliations and indignities the poor are made to undergo in tones of irony and ribald laughter as well as defiance and complaint. It is a wonderfully enjoyable and moving work.

---

* By D. H. Lawrence: 'Tragedy ought really to be a great kick at misery.' *The Letters of D. H. Lawrence*, Volume I, edited by James T. Boulton (Cambridge: Cambridge University Press, 1979), p. 459. McGahern had reviewed the fourth volume of Lawrence's *Letters* in 1987.

From 'A Revolutionary Mind'

Ernie O'Malley: IRA Intellectual, by Richard English

[...]

In his biography of O'Malley just published, Richard English fills out the facts of the life in some detail: he is plainly fascinated by O'Malley, appears to have read everything written on or around the period, and he received much help from the O'Malley family and was given access to papers.

In his preface he makes it clear that he has less interest in the life, in the sense of a conventional biography, than in using an understanding of the life and work to explain the Irish revolution, Irish nationalism, nationalism in general and the tradition of physical force in modern Irish history.

The first third of the work deals with the life in order to provide a biographical foundation for his stated aims, and in doing so he outlines his perception of the revolutionary strategy of that war: 'The Anglo-Irish war, therefore, witnessed a combination of alternative politics and alternative militarism; Sinn Féin set up their own government to rival British legitimacy in Ireland, while the IRA engaged in a determined campaign to undermine British rule by military means.'

It is no accident that O'Malley's books are permanently on display in Sinn Féin windows, and English quotes a strange reading by Gerry Adams of the meaning of *On Another Man's Wound*. In the most lucid and interesting chapter he writes about O'Malley the revolutionary and examines the thinking behind the strategy of the war.

[...]

O'Malley was in the middle of organizing his forces to continue the war when the Treaty was announced, and he was bitterly disappointed. He argued that the people had been coerced into a settlement by the British and consequently had not been given a real choice. The tactics that had worked so well against the British no longer worked. However much it was disputed, the new State had acquired legitimacy. Kevin O'Higgins was to state this view with remarkable clarity at the very outset of the Civil War:

if Civil War occurs in Ireland it will not be for the Treaty. It will not be for a Free State versus anything else. It will be for a vital, fundamental, democratic principle – for the right of the people of Ireland to decide any issue, great or small, that arises in the politics of this country.

Richard English is convincing on all of this in his analysis of the revolutionary mind. O'Malley's vision of Irish nationality was romantic, quasireligious, with a strong emphasis on the spiritual; and it was invested in the people, as long as the people did not dispute or choose to misinterpret their investiture.

The succeeding chapters are less convincing. In the part entitled 'The Intellectual' he strives to make O'Malley bear a weight he is unable to carry. He is on even more uncertain ground in 'The Companion', where he attempts to draw conclusions from O'Malley's marriage and his friendships. The wide reading drawn upon in support of his conclusions can be confusing and sometimes irrelevant.

The historical accuracy of O'Malley's memoirs has often been disputed. English is aware of this but takes it no further. Surely an investigation would tell us more about O'Malley than the use of tangential figures, even those as worthy as Edward Said, to support arguments about O'Malley's approach to the arts?

The war was the most intense experience of O'Malley's life. Several times he mentions that he did not expect to live through the war. After such an experience, no matter what shape his life was to take, it could not have been other than difficult. A number of times he could have entered politics, but he rejected the offers. His character was ill-suited to compromise or obfuscation. In the libel case over *On Another Man's Wound*, he discovered that what people believed in private they would not support in court.

He became a difficult marginal figure in a country he had helped to create. The myth that he had been prepared to follow, no matter what the cost to himself or to others, had turned into an inward-looking, pedantic theocracy that he was forced to live in.

There are fascinating glimpses of this life in Richard English's biography. We see O'Malley living and farming, not very successfully, in Mayo; chairing a meeting in Dublin of Republicans in sympathy with the anti-Franco forces in Spain, when the Hierarchy and most of the country were rabidly for Franco. He worked as an adviser to his friend John Ford on *The Quiet Man* and *The Rising of the Moon*, promoted and wrote about the work of another friend, Jack Yeats, and many other painters. He was friendly with several writers, and visited Beckett in Paris. He successfully resisted an attempt to evict him from his house near Newport during the divorce, and retained custody of one of his children. He sent his son to school in England and looked towards London as the centre of culture.

I believe that by using the life as a basis for a number of theses, Richard English misses out on something that could be much more fascinating, a full life; and all the admirable things, and the less than admirable, would come to us more powerfully through suggestion rather than exposition.

Perhaps the depth of O'Malley's disaffection can be guessed at in his response to an objection that one of his friends at this time was a Fascist: 'As if that made any difference. I can't carry round my wars with me all the time. Goodness knows I have enough hangover from fighting against an Empire to quarrel with ideologies. People are more important to me now, anyhow.'

On the Turning Wheel of the Year

Northern Lights: A Poet's Sources,
by George Mackay Brown

George Mackay Brown was born in Orkney in 1921 and died there in 1996, a place he rarely left. In the late 1950s he studied under the poet Edwin Muir at Newbattle Abbey, outside Edinburgh, but returned home as soon as he graduated. It was Edwin Muir who introduced his first book of poems. Awarded the Society of Authors' Travelling Fellowship in 1968, he refused to travel further than Ireland, where he stayed with his friend and admirer Seamus Heaney. He visited England for the first time in 1989. When his last novel, *Beside the Ocean of Time*, was shortlisted for the Booker Prize in 1994, he refused to travel to London for the dinner in the Guildhall.

He had already travelled far in a rich harvesting (a favourite word of Brown's) of poems, stories, novels, essays, plays, books for children, moving easily between verse and prose, generations and centuries. His language is poetic and true and moves swiftly in simple lines and sentences, often in very short paragraphs: 'The girl brought them shell-fish. They left the empty shells on a stone. They rowed North.' It is interesting that one of the most exciting living short-story writers, Alistair MacLeod, different in temperament and much more sparing than Mackay Brown, likewise moves with the same imaginative ease from present-day Nova Scotia to Colmcille on Iona to the generations that left Skye at the time of the Clearances, as if they were all part of the same eternal day.

The editors of *Northern Lights* state that by intertwining verse and prose they seek to follow 'the example of its great predecessor *An Orkney Tapestry*'. George Mackay Brown began his writing career as a local correspondent for the *Orkney Herald* in the 1940s. As well as reporting football matches and council meetings he wrote a weekly essay, and fifty years on he was still writing a similar column for the *Orcadian*. These pieces were very popular, appearing every week almost without a break for twenty-five years.

A great part of *Northern Lights* is made up of selections from these columns, arranged according to the 'turning wheel of the year'. They are interesting for the occasional fresh insight and vividness of phrasing and the underlying attractiveness of Mackay Brown's personality; but very few weekly columns can survive this transition, and these pieces are, for the most part, no exception. It is hard to imagine them interesting anyone who hasn't already some knowledge of Mackay Brown's work.

Also published for the first time is a diary he kept during a visit to the Shetland Islands in 1988, one of the rare visits abroad. There is a rendering of various Orkney and Shetland legends. What emerges gradually is that the editors are scraping an already well-scraped barrel. George Mackay Brown published an enormous body of work in his lifetime and was a watchful, intelligent critic of his own work. Nearly everything new in *Northern Lights* he had chosen not to publish and most of the inclusions prove him to have been right.

The one exception, and the saving grace of the volume, is the section entitled 'Finished Fragrance', particularly the portraits of his mother and father, Mary Jane Mackay and John Brown, tailor, mimic and postman. The pair met and married when she worked as a waitress and chambermaid in the new Stromness Hotel, and they had six children, five of whom survived. In these moving portraits they are truly honoured, and Mackay Brown's method serves him and them superbly. He makes himself as anonymous as the old ballad makers, allowing the portraits to emerge in their own unfettered light with an artfulness that is all the more effective because it is nowhere visible and consciously simple.

Brought up a Presbyterian, Mackay Brown became a Roman Catholic in 1961. *Following a Lark*, his last collection of poems, he described as written mainly in praise of the light, adding that he hoped it might also 'glorify in a small way the Light behind the light'. In the final poem, 'A Work for Poets', he sets out both his own epigraph and his idea of the function and place of poetry:

To have carved on the days of our vanity
A sun
A ship
A star
A cornstalk

Also a few marks
From an ancient forgotten time
A child may read

That not far from the stone
A well
Might open for wayfarers

Here is a work for poets –
Carve the runes
Then be content with silence

Pieces of Yeats

The Life of W. B. Yeats: A Critical Biography,
by Terence Brown

In his preface, Terence Brown writes that this critical biography would not be possible without the work of the previous scholars and writers on Yeats that he is able to draw on. These are many, and all are acknowledged. He also states that he wishes the work to be open to the general reader.

The early chapters have the rich detail of William M. Murphy's sympathetic biography of John Butler Yeats. They cover much the same ground, but the methods are very different. This can be seen in Brown's treatment of J.B.Y.'s extraordinary decision to give up the law for art and move from Dublin to London to study drawing at Heatherley's Art School, leaving his wife and two children with her parents in Sligo.

Brown draws on both Murphy's partisan account and on Gifford Lewis's study of *The Yeats Sisters and the Cuala*: to Murphy it was a necessary if reckless artistic impulse; Lewis saw it as an act of a profoundly irresponsible man who sacrificed his family for the sake of a feckless whim. Brown gives his own reasons why Gifford's judgement is too severe and narrow, but he is almost equally distant from Murphy's warm advocacy. Brown resorts to this method frequently. It could degenerate into fair-minded dullness, but instead it adds to the richness of the text, partly because he has such command of his many sources that he is able to thread them so unobtrusively together that they seem part of a single narrative. And when it is necessary, he is never shy of speaking bluntly.

Throughout the work he is alert to social and cultural change and the effects of such change. In a few pages he is able to trace the disastrous effect of the rise of the mass market on the lives of the poets who belonged with Yeats to the Rhymers: 'In an apparent paradox, it was increased literacy which put the role of the man of letters in question', and he argues how the ensuing fragmentation of the serious literary market place led indirectly to the *fin de siècle* of the 1890s.

He is equally alert to political change, which is even more necessary as he sees Yeats's extraordinary career, in its many aspects, reflecting this country's complicated relationship with Britain, and certain of his works are seen as interventions in that history. With the same careful selection and threading of quotation, he is able to evoke atmosphere:

We glimpse Yeats again in this Edwardian twilight on the brink of European dark, in the spring of 1914 at dinner in Sir Edmund Gosse's fine house in Regent's Park, 'a pattern of talk . . . dancing to and fro across the table . . . easy and effortless' [. . .]. It is a striking vignette: 'Beyond Yeats's dark hair and heavy chin like that of some prelate not too ascetic, and Sickert's aquiline profile, the open windows showed heavy garden laburnums pale in candlelight against the sombre leafage of the park' . . .

Similarly, Brown cites many critics and writers, patiently and unobtrusively, as he searches to explain the poet's work. At the heart of this search is Yeats's lifelong fascination with the occult. Here Brown turns to that clearest of clear minds, E. R. Dodds, author of *The Greeks and the Irrational*, who as a young man knew Yeats in Dublin and was later to be a sceptical member of the British Society of Psychical Research. In his autobiography, Dodds distinguishes between two approaches to psychic phenomena, though sometimes they are mixed in individual minds. 'The one was that of the occultist who sought experience rather than explanation, the other that of the psychic researcher who wishes to "abolish" the occult in the clear light of day.' Dodds thought Yeats an occultist, whereas he numbered himself among the psychic researchers. Brown, characteristically, thinks that for all his dedication to the occult there was much of the investigator in Yeats, and it is in this light that he comes to examine that most perplexing of Yeats's works, *A Vision*.

Yeats married George Hyde-Lees amid doubts and hesitations:

It was Lady Gregory who managed to bring the reluctant but lonely prospective husband to the sticking point, having first been persuaded that Yeats's intentions were in fact honourable, if ill-expressed. Some home truths must have been spoken. The mistress of Coole was particularly scathing about Yeats intending to marry Hyde-Lees in the clothes he had purchased to woo Iseult [Gonne].

The marriage almost ended during the honeymoon. To distract her husband from his depression, the young bride faked a session of automatic writing, to discover that she had a ready facility. Yeats was fascinated:

It was a gift she was to exploit to remarkable effect in the early years of a marriage which might otherwise have foundered. For it quickly made her a daily focus of the poet's almost insatiable curiosity about the paranormal, about the possibility of spirit communication, and gave her the means by which she might direct, without obviously appearing to do so, a conjoint exploration of their relationship.

What began in faking led to the extraordinary collaboration that was to grow into A Vision. Brown suggests that the collaboration could also have contained elements of analysis such as Jung was conducting at the time. Brown handles this most difficult material with the same delicacy and insight he brings to his reading of the poet's work.

The risk in any critical biography is the preservation of a balance. In the greater part of the book this is kept and sensitively held, but there are times in the second half of the book when I felt the balance swings too heavily toward academic criticism, and as a result the narrative appears to hurry in the compelling closing chapters, as if there was an awareness that it had lingered too long elsewhere. The work is fascinating and a pleasure to read, Brown an illuminating and companionable guide throughout its extraordinary intricacies, and it made this general reader want to revisit certain plays, and the magical poems.

A Classic Gathering of the Classics

Irish Classics, by Declan Kiberd

In the introduction to his latest work, *Irish Classics*, Declan Kiberd gives a number of definitions of a classic – such as Mark Twain's: 'a book nobody wants to read but everybody wishes to have read' – before giving his own clear view:

For me a classic is like a great poem, 'news that stays news'. It is in fact the sort of book that everybody enjoys reading and nobody wants to come to an end. It owes its reputation, undoubtedly, to its initial impact on its own generation, without which few books ever survive: but after that it displays a capacity to remain forever young and fresh, offering challenges to every succeeding generation which must learn anew how to be its contemporary. It reads each passing age at least as intensely as it is read by it.

In the concluding chapter, Kiberd tells us something of what he hoped to achieve. In paying generous tribute to his late teacher, the critic and biographer Richard Ellmann, he asserts that Ellmann's influential writings on Yeats and Joyce, Wilde and Beckett, had the strange effect of convincing a whole generation of readers that the great Irish modernists were not, in any meaningful sense of the word, 'Irish'.

The central argument in *Irish Classics* is a direct reversal of Ellmann's:

my contention is that, for writers as disparate as Ó Bruadair and Yeats, to be Irish was to be modern anyway, whether one liked it or not. That is what links the artists covered here: each has had to cope, in his or her way, with the coercive onset of modernity. Each has generated a narrative that seeks to salvage something of value from the past, even as the forces of the new world are embraced.

I would be prepared to take either view, Ellmann's or Kiberd's, depending on what is made of the particular view.

Professor Kiberd takes the Flight of the Earls as his starting point and he observes that what fell with Hugh O'Neill was not a Gaelic civilization, so much as an aristocratic order. In fact, the flight reflected changes that had already taken place, some of them for the good, such as the freeing of the serfs. The bardic order had been completely tied to the aristocratic, and were themselves unapologetically aristocratic, with great, often hereditary, powers and privilege:

For four centuries they had shown nothing but contempt for the common people: and they had developed a mandarin language which was comprehensible only to the elite. That language, priding itself on its archaic qualities, over the centuries had grown resistant to further development or change. The virtuosity of the poets was, for the most part, of that kind which leaves an artist invulnerable to criticism and yet incapable of evolution. Now the *filí* found that, if they wished to survive, they would have to employ the language of a more vulgar market.

The result had the effect of reviving a tradition that had long been closed and moribund and resistant to change. The meditation ranges far and wide as he compares the collapse with later European situations, when the loss of status and power resulted in the release of new energies. I found this whole section fascinating. Here begin the dualities that are essential to Kiberd's central argument: 'A tradition is never more vital than when facing extinction; each articulation of the collapse of one civilisation ends up becoming the master narrative of another.'

He writes well about the rise of the English language, the decline of Irish, the effects of bilingualism, the Anglo-Irish themselves, who were English within Ireland but were seen as Irish in London, the face and the mask . . .

These various revivals in the face of extinction are traced through the works of the great Gaelic poets of the seventeenth and eighteenth centuries: Seathrún Céitinn, Ó Bruadair, Séamas Dall Mac Cuarta, Aogán Ó Rathaille and others. There are illuminating and sometimes moving readings of well-known poems such as 'A bhean lán de stuaim' (O woman full of wantonness, attributed to Céitinn) and Mac Cuarta's

'Fáilte don Éan' (Welcome to the sweetest bird on the branches) to less familiar poems. In each case the background and the society of the poem is given. Alongside the Gaelic texts are Kiberd's prose translations in clear English.

With the Swift of the *Drapier's Letters* and *Gulliver's Travels*, we are on more familiar ground. Swift is followed by two particularly delightful essays on Goldsmith's 'The Deserted Village' and *She Stoops to Conquer*. There is Sheridan's *The School for Scandal,* Merriman's *Midnight Court* and Eibhlín Dhubh Ní Chonaill's *Caoineadh Airt Uí Laoghaire*. Here, he describes what remained of wealthy Catholic society under the Penal Laws and the tensions within and around that society, and identifies how an individual talent, akin to Sylvia Plath's, merged with a formal oral tradition to create that great lament.

He writes on Edmund Burke, Wolfe Tone's Journals, Maria Edgeworth's *Castle Rackrent* and Carleton's *Peasantry*. The traditional novel is seen as the form most dependent on an agreed idea of society and seen as the greatest casualty in this disjointed world. Yet, three favourites of mine are chosen: George Moore's *A Drama in Muslin*, Kate O'Brien's *The Ante-Room* and *The Silver Fox* by Somerville and Ross.

Ulysses, the novels of Beckett, *Cré Na Cille* and *At Swim-Two-Birds* are seen as subversive or anti-novels. The reading of *At Swim-Two-Birds* manages to be both affectionate and funny. There is no single essay on Beckett but his work is referred to throughout the book. In fact, he is probably the dominant presence.

Of *Ulysses*, Kiberd says, in a lively, provocative essay: 'His book is really a collection of short stories in the drag of a novel and so it captures something of the old storyteller's authority, even as it harnesses the leaflets, papers and posters of the modern city.' Sean O'Casey's Dublin plays are linked with Liam O'Flaherty's *The Informer*. He writes on Shaw's *Arms and the Man*, Augusta Gregory's *Cuchulain*, the Blasket writers, Hyde's *Love Songs of Connacht*, Yeats, Patrick Kavanagh, Louis MacNeice and Seán Ó Ríordáin.

Kiberd's great learning is worn lightly, with wit, with intelligence, with feeling, with courtesy – what is not useful is always set aside with regret, never with conceit or venom. The narrative is constantly enlivened by small human details. I was surprised to discover that the distinguished linguist Carl Marstrander was a Norwegian pole-vault champion and used the oar of a curragh as a pole to launch himself over Tomás Ó Criomhthain's house.

With the skill of a good novelist he can etch in backgrounds from his wide reading that, for one reason or another, the novelist did not choose to describe:

Had Moore gained entry, he might have found the Castle ball a ritual more suited to social comedy than political satire. For example, the old Viceroy Lord Spencer was expected to kiss each debutante as she was presented. He had a flaming red beard, but it soon turned snowy white from all the face-powder deposited on it by blushing girls . . . The State Steward was notorious for falling asleep (sometimes on his feet) at these occasions. His job was to deal with formal complaints, as when a dispute arose because the Earl of Clonmel had sat down heavily on the lap of a lady dowager, drunkenly mistaking her for a well-upholstered armchair.

I have cavils. His intellectual energy can sometimes draw him into making connections that appear far-fetched. At other times, certain readings are too overtly political for my taste. I found that while certain writers answer beautifully to his meditations and arguments – 'Synge's *Tristes Tropiques*: *The Aran Islands*' is a happy example – there are others, such as Swift, that resist his reading.

Finally, his closing narrative leads him by questionable paths to the duality of the Belfast Agreement. I believe literature and politics to be, at best, uneasy bedfellows. In bringing them together here, Kiberd gives to literature more worldly importance and influence than it ever has. Too much importance generally brings no great good to women or to men or beasts or books. Kiberd cites Sir Patrick Mayhew and how Mayhew was moved and influenced by the reading of letters Ernie O'Malley wrote while in prison: O'Malley found solace and comfort while wounded and close to death in an IRA campaign in reading a pocket edition of Shakespeare's sonnets.

I would have been happy to see *On Another Man's Wound* numbered among Kiberd's Irish classics because I think of it as the only work to have emerged directly from the violence that is fit to be set beside Wolfe Tone's Journals. But anybody with a knowledge of O'Malley's book would know that a man of Mayhew's background, because of the class and caste system of empire, will always feel closer to an IRA man who reads Shakespeare than to an English soldier who looks to the *Sun* or *News of the World*. I have always felt that the least complaining victims of empire and postcolonialism have been the English working classes.

It would be extraordinary if there were not some disagreement in the course of such a wide-ranging and ambitious work that could, in time, itself become a classic. His theme, whatever one may think of the argument, has the practical effect of giving a spine or central idea to a work about writers that have often little more in common with one another than the fact that they wrote well.

All good writing is local and is made universal through clear thinking and deep feeling finding the right expression, and in so doing reflects all the particular form is capable of reflecting, including the social and the political. Consequently, in addition to reporting back from the war zones of scholarship with discernment and wit and zest about the exciting 'news that stays news', he has also, probably inadvertently, written one of the most fascinating, enjoyable and original histories of Ireland, because of that other duality within his subject matter: the local becoming the universal.

How They Lived up in the Big House

The Big House in Ireland, by Valerie Pakenham,
with special photography by Thomas Pakenham

In the North Roscommon I grew up in, the high demesne wall of Rockingham extended for several miles. All the stone gatehouses were picturesque and no two were alike, and from their gates the long avenues ran to the Nash mansion that overlooked Lough Key. There was a chapel of ease, a harbour, boathouse, lawns, tennis courts, gardens, stables, a farmyard, tied cottages, woods and parkland, even an elaborate system of tunnels that allowed goods to be carried into the kitchens out of sight of the Great House.

With a retinue of servants, farmhands, stable lads, gardeners and gamekeepers, the estate was a closed world within a world. The social occasion of the year was the pheasant shoot and the great annual ball when the gentry gathered from several counties and the British ambassador came from Dublin. Rockingham House burned down in 1957 and the estate was split into farms.

A few miles away stood Woodbrook House. It had one tiny gatehouse and no walls and it was given fame by David Thomson's book *Woodbrook*. The Kirkwoods lived there, under the leaking roofs, and occasionally they were rescued from their habitual genteel penury by their racehorses. The only annual ball was when they gave their barns to the local wrenboys on St Stephen's Night for their dance. Around the same time as Rockingham burned down, Woodbrook passed into the hands of the gentle Maxwells, old retainers of the Kirkwoods.

Valerie Pakenham brings these and other houses to life in *The Big House in Ireland*, from their beginnings in the seventeenth century to the houses that have survived into the present century. In seventeen chapters she details in formal order various aspects of these houses and their histories – their buildings, the laying out of their parks and gardens, their furnishings, their inhabitants and their relationships with one another and the people outside their walls at various points in the history of the country.

The introductions are clearly written, out of affection and deep knowledge, and they are followed by relevant extracts from the writings of people who lived or stayed in these houses, culled from memoirs, letters, diaries and private collections of family papers. My one complaint is that they are generally too short and various and tend to confusion following the clear introductions. They are probably better dipped into than taken whole.

Among the writers she draws on are Maria Edgeworth, Swift, Martin Ross, Edith Somerville, Lady Gregory, George Moore, Elizabeth Bowen, David Thomson. In the general climate of affection, a place is given to dissenters, such as de Tocqueville and Engels. Here is Engels writing to Karl Marx in 1856: 'Their country seats are surrounded by enormous, wonderfully beautiful parks, but all around is waste land, and where the money is supposed to come from it is impossible to see. These fellows ought to be shot.'

The book is beautifully produced. The photographs, illustrations and reproductions are all interesting, and some are more than that.

Heroines of Their Lives

Hateship, Friendship, Courtship, Loveship, Marriage,
by Alice Munro

In volume after volume of short stories, Alice Munro has created a world that is uniquely her own and yet is familiar and close, reflecting and touching on the realities of the lives of many readers. She has won both a high and a popular reputation in a time when the short story is almost as isolated on the margins of popular culture as the poem. From the very beginning, Munro's stories were distinguished by their individuality, the vigorous use of the rhythms of ordinary speech, a clarity of image and phrase, a sensuousness that never cloyed, a subtle psychological awareness, a hard honesty. She has an imaginative boldness.

Behind the fictional disguises, the biography of a recognizable heroine emerges. She is born into a poor dairy farm in Ontario at a time when such farms are going out of business. A parent dies. There is a wide, close circle of relatives, all vividly realized. The family moves to a small town on the edge of the 'flat, scrubby unremarkable countryside', where they run a small store, work as travelling salesmen or in department stores. The heroine is bright and attractive and gets to university. There she meets a man from a wealthy family. They marry and move to his home on Vancouver Island and have children. There is something unsatisfactory about the husband, as there is about many of Munro's men, especially if they are in any way academic or intellectual. The fathers and relatives and men who work physically or pursue practical disciplines are brought to more vivid life. As soon as she enters her husband's wealthy family, the woman discovers that it is far from what she imagined or dreamed of, and the working-class world that she used to be secretly ashamed of now appears in a fresh light, jovial and contented in comparison.

The couple quarrel incessantly. The heroine forms relationships with wives in similar middle- or upper middle-class marriages, and takes a lover. In 'Differently', the husbands are discussed openly: 'They looked at each other bleakly, and laughed. Then they announced – they admitted – what weighed on them. It was the innocence of these husbands – the hearty, decent, firm, contented innocence. That is a wearying and finally discouraging thing. It makes intimacy a chore.' They divorce, and we follow her through the vicissitudes of her newly independent state. In some of the stories, she appears as a television reporter, as an actress, as an editor, as an assistant in a bookstore, moving through a world of romantic possibilities, affairs, sexual strife, the claims of her children and her own family, usually her father. She makes no claim to virtue or goodness, but she is wonderfully honest and vital: she misses nothing. I know of nobody who writes as well as Munro about 'the hardhearted energy of sex':

She sat on the stool and watched the street – patient, expectant, by herself, in a finely balanced and suspended state.

She saw Miles' reflection – his helmeted ghost parking his motorcycle at the curb – before she saw him . . . That was what they did. They sat for a while on the logs. Then, though the beach was not quite dark or completely deserted, they made love in the imperfect shelter of some broom bushes. Georgia walked home, a strengthened and lightened woman, not in the least in love, favored by the universe . . . And Georgia herself, watching her children on the roundabout, or feeling the excellent shape of a lemon in her hand at the supermarket, contained another woman, who only a few hours before had been whimpering and tussling on the ferns, on the sand, on the bare ground, or, during a rainstorm, in her own car – who had been driven hard and gloriously out of her mind and drifted loose and gathered her wits and made her way home again . . . Trouble began, perhaps, as soon as they said that they loved each other . . . But you would have thought that after such scourging she'd have scuttled back into her marriage and locked its doors, and appreciated what she had there as never before.

That was not what happened. She broke with Ben. Within a year, she was gone. Her way of breaking was strenuous and unkind.

In the early stories, Munro details with loving slowness how the shades of the prison house begin to close upon the growing girl, burdening her with the darkness of the life of adults. By the time 'Royal

Beatings' is reached, we find the girl, now full of wile, enacting with her father and stepmother rites that will be echoed later in scenes of marital fury. By now, she has acquired a girl friend, as later, when married, she will have a woman friend who serves as ally, conspirator, a distraction and a sounding board. Once these alliances collapse, depths of hidden rivalry are often revealed, as well as a savage solitude.

In her later stories, Munro has turned to reconstructions of an early Canada. These reconstructions in their largeness of feeling and range, their historical imagination, recall more the great Russians than the work of her contemporaries. Munro writes as vividly about these early people as if they were her contemporaries, and this gift is closely allied to another aspect of her vision, that life in its essence does not alter greatly from generation to generation:

The odd thing is that my mother's ideas were in line with some progressive notions of her times, and mine echoed the notions that were favored in my time. This in spite of the fact that we both believed ourselves independent, and lived in backwaters that did not register such changes. It's as if tendencies that seem most deeply rooted in our minds, most private and singular, have come in as spores on the prevailing wind, looking for any likely place to land, any welcome.

. . . What holds anybody in a man or a woman may be something as flimsy as a Romanian accent or the calm curve of an eyelid, some half-fraudulent mystery.

In some of the reconstructions, the transference of her central themes to a remote and more repressed time works uncertainly. The sudden shifts of focus can appear as violent strategies of closure when they fail to bring such disparate points together. Part of the difficulty may be in the very limitations of the short story, which is unable to contain this largeness that she so ably bends and shapes to her purposes elsewhere. When they succeed, they are a triumph, and Munro's failures are often more exciting than modestly contained successes.

In the sharpness of her social awareness there is humour, but it is as if she deliberately refuses to resort to humour, seeking to go further: 'I got a call at work, and it was my father', begins the reflective and moving 'The Progress of Love':

My father was so polite, even in the family. He took time to ask me how I was. Country manners. Even if somebody phones up to tell you your house is burning down, they ask first how you are.

'I'm fine,' I said. 'How are you?'

'Not so good, I guess,' said my father, in his old way – apologetic but self-respecting. 'I think your mother's gone.'

Much of the world Alice Munro has made her own reappears in *Hateship, Friendship, Courtship, Loveship, Marriage*, and by now desire has become, in part, memory and reflection. In 'What is Remembered', Vancouver and Vancouver Island are revisited. The couple is not as individual nor as richly solid as the earlier couples; they are more like sketches. The pair take the ferry to attend a funeral near Vancouver. The husband has to return to the Island, while the wife goes to visit an old friend of her family who is now in a nursing home. A doctor she meets offers to drive her there. The visit is made, and they spend the day together before going to a borrowed room. Afterwards, he gives no sign of wishing to take the encounter further, and the wife, in a confusion of feelings, returns to her husband and children. All of the action takes place in memory and has more the air of essay and reflection than story, but the exacting prose is as arresting as ever as it explores the paths not taken.

In 'Nettles', the vein is riskier but similarly reined in. A couple who knew each other and were close when young meet unexpectedly at a friend's house where they are staying over the weekend. The man is now married. The woman is divorced and in an unsatisfactory affair:

When I met him I tried to be carefree and to show an independent spirit. We exchanged news – I made sure I had news – and we laughed, and went for walks in the ravine, but all I really wanted was to entice him to have sex with me, because I thought the high enthusiasm of sex fused people's best selves. I was stupid about these matters, in a way that was very risky, particularly for a woman of my age.

The new couple explore the life they knew and the shape their lives have taken since their paths separated. On a golf course they are at ease with one another, the woman content to follow the man as he plays, when a violent rainstorm forces them to shelter in woods. One form of violence or another is always close to Munro's sense of the primacy of sex, but what comes of their imprisonment in the storm, however, is not sex but 'love that was not usable, that knew its place'.

In the rich and surefooted 'Family Furnishings', we return to the small farms of the father's youth, as the bells ring out to celebrate the end of the First World War. This small closed world of the families, with their low horizons and working-class manners and rigid codes, is lovingly evoked. Struggling out of this world towards freedom and independence are two women: Alfrida, a sophisticated older figure with an obliterated past who works on a newspaper and brings home the dangerous glamour of cities; and the clever daughter we have come to know so well. These two women, in their different ways, not all that flattering to either, put this older traditional world in a corner. Here, the various fictional disguises are abandoned. The younger woman is revealed as the writer who will one day weave the material into a story:

I did not think of the story I would make about Alfrida – not of that in partic-ular – but of the work I wanted to do, which seemed more like grabbing some-thing out of the air than constructing stories. The cries of the crowd came to me like big heartbeats, full of sorrows. Lovely formal-sounding waves, with their distant, almost inhuman assent and lamentation.

This was what I wanted, this was what I thought I had to pay attention to, this was how I wanted my life to be.

The opening movements of the title story, 'Hateship, Friendship, Courtship, Loveship, Marriage', evoke dramatically both the small town at a time 'before the trains stopped running on so many of the branch lines' and the vast unruly spaces of Canada the railroad served. For a long time it holds the promise of an important novel. Tidied into the shorter form, the two conniving girls essential to the plot are unable to support either the weight of the material or the unlikely happiness their connivance has brought into being. Even so, the loneliness of un-connected lives in the small towns and the vastness and unruliness of the frontier spaces that is caught are palpable.

Hand in hand with her sense of the primacy of sex, Munro has always been keenly attuned to all signs of ageing. What was always there in the shadows of the early work is now in the foreground. In 'The Bear Came over the Mountain', the wife of a devoted childless couple develops Alzheimer's, goes into a home, and forms a romantic attachment to one of her fellow inmates. The whole is skilfully delineated, but throughout there is a sense that the material belongs more to the Surrealists or to the savage genius of a Gogol than to Munro's naturalism; and it does not help that the eyes and ears of the narrative is another of her colourless academics. 'Comfort' is more fully realized. Another childless couple, he a biology teacher – headstrong, difficult, abrasive – runs into trouble with Christian fundamentalists over the teaching of evolution, and the ruckus is only resolved when he falls terminally ill and resigns. In places, the prose takes on an unusual forcing note, and the small offstage scenes are managed more happily than the central theme.

The marvel of the volume is 'Floating Bridge', which triumphantly joins Munro's new concerns to her old strengths. In both time and place, it is the least complicated of the stories. Again, there is a lightweight husband, a social worker with a special interest in delinquents. His younger wife has cancer. They hire a girl who was once one of his charges to help them through the final stages of her illness. To the wife, the girl has 'a disagreeable power'. In an old van, in the intense heat of August in Toronto, they set out on a quest for the girl's good shoes that takes them to a trailer beside an abandoned farmhouse outside the city where she and her sister live with her foster parents. They are invited into the trailer.

This is too much for the wife to face, but she encourages her husband to accept, content to be alone. In the fierce heat she is drawn to the coolness of a field of corn, enters the narrow rows, and gets lost. As someone leaves the trailer, the barking of the dogs allows her to find her way back to the van. The man has come from the trailer to see if she is all right, to press her to join them within, and starts to tell a long joke. Tired and bored by the demands of listening, she hears in her head the pronouncements of various oncologists during the treatment of her illness. 'It's too much', she says out loud to one of the pronouncements. The man from the trailer takes this as a rude criticism of his joke, and goes back in. The natural son of the foster mother comes along on a bicycle. He is a younger version of the helmeted motorcyclist who appeared in 'Differently', more innocent, less experienced. Each in their different season could double as the muse of poetry she is forced to follow. They talk and, despite the havoc her illness has wrought and the differences of age, discover that they have things in common. Within the van he sees the keys in the ignition and offers to drive her home. Taking her through a swamp, they pause to view the night on a floating bridge. Everything is true and breathtakingly sure and is as good as Alice Munro has ever written, which is to say that it is written as well as anybody who has written well in her time, and with her own uniqueness.

Kiltubrid, County Leitrim

Kiltubrid, County Leitrim: Snapshots of a Rural
Parish in the 1890s, by Liam Kelly

I have enjoyed and admired all of Liam Kelly's books: *Kiltubrid* (1984) and *The Face of Time* (1995), his book of moving photographs Leland Duncan took of the people and places close to Annadale House towards the close of the nineteenth century; *A Flame Now Quenched* (1998) concerned itself with rebels and Frenchmen in Leitrim in the years 1793 to 1798. And now we have *Kiltubrid, County Leitrim* in the Maynooth Studies in Local History series. All these books are, in the best sense of the term, local histories.

The book examines the lives of the Kiltubrid people throughout the nineteenth century through the dwellings they inhabited, the land they tilled and how they tilled that land, the patterns of emigration and its effect on the communities. People did not live in Ireland then; they lived in small, intense communities which could vary greatly in character, and even morale, over the course of a few miles. When I returned to live here more than thirty years ago I was told by a man in Fenagh of some [neighbour] who was hard up: 'He had to go abroad for a woman.' I thought this was interesting: that the local man in question had married a Frenchwoman or an Italian, but when I enquired I was told in no uncertain terms that he had to go to Cloone for a woman. The implication was that nobody local would have him.

Liam Kelly reveals that Kiltubrid was too large an entity to contain a single community and that there were, in fact, three separate communities that had very little to do with one another within the parish, which was particularly reflected in marriage patterns and later by the farming practices and rivalries between the different football teams.

The progress of housing is traced. In the beginning was the single room. A man kept his cow in one end of the room and his spouse in the other and, gradually, those dwellings improved with a slowly increasing prosperity. It was unusually slow and difficult because of the poor land and poor farming practices. Leitrim could support few horses. Their beast of work and transport was the humble ass. Through photographs and different records, the book looks at the stories of the people, the food they survived on, the clothes they wore. The great drama of their lives was not glory but survival. They were a tough, resilient people who survived famine, hardship, emigration and poverty.

Up to now history has concerned itself with wars and governance, empires, whole civilizations as they rose and fell, what a friend of mine close to Laura Lake describes as 'Importances'. Liam Kelly turns his attention to the ordinary people who are our past. To see them truly is to see ourselves more fully, without bogus glorification or sanctification of the past. I find these local histories as fascinating as some of the great histories of state. For one thing they are closer to our lives and in writing this book Liam Kelly has served us supremely well.

Notes and References

The essays are taken from the following sources. For material that has been previously published in books, newspapers or magazines, references are given to the original place of publication and all known reprints. Previously unpublished material, now available in the John McGahern Collection at the James Hardiman Library of the National University of Ireland, Galway, is identified with the abbreviation NUIG followed by the appropriate file number. Note, though, that some new archive material had not yet been catalogued at the time of going to press.

Unless otherwise stated, the titles are those under which these pieces appeared on their original publication or, for previously unpublished material, that which appears on the source manuscript or typescript.

I WRITING AND THE WORLD

'Five Drafts'   Unpublished typescript. NUIG P71/uncatalogued.

'The Image: Prologue to a Reading at the Rockefeller University [1968]'   *The Honest Ulsterman* 8 (December 1968): 10. Published in French translation in John McGahern, *Lignes de fond: précédé de L'image*, translated by Pierre Leyris (Paris: Mercure de France, 1971), 17–18.

'The Image [1991]'   *Canadian Journal of Irish Studies* 17.1 (July 1991), Special issue on John McGahern: 12. Reprinted in *L'Œil-de-bœuf: Revue littéraire trimestrielle* 9–10 (May 1996): 74–5.
Variations:
in terror or in laughter once: the otherwise identical 1996 version switches this around to read 'in laughter or in terror once'.

'Playing with Words'   Unpublished. Untitled typescript with handwritten revisions and corrections, c.1985–8. NUIG P71/1298.
Variations:
that will not go away: NUIG P71/1299, a typescript of a shorter version of the same essay.

If I have any quarrel today with 'The Image': in the typescript (NUIG P71/1298)
this reads 'If I have any quarrel today with the above', as it suggests repeating
the text of 'The Image' within this essay.

that older, healing word: the word order has been adapted here to aid the
meaning, as a handwritten revision to the last line of the typescript appears
to suggest the phrase 'that older word, healing – magic'.

'The Local and the Universal'   Unpublished. Lecture given at the official opening
of the 34th Listowel Writers' Week, 2 June 2004. Typescript entitled 'Writers'
Week, Listowel 2004'. NUIG P71/uncatalogued.

Note on the text: in the typescript, McGahern inadvertently switches the words
'local' and 'universal' in the central epigram taken from Miguel Torga's *The
Creation of the World*: 'The local is the universal, but with the walls taken
away' [sic]. I have changed those two words back in order to aid the meaning.

'History (On meeting J. C. Beckett)'   Unpublished. Opening paragraph of an
untitled typescript. NUIG P71/uncatalogued.

'Madness/Creativity'   *La Licorne* 32 (1995), Special issue on John McGahern: 9–10.

II PLACES AND PEOPLE

'Time Regained: Photographs of County Leitrim'   Published as an untitled
foreword in Liam Kelly, *The Face of Time: Leland Lewis Duncan 1862–1923:
Photographs of County Leitrim* (Dublin: Lilliput Press, 1995), 5.

'County Leitrim: The Sky above Us'   The material of this essay was published in a
number of different versions:

'County Leitrim'   *32 Counties: Photographs of Ireland by Donovan Wylie: With
New Writing by Thirty-Two Irish Writers*, edited by Donovan Wylie (London:
Secker & Warburg, 1989), 165–7.

'No Escaping Wind from Drumshambo'   *Irish Independent* 13 July 1991:
Weekender 12.

'The Plain Ways of Leitrim'   *New York Times Magazine* 17 May 1992:
Sophisticated Traveller 26–34.

'Ireland: All Quiet on the Western Front'   *Guardian* 3 July 1993: Weekend 43.

'Down by the Lazy Rivers'   *Irish Independent* 10 July 1993: Weekender 4–5.

'The Sky above Us'   *Ireland of the Welcomes* 45.5 (September/October 1996),
Special Issue on 'New Irish Writing', edited by Derek Mahon: 39–42.

Note on the text: The material that makes up McGahern's essay on his native
county Leitrim was habitually revised, lengthened and shortened again
between its various incarnations. This is probably due largely to the rigours
of magazine publication, with its often strict word-count limits. The text of
the essay as it is printed here is based on 'All Quiet on the Western Front'

(1993), as it is the fullest single text available; but it *also* incorporates or reinstates material from other versions where appropriate – material that was either newly added in the later (1996) version, or which had had to be excised (probably for considerations of length) from any of the earlier versions. Such reinstated or added material is listed below.

Variations:

From there . . . at Roosky: 'County Leitrim' (1989).

The upper Shannon . . . Drumsna to Roosky: 'County Leitrim' (1989).

What looks . . . folly: 'The Sky above Us' (1996).

twelfth-century: 'The Sky above Us' (1996). 'Plain Ways of Leitrim' (1992) prints '13th-century'.

Strokestown Park House: 'The Sky above Us' (1996).

curator: 'The Sky above Us' (1996). 'All Quiet' (1993) prints 'administrator'.

Except for football . . . them: 'County Leitrim' (1989) and 'No Escaping Wind from Drumshambo' (1991).

. . . (New York or Sicily): 'The Sky above Us' (1996).

The dramas . . . enormous store: 'County Leitrim' (1989). 'No Escaping Wind from Drumshambo' (1991) also places this section here.

The site . . . too often: 'The Sky above Us' (1996). McGahern had originally written this in the present tense: 'The site of the one public telephone is a major focus. For the time being, anyhow, it stands outside the Fianna Fáil bar, but a change of government could see it on the move again, all of thirty yards to the other side of the road.' See: 'County Leitrim' (1989) and 'All Quiet on the Western Front' (1993).

all that remains . . . St Colmcille: 'County Leitrim' (1989).

A purpose-built . . . ancient site: 'County Leitrim' (1989).

I like the town best . . . its own bar: 'County Leitrim' (1989).

'Galway, Western Ireland's Lilting Heart'   *New York Times Magazine* 14 May 1995: Sophisticated Traveller 36–44, 80.

'"What Are You, Sir?" Trinity College Dublin'   Untitled essay in *Trinity College Dublin and the Idea of a University*, edited by C. H. Holland (Dublin: Trinity College Dublin Press, 1991), 349–54. Reprinted with revisions and abridgements as 'What Are You, Sir?', *Irish Times* 9 March 1992: Weekend 1–2.

Note on the text: The text printed here is largely that of the original untitled essay from *Trinity College Dublin and the Idea of a University*, as it is slightly longer than the expurgated *Irish Times* reprint. Some of McGahern's handwritten corrections on a photocopy of the original essay (marked in hand: 'For I Times '92': NUIG P71/uncatalogued) have been incorporated.

Variations:

to boot: 'What Are You, Sir?' (1992).

still (in 'the Reserved sin *still* hovered over'): 'What Are You, Sir?' (1992).

roistering: 'What Are You, Sir?' (1992).

wearing the scarves: 'What Are You, Sir?' (1992).

each single strike seems to count: 'What Are You, Sir?' (1992).

bowsie: 'What Are You, Sir?' (1992) (the original edition has a blank space:
'_____').

'Blake's of the Hollow' Unpublished/publication unknown. Untitled typescript with handwritten corrections. NUIG P71/uncatalogued.

'Dreaming at Julien's' *Irish Independent* 11 April 1998: Magazine.

'Morocco, the Bitter and the Sweet' *New York Times Magazine* 14 September 1997: Sophisticated Traveller 18–20, 32–4.

'An Irishman in Newcastle' Unpublished. Untitled typescript. NUIG P71/uncatalogued.
Note on the text: The occasional [ ] that appear in this essay indicate blank spaces left in the typescript.

'The Bird Swift' *PS . . . of course: Patrick Swift 1927–1983*, edited by Veronica Jane O'Mara (Oysterhaven, Co. Cork: Gandon Books, 1993), 147–55.

'A Poet Who Worked in Prose: Memories of Michael McLaverty' *Sunday Independent* 29 March 1992: Living & Leisure 10.

'Dick Walsh Remembered' Published as an untitled foreword in *Dick Walsh Remembered: Selected Columns from* The Irish Times *1990–2002* (Dublin: TownHouse, 2003), 11–18.

III AUTOBIOGRAPHY, SOCIETY, HISTORY

'The Solitary Reader' This essay was published in a number of different versions:
'Amongst Books' *Culture in Dublin 1991: An* In Dublin *Guide* ([January] 1991): 16–21.
'Those Dangerous Mirrors Reflecting Our Lives' *Daily Telegraph* 27 April 1991.
'Me among the Protestants: A Bookish Boyhood' *New York Times Book Review* 28 April 1991: 1, 25–7.
'Legends that Shaped My Life' *Irish Independent* 4 May 1991: Weekender 8.
'The Solitary Reader' *Canadian Journal of Irish Studies* 17.1 (July 1991), Special issue on John McGahern: 19–23.
'The Devil Finds Work for Idle Hands' *The Agony and the Ego: The Art and Strategy of Fiction Writing Explored*, edited by Clare Boylan (Harmondsworth: Penguin, 1993), 97–104.
'Reading and Writing' *Irish Writers and Their Creative Process*, edited by Jacqueline Genet and Wynne Hellegouarc'h (Gerrards Cross: Colin Smythe, 1996), 103–9.

'Reading and Writing' *De Valera's Irelands*, edited by Gabriel Doherty and Dermot Keogh (Cork: Mercier Press, 2003), 132–7.

'Words as Sweet as Honey' *Guardian* 1 February 2003: Saturday Review 31.

Published in French translation as 'La création romanesque', translated by Margie Debelle, in *Le Processus de la création chez les écrivains irlandais contemporains*, edited by Jacqueline Genet and Élisabeth [Wynne] Hellegouarc'h (Caen: Presses Universitaires de Caen, 1994), 141–8.

Note on the text: This essay was published no fewer than ten times in a dozen years, between 1991 and 2003, so it is hardly surprising that it was occasionally revised between its various publication dates. The body of the essay is identical in all versions, with the exception of 'Me among the Protestants', which incorporates a few minor revisions, probably intended specifically for North American readers; the opening and conclusion, however, varied occasionally between appearances.

Variations:

I came to write . . . pure luck: 'Reading and Writing' (1996 and 2003).

I had great . . . become a writer: all the 1991 versions ('Amongst Books' to 'The Solitary Reader'), except 'Me among the Protestants'.

I came to write . . . become a writer: an amalgam of the two different versions of the opening paragraph (see the two previous notes) was printed in this way in 'The Devil Finds Work for Idle Hands' (1993).

When I began to write . . . their true reader: 'The Devil Finds Work' (1993) and all later versions.

I think every writer . . . I bowed to A. N. Wilson: all the 1991 versions ('Amongst Books' to 'The Solitary Reader').

where the Booker . . . to be announced: 'Me among the Protestants' (1991).

'Censorship' Unpublished. Untitled typescript missing one page: that page is taken from an earlier typescript with handwritten revisions. NUIG P71/uncatalogued.

'Why the Booker is Such a Hard Bet' *Irish Independent* 23 October 1993: Weekender 3.

'Schooldays: A Time of Grace' *A Time of Grace – School Memories: Edmund Rice and the Presentation Tradition of Education*, edited by Matthew J. Feheney (Dublin: Veritas, 1996), 130–5.

'My Education' Untitled essay in *My Education*, edited by John Quinn (Dublin: TownHouse, 1997), 256–63. Reprinted as 'My Education', *Leitrim Guardian: Leitrim's Annual County Magazine* 30 (1998): 79–82.

'*Ní bheidh sibh ar ais*: St Patrick's College Drumcondra' Unpublished. Speech delivered on 8 November 2003, on the occasion of McGahern's receipt of an

honorary doctorate from St Patrick's College, Drumcondra, where he had been
a student between 1951 and 1953. Untitled typescript. NUIG P71/uncatalogued.
Variation:
They gave us . . . no bad thing: This sentence was crossed out in hand in one of
  the typescripts.

'In the Beginning Was the Word' Unpublished.
  Note on the text: McGahern used this anecdote on several occasions, employing
    it to illustrate a variety of points about different subjects. The text of the
    essay as it is printed here is based on the untitled typescript, marked 'Final' in
    handwriting, of a lecture delivered to Equity (the Irish Actors' Union) on the
    occasion of their fiftieth anniversary (NUIG P71/1073). The final paragraph is
    taken from an untitled typescript that connects the anecdote about the
    reading at Goshen College with an account of the repressive and insular
    intellectual climate of the Ireland of McGahern's youth (NUIG P71/1317).
  Variations:
  when I was teaching at Colgate University: Untitled typescript. NUIG P71/1317.
  of English: Untitled typescript. NUIG P71/1317.
  immediate: Untitled typescript. NUIG P71/1317.
  since they believed . . . counterfeit usurpers: Typescript with handwritten
    revisions with title 'Equity' written in hand. NUIG P71/1072.
  we had been dreaming: Typescript with handwritten revisions. NUIG P71/1072.

'It's a Long Way from Mohill to Here . . .' *Irish Independent* 14 June 1989: 10.

'Shame in a Polling Booth' *Irish Independent* 28 November 1992: 20.

'From a Glorious Dream to Wink and Nod' *Irish Times* 3 April 1991: 9.

'Whatever You Say, Say Nothing' *Irish Times* 26 October 1999: 13. Reprinted in
  Eye on the Twentieth Century: A Decade by Decade Look at the Past 100 Years: a
  supplement with the *Irish Times* 30 December 1999: 27.

'The Church and Its Spire' *Soho Square 6: New Writing from Ireland*, edited by
  Colm Tóibín (London: Bloomsbury, 1993), 17–27. Extract printed as 'Hell and
  Damnation', *Irish Independent* 31 July 1993: Weekender 1, 4.

'God and Me' *Granta: The Magazine of New Writing* 93 (Spring 2006): *God's
  Own Countries*: 63–5. Extract printed, with an introduction and commentary by
  Ian Jack, as 'Saving Grace', *Guardian* 8 April 2006: Saturday Review 12.

'The Christmas Rose' *Irish Independent* 23 December 1995: Weekender 16. Extract
  printed in *Leitrim Guardian: Leitrim's Annual County Magazine* 29 (1997): 6.

'In the Spirit of Christmas' *Irish Independent* 15 December 1990: Weekender 13.

'Life as It Is and Life as It Ought to Be' *Irish Independent* 31 December 1993: 21.

'Rural Ireland's Passing' *Irish Independent* 29 January 2000: Weekend Review 1. Reprinted in *It's Us They're Talking About: Proceedings from the McGlinchey Summer School* 4 (June 2002): 87–9.

'Terrible Tales from the Mart' *Irish Independent* 27 December 1997: 10.

IV LITERATURE

'A Literature without Qualities' Unpublished typescript with handwritten corrections and additions. NUIG P71/uncatalogued.

> Note on the text: Another typescript (NUIG P71/1314) places the handwritten note on the margin of p. 2 of the first typescript at the end of the essay, where it has also been included in this volume, as an afterthought to the conclusion of the main argument.

'Mr Joyce and Mr Yeats' Published as an untitled foreword in Neill R. Joy, 'James Joyce Exhibition Catalogue', *Philobiblon: The Journal of the Friends of the Colgate University Library* 11 (Spring 1979): v–vi.

'*Brian Westby*' *Threshold* 28 (Spring 1977): 37–50. Reprinted in *Retrospective Adventures: Forrest Reid, Author and Collector*, edited by Paul Goldman and Brian Taylor (Aldershot: Scolar Press, in association with the Ashmolean Museum, Oxford, 1998), 11–15.

'*Dubliners*' *James Joyce: The Artist and the Labyrinth*, edited by Augustine Martin (London: Ryan Publishing, 1990), 63–72. Reprinted in *Canadian Journal of Irish Studies* 17.1 (July 1991), Special issue on John McGahern: 31–7. Reprinted as 'ReJoycing in *Dubliners*', *Irish Independent* 15 June 1991: Weekender 9.

'The Stories of Alistair MacLeod' Published as an untitled foreword in Alistair MacLeod, *Island: Collected Stories* (London: Jonathan Cape, 2001), vii–xiv.

'Knowledge of the World: John Williams's *Augustus*' Published as an untitled introduction in John Williams, *Augustus* (London: Vintage Classics, 2003), vi–xiii.

'A Matter of Love: John Williams's *Stoner*' Published as an untitled introduction in John Williams, *Stoner* (London: Vintage Classics, 2003), vi–xii.

'The Letters of John Butler Yeats' Published as an untitled introduction in John Butler Yeats, *Letters to His Son W. B. Yeats and Others 1869–1922*, edited by Joseph Hone, abridged and with an introduction by John McGahern (London: Faber and Faber, 1999), 1–25. Published in French translation as *Lettres à son fils, le poète W. B. Yeats, et à d'autres correspondants: 1898–1922*, translated by Anne Morin (Paris: José Corti, 2000).

433

'In Pursuit of a Single Flame: Ernie O'Malley'   The material of this essay was
    published in a number of different versions:
'In Pursuit of a Single Flame', *Irish Times* 17 February 1996: Weekend 8.
'Return of the Revolutionary' (Review of *On Another Man's Wound*, by Ernie
    O'Malley), *Irish Times* 8 June 2002: Weekend 10.
'Make Them Criminals: A Classic of Ireland's Wars', *Times Literary Supplement*
    17 June 2005: 12–13.
See also McGahern's review of *Ernie O'Malley: IRA Intellectual*, by Richard
    English: 'A Revolutionary Mind', *Irish Times* 11 April 1998: Weekend 4, an
    extract from which is printed elsewhere in this collection.
Note on the text: McGahern published several essays and reviews on Ernie
    O'Malley, as well as a review of Richard English's *Ernie O'Malley: IRA
    Intellectual*. These essays and reviews, including that of English's book, all
    draw on the same material and necessarily repeat one another. The text of the
    essay as it is printed here is largely that of the last published version, 'Make
    Them Criminals', as it is much longer and in places more refined than either
    of the earlier versions; but, where appropriate, it also incorporates some
    relevant material from the earlier versions that had been omitted from that
    latest text, in particular McGahern's memory of teaching one of O'Malley's
    nephews in Clontarf in the late 1950s, which has been reinstated for inclusion
    here.
Variations:
When I was teaching . . . a nephew of Ernie O'Malley when: 'In Pursuit of a
    Single Flame' (1996).
soon after his death . . . O'Malley's writing: 'Return of the Revolutionary'
    (2002).
Like many writers . . . the page: 'Return of the Revolutionary' (2002).
The clear writing . . . certain paintings: 'In Pursuit of a Single Flame' (1996).
A few months before: 'In Pursuit of a Single Flame' (1996).
O'Malley the soldier . . . to the writer: 'In Pursuit of a Single Flame' (1996).
The signatories of the proclamation . . .: 'Make them Criminals' (2005)
    erroneously lists Major John MacBride among the signatories of the 1916
    Proclamation.
In 1932 . . . a general's pension: 'A Revolutionary Mind' (1998).
was highly praised . . . are accurate: 'Return of the Revolutionary' (2002).
The work as a whole . . . has been denied: 'In Pursuit of a Single Flame' (1996).
It is probably true . . . to himself or others: 'Return of the Revolutionary' (2002).

'What Is My Language?'   *New Readings of Old Masters*, edited by Mary Massoud
    (Cairo: Macmillan, 2004), 205–19. Reprinted with revisions in *Irish University
    Review* 35.1 (Spring/Summer 2005), Special issue on John McGahern: 1–12.
    Most of the long central reflection on Ó Criomhthain's classic book (beginning

from the paragraph that starts 'I turn to a work that has no obvious artifice' to the quotation from the end of the book about Ó Criomhthain's memory of his mother) had, prior to being incorporated by McGahern into this longer essay, been published as an essay in its own right, entitled simply '*An tOileánach*', first published in *Canadian Journal of Irish Studies* 13.1 (June 1987): 7–15. Reprinted with revisions in *Irish Review* 6 (Spring 1989): 55–62. That essay was also published in an Irish translation, translated by Tomás Mac Síomóin, in *Scáthán* [no volume number] (1985): 6–11. Reprinted in *Tomás an Bhlascaoid*, edited by Breandán Ó Conaire (Indreabhán, Conamara: Cló Iar-Chonnachta, 1992), 301–11.

Note on the text: The two published versions of 'What Is My Language?' are identical but for their concluding paragraphs, beginning after the question 'What, then, is my language' is posed. The text as it is printed here is that from the *Irish University Review* Special issue on McGahern, as it incorporates McGahern's most up-to-date revisions; but it reinstates one paragraph he had deleted from this revised version of the essay, as well as two sentences from the original essay on *An tOileánach* that were omitted from 'What Is My Language?'

Variations:

There are no . . . the daffodil: '*An tOileánach*' (1987 and 1989).

I believe that this island lies closer . . . in our youth: '*An tOileánach*' (1989).

I will not . . . a length: 'What Is My Language?' (Massoud ed. 2004).

That language . . . the Irish language: 'What Is My Language?' (Massoud ed. 2004).

V PREFACES AND INTRODUCTIONS

'Preface to the Second Edition of *The Leavetaking*'   John McGahern, *The Leavetaking*, second, revised edition (London: Faber and Faber, 1984), 5.

'Preface to *Creatures of the Earth: New and Selected Stories*'   John McGahern, *Creatures of the Earth: New and Selected Stories* (London: Faber and Faber 2006), vii–viii.

'Introduction to *The Power of Darkness* [1991]'   Originally printed with the title 'Fear of Famine' as a Programme Note for the original Abbey Theatre production of the play at the Dublin Theatre Festival in October 1991, directed by Garry Hynes. Published with slight revisions in John McGahern, *The Power of Darkness* (London: Faber and Faber, 1991), vii–viii.

'Introduction to *The Power of Darkness* [2005]'   Introduction by the author to a radio production of the play, produced by Kevin Reynolds. Broadcast as part of the *Sunday Playhouse* series on RTÉ Radio One, 2 April 2006. The text as it is printed here is based on two draft typescripts with handwritten revisions, probably McGahern's recording notes (NUIG P71/uncatalogued); but it also incorporates some further amendments to the text of those drafts in accordance with the finished recording, which can be listened to at: http://www.rte.ie/radio1/sundayplayhouse/.

VI REVIEWS

'Fact and Factotum'   Unpublished typescript with handwritten corrections. NUIG P71/936. The book appeared in 1968.

'Everybodies'   *Listener* 23 April 1970: 554–5.

'Authors' Domains'   *Listener* 18 March 1971: 345.

'An Island Race'   *Hibernia* 5 October 1973: 13.

'Memories of Newcastle'   *Times Literary Supplement* 13 February 1976: 159.

'A Bank of Non-Sequiturs'   *Sunday Independent* 4 January 1981: 15.

'Local Hero'   Unpublished. 1986. Untitled typescript. NUIG P71/1066.

'New Victory for Gilchrist'   *Evening Herald* 13 June 1986: 26.

'A Solid Gold Novel'   *Evening Herald* 11 July 1986: 18.

'Who's a Clever Chap?'   *Evening Herald* 1 August 1986: 18.

'Sicily – A Land of Extremes'   *Evening Herald* 5 September 1986: 24.

'A Plain Tale from a Desert Island'   *Evening Herald* 10 October 1986: 25.

'Simenon – Far from Maigret'   *Evening Herald* 28 November 1986: 29.

From 'Critic's Choice'   *Evening Herald* 19 December 1986: 23.

'The Hero We Didn't Know'   *Evening Herald* 1 and 2 January 1987: 18.

'A Family at War?'   *Evening Herald* 16 January 1987: 16.

'When the Magic Fails'   *Evening Herald* 6 March 1987: 22.

'Journey along the Canal Bank'   An abridged version of this essay was published in the *Evening Herald* 15 May 1987: 23.
  Note on the text: The text of the review as it is printed here is that of an untitled typescript NUIG P71/uncatalogued. The text that appeared as a review in the *Evening Herald* appears to be an abridged and slightly amended version of that longer text.
  Variations:
  much (in 'not a quality *much* associated with Kavanagh'): *Evening Herald* edition (1987).

In one of the lectures printed here . . . : Evening Herald edition (1987).
A philistine Church . . . the greater mathematician: Evening Herald edition (1987).
The main difference . . . more completely cut off: Evening Herald edition (1987).
. . . of this kind of doggerel as: Evening Herald edition (1987).

From 'Higgins Goes to the Brinks' *Evening Herald* 12 June 1987: 25.

'It's All in the Mind' *Evening Herald* 24 July 1987: 21.

'Poor Account of Chilean Life' *Evening Herald* 31 July 1987: 19.

'Yours Sincerely, D.H.L.' *Evening Herald* 11 September 1987: 23.

'Getting Flaubert's Facts Straight' *Irish Times* 29 April 1989: Weekend 8.

'Sagas from the North' *Irish Times* 1 July 1989: Weekend 8.

'The Man Who Fell in Love with His Dog' *Irish Times* 23 September 1989: Weekend 8.

'The Life, the Work and the Hurt' *Irish Times* 17 March 1990: Weekend 9.

'An Immaculate Mistake' Unpublished/publication unknown. Untitled typescript. NUIG P71/1059. The novel appeared in May 1990.

'Travails with the Not So Merry Pranksters' *Irish Times* 7 July 1990: Weekend 8.

'On the Edge of the Dream' *Irish Times* 18 August 1990: Weekend 4.

'Patriot Games' *Sunday Times* 21 October 1990: Books 11.

'The Beautiful and the Damned' *Irish Times* 29 June 1991: Weekend 9.

'Cool World' Publication unknown. The text is taken from a photocopy of a faxed proof or cutting of the review, marked by the fax machine: 'Oct. 06 '92 . . . CONDE NAST PUBLI'. Private Collection. The novel appeared in May 1992.

'The Adult Mysteries' *New York Times Book Review* 12 September 1993: 7.

'The Forging of the State' *Irish Times* 23 July 1994: Weekend 8. Reprinted as 'Des intellectuels et de la nation' [in English], *Études Irlandaises* 20.1 (Spring 1995): 239–43

'Shadows of a Summer Night' *New York Times Book Review* 27 March 1994: 10.

'A Legend after His Own Lifetime' *Irish Times* 12 November 1994: Weekend 8.

'A Critic Who Was One of the Elect' *Irish Times* 23 September 1995: Weekend 8.

'The Tragical Comedy of the Men of Ireland' Published in French translation, translated by Daniel Bismuth, as 'La comédie tragique des hommes d'Irlande', *Le Monde* 5 September 1997: Le Monde des livres v. Unpublished in English.

Note on the text: The review was originally published in French translation. This English text is that of an untitled typescript with handwritten corrections by McGahern: NUIG P71/1020. The final paragraphs, which appear with an over-abundance of handwritten amendments in that typescript, have been revised according to the copy of a fax of the corrected typescript containing handwritten corrections by McGahern NUIG P71/uncatalogued.

Variations:

The same setting . . . Beckett's first novel: In the typescript, this sentence comes before the quotation about Oliver Shepherd's statue of Cuchulain.

One of the finest Irish novelists of this century . . . in Morocco: This aside about Kate O'Brien was crossed out in the typescript, but has been reinstated for inclusion in this volume.

The reference to . . . : occurs in the published (French) text only.

From 'A Revolutionary Mind' *Irish Times* 11 April 1998: Weekend 4.

'On the Turning Wheel of the Year' *Irish Times* 3 July 1999: Weekend 8.

'Pieces of Yeats' *Irish Times* 27 November 1999: Weekend 10.

'A Classic Gathering of the Classics' *Sunday Business Post* 19 November 2000: 41.

'How They Lived up in the Big House' *Irish Independent* 13 January 2001: Weekend 11.

'Heroines of Their Lives' *Times Literary Supplement* 9 November 2001: 23–4.

'Kiltubrid, County Leitrim' Unpublished typescript with handwritten corrections and a handwritten insert. NUIG P71/uncatalogued. The book appeared in September 2005.

Index